URBAN LEVIATHAN

MEXICO CITY

IN THE

TWENTIETH

CENTURY

DIANE E. DAVIS

URBAN

TEMPLE UNIVERSITY PRESS　PHILADELPHIA

LEVIATHAN

MEXICO CITY

IN THE

TWENTIETH

CENTURY

Temple University Press,

Philadelphia 19122

Copyright © 1994 by

Temple University.

All rights reserved

Published 1994

Printed in the United States

of America

The paper used in this publication meets
the minimum requirements of American
National Standard for Information
Sciences—Permanence of Paper for
Printed Library Materials, ANSI
Z39.48-1984   ∞

Library of Congress

Cataloging-in-Publication Data

Davis, Diane E., 1953–

   Urban leviathan : Mexico City in

the twentieth century /

Diane E. Davis.

      p.   cm.

   Includes bibliographical references
and index.

   ISBN 1-56639-150-4 (cloth). — ISBN
1-56639-151-2 (pbk.)

   1. Urbanization—Mexico—
Mexico City—History—20th
century. 2. Mexico City (Mexico)—
Politics and government. 3. Mexico
City (Mexico)—Economic
conditions.   I. Title.

HT384.M62M483   1994

307.76'0972'53—dc20   93-23069

CONTENTS

Photographs follow pages 136 and 218

LIST OF ABBREVIATIONS

AGN   Archivo General de la Nación; National Archive

AVCC   Actas y Versiones del Consejo Consultivo de la Ciudad de
            México; Minutes of the Consultative Council of Mexico City

CANACINTRA Cámara Nacional de la Industria de la Transformación;
            National Chamber of Manufacturing Industries

CCM   Confederación de la Clase Media; Confederation of the
            Middle Class

CEPES   Centro de Estudios Políticos, Económicos y Sociales del Distrito
            Federal; Center of Political, Economic, and Social Studies on the
            Federal District

CGOCM   Confederación General de Obreros y Campesinos Mexicanos;
            General Confederation of Mexican Workers and Peasants

CGT   Confederación General de Trabajadores; General Confederation
            of Workers

CNC   Confederación Nacional Campesina; National Peasant
            Confederation

CNOP   Confederación Nacional de Organizaciones Populares; National
            Confederation of Popular Organizations

CONAMUP   Coordinadora Nacional de Movimientos Urbanos Populares;
            National Coalition of Urban Popular Movements

CONCANACO   Confederación de Cámaras Nacionales de Comercio;
            Confederation of National Chambers of Commerce

CONCANACOMIN Confederación de Cámaras Nacionales de Comercio y
            Industria; Confederation of National Chambers of Commerce
            and Industry

CONCAMIN Confederación de Cámaras Industriales; Confederation
of Industrial Chambers

COP Confederación de Organizaciones Populares; Confederation of
Popular Organizations

COPARMEX Confederación Patronal de la República Mexicana;
Employers' Confederation of the Mexican Republic

COVITUR Comisión de Vialidad y Transporte Urbano; Commission on
Roadways and Urban Transport

CROM Confederación Regional de Obreros Mexicanos; Regional
Confederation of Mexican Workers

CTM Confederación Nacional de Trabajadores Mexicanos; National
Confederation of Mexican Workers

DDF Departamento del Distrito Federal; Department of the Federal
District

FNOC Frente Nacional de Organizaciones y Ciudadanos; National
Front of Organizations and Citizens

FNTE Federación Nacional de Trabajadores del Estado; National
Federation of State Workers

FSODF Federación de Sindicatos Obreros del Distrito Federal;
Federation of Labor Unions of the Federal District

FSTDF Federación de Sindicatos de Trabajadores del Distrito Federal;
Federation of Workers' Unions of the Federal District

FSTSE Federación de Sindicatos de Trabajadores al Servicio del Estado;
Federation of State Workers' Unions

GATT General Agreement on Tariffs and Trade

ICA Ingenieros Civiles Asociados; Associated Civil Engineers

ISSTSE Instituto de Seguro Social para Trabajadores en Servicio al
Estado; State Workers' Social Security Institute

ISTME Ingeniería de Sistemas de Transporte Metropolitano;
Metropolitan Transport Systems Engineers

PAN Partido Acción Nacional; National Action Party

PARM	Partido Auténtico de la Revolución Mexicana; Authentic Party of the Mexican Revolution
PNR	Partido Nacional Revolucionario; National Revolutionary Party
PRI	Partido Revolucionario Institucional; Institutional Revolutionary Party
PRM	Partido de la Revolución Mexicana; Party of the Mexican Revolution
PPS	Partido Popular Socialista; Popular Socialist Party
PSUM	Partido Socialista Unificado de México; Unified Socialist Party of Mexico
SEDUE	Secretaría de la Desarrollo Urbano y Ecología; Ministry of Urban Development and Ecology
SUTGDF	Sindicato Único de Trabajadores del Gobierno del Distrito Federal; Federal District Government Workers' Union

PREFACE AND ACKNOWLEDGMENTS

This study of political conflict and urban development in Mexico City takes as its point of departure national history and its embeddedness in a particular spatial context. Mexico's unique urban and revolutionary heritage established the centrality of its capital city in national politics and the economy from as early as 1910, and even before. This centrality ensured that the tale of twentieth-century Mexico City was intricately linked to national processes of postrevolutionary political consolidation and economic development. After violently seizing power in the capital, Mexico's revolutionary leadership helped cement its social and political bases by fostering the spatial and economic reconstruction of Mexico City during the 1920s and '30s. Yet this same strategy, when pursued during the '40s and '50s, spurred questions from state and class actors about the nature and pace of Mexico City's urban development and about the national project of urbanization-led industrialization. Conflicts over the spatial character and growth of the capital city emerged with full force in the '60s and continued throughout the '70s, calling into question national development strategies and exposing insurmountable contradictions in Mexico's incorporated political system, especially in the relationships within and between state and class actors, both local and national. By the '80s, these contradictions threatened the efficacy of existing institutional mechanisms of urban governance and their articulation with national party structures, thereby weakening the foundations of one-party rule.

In the upcoming pages, we explore these state and class conflicts over Mexico City's urban development and assess their local and national political implications. In so doing, this work builds on a historical tradition of scholarship that links the urban and national domains through an analysis of the state and classes, on one hand, and through a focus on territory and space, particularly the built environment, on the other. It argues that both urban development patterns and their political consequences are uniquely influenced by the territorial overlap of local and national actors and political institutions in Mexico City. That is, Mexico City's unique pattern of concentrated urban growth emerges as a result of local and national political struggles over its size and character; and these struggles, in turn, shape the institutional relationships between local and national state and class actors, and thus the dynamics of one-party rule in twentieth-century Mexico.

This book could not have been completed without encouragement from many, starting with Maurice Zeitlin, Manuel Castells, and Ivan Light during my graduate studies in California. I also want to thank colleagues at the Graduate Faculty of the New School for Social Research, where I have had the opportunity to work closely with Charles Tilly, Janet Abu-Lughod, Ira Katznelson, and various others who deepened my commitment to exploring the historical relationships among cities, classes, and states. Others, both here and in Mexico, also played an important role along the way. My gratitude goes to Susan Eckstein for continued friendship and intellectual support over the last several years. Her informed comments on my work, sure insight, and sound advice have been much appreciated, as has her willingness to aid my career development in myriad ways. I also owe thanks to Alejandro Portes, Theda Skocpol, Michael Peter Smith, Michael Timberlake, and John Walton, all of whom graciously commented on drafts or related presentations, in one form or another, of parts of this book over the years.

In Mexico, countless people deserve recognition for facilitating the field research process, sharing scholarship and ideas, and keeping me true to the facts. They include Antonio Azuela, Helga Baitenmann, Elsa Blum, Vivane Brachet Márquez, Javier Caraveo, Guillermo Cosio Vidaurri, Miguel Covían Pérez, Miguel de la Torre, Jorge Gamboa de Buen, Hugo García Perez, Gustavo Garza, Fernando Giffard, Valentín Ibarra, Carlos Jiménez Macías, Jorge Legoretta, Ignacio Marván, Alejandra Massolo, Alejandra Moreno Toscano, Bernardo Navarro, Manuel Perlo, Marta Schteingart, Carlos Sirvent, Alicia Ziccardi, and numerous other friends, scholars, informants, party activists, and archivists who shared their valuable time and insight. I could not possibly begin to list all by name, but this project would not have been possible without their cooperation. I am especially indebted to Dr. Victoria San Vicente of the Mexican National Archives, and to Roberto Rock, of El Universal, for their help in securing photographs.

Institutional and financial support was generous, and for that I am truly grateful. Because the book has been so long in coming, and is now but a distant cousin of the dissertation research that initiated my interest in the topic in 1980, many deserve acknowledgment. Financial support for master's and doctoral studies came from the University of California at Los Angeles; the NDEA Title VI program funded my two years as a fellow of the UCLA Latin American Center. Fieldwork support in Mexico came from the University of California system, the Fulbright-Hays Program, the Tinker Foundation, the Social Science Research Council, Harvard University, and the Howard Heinz Foundation. A New School Faculty Development Grant provided support for

PREFACE AND ACKNOWLEDGMENTS

manuscript preparation; and among those who worked tirelessly were Kim Geiger, Andy Schlewitz, Kumru Toktamis, Guy Baldwin, and Fred Murphy.

Many research institutions provided facilities as I worked on various sections and stages of the manuscript, and they also deserve a word of recognition. They include the Population Studies Program at Brown University, the Gordon Public Policy Center at Brandeis University, the Department of Urban Studies and Planning at MIT, the Center for Studies of Demography and Urban Development (now called the Center for Studies of Economy and Urban Development) at the Colegio de México, and the Center for Sociological Studies, also at the Colegio de México. Among those who lent encouragement at these institutions whom I have not already mentioned, I especially want to thank Orlandina de Oliveira, Ralph Gakenheimer, Calvin Goldscheider, Sidney Goldstein, Martin Levin, José Luís Reyna, Judith Tendler, and the late Luis Unikel.

Last, I thank my family and friends, especially my husband, Bish Sanyal, for putting up with me as this project grew larger, more complex, and more time-consuming. I am sure they are as happy as I to finally see some closure.

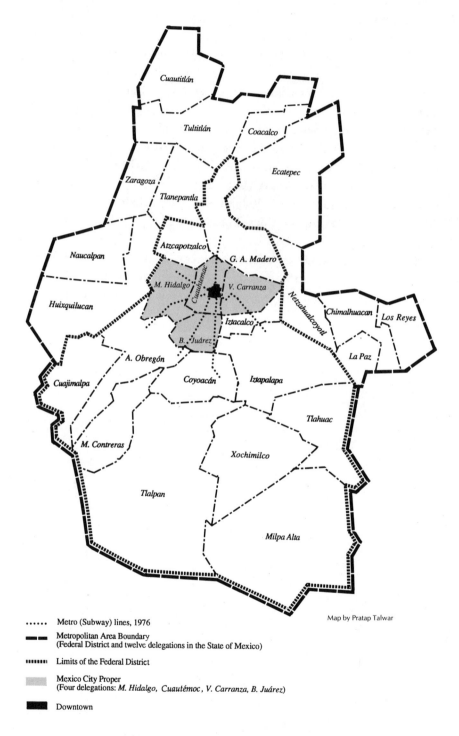

Cuautitlán

Tultitlán

Coacalco

Ecatepec

Zaragoza

Tlanepantla

Atzcapotzalco

Naucalpan

G. A. Madero

M. Hidalgo

Cuauhtémoc

V. Carranza

Iztacalco

Netzahualcoyotl

Chimalhuacan

Los Reyes

Huixquilucan

B. Juárez

La Paz

A. Obregón

Coyoacán

Iztapalapa

Cuajimalpa

Tlahuac

M. Contreras

Xochimilco

Tlalpan

Milpa Alta

Map by Pratap Talwar

······ Metro (Subway) lines, 1976

▬ ▬ Metropolitan Area Boundary
(Federal District and twelve delegations in the State of Mexico)

▪▪▪▪▪▪ Limits of the Federal District

Mexico City Proper
(Four delegations: *M. Hidalgo, Cuautémoc, V. Carranza, B. Juárez*)

Downtown

Mexico City Metropolitan Area

1

LAYING THE FOUNDATIONS

Glorious Mexico City, once known as the city of palaces, is now gasping for breath in a sea of people, poverty, and pollution. Though the reasons are many, distinguished author and activist Octavio Paz echoes common sentiment when he blames Mexico's political leaders for this insufferable situation. He chastises the ruling party for its incapacity to foresee the disastrous consequences of what he considers a thoughtless cult of out-and-out development and industrialization. Paz minces no words in his indictment: "As they were intent on 'modernizing' the country, none of [Mexico's] rulers—all of them surrounded by 'expert' counselors and ideologists—realized in time the perils of the population's excessive and uncontrolled growth. . . . Nor did they take measures against the demographic, political, economic, and cultural centralization that has converted Mexico City into a monstrous inflated head, crushing the frail body that holds it up."[1]

To those familiar with Mexico and its capital city, Paz's words ring true. Worse than a planner's nightmare, Mexico City is a depressing testament to administrative chaos and the excesses of rapid and concentrated industrial development. Since initiating industrial development in the 1940s, Mexico's capital has been transformed from a charming city with wide boulevards, an almost leisurely lifestyle, and a population of around 1.8 million to a living hell with nearly 16 million residents in the metropolitan area.[2] It is now neck and neck with Tokyo for the dubious honor of being the world's largest city, and it shows in the daily disorder of urban life. Clearly the capital city was not always this way. Yet because Mexico's ruling political party, the Partido Revolucionario Institucional (PRI), concentrated national investments and industrial infrastructure in this central locale, Mexico City grew by leaps and bounds. Between the 1940s and 1960s, the capital city more than doubled in size as it proudly showcased the nation's economic growth. The capital came to be synonymous with seemingly unlimited employment opportunities, wealth, and urban and economic development. By the early sixties, Mexico City boasted Latin America's first skyscraper, rising standards of living, a sophisticated cultural life, and some of the developing world's most modern urban amenities, including a gleaming new rapid transit system. The economy flowered and the capital city sparkled as the symbol of the country's successful confrontation with modernity; in turn, Mexico's citizens lent relatively solid political support to the PRI and its one-party rule.

Almost as rapidly as it came, however, this urban-based miracle turned around. By the late 1970s and early 1980s, Mexico's import-substitution industrialization strategy had reached a point of saturation, and so too had Mexico City. Local officials were hard-pressed to meet the administrative demands of the monstrous city. In the capital, where most industries were located, investment and productivity declined precipitously, spurred by an economic crisis associated with massive foreign debt obligations and skyrocketing urban infrastructure expenditures incurred in the process of rapid industrialization. Visible changes in the capital city's social, spatial, and political landscape, in short, chronicled both the nation's rapid ascent and its apparent decline. Near-lethal levels of pollution from industrial firms that had made the industrialization miracle possible were strangling the local population. By 1990, as ozone levels reached dangerous heights, the government was routinely closing schools and factories and systematically restricting automobile usage with an elaborate system of vehicle permits. The overconcentration

CHAPTER ONE

of vehicles, population, and industry also produced severe scarcities in urban services. With high demand and limited fiscal resources, critical services like electricity, water, housing, and public transportation became almost too costly for the government to administer or provide, at least at the rate demanded by this ever-expanding metropolis and its impoverished residents.

In response to these service scarcities, increased pollution, skyrocketing expenditures, and other urban and administrative problems associated with unlimited urban growth, Mexico City's residents have ever more frequently taken to the streets and made vocal demands on ruling party leaders to address deteriorating urban conditions. However, the economic crisis has imposed strict limits on social expenditures, and because of the sheer enormity of the problem, little has been accomplished. As a consequence, over the past decade or so well-organized networks of urban social movements in the capital city have boldly challenged the ruling party and its monopoly on urban policy decisions. And the results have been formidable: The PRI can no longer easily count on social or electoral support in Mexico City, where several autonomous urban social movements are demanding democracy and laying a solid foundation for the development of a more competitive political system. In the 1988 presidential election, for example, opposition candidate Cuauhtémoc Cárdenas carried Mexico City and sent shockwaves through the PRI by challenging its political hegemony in the capital and the nation at large. Although Cárdenas repudiated the PRI for numerous shortcomings, urban problems and the incapacity of local residents to make critical decisions about urban services in Mexico City, owing to the absence of local democratic institutions, were among the most critical and widely discussed issues in his campaign. Since then, the PRI has been quick to address the political fallout from the Cárdenas challenge. This was first evidenced in a 1989 symposium sponsored by the Mexico City mayor's office that committed the PRI to exploring the relationship between democracy and urban development in the Mexico City metropolitan area. Among the most-discussed issues were planning, democracy, participation, and quality of life; urban expansion and the transformation of local and national political institutions; and the urban policy platforms of Mexico's ruling and opposition parties.

CITY, CLASS, AND CORPORATISM: AN OVERVIEW

So what accounts for Mexico City's rise as a gigantic and overpopulated industrial center, one that sustained the political and economic successes of an entire nation? And why have we seen such a dramatic reversal of fortune in the last two decades, such that Mexico City's growth and administration have themselves become serious problems? What are the implications for both local and national politics, especially the power of the PRI and the future of one-party rule in Mexico? To ask these questions is to seek the origins of the capital city's urbanization patterns and to consider their interrelationship with industrialization and national political development. Of course, one cannot comprehensively address all the multiple determinants of political and economic development in Mexico, urbanization-related or otherwise, in a single account. But it is possible to pose a more narrowly defined set of leading questions that help us understand these big structures and large processes, as Charles Tilly would call them: What explains the rapid and uncontrolled urban development of Mexico City over the past seventy years, and how have administrative practices and urban development policies introduced in the capital during this time period been influenced by—and in turn influenced— local and national politics?

By posing these questions, I share Octavio Paz's concern for linking Mexico's political history and many of its current political problems to the growth and dynamics of its capital city. Yet I use a slightly different theoretical perspective to untangle urban and political dynamics. Rather than pin the blame only on Mexico's political leaders, their personal ideologies of development, or their modernist biases toward industrialization and urbanization, I argue that Mexico City's urban development patterns—and their political consequences—are rooted in historically grounded conflicts and alliances among state and class actors; these conflicts and alliances have both produced and emerged in response to efforts to manage the servicing, land use, and growth of the capital city, as well as to control local politics. Furthermore, I argue that these conflicts and alliances are made particularly troublesome and consequential by one characteristic that differentiates this city's experience from many others': the fact that Mexico City is also its nation's political and economic capital. Mexico City is home not just to so-called "local" populations, or residents concerned with the production and consumption of their everyday lives. It is also home to national political institutions and actors with national constituencies and national developmental concerns. Indeed, Mexico City hosts most of the nation's foreign and domestic investment, the nation's largest concentration of both working and middle classes, the headquarters of the ruling party, and all three corporatist structures for national political participation.

All this means that political conflicts over Mexico City's administration and urban development have engaged national-level state and class actors and institutions as much as local ones. Precisely because Mexico City is the political and economic center of the nation, in fact, Mexico's leaders have denied the capital's local residents their own independent structures for democratic participation, in order to prevent residents with neighborhood or other more parochial concerns from interfering with urban administrative goals and national development plans. This, in turn, has meant that until recently, Mexico City's populations have been forced to use national political structures to express local concerns. As a result, policy conflicts and administrative decisions about the growth, nature, and spatial or sectoral character of Mexico City have had direct repercussions on the national economy, on national corporatist political structures, and on the balance of power in national politics. Depending on whether they were more concerned with the local or national domains, and depending on their allegiances to specific classes or class-based sectors within the party, Mexico's national political leadership has frequently come to blows with local populations over Mexico City's development, thereby irreparably dividing the PRI. The results have been clear: a slow but steady weakening of state power vis-à-vis Mexico City populations and growing tension within and between its class-based corporatist sectors, especially as the city grows out of control.

In view of the unique overlap of local and national dynamics in Mexico, the politics of urban development that I explore in this book play themselves out on two levels simultaneously: the local, or urban, and the national domain. One of the main propositions I advance is that it is precisely the political and economic interrelationships between local and national actors and institutions that have produced Mexico City's disastrous urban development trajectories. A second proposition is that this unique set of interrelationships links administrative and policy decisions about urban development in Mexico City to several fundamental institutional transformations in the corporatist political system. To make these claims is not to say that conflicts over servicing and administration in Mexico City have been the *sole* determinants of national political transformations within the PRI and Mexico's incorporated political system. Outside the capital city, rural populations and changing relationships within and between peasants and the state have also played a part in either supporting or challenging the ruling party and its macroeconomic policy positions. So too have capitalists and laboring populations in other regions and even outside the nation's borders. Nor is it to argue that within Mexico City itself class dynamics or struggles in the workplace, especially as they produce tensions and relationships between capital and labor, are inconsequential or secondary to urban administrative and policy concerns. Clearly, tensions between capitalists and Mexico's working classes have worried Mexico's political leaders and influenced many of the PRI's most important political and economic policy decisions, both on the local and the national level. What I do claim, however, is that conflicts over services and administration in Mexico City have involved the nation's most critical state and class actors, including capitalists and the working class; they have involved national-level actors and institutions; and both these sets of conflicts have had national political repercussions, not just local, urban ones.

Just as no study of the politics of urban development in Mexico City is complete without an understanding of the ways that national actors involve themselves in local struggles over urban policy, either in conflict or alliance with local actors, then, no study of national politics or corporatism in Mexico would be complete without an eye to the conflicts and alliances that emerge in the course of struggles over urban development in its capital city. Of course, in the complex whole under study in this book, it is easier to understand urban development trajectories within the context of the national political scene than to understand the national political dynamics of corporatism within the context of conflicts over Mexico City's growth and servicing. Nonetheless, this should not—and will not—stop us from using an examination of local and national conflicts over Mexico City's size, nature, and administration to raise new questions about corporatist politics and their dynamics in Mexico as a whole.

Yet let us pause for a moment. Can we really say anything meaningful about Mexico's overall political development trajectories with a focus only on Mexico City and the service and administrative conflicts that have unfolded there? What about Monterrey industrialists, Sonoran agriculturalists, Campeche oil, Chiapas indigenous populations, Jalisco Catholicism, Morelos peasants, to name but a few of the potent national political forces in Mexico's history? Should we not consider their relative impact on the consolidation and weakening of corporatism and one-party rule? Such questions are important for defining the limits of this study as well as for highlighting this book's uniqueness and its possibilities. Clearly, one cannot chart each and every factor or force in Mexico's national political transformations over the past seventy years with a focus solely on forces and conditions in its capital city, let alone with a singular focus on urban development conflicts there. But that is not to say that through a focus on Mexico City and an examination of service and administrative conflicts that we cannot capture some critical aspects of national political development or corporatism that have been ignored in studies of other conflicts, forces, or regions. It is not necessary to prove that other regionally based forces and factors did *not* matter in Mexico's corporatist politics, for example, in order to claim that urban forces and conditions *did*. The mere fact of demonstrating any significant role played by conflicts over urban development in national politics is enough to challenge past ways of seeing and perhaps even to establish the terms of a new debate on Mexico's political development.

Yet make no mistake, to make this caveat is not to cede the point. Conflicts in and over Mexico City's centrality and growth have involved regional forces and conditions more than most people imagine. Accordingly, when I underscore the critical role played by urban development conflicts in national political transformations, I do not ignore other classes or regional dynamics. On the contrary, I call attention to the connectedness between urban and national politics in Mexico, and to the impact of regional populations and competing class forces in struggles over services and administration in Mexico City. To ignore the dynamics of urban development in Mexico City and the ways in which it emerges from and produces local-national tensions, I will argue, may be to misread the complex and multifaceted determinants of Mexico City's growth and of national politics in Mexico. To consciously consider these urban dynamics, however, and to examine the political conflicts they engender among the local and national state and class actors, is to gain new insight into salient developments in Mexico's corporatist political system, and into the fate of one-party rule.

A NEW POINT OF DEPARTURE

Studies by urban scholars like Harvey Molotch and John Logan, Roger Friedland, Norman and Susan Fainstein, Todd Swanstrom, and J. Allen Whitt have all made great strides in examining state and class determinants of urban development patterns, especially the ways in which the requisites of capital determine policies affecting the built environment or the ways in which governing officials mediate class-based conflicts over urban development policies. Yet these authors tend to use as their points of departure *either* local *or* national capital, classes, and the state. They rarely explore the connections between the local and national domains, perhaps because they do not examine developing countries like Mexico, where the overlaps and articulations are so clear. Occasionally, a scholar of the advanced capitalist world will focus on national and international forces in the development of cities, as recent work by Richard Child Hill on Detroit demonstrates. Still, the tendency in the existing literature on urban development in U.S. cities is to examine local determinants and to see national or international forces and conditions mainly as context for locally bounded state and class struggles over urban growth. With the exception of John Mollenkopf's *The Contested City*, the articulations of several levels and their impact on each other are rarely explored.

While we might expect analysts of American cities to focus mainly on local dynamics and ignore the national, since in this country cities preserve a notable degree of fiscal and administrative autonomy from the national government, we surely would not expect such findings from those studying urban patterns in the context of a developing country such as Mexico. Much urban research conducted during the sixties and seventies demonstrated that there were clear economic and spatial relationships between urban and national development trajectories, especially in Latin America, such that the nature, composition, and employment and growth patterns of third-world cities were linked to national and international processes of dependent development.[3] Yet despite the widespread acceptance of these conclusions, or perhaps because of them, the existing literature on urban policy and urban politics in Mexico has failed to take seriously both the local and the national dimensions of the urban development process. The basic problem is that most urban scholars of Mexico are weak exactly where urbanists of the advanced capitalist context are strong: Analysts of Mexico have generally ignored the specifically local state and class dynamics of urban development patterns and focused instead on national (or even international) dynamics and determinations. The upshot is that there exists practically no work on the politics of urban development in Mexico City that helps us understand what happens when local classes confront the national as well as the local state, when the local state (read Mexico City's government) must confront nationally organized and powerful classes, or when we see alliances or conflicts between the local state, the national state, locally organized classes, or nationally organized classes.

For example, one of the few published works that seeks to account for Mexico City's urban development, written by Gustavo Garza, focuses primarily on the investment decisions of capitalists during the drive toward national industrialization.[4] According to Garza, capital has its own overdetermining logic, which is accumulation, and which drives investment decisions in Mexico City. Garza's is a thorough and provocative piece of work with massive amounts of material and data that provide incontrovertible evidence of the industrialization-led urban growth of Mexico City. However, like so many other works by scholars of Mexico, this book subordinates local developments to national dynamics. This may be explained by the preoccupation with capital and the all-powerful Mexican state, which is conceptualized as a series of nationally constituted government institutions controlled by the PRI. Indeed, Garza suggests that the PRI-dominated Mexican state has facilitated the urbanization process by introducing national policies that facilitate capital investment in Mexico City. But the possibility that local politics in Mexico City may run counter to the national policies of the Mexican state, or impede the process in any way at all, is ignored. So too is the possibility that local and national capitalists may use different strategies of accumulation, or may have different ways of investing in space.

Garza's tendency to trace urban development patterns to a more universally understood logic of capital-labor-state dynamics that is overdetermined at the national level is perfectly consistent with the general approach to urban studies coming from most of Mexico's top urbanists, sociologists, and political scientists. Scholars such as Martha Schteingart, Susan Eckstein, Alan Gilbert and Peter Ward, Antonio Azuela, and Manuel Perlo have analyzed urban policies and spatial patterns within Mexico City through a focus on the power of the national state and the general logic of capital accumulation. They too tend to see local dynamics, be they state or capital-specific, as indistinguishable from national ones, at least to the extent that they consider the most relevant political decisions about urban policy in Mexico City as being made by the president or the PRI under the pressure of nationally powerful capital, or through the investment decisions of nationally powerful capitalists. Many of these urbanists assume that there is little independent political or economic determination of urban outcomes on the local level because they see the Mexican state (or the PRI) in alliance with capital and pitted against the urban working classes or urban poor, with this state-capital alliance characteristically triumphant in urban conflicts, regardless of local and territorial dynamics or the involvement of local populations. Gilbert and Ward note, for example, that in order to understand urban servicing problems of cities like Mexico City (as well as Bogotá, Colombia, and Valencia, Venezuela), we must "understand the nature of the state, the prospect of the economies, and the broad structure of interest groups."[5] This approach is also exemplified in Susan Eckstein's claim that the PRI's power over urban populations was constant in three different neighborhoods in Mexico City, despite the clear socioeconomic differences between them, mainly because the Mexican state's policies vis-à-vis the urban poor are generally overdetermined by its overall political objective and its favoritism toward the interests of capital.[6] It is only Wayne Cornelius's *Politics and the Migrant Poor in Mexico*, in fact, that even tries to identify local political relationships between the PRI and Mexico City populations as determined by more than the overwhelming power of the Mexican state and/or capital. In Cornelius's case, urban outcomes have a lot to do with the social composition of certain neighborhoods, especially as understood with respect to the migrant status of local residents.

All this is not to say that most urban scholars of Mexico would not see the local and national domains as conceptually distinct, if pressed. Nor is it to say that most urban work on Mexico does not empirically distinguish between the urban policy actions and responses of local as opposed to national actors in the arguments they make. However, the conceptual distinctiveness of the urban and national domains—and the socially produced overlaps and attendant tensions between them—is not explicitly laid out as a central problematic. Nor is the fact that local and national dynamics, either in terms of class relations or the state, let alone urban policy priorities, might be different from each other. What comes through in these accounts, instead, is that the most critical actors in determining urban policies and patterns in Mexico City politics are capitalists and the PRI-controlled state, whose logic of power or accumulation is anything but place-specific. Working classes or low-income groups on the local level may fight against these forces; but even their relationships or conflicts with the state or capital are class-specific ones that result from accumulation logic and one-party rule, and have very little to do with the territorial specificities of citizens' lived experiences in Mexico City.

In this book I depart from these past works on urban policy, administration, and urban development in Mexico. Unlike much of the previous work cited above, I recognize that although urban and national dynamics frequently intersect with each other, they are analytically distinct and should be treated as such. Moreover, I argue that in order to understand the urban and administrative development of Mexico City, and its impact on national politics, we must be able to assess the tensions and overlaps between the urban and national domains, explore the ways in which these tensions and overlaps play themselves out in conflicts over Mexico City's administration and growth, and show how these urban conflicts influenced both local and national balances of state and class power.

One clear advantage of distinguishing between local and national state and class actors is that we can take seriously the actions and involvements of certain individuals and social groups that are generally ignored in studies of politics and change in Mexico. For example, even though middle classes are rarely seen as playing any role at all in Mexico's politics, due to the preoccupation with capital, labor, and the national state, when we analyze the urban level on its own we find that in struggles over Mexico City's growth and development, middle classes are absolutely key. This owes partly to their location in the areas of the city where transport infrastructure, land usage, and growth were most consequential and vigorously contested. To the extent that middle classes were critical in these local struggles over Mexico City's growth and servicing, then, and to the extent that they frequently took a position different from that of capitalists, labor, and the national political leadership on these local issues, they can be considered important actors in local-national struggles, and thus in larger changes in Mexico's corporatist politics.

In addition to recognizing the central participation of middle classes, once we distinguish local from national dynamics, one additional group of actors that must be examined closely consists of those involved in the so-called local state. This primarily means Mexico City's mayor and an extensive cadre of local-level politicians and administrators who may be members of the PRI but who also have slightly different linkages to social classes, both local and national, and to the rest of the party and its corporatist institutions. Once we acknowledge the existence of these local actors, and we recognize that the dynamics of the local state and its relationship to classes may be different from those of the national state, we must consider the possibility of conflicts between these two domains of the PRI. These conflicts can be absolutely critical obstacles to urban policymaking, the power of the PRI, and the overall legitimacy of one-party rule. To those who fail to distinguish local and national dynamics, however, such conflicts are elusive, at least enough so to wonder whether prevailing views of party and state hegemony might be fundamentally flawed.

Last, by recognizing differences in local and national state and class actors, as well as their conflicts with each other, we can expose yet another bias in the existing literature on Mexico: the tendency to see all relevant politics and decisions in Mexico as made by a relatively autonomous and all-powerful executive branch, through the wheeling and dealing of national bureaucrats and through the self-selection of their political cadres, or teams. This approach may be best exemplified in the work of political scientists like Roderick Camp, Peter Smith, and Gabriel Székely and Daniel Levy. These scholars tend to take the same view of Mexican politics as do the politicians themselves: that party bureaucrats' own personal networks and relations are the fundamental driving forces of policy, politics, and change in Mexico. Not only do local-national divisions in the state or bureaucracy fail to matter in their view; neither do the party's formal institutional structures, classes, or civil society. Yet if we acknowledge that local residents—in this case middle classes and a myriad of others in Mexico City—matter in urban and national policymaking, the assumption that relatively autonomous national bureaucrats chart the course of all Mexican politics is highly tenuous. These assumptions are also called into question once we acknowledge that local politicians can take—and have taken—stances on urban policies that pit them against cadres of national-level bureaucrats, the president, and the party leadership. If Mexico scholars focus only on national political teams or cadres of national bureaucrats, they merely reproduce the same misleading view of other urbanists: that an all-powerful national party apparatus overdetermines all policy and political developments in Mexico. But by recognizing the distinction between local and national state and class actors, scholars are free to analyze the heterogenous complexity of the Mexican state and to search for determinants of national political development in civil society and local politics as much as in the composition and orientation of an autonomous national bureaucracy.

FROM ANALYTIC FRAME TO THEORY AND METHOD

What does it mean, theoretically, to distinguish local and national actors and institutions in the study of Mexico City's administration and urban development? In addition to challenging prevailing approaches to Mexican politics, it means to take space seriously, which means to reject structuralist explanations that impute fixed and overdetermined interests to state, class, or bureaucratic actors. "Spatiality," says Edward Soja, "situates social life in an active arena where purposeful human agency jostles problematically with tendential social determinations to shape everyday activity, particularise social change, and etch into place the course of time and the making of history."[7] To take space seriously also means to consider that class and state power and action may be contingent on location in a local, as opposed to national, domain, for example. John Urry makes this clear as he states

> what would be obvious or taken for granted by anyone coming from a geographical/spatially inclined perspective. That is, the description of a national class structure may conceal significant geographical variations as a result of which few individuals actually live in a "local" class structure which is isomorphic with the national. Much sociological work on social class either assumes that what is true at the national level is also true on the local level, or that local studies can be fairly unproblematically taken as representative of the national. . . . [Yet] any particular distribution of empirical events (such as their spatial patterning) is the product of the complex interdependence of different social entities with varying causal powers.[8]

Spatial factors not only establish parameters on action, then, they also interact with social forces and structures and conditions to construct action. For sociologist Anthony Giddens, this means that space is the context for the construction of human agency, and geographers Michael Storper and Richard Walker agree. "Political and economic processes in general are profoundly shaped by their geography, and . . . any theoretical apparatus in the social sciences which ignores the geographical dimension of these processes (as nearly all do in the twentieth century) does so at its own peril."[9] To the extent that recent scholarship has made great strides in taking history seriously and examining how it articulates with state and class power and action, then, it must do the same with space.

What this implies here, in our study of Mexico, is the conscious situation of critical social actors, organized labor or bureaucrats, for example, in their spatial context. Indeed, if a nation's most active, visible, and powerful laborers and state workers are living, organized, and politically concentrated in a particular city, as has generally been the case in Mexico, then this fact should be as central to any study of their actions as is their class or occupational identity. Unfortunately, however, both in the study of Mexico and in the political and social sciences in general, spatiality is all too frequently ignored. Many analysts treat state and class actors as if they were free-floating in space; and most scholars far too easily jump from a focus on certain actors, Mexico City–based most likely, to making grand generalizations about national politics, without analytically distinguishing the local and national domains and without seeing that specific actors may be responding as much to local conditions and constraints as national ones. Once attention is paid to spatiality, however, we will have a more complete understanding of why social actors do what they do, which in turn gives us a better grasp of their impact on national political transformations. As Edward Soja argues, implicit in the understanding of spatiality is the assumption that social and political change are embodied in the redefinition or reconstruction of space, physical as well as social and vice versa.[10] To recognize this in our case is to consider that any struggles over Mexico City's growth and spatial character also challenge the political and social relations of state and class actors, especially their local-national articulations.

Once we start from the assumption that the actions and power of state and class actors in Mexico are determined in a particular spatial context, we not only understand the complex local and national politics of urban development conflicts; we also have a basis for questioning prevailing arguments about social and political change that presuppose general patterns of state-class relations and power, independent of social or spatial context. And this questioning, in turn, pushes us to take a slightly different view of the nature and role of theory in the social and political sciences. Rather than building theory around universal claims about state and class actors, for example, we accept a view of theory already well articulated and proposed by Jonathan Arac and Barbara Johnson, that theory is neither a system with presupposed outcomes nor a method that provides incontestable answers, but an interrogative process of critical thinking.[11] In other words, theory does not have to be an alternative logic standing above or outside the world, that is true in all times and places; it is the process of knowing and presenting the world. This process should include an understanding of both social actors and structures in the movement of history, and should be able to both accommodate and give larger meaning to the uniqueness of certain historical experiences, especially as they are imbedded in space. In this interrogative view of theory building, moreover, narrative becomes extremely important, primarily because it helps root theory and explanation in the discovery of historical developments, rather than in the association of laws and causation with regularities among events. According to Andrew Sayer, who has made important strides in examining the tensions between contextualizing and law-seeking approaches in the social sciences, history does not elude theory because of any lack of regularities in what it studies. Theory can grasp unique as well as repeated events, and it does so in the narrative process. In contrast to analysis, which is concerned with "abstracting common, widely replicated structures and mechanisms which endure through a number of different concrete histories . . . , the power of narrative derives from the way in which the depiction of events chronologically, in a story, gives the appearance of a causal chain of logic and the sense of movement towards a conclusion." [12]

In the upcoming pages we offer what Sayer might call a realist narrative (a term that is a welcome alternative to the empiricist label heaped on much historically grounded sociology), and what we prefer to think of as the union of theory and historical method. We take seriously constituent actors' accounts, when they are available, rather than dismissing them in order to maintain the purity of some a priori theoretical propositions; and we insist on critically analyzing these accounts in order to understand the how, where, and why of them and the larger developmental processes to which they refer.

URBAN TRANSPORT CONFLICTS IN MEXICO'S POLITICAL HISTORIOGRAPHY

In designing a research framework and analytic focus to drive our narrative account of the dynamics of Mexico City's administration and development, the work of urban sociologist Manuel Castells serves as a valuable starting point. One of the critical questions Castells posed in his early work was whether so-called urban processes were autonomous from nonlocal ones, be they national or international, and how, given this question, we should both delimit and study the urban domain.[13] In seeking answers to this fundamental theoretical question, Castells introduced the notion of collective consumption. He claimed that the provision and administration of collective consumption services, such as transport, housing, and other related infrastructure provided collectively to residents in large agglomerations, are the central axis around which the social and spatial development of cities occurs. Thus, according to Castells, in order to understand urbanization—or the growth of cities—one must understand the nature, logic, and social and spatial dynamics of collective consumption. Castells's is an approach to cities and to the built environment that is not necessarily based on rigid size or spatial designations, as were studies by urban sociologists before him. In contrast to earlier approaches, Castells starts from the proposition that the size, nature, and boundaries of the city—or urban domain—are socially produced, and this occurs through struggles over collective consumption.

Castells's notion of collective consumption has been highly controversial; and a decade after its initial popularization we see few works that still employ this concept. This may have to do with the limitations of this notion when used as a defining feature of cities and "the urban," since many of the infrastructural services Castells grouped under the rubric of collective consumption are neither collective nor specific to cities. Housing, for example, which Castells has analyzed in great detail throughout the body of his work, is produced and consumed both publicly and privately. And obviously, housing and myriad other infrastructural services also pegged by Castells, like electricity and transport, exist outside cities as well as within them. Yet despite these definitional problems, the notion of collective consumption stands as a useful starting point for the study of conflicts over growth, administration, and urban development in Mexico City, especially for a study like this, which takes the social and spatial boundaries between local and national domains as a problematic yet driving force in both urban and national development. Among the wide range of urban infrastructural services that are central to the administration and development of Mexico City's built environment, especially to the capital city's extension in and over space, transport is perhaps the most critical. It tends to be one of the most contentious and problematic issues for governing authorities, precisely because it engages perhaps the widest variety of disparate class and social actors. Unlike housing, for example, which tends to be of greatest concern to lower classes denied access to market allocation of housing, transport services touch on almost all social and class actors in the city in one way or another, independent of income level, mainly because they are essential to intraurban mobility and local economic prosperity. If the movement of goods and people is restricted, so too are work opportunities, market transactions, and thus the city's and region's economic health. Likewise, if Mexico City is prevented from growing in space, via certain transport infrastructure or services, both local and national economic dynamics are affected, as are the daily experiences of a city's residents, independent of their income level. Equally important, because different urban transport options become increasingly expensive as cities grow in size, over time the need for transport forces state and class actors to make difficult administrative decisions as they weigh local fiscal and political concerns about transport against demands for other social expenditures. All this suggests that urban transport policies, or the lack of them, not only help determine a city's spatial character and potential size; they also concern both local residents and national-level actors, albeit for different reasons perhaps. To the extent that one of our concerns here is to assess how the connection between urban and national domains plays itself out in struggles over Mexico City's development, transport conflicts emerge as illustrative in several critical periods under study.

That the administration and provision of urban transport services in Mexico City is central, both to local and national politics as well as to the urban development of the capital city, is not merely an esoteric academic proposition. Quite the contrary. Urban transport in Mexico City has been so fundamental to the history of the nation and the experience of its residents that it constantly emerges in the popular idiom and in literary works as a metaphor for political change and as a source of collective self-understanding. "Irémos en camión." We'll go by bus. Those simple words by Salvador Novo, honorary chronicler of Mexico City, begin an engaging account of life in the capital in the first half of the twentieth century. Although the intent of this essay is to underscore the capital's centrality in the nation's political and economic life after the 1910 Revolution, it also makes a claim for the larger importance of urban transport in the nation's cultural imagery. Novo weaves a tale of the city's urban growth and the nation's social and political development through a focus on *tranviarios* (trolley workers) and later on *camioneros* (bus drivers). In speaking to the rhythm of the city's development, to occupation and class formation, to the political and social impact of the Revolution, to the origins of popular language, and even to the emergence of bureaucratic corruption, urban transport is central to Novo's narrative.[14] Novo gives evidence of the ways in which providers and regulators of urban transport sprang from the 1910 Revolution, guided the still unconsolidated social and political order, and became entrenched in citizens' and governing officials' common practices. His dramatic exposition also focuses our attention on central city streets of the capital—like Calle Tacuba—where conflicts over transport access and land usage would throw local residents and authorities into battle as the postrevolutionary decades unfolded. And the *camioneros* Novo's pen caresses with such great care have made their mark on Mexican politics in ways that reflect their power and that, in turn, have kept urban transport issues at the forefront of policy and debate. These *camioneros* have become some of Mexico's wealthiest men and have consistently held positions in the Senate and Congress—and even governorships—for the past forty-five years.

Of course, many different urban services have affected Mexico City's development in some way; and many have been central to political struggles and cultural life. Housing stands out in this regard and has been analyzed by several authors in the past, sometimes even with a view to its national developmental implications. Yet not all urban services and urban development conflicts can be treated with equal care and consideration, owing to obvious constraints. Moreover, few urban services have had such a direct impact on Mexico City's growth—both its population increase and spatial expansion—as has transport. Equally important, perhaps, even though urban transport conflicts and concerns consistently emerge as politically salient and highly contentious in Mexico City, they—unlike housing—have not been examined as systematically by sociologists, political scientists, or historians. For all these reasons, urban transport serves as a central object of study in this account of Mexico City's urban development.

This does not mean that I will ignore all other urban infrastructural service controversies in Mexico City, especially when they are central to understanding local or national political conflicts over Mexico City's growth and administration. In certain crucial periods of time, for example, provision of housing was as contentious and central to Mexico City's development as was transport. But in order to delimit the focus of this study, and to give transport its analytic due in studies of the capital city's social, spatial, and administrative development, I pay special attention to urban transport policies.

In the earliest periods under study, immediately after the Revolution, our central focus will be the government's efforts to revive trolley service and the conflicts over its provision and administration. In the intermediate periods, during Mexico City's industrial take-off, I focus on public bus service and the political and administrative conflicts that ensued over street widening, downtown development, and other related urban redevelopment policies that generated political controversies. In the later period I focus on Mexico City's downtown subway system and the conflicts generated by its proposed introduction and subsequent implementation. In each set of transport conflicts, I examine the ways in which both local and national state and class actors participated, as well as the points of contention between them and their articulation with local and national politics.

As will be clear shortly, how each set of transport conflicts was "resolved" often had more to do with the power of national actors than of local ones. That is, state actors representing national political institutions rather than local ones, or class actors who were organized in national rather than Mexico City federations, generally prevailed in controversial urban policy decisions. Yet the consistent subordination of local concerns to national ones, at least in the area of urban transport policy, often had unforeseen implications for Mexico City's urban growth and for the power of certain state or class actors to influence future urban development, both local and national. For one thing, it helped set the terms of debate over transport policy and over urban development trajectories in subsequent periods. For another, these patterns of national determination generated local conflicts that ultimately altered the political balance of power, both locally and nationally, and within the ruling party as a whole. That is, despite the consistent triumph of national forces in local transport struggles, local populations did not stand quietly by. When it became clear that transport policies proposed for the capital were geared exclusively toward the demands of national actors and institutions, local populations went beyond making demands about transport, and challenged both political structures and one-party rule.

This dynamic set national party leaders scrambling, since it meant that to triumph with a specific urban development policy also meant to challenge the party's national legitimacy. In the wake of serious transport conflicts, national leaders sought to buttress past alliances and create new ones, in order to restore their legitimacy with Mexico City populations and still keep competing urban development forces loyal to the party. It was a juggling act that produced the peopled, polluted, and poverty-stricken capital city. More important, perhaps, it was a juggling act that pushed party leaders to introduce fundamental reforms in both local and national political institutions and practices, some of which were successful and others of which were not. In the long run, these reforms helped transform political relations within and between local and national state and class actors, and by so doing posed an unexpectedly serious challenge to the political structures of corporatism and the ruling party's capacity to maintain power.

STRUCTURE OF THE BOOK

The book proceeds chronologically, charting conflicts over the servicing, administration, and spatial development of Mexico City, starting in 1910 and ending in 1988. Each chapter can and should stand on its own as an account of salient urban policy and development conflicts and their local and national political implications during a particular historical time period. Still, the book is also meant to be read as a document whose whole is greater than the sum of its parts. Accordingly, developments in each chapter and period lay the groundwork for those emerging in subsequent chapters. This method not only allows a rooting of present conflicts and reforms in past ones, it allows the reader to see how pressures and small-scale institutional changes in Mexico City that may appear minor in a single period of time accumulate to produce chaotic urban development trajectories and a fundamental transformation in corporatism and one-party rule.

The book's format is relatively straightforward. Chapter 2 begins by high-lighting the national and local political conditions that spurred the revolutionary leadership to foster the urban reconstruction and development of Mexico City. Both Chapters 2 and 3 discuss the urban service conflicts and concerns in the capital before Mexico City hosted the nation's urbanization-led industrial development (1910–1943). It is during this period that we see how decisions about the servicing and administration of Mexico City's built environment, especially in the areas of housing and transport, set the stage for collaborative relations between capital and labor and for the foundation of the CNOP, both of which contributed to the political consolidation of corporatism and one-party rule. Chapters 4 through 6 examine the period of rapid urban and industrial development in the capital, and they highlight the ways in which controversies over the provision and administration of urban services, especially those linked to the city's rapid growth, like the subway, produced conflicts within the corporatist political system (1944–1973).

Chapters 7 and 8 bring the discussion up to date (1973–1988). They show how anarchic processes of urban development and the extension of costly urban services, such as the subway, brought urban fiscal crisis and urban social movements, both of which challenged corporatist political structures. When these urban problems interfaced with a national political and economic crisis, they called into question the fit between local and national politics and the political balance between different class-based sectors of the PRI. Chapter 8 also raises some hypotheses about the ways in which these urban-based conflicts have affected Mexican corporatism today and the future of one-party rule. Chapter 9 concludes with a recap of the nature and national political impact of urban development conflicts, and discusses the theoretical implications of this evidence for understanding the capital city, classes, and corporatist politics in twentieth-century Mexico.

2

THE URBAN TERRAIN OF

POSTREVOLUTIONARY

STATE BUILDING, 1910–1929

Mexico's 1910 Revolution succeeded in toppling the dictatorship of Porfirio Díaz, but it also created two critical problems that confronted revolutionary forces in the years immediately following Díaz's defeat. One was the disruption of the economy and the dire need to restart the engines of economic growth. The other was a struggle within the revolutionary leadership over the ideological direction the Revolution was to take and the power to be granted to rural versus urban classes in constructing that path. These two problems were integrally linked. Efforts to restart the economy were to be predicated on decisions about placing priority on agricultural versus industrial development, and about the economic centrality of Mexico City. These decisions, in turn, not only had implications for Mexico City's urban development, but they also affected which ideological factions of the revolutionary leadership were to triumph and with which bases of support.

In theory, Mexico's Revolution could have taken several different paths after 1910. Given the involvement of *agraristas* like Emiliano Zapata and Pancho Villa, given the fact that rural populations with agrarian sentiments had struggled most actively in the armed struggle, and given the overwhelming anti-Americanism that prevailed at the time, it would have been perfectly logical for Mexico to have followed an ideological course not unlike that taken by Cubans in their revolution five decades later. That is, Mexico's revolutionary leaders could have built an anticapitalist social and political order structured around the objectives of rural development. But they did not. Within the revolutionary leadership, political factions oriented toward a broad variety of urban populations prevailed, to the exclusion of *campesinos*, such that the development policy of choice in those critical early years after the Revolution was urbanization-led industrialization, not rural development. Moreover, the goals of national industrialization were purposefully linked to the goals of reviving the urban economy in the capital, not only industry but also commerce and services for the urban middle classes. This, in turn, meant that both small and large capitalists, especially local manufacturers and *comerciantes* in Mexico City, also had a say in Mexico's postrevolutionary political and economic development, in marked contrast to the Soviet Union after 1917, where the party-state prioritized the proletariat and singularly commanded the economy in the absence of a strong capitalist class.

This is not to say that Mexico's party-led state failed to become actively involved in the project of national industrialization, or that the desires of capitalists always prevailed. Nor is it to say that because of an urban orientation, agrarian demands and the social concerns of rural populations were entirely absent from postrevolutionary politics and policy in Mexico. Perhaps the most renowned of all twentieth-century Mexican leaders was General Lázaro Cárdenas, who collectivized significant portions of agriculture, concentrated resources in agricultural development, and constructed the Mexican political system around direct participation by peasants, in addition to urban-based industrial workers. However, this rural orientation did not fully come to the fore until Cárdenas came to power in 1934, more than two decades after the revolutionary upheaval. By that time, Mexico had already started to head down a less radical path, one that prioritized economic development and political stability in Mexico City, at the expense of most other regions. This preoccupation ensured that the capital city would receive disproportionate amounts of national resources and that its principal resident populations—bureaucrats, middle classes, and urban-based industrial laborers—would hold disproportionate political sway in determining national policies.

That Mexico followed this path was not necessarily inevitable. Regional forces in the revolutionary leadership, like Villa and Zapata, voiced opposition to the liberal vision of industrialization and modernization promoted by Francisco I. Madero, Venustiano Carranza, Alvaro Obregón, and later Plutarco Elías Calles. Had Villa's or Zapata's rural forces triumphed, we probably would not have seen the political and economic subordination of regions to the center that has characterized twentieth-century Mexico. We also would not have seen the rapid industrial development of the capital city and the overwhelming concentration of political power and institutions there. So what made it possible for the more liberal forces in the Revolution to defeat their rural counterparts and to establish the urbanization-led industrial development of their country? And what were the implications for the servicing, administration, and growth of Mexico City?

Although the reasons for ignoring rural populations and pursuing urbanization-led industrialization were many, one factor that was absolutely critical was the revolutionary leadership's reliance on political support in Mexico City proper, which also had direct implications for local servicing and administration. To the extent that political leaders like Carranza and Obregón sought the support of Mexico City populations in their struggle against Zapata and Villa, they formed a united front and increased their chances of successfully seizing state power in the capital; and to the extent that these revolutionary leaders could reconstruct the built environment and revive the Mexico City economy, they were better able to guarantee the support of these local populations, ranging from owners of businesses both large and small to artisans and members of the comfortable middle classes, who understandably were eager to see a return to normalcy in the capital. Once Mexico City populations were targeted as critical political allies by certain factions in the revolutionary leadership, moreover, servicing and reconstruction of the city continued as a priority for national political leaders, especially Madero, Carranza, and Obregón. Pressures for repayment of national debts that had accumulated during the dictatorship of Porfirio Diáz also reinforced this dynamic. Madero and his immediate successors found that before lending much-needed political or financial support to any new regime, foreign lenders and their home governments were anxious to see evidence of economic renewal and political calm, especially in the capital city, where many factories and the institutions of state were located. Accordingly, the process of postrevolutionary political consolidation in the 1910s and 1920s went hand in hand with efforts to redevelop Mexico City and reconstruct its built environment in accordance with the servicing demands of local populations, workers, capitalists, and middle classes alike. In the immediate postrevolutionary period, then, the stability and ideological direction of national politics depended in no small part on local politics, administrative dynamics, and economic development in the capital city.

Administering, constructing, and reviving Mexico City were easier said than done, however, because these goals required fancy footwork and crafty political alliance-making. The city was in virtual chaos. After several years in the throes of battle, the problems in the capital were many. Employment was down, industry and commerce were stalled, and many local services were barely operating. Much of this was a result of the destruction of Mexico City's infrastructure during the Revolution. As home to foreign elements, Díaz loyalists, and the Porfirian state, the capital city had suffered serious attacks in the final stages of battle, attacks that damaged critical roads and buildings, halted many economic activities, and caused a substantial proportion of the city's foreign capitalists to return to their countries of origin. Thus the problems were great and the resources were few, especially with capital flight and the loss of local tax revenues that followed the cessation of economic activity. Moreover, reviving the economy and administering local services in conditions of scarce government revenues often meant turning to the private sector, foreign lenders, or both for necessary financial resources. Yet this put the revolutionary leadership in a potentially tricky political situation. Because the Revolution had been fought partly over the penetration of foreign capitalists, it was difficult to turn abroad for urban reconstruction money. Local firms had few resources of their own, however, and tax revenues were stalled until the restoration could begin. Complicating matters, many of Mexico City's critical urban infrastructural services, like transport and electricity, were still under foreign ownership. To nationalize them or intervene directly in their administration might facilitate the process of urban reconstruction; but it would also imply a stronger antagonism to foreign capital than many in the revolutionary leadership wished to exhibit at this early stage. Thus, even though there may have been strong support for urban redevelopment from Mexico City's resident populations, there was little consensus over how to bring it about in conditions of economic scarcity without offending foreign capitalists, especially those involved in urban services.

Prioritizing urban redevelopment frequently meant subordinating class-specific demands to larger urban objectives, and this too called for real political skill, not only because class issues were a principal rallying point both during and immediately after the Revolution, but also because the demands of some classes were more consistent with urban redevelopment objectives than were others. For example, efforts to revive the local economy and restore urban infrastructural services most directly benefited the city's middle classes, especially small shopkeepers and employees, most of whom relied on local economic prosperity and infrastructural services for their livelihood. This was not true for industrial laborers, however, and because of this the revolutionary leadership also had to pay special attention to the city's working-class organizations while it concentrated on urban development. Yet keeping labor's demands in the forefront posed an additional problem for the revolutionary leadership, at least to the extent that local factories and businesses also had to prosper if the urban economy was to restart. This did not bode well for wage and workplace demands, and thus it held the potential to generate opposition from labor. With urban redevelopment plans, then, revolutionary leaders had to burn the candle at both ends, so to speak: they had to give incentives to business to revive activities while also extending the olive branch to workers in those same enterprises. This task was difficult in general, but in the urban service sector, which, after all, was so central to urban redevelopment, this task was practically impossible. Given the difficulties involved in facing these daunting challenges, the revolutionary leadership avoided administrative actions or urban development policies that were too partisan, that threatened to alienate potential bases of urban political support, or that brought more political infighting within the revolutionary leadership. Still, conditions in the capital city were such that some concerted effort at urban redevelopment was absolutely necessary, especially if the objectives of restoring the local economy, and thus consolidating political power, were to be achieved.

In the upcoming pages we discuss this complex problematic of urban administration and policymaking, and explore its political implications. With the city and the nation up for grabs during much of the period discussed in this chapter, many actors appeared on the scene to make claims and shift alliances, including the organized working class. Our purpose is as much to introduce these actors—most of whom continued to be key players in later periods—as it is to discuss their involvement in, and impact on, urban administration and development in this watershed moment. As such, we pay especially close attention to the details of labor and state conflicts over administration and reconstruction in the capital, even though they may be only indirectly related to questions of urban policymaking; we also discuss divisions in the working class that resulted from state and class efforts to address Mexico City's urban problems in the immediate postrevolutionary period, even though these too tend to move our attention away from the urban domain. We focus on these actors and conflicts, however, because their initial struggles and divisions laid much of the organizational and jurisdictional foundation for local politics in the capital and for corporatism in Mexico. These actors' involvement in the social, political, and economic life of Mexico City, moreover, highlights the importance of transport conflicts in the postrevolutionary period and explains the appearance of several new players in the union movement and in urban politics, like bus drivers, who would come to play a central role in local and political struggles over urban administration, servicing, and growth discussed in later chapters.

We begin our account of these ground-laying developments with an examination of the chaotic urban conditions in Mexico City after 1910 and the ways in which these conditions helped link a broad coalition of Mexico City populations to each other and to certain national factions of the revolutionary leadership. Next we consider the impact of common urban concerns about the built environment, especially housing and transport scarcities, on the growing political power of transport workers and on the formal collaborations between the state and Mexico City labor organizations in the late 1910s. These collaborations soon became essential for both national political leaders and local populations, not only for the purposes of restoring urban services, but also for consolidating political power vis-à-vis middle classes. Last, we discuss the political tensions that emerged within Mexico City labor movements during the 1920s as national political leaders sought to facilitate urban development.

Throughout the two decades after 1910, the revolutionary leadership's urban development objectives and the conflicts they produced threatened to undermine the class-based demands of certain Mexico City populations, even as they were crafted to ensure the support of others. This contradiction fueled an upsurge of labor unrest in the city, especially around urban transport provision. But with transport provision in chaos as a result, the revolutionary leadership became even more resolute in subordinating class-specific priorities of local labor organizations to urban development objectives in the capital. They did so by granting greater institutional and political power to those local, class-based federations that controlled urban transport services; and once these local labor organizations were privileged in this manner, a new set of political conflicts and tensions emerged, particularly as these local labor federations captured unparalleled political power. The result: From 1910 to 1928 the tables turned in terms of the articulations between local and national politics, such that national political dynamics were now subordinated to local ones, rather than vice versa. That is, labor organizations that first began with a Mexico City membership and a concern primarily with local prosperity had by 1928 gained sufficient political clout to challenge the national revolutionary leadership and to control local political institutions for their own national, as well as urban, political purposes. This not only created new political tensions in the national political leadership; as the decade of the 1920s ended, it also produced an entirely new approach to the servicing and administration of Mexico City, including the elimination of democratic rule in the capital.

THE CITY IN SHAMBLES

After the 1910 Revolution, the two most serious urban problems in the capital were housing and transport scarcities. Mexico City's population first began to increase markedly as the capital went through a phase of rapid industrial growth between 1900 and 1910. Much of the growth was due to rural-urban migration during the final years of the Porfiriato, as peasants were driven off their lands by the commercialization of agriculture. Ongoing revolutionary struggles during the century's first decade further pushed rural populations into the capital city, where the situation was comparatively less violent than in the countryside. As the future for the rural peasantry became less clear, due to the destruction of many haciendas and their surrounding villages during revolutionary battles, the pace of migration intensified. The overall population in Mexico City soared from 541,516 in 1900, to 729,153 in 1910, an increase of 33 percent; by 1921 the population rose another 26 percent to 903,063 (see Appendix B).

With the tremendous population increases, housing and social conditions in the capital deteriorated. According to urban historian María Dolores Morales, the urban poor figured prominently in these increases, a fact that translated directly into a densely occupied and underserviced housing stock.[1] The disproportionate concentration of urban poor was partly due to the fact that many of the city's wealthier trading and commercial families fled with Díaz's imminent defeat, leaving the most economically disenfranchised classes still in the city. Yet it also was due to ownership concentration and real increases in the number of urban poor, as rapid rural-urban migration spurred by unemployment in the countryside caused Mexico City's population to increase more rapidly than employment prospects. As the net urban population increased, formal sector employment decreased, due largely to the proletarianization of artisan professions, which began in the late 1880s and continued through the 1910 Revolution. And amid the poverty accompanying the unemployment of these traditional craftsmen and artisans, urban living conditions sank to a low point. In his seminal work on Mexican industrial workers at the time of the Revolution, Rodney Anderson notes that in the first decades of the twentieth century, the "growing class of dispossessed artisans, whose talents were less needed in the industrial age," crowded into the working-class barrios of the cities and towns, mostly in Mexico City. Anderson notes that "the unemployed poor and urban workers alike lived in the same crowded conditions, with no plumbing and no water, amid filth and disease."[2] A turn-of-the-century survey, also cited by Anderson, showed that in Mexico City density rates had reached an average of seven inhabitants per room and that "16 percent of the city's population had no home at all, many paying a few *centavos* a night to stay in the public lodging houses."[3]

After 1910, Mexico City's real estate market also began to experience a boom, spurred by the rapid sale of church and other corporate properties in the midst of the anticlerical fervor that greeted the new century and fueled the Revolution.[4] The destruction of many haciendas by Zapatista and Villista forces, Porfirio Díaz's political defeat, and uncertainty in the provinces further fueled the urban land market by propelling rural elites to the city, where conditions seemed more predictable. Mexico City soon became the new home for "the heirs of the large rural landlords (*latifundistas*), who quickly became urban landlords (or *grandes latifundistas urbanos*) and whose large-scale ownership of urban property infused life into Mexico City's real estate market."[5] Because many of the capital city's prosperous foreign families temporarily fled the country during the revolutionary upheaval, these new urban *latifundistas* were able to acquire valuable parcels of unpopulated Mexico City lands at cheap prices, particularly on the edges of the metropolitan area. By holding these lands off the market until they were able to command a relatively high price, competition for scarce properties accelerated. These actions both heated the land market and exacerbated the housing problem, since the valorization of real estate and conscious efforts to keep abandoned urban properties off the market drove housing and rental costs up almost immediately. With the majority of urban residents paying rent to urban landlords, both new and old, popular concern about urban infrastructural scarcities mounted, especially in the area of housing.

While housing struggles captured some of the energy of Mexico City's residents in the two decades surrounding the Revolution, urban populations also made extensive demands for transport, mainly trolley service, which was the principal means of transport in the capital. Claims for roadway infrastructure and urban transport provision have not been as well documented as housing struggles in the early period, the latter of which are discussed with much insight and careful detail in the work of Manuel Perlo Cohen.[6] A closer look at conditions in Mexico City in the 1910s and 1920s, however, suggests that transport deficiencies spurred the ire of residents almost as much as housing scarcities, and that conflicts over transport soon replaced housing struggles as one of the period's most contentious and consequential urban problems. Indeed, most documentary accounts suggest that the existing transport system—electric trolleys installed during the Porfiriato—was woefully inadequate to serve the capital's growing population.[7] Also, because Mexico City's rapid growth and attendant proletarianization displaced many of its poorer residents from central city areas, low-income and traditional residents could no longer walk as easily between home and work and were thus forced to rely on public transport in greater numbers.[8] A basic source of the problem was that transport services did not increase as rapidly as demand. During the first decade of the twentieth century, before the overthrow of Porfirio Díaz, more government investment was poured into road construction and pavement than into collective transport, in an effort to facilitate the residential dispersion of an increasingly prosperous middle class to the south and to foster individual modes of transport. Thus transport infrastructure was already inadequate to the task, even before the dramatic postrevolutionary increase in population. After the Revolution, with a new spurt of growth in the city, serious inadequacies surfaced and generated both government and popular concern. Yet it took several years for the Revolution's new leadership to ensure adequate trolley services, since rebel attacks on electrical installations—which provided the energy for trolley services—continually disrupted service.[9] Protests by trolley workers (known as *tranviarios*) against foreign ownership of this critical service also hampered urban transport provision.

THE REVOLUTIONARY LEADERSHIP AND URBAN POLICY: FROM A LIBERAL TO A LABORIST STRATEGY

When Francisco I. Madero assumed Mexico's presidency after Porfirio Díaz's ouster in 1911, he faced both a city in crisis and a highly unstable political environment. Because local populations lacked basic transport and housing services, they clamored for immediate improvements. Yet as Mexico City residents stood poised to assess Madero's capacity to revive the city and restore its activities to normalcy, they, like the rest of the nation, also made demands on the new government to demonstrate its political colors, so to speak. Madero was prepared to respond, in order to legitimate his hold on power, but demonstrating a commitment to democratic politics took precedence over a commitment to bettering urban services. This was made clear by his efforts to restore a municipal form of urban government. Because his predecessor, Porfirio Díaz, had limited the capacity of local municipalities in the nation's capital to popularly elect representatives and make major urban policy decisions, a battle cry of the liberal forces in the Revolution had been to establish the municipality as a central element of Mexican democracy. As spokesman for the liberal forces in the Revolution, President Madero reintroduced the municipality as the principal unit of urban governance and policymaking, a change that he implemented in 1911. This reform, in essence, restored local democratic practices that had been eliminated by the Díaz dictatorship for the purposes of centralizing control and decision making in the capital. Madero's decision to revitalize the *municipio*, as the sublocal territorial jurisdiction was called, was made mainly for political purposes, with the aim of marking a break from the immediate past and of legitimizing his rule among populations in the capital. Yet the fiscal and administrative consequences of this urban reform were not very well anticipated, and the results were indeed disastrous for urban servicing and political stability, two problems that plagued both Madero and his successors.

First of all, the restoration of municipal autonomy initiated under Madero produced serious political infighting in the capital, as competing parties and ideological factions fought to control each territorially distinct sublocal jurisdiction. In addition, municipal infighting exacerbated problems of urban service coordination, particularly in the area of transport, because each *municipio* sought to enact separate legislation and play competing providers of urban services off against one another. Also, given the small size of these newly autonomous units of Mexico City governance, local revenue bases were insufficient for the major infrastructural investments such a large and important city required. Ultimately, the Madero government and its successors came under pressure to introduce other urban policy measures that would help efficiently and adequately restore urban services in the capital. A 1913 Reglamento de Circulación de Vehículos and the creation of the Oficina del Tráfico in 1915 were among the first of these measures imposed with federal authority on the city as a whole. The vehicle circulation laws set restrictions on traffic flow in the capital, and the new traffic office licensed carriages and motor vehicles to provide transport services. Yet it soon became clear that introducing laws to regulate existing services would neither solve transport problems nor eliminate the growing political conflict in Mexico City, which continued due to municipal infighting and to the generally unstable political situation. New and improved services needed to be offered, too, especially if the city was to thrive once again.

Some of the most pressing problems facing the revolutionary leadership involved rebuilding transport infrastructure that had been destroyed, and extending existing transport and housing services that previously were inadequate or that could not be efficiently provided by individual *municipios*. Given the revolutionary leadership's commitment to social justice, services geared toward the masses that required some public regulation and support, like transport, were targeted priorities. As such, new efforts were made to restore and expand the city's trolley network, although the limited resources available made these attempts only partially successful. With pressing needs and limited fiscal resources, governing officials and local administrators had to seek other strategies to redress the problem, including the imposition of strict work regulations on those providing urban services. The purpose of these regulations was to ensure that Mexico City workers would work long hours at low wages in order to protect the city's already overdrawn economic base.[10]

Those employed in urban service provision were under particularly intense pressure to provide long hours and comprehensive services, given both the new government's and the private sector's priorities to restore critical infrastructural services in the nation's capital. This did not sit well with the Mexico City labor movement, however, which is perhaps best evidenced by a series of strikes that hit the capital in the Revolution's aftermath. Starting in 1914, trolley car operators in Mexico City staged strikes over low wages and long working hours that were so severe that the still fragile constitutionalist government of Venustiano Carranza, who headed a provincially based faction of the revolutionary leadership that had come to power after President Madero's assassination in 1913, was forced to intervene in the administration of the foreign-owned Compañía de Tranvías to "guarantee urban transport services" in the capital.[11] In 1915 and 1916, moreover, two successful strikes over wages and work conditions brought the capital to a standstill. Both involved urban service provision. One was waged by trolley workers who were being pressured to restore urban transport service to prerevolutionary levels. Another was called by electricians working for the foreign-owned Compañía de Tranvías, who were charged with reconstructing and expanding the city's electricity networks. Electricity not only fed the trolley system; it also serviced urban households and local businesses. Complicating matters, at around the same time, a strong renters' movement (inquilinarios) was developing in Mexico City and in several other cities that faced similar problems with speculation and rapid population increases from rural displacement, including Mérida and Veracruz.

As he faced growing labor conflicts among urban service workers and a mobilized renters' movement, Carranza and his provincial allies in the revolutionary leadership found it even more essential to negotiate a series of work settlements and urban policy accommodations in order to guarantee labor peace in the capital, where their political connections were still tenuous. Wages and working conditions in the city's most critical service, urban transport, were a sticky mess to untangle, however, and the governing revolutionary leadership avoided this cause like the plague in its efforts to consolidate power. Carranza steered clear of direct intervention in transport activities because the Compañía de Tranvías was an important ally for his still unconsolidated governing coalition in its attempts to restore the urban economy. The Compañía had long absorbed the cost of most of Mexico City's street paving and several other critical urban infrastructural services.[12] Moreover, this foreign-owned trolley company (Compañía de Tranvías) was jointly owned by a foreign-owned electric company (Compañía de Luz y Fuerza), which further explains why major labor concessions or radical policy changes in this sector were avoided. Few in the national revolutionary leadership cared to alienate the Compañía de Luz y Fuerza by consistently siding with its striking workers, since the firm's foreign owners could cause serious diplomatic problems for any revolutionary faction attempting to consolidate its claim to govern the national state. Also, this foreign-owned utility provided much-needed electricity to the city's businesses and residences, who constituted important political bases of support in those moments of vulnerability. Perhaps most important, the Compañía de Luz y Fuerza was a principal source of necessary cash for all manner of urban expenditure and reconstruction, and the revolutionary leadership was not willing to jeopardize this scarce resource and thus risk bankruptcy or urban chaos in the capital.[13]

Precisely because foreign involvement in trolley service and electricity generation limited their capacity and desire to directly intervene in the transport sector, the revolutionary leadership turned to another critical urban service, housing, as a way to make political concessions to striking Mexico City laborers and to restore enough social peace to bring the local population to its side. Not only did the absence of foreign investment in the housing sector make intervention in the provision of this equally critical aspect of the built environment less controversial than transport, housing problems did not necessarily require direct or massive government resources, which were sorely lacking. Mere changes in the regulation of rent hikes and land usage sufficed to demonstrate a commitment to bettering housing conditions, whereas to fully accommodate transport concerns would require either nationalization of transport, a problematic political issue, or direct provision of public transport services, a costly fiscal obligation. Starting in late 1915, then, the national revolutionary leadership temporarily shifted its attention away from transport and began to tackle the local problems of housing in Mexico City. In September of that year, Carranza responded to the growing demands of the renters' movement and decreed that unoccupied houses for both residential and commercial usages would have to be rented for a period of three months

at a regulated price of less than fifty pesos a month.[14] In 1916, one year before the establishment of the first postrevolutionary constitution, Carranza's
national minister of justice continued this line of reform and imposed strict
regulations on tenants' evictions. In the same year, Mexico City's governing
officials "decreed that urban landlords could not rent at a price higher than
those set on April 1, 1916, under penalty of 300 to 500 pesos or incarceration
for 15 to 30 days."[15]

Most of these policy reforms were nationally, and not just locally, decreed.
By 1917, when Mexico's new constitution was formulated, housing rights
were formalized in two specific clauses within the section on rights for the
working classes, known as Article 123. These clauses obliged all employers to
provide comfortable and clean housing when more than one hundred workers
were employed, a situation that was common in Mexico City, or when the
place of employment was outside a major population center. This clause also
mandated public support for the establishment of social cooperatives to construct affordable and hygienic housing for workers, most of which were subsequently located in the capital. The new constitution also addressed issues of
affordability, decreeing that employers must provide their laborers with sanitary dwellings at a rental not "exceeding one-half of one percent per month
of the assessed value of the properties."[16]

URBAN CONDITIONS AND THE MEXICO CITY LABOR MOVEMENT

Despite the fact that these changes were formalized in the new national
constitution as rights for all Mexican citizens, the housing reforms in this
immediate postrevolutionary period were not necessarily introduced with the
general population in mind. Nor should they be considered merely as general
accommodations made by a new revolutionary state for the purposes of fostering national legitimacy in the still unstable political environment. They were
as much specific political agreements made by a specific faction of the revolutionary leadership with critical and well-organized sectors of the Mexico
City labor movement, starting first with the Casa del Obrero Mundial, a
federation of unions and assorted mutualist associations in the nation's capital
that emerged out of the ashes of the Revolution. These Mexico City–based
agreements over housing soon set the terms of national debate over the urban
policy orientation of the Carranza government, even as they also initiated the
government's efforts to better urban conditions in Mexico City in particular.
Equally important, they set the stage for a new state-labor collaboration that
would develop into a national politics of corporatism in subsequent decades.

The importance of establishing state-labor collaborations, and of using housing and other urban policies to do so, first became clear when the revolutionary movement was in chaos after Madero's assassination and when Venustiano Carranza, Pancho Villa, Emiliano Zapata, and later Victoriano Huerta were all actively struggling for political control in the capital. In September 1914, Carranza established an informal alliance with the Casa del Obrero Mundial; in return he pushed through favorable measures for urban renters. His concern probably was as much to take the steam out of a highly visible renters' movement, which was becoming more closely linked to the labor movement and moving it leftward, as it was to consolidate his political bases with urban workers. Yet by gaining the support of the labor leadership in the Casa in exchange for his agreement to support their demands for urban housing reforms, Carranza cemented perhaps the most important political alliance of his career. On February 17, 1915, the political relationship between Carranza and the Casa del Obrero Mundial was formalized in the form of a pact, which both parties signed with the additional support of Alvaro Obregón, a revolutionary leader closely tied to the Casa and the labor movement. In the document that formalized the collaboration, housing was the only concrete policy issue articulated; the remaining eight clauses addressed issues of more general concern, such as preserving order and reducing bloodshed.[17]

To be sure, Carranza's strategy was not necessarily to embrace workers' class-specific demands or even to advocate far-reaching reforms in housing policy. During his years in power, in fact, Carranza limited the nature and larger bases of labor organization while still rhetorically advocating workers' rights to strike. Thus he was careful not to completely alienate small property owners and other petit bourgeois sectors with his labor stances. Rather, his efforts to toe a centrist line prevailed over any prolabor ideological orientation or political alliance. This was clear as early as 1916 when, after temporarily strengthening his position vis-à-vis Zapatista forces, Carranza both reversed some of the restrictions on rent hikes and militarily repressed striking workers in Mexico City.[18] If anything, then, Carranza's strategy of making alliances with the urban labor movement on the housing issue were part and parcel of his larger objectives of maintaining power over peasant forces in the revolutionary movement and establishing peace and economic prosperity in Mexico City. For that reason, the housing platforms Carranza supported, both in Article 123 of the constitution and in the pact with the Casa del Obrero Mundial, were confined mainly to bettering housing conditions and the built environment without undermining his commitment to private ownership. General decrees about universal rights to housing or rent control that might challenge the capitalist logic of private property were absent, as were clauses that gave the labor movement full autonomy with the power to seriously undermine either capital or the state.

Carranza's limited ideological commitment to the labor movement's workplace concerns, or their class-specific demands, raises some important questions about the origins and larger political implications of the state-labor pact over urban housing formulated in 1915. Was this just an early example of the Mexican political system's capacity to co-opt, or of Mexican labor's clientelistic orientation? Or was it a marriage of convenience formed in the coincidence of local and national concerns over urban policy? Most scholars prefer the first two explanations, and they cite Carranza's pact with the Casa as evidence of the failures of the labor movement and the hegemony of the state in postrevolutionary Mexico. Jean Meyer goes so far as to suggest that this collaboration between the Carranza forces and the Casa was "a fatal step which . . . place[d] the Mexican labor movement under the tutelage of the government, a tutelage which has persisted until today."[19] Others similarly claim that the "collaboration of the Casa with Carranza marked the alliance of the labor movement with the bourgeois wing of the 'revolution' in exchange for a few concessions."[20] They based their assessment on the fact that after receiving some initial concessions from Carranza on housing, the leadership of the Casa del Obrero Mundial promised to "suspend trade union and syndicalist organizing and enter into a different phase of activity in view of the urgent need to propel and intensify the revolution"—which, in the most immediate terms, meant taking up arms for Carranza against competing rebel forces.[21] Raul Trejo Delarbre further claims that because the Casa then organized its members into military units (six known as the Batallones Rojos, or Red Battalions, made up of almost ten thousand men each) to defend the constitutionalist government of Carranza, "the workers from the Casa demonstrated that they had a great capacity for organization, but they used their strength to combat their class brothers, headed by Villa and Zapata in revolt against Carranza."[22] And Mexico's leading political historiographer, Arnaldo Córdova, is harsher still in his assessment of the Casa's pact with Carranza: "Urban [read: Mexico City] workers, led by a handful of opportunist leaders, experienced a period of complete confusion. Unable to form an independent proletariat and to put forward a program for society based on their own class interests, they were overcome and strangled by the forces imposed upon them externally."[23]

On one level, such indictments of the strategy pursued by the Casa leadership in alliance with Carranza indeed are warranted. The state-labor collaboration the Casa-Carranza pact embodied, the concessions about trade union organization the Casa granted, and the conflicts these actions ultimately produced within the labor movement all prevented a flowering of some of the more radical tendencies that first burgeoned during the revolutionary movement against Porfirio Díaz. Indeed, to the extent that many workers' demands for proletarian revolution were extinguished, and collaborative practices continued in Mexico for decades to come, these initial alliances had negative repercussions for the development of a radical and independent labor movement in Mexico. But insofar as such indictments of the Casa-Carranza collaboration tend to attribute such decisions to misguided ideologies or to the corrupt practices of labor leaders, they ignore the fact that such alliances were grounded in the real conditions of deteriorating urban life facing a heterogenous and still developing urban labor movement that sought better living conditions in the capital city, where a majority of workers resided.

The Casa leadership had good reasons to collaborate with Carranza over urban housing and other urban redevelopment concerns. Not only were housing scarcities and skyrocketing rents some of the most immediate and serious problems facing the Mexico City population at the time, as noted earlier, there still existed a possibility that through such an alliance, the Mexico City labor movement might wield some power with Carranza and within the revolutionary coalition itself, especially if it found an issue of mutual interest for negotiation. At this point in the postrevolutionary process, Carranza's general platform and conservative ideological orientation were not yet etched in stone, nor had insurmountable conflicts between labor-oriented revolutionary leader Alvaro Obregón and Carranza fully surfaced. Thus the Casa had clear incentives to collaborate with the government then in power, especially at this early stage.

The informal September 1914 alliance that labor made with Carranza, for example, followed the Casa's painful failure to assert its own objectives with liberal president Francisco I. Madero.[24] It also occurred on the heels of the assassination of General Victoriano Huerta, who had deposed Madero in early 1913. Huerta was a reactionary general allied with many ex-Porfiristas who started as a friend of labor but soon demonstrated his malevolent stance through forceful efforts to outlaw the Casa in May 1914. When the field was again open for a new revolutionary leader after Huerta's assassination, the Casa was eager to see a figure who would not repeat Huerta's repression or Madero's neglect. Carranza seemed to fit the bill, particularly when he made the first historic agreement over housing scarcely four months later, in exchange for the Casa's political support. Carranza's still warm political ties to Alvaro Obregón, another northern revolutionary general known for his open links with the Casa and the Mexico City labor movement, further greased the wheels of collaboration.

Yet Carranza clearly wanted to negotiate too, even with those union forces with whom he did not see eye to eye on political ideology. Indeed, Carranza could not afford to lose labor's support in Mexico City, since in 1914 and 1915 he was facing threats to his power from Emiliano Zapata's new, yet tentative, alliance with Pancho Villa, another northern-based constitutionalist revolutionary whose political vision, like Obregón's, matched labor's more closely than did Carranza's. This may help explain why Carranza continued to respond to urban workers' demands about the city's deteriorating environment with minimal housing reforms even when the urban landowners and nationalist entrepreneurs who were his principal ideological allies (Carranza himself came from a landowning family) may not have agreed. With Carranza worried about maintaining power vis-à-vis other contending revolutionary leaders, he crafted his political alliances and labor concessions to meet the exigencies of the moment. The upshot was, as John Mason Hart so aptly notes, that "the Casa del Obrero benefitted from the government's [Carranza's] attempt to maintain a base of support in central Mexico against the Constitutionalist rebellion in the North." [25] Of course, Carranza's willingness to negotiate with labor around urban services was not the only factor that explains his concessions to the Casa and his subsequent collaboration. As suggested earlier, the fact that the urban labor movement was still relatively weak and thus unable to negotiate around more radical class or workplace demands was also a crucial determinant in this partnership.

The Casa's organizational presence had been formalized only in 1912, as an umbrella syndicate of six unions, themselves founded as recently as 1909 and 1911. [26] Also, at the time Carranza extended the olive branch of peace, the Casa leadership faced a reduced constituency, "due to exile and repression" after the Huerta fiasco. It now hoped to take advantage of Carranza's tentative openness to "organize the workers quickly while the constitutionalists still needed them." [27] That is, the collaboration around this relatively benign demand may have been imagined as the stepping-stone toward a strengthened position for the labor movement. Equally noteworthy, employment and urban living conditions for the urban labor force were so precarious during the period between 1914 and 1918 that rejecting an opportunity to wrench concessions from Carranza on critical urban services like housing might be politically detrimental to the credibility of the still fragile and relatively weak labor movement. This was especially so if the Casa wanted to consolidate its organizational position as the representative of urban workers. Estimates hold that close to twelve thousand urban workers were killed during the revolutionary uprising, which reduced the ranks of the urban labor movement. Postrevolutionary efforts to reorganize urban laborers were also made difficult by the precarious social and economic conditions in the capital. Factories were slow to start up, investment was limited, employment was down, prices were up, and public dissatisfaction was high. This coincidence of economic decline and political uncertainty made both the nascent labor movement and Carranza willing to bargain with each other over servicing the built environment in Mexico City. According to historian Ramón Ruiz, many felt that Carranza was pressured to make some peace with labor in order to cement his policy of national conciliation and cooperation among businessmen.[28] Labor and the Casa, on the other hand, felt pressured to struggle for the basic necessities of urban life, often to the point of forgoing some of the more radical, work-centered demands in order to assure urban concessions and a more solid political position.

URBAN SERVICES AS A COMMON FOCUS

Why were urban services, especially housing, the basis for this compromise? Partly because the organized labor movement in Mexico City in the 1910s and 1920s was a heterogeneous collection of workers in disparate activities who shared few common workplace concerns. What held them together was not a clear class consciousness so much as a strong mutualist tradition, a rabid anti-foreign sentiment, and a resurgent urban identity and pride in Mexico City that differentiated them from the encroaching rural peasantry. These factors combined to make urban problems and services in the capital one of the most obvious and least divisive bases for the Casa's negotiation with the nation's governing forces after 1914, who at that point resided in Mexico City, too.

The impact of the urban experience on the identities and political actions of Mexico City workers can become clear only with a closer look at the Casa and its constituents. Besides a smattering of youth groups and mutual aid societies, the Casa included such professions as "tailors, restaurant workers, weavers, stonecutters, textile factory workers, carriage drivers, mill workers, chauffeurs (of urban transport, including trolley workers), shoe factory workers, mechanics, blacksmiths, schoolteachers, plumbers, tinsmiths, beltmakers, buttonmakers, retail clerks, bakers, models, draftsmen, seamstresses, and bookbinders."[29] Other early documents for the Casa list as well the following headings for its members: professionals, intellectuals, painters, employees, and women of "diverse specialties."[30] Clearly, the Casa was diverse with respect to the occupational and class identities of its affiliates (see Table 1). It housed three different categories of workers: (1) artisans and petit bourgeois elements working in settings with minimal supervision

TABLE 1

Organizations Affiliated with the Casa del Obrero Mundial (House of the World Worker), 1913–1914, by Occupation and Specialization

Construction, Building, and Urban Services

1.	Gremio de Carpinteros	Carpenters Union
2.	Unión de Canteros	Union of Quarriers
3.	Sindicato de Canteros	Quarriers Union
4.	Sindicato de Albañiles	Brickmasons Union
5.	Sindicato de Plomeros y Hojalateros	Plumbers and Tinsmiths Union
6.	Sindicato de Conductores de Coches de Alquiler	Coach Drivers Union
7.	Sindicato de Choferes	Chauffeurs Union
8.	Sindicato de Modelistas y Moldeadores	Molders and Casters Union
9.	Federación de Obreros y Empleados de la Compañia de Tranvías	Workers and Employees Federation of the Streetcar Company
10.	Sindicato Mexicano de Electricistas	Mexican Electricians Union
11.	Sindicato de Repartidores y Vendedores de Pan	Union of Bread Sales- and Deliverypersons
12.	Sindicato de Trabajadores del Distrito Federal	Workers Union of the Federal District

Skilled Artisanry, Craftwork, or Other Small-Scale Activities

1.	Sindicato de Talladores, Ebanistas y Carpinteros	Union of Wood Carvers, Cabinetmakers, and Carpenters
2.	Ramo de Zapatería	Shoemakers Branch
3.	Operarios de los Talleres Valentín Elcoro*	Workers of the "Valentín Elcoro" Works*
4.	Sindicato de Zapateros	Shoemakers Union
5.	Sindicato de Operarios Sastres	Tailoring Workers Union
6.	Sindicato de Talabarteros	Leatherworkers Union
7.	Sindicato de Toneleros	Barrel Makers Union
8.	Sindicato de Tipógrafos	Union of Linotype Operators
9.	Sindicato de Rayadores, Encuadernaderos y Foliadores	Union of Line-drawers, Binders, and Page-numberers
10.	Sindicato de Mecánicos	Mechanics Union
11.	Sindicato de Bizcocheros	Confectioners Union
12.	Gran Liga Nacional de Sastres	Grand National League of Tailors

TABLE 1 continued

Proletarianized Labor

1.	Sindicato de Trabajadores y Empleados de los Molinos de Nixtamal	Workers and Employees Union of the "Nixtamal" Mills
2.	Obreros de las Fábricas de Fósforos y Cerillos	Match Factory Workers
3.	Obreros de la Linera	Workers of "La Linera"
4.	Obreros de la Fábrica el Salvador	Workers of the "El Salvador" Factory
5.	Obreros de la Nueva Industria	Workers of the New Industry
6.	Obreros de la Carolina	Workers of "La Carolina"
7.	Obreros Ferrocarrileros de la División Estado de Hidalgo	Railroad Workers, Hidalgo State Division
8.	Operarios de la Impresora del Timbre	Workers of the Postage Printing Plant
9.	Sindicato de Pureros de La Antigua Rosa de Oro*	"Antigua Rosa de Oro" Cigarmakers Union*
10.	Sindicato de Cigarreras de la Compañía Mexicana*	"Compañía Mexicana" Cigarette-makers Union [female]*
11.	Federación de Obreros de Hilados y Tejidos**	Spinners and Weavers Federation**

Commercial, Clerical, and Other Professional Services

1.	Sociedad Caja de Ahorros	Savings Bank Association
2.	Sindicato de Dependientes de Restaurantes	Union of Restaurant Employees
3.	Sociedad de Empleados Libres del Comercio del Distrito Federal	Association of Free Commercial Employees of the Federal District

Mutualist Organizations

1.	Sociedad Mutua de Señoras Tesoro del Hogar	"Household Treasure" Ladies Mutual Society
2.	Círculo Patriótico El Centenario de la Independence	"Centennial of Independence" Patriotic Circle
3.	Sociedad Mutua El Inmortal Morelos	"Immortal Morelos" Mutual Society
4.	Sociedad Auxilio	Aid Society

TABLE 1 continued

5. Sociedad Mutualista de Auxilio, Amistad y Progreso	Mutualist Society of Aid, Friendship and Progress
6. Centro Cosmopolitana de Dependientes	Employees Cosmopolitan Center
7. Sociedad Verdad y Trabajo	Truth and Labor Association
8. Sociedad Esperanza	Society of Hope
9. Sociedad Instructiva y Recreativa Guillermo de Landa y Escandón	"Guillermo de Landa y Escandón" Educational and Recreational Association
10. Sociedad Mutua de Carpinteros Ignacio Altamirano	"Ignacio Altamirano" Mutual Society of Carpenters
11. Benemérita Sociedad Minerva de Tejedoras	"Distinguished Society of Minerva" Women Weavers
12. Sociedad Benemérita del Ramo de la Sastrería	Distinguished Society of the Tailoring Branch
13. Sociedad Alianza	Alliance Society
14. Sociedad Fraternal de Profesores	Teachers Fraternal Association

Other Unclassified Associations

1. Partido Socialista de México	Socialist Party of Mexico
2. Sociedad de Jóvenes Trabajadores	Young Workers Association
3. Quinto Comité del Partido Popular Obrero	Peoples and Workers Party, Fifth Committee
4. Gran Liga Obrera	Grand League of Workers

*These organizations are grouped under artisan activities because their workers are employed in small workshops (*talleres*) rather than in large factory settings, as in the category Proletarianized Labor. See John M. Hart, *Anarchism and the Mexican Working Class, 1860–1931* (Austin: University of Texas Press, 1978).

**These professions are included in this category because textile industries are considered highly capitalized and proletarianized after 1913. See Hart, cited above.

Sources: Luis Araiza, *Historia del movimiento obrero mexicano*, vol. 3 (Mexico City, 1965), 38–39; Rocío Guararrama, *Los sindicatos y la política en México: la CROM (1918–1928)* (Mexico City: Ediciones Era, 1984), 31.

(for example, retail clerks, carriage drivers, plumbers, restaurant workers); (2) those in more professional occupations (schoolteachers, professors, "intellectuals"); and (3) those in more proletarian professions (textile, mill, and shoe factory workers).

It was this diversity that drove Frank Tannenbaum to suggest that the Casa was not a movement so much as "a propaganda [*sic*] center where all sorts of ideas were discussed."[31] Indeed, for some, to join the Casa meant to support proletarian struggle along more orthodox Marxist lines; for others, membership in the Casa inspired socialist ideals without revolutionary praxis; and for still others, affiliation with the Casa merely justified a call for liberal democracy and a restoration of the nation's industrial infrastructure to native Mexican hands. There were even those who saw membership in the Casa primarily as a basis for restoring the artisan foundations of the urban economy.[32] Clearly, as the country faced rapid, foreign-dominated industrial development alongside persisting traditional preindustrial activities characteristic of a mercantilist, exporting economy, finding a common identity in class terms was difficult. If anything, the Mexico City "workers'" movement was a jumbled morass of occupations and ideologies with no clear contours. This understanding, in fact, was clearly expressed in the first labor regulations codified in Article 123 of the new constitution—which, it is important to remember, emerged out of the Casa-Carranza pact. Social benefits guaranteed in the labor articles of the constitution were not geared toward just the traditional working class, but were also formulated with explicit reference to skilled and unskilled workers, employees, domestic servants, and artisans.

Given the variety of occupational and ideological divisions in the Casa and the labor movement as a whole, it is no surprise that the urban labor movement was plagued by ideological divisions and disagreements over workplace priorities and strike tactics. Nor is it a surprise that the Casa was hardly in a position to struggle actively over class-specific demands or reject collaboration with the state over the built environment and its urban servicing priorities, such as housing. The prevalence of many mutualist organizations within the Casa brought many of its members to reject proletarian tactics like strikes and instead emphasize demands relating to urban living conditions and the need for mutual aid among members.[33] The fact that the urban labor movement held so many artisans, and so few factory workers,[34] further prevented the language of class warfare from dominating the Casa's activities and its political bargains.

Yet despite their occupational and ideological differences, these disparate groups within the Casa still managed to find a reason to act collectively, and urban issues appeared to be one of the few common denominators of political unity, insofar as they were often the least divisive and most mobilizing concern unifying the Casa and its membership. In addition to those factors already noted, there were several other considerations that contributed to this sense of unity. Perhaps the most striking was the antirural sentiment shared by many of Mexico City's urban workers, which was fueled by the labor market competition presented by a steady stream of rural migrants. One of the undeniable legacies of the Revolution was the high degree of urban antagonism toward rural *campesinos*, who were seen by many Mexico City residents as dirty, uneducated, and uncivilized. After the fall of Porfirio Díaz much physical destruction occurred in Mexico City proper as the result of struggles between Zapata and other revolutionary leaders, a fact that further spurred urban residents' antagonism toward rural populations. Between 1910 and 1919, Zapata's peasant forces made frequent raids on the urban areas lying to the south of the city, destroying parts of the built environment, the economy, and employment opportunities for urban residents. These attacks accelerated and intensified in mid-1914, at around the same time as the Casa was most intent on organizing itself as the principal institutional mouthpiece for urban workers. Press accounts assert that Zapata's advance on Mexico City in July 1914 was so violent that it forced the closing of textile mills in the peripheral communities of San Angel and Contreras and spread terror throughout various neighborhoods in the metropolitan area.

Peasant attacks in 1914 and 1915 not only continued to thwart the return of stable employment conditions and political stability in the capital; they also generated hostility among urban workers, who felt that rural populations were not faced with the same difficult circumstances now that the principal locus of battle had shifted to Mexico City. Ramón Ruiz notes that "despite the legion of military engagements and the pillage of villages by armed bands, most peasants continued to till the land and to feed, if poorly, their families." This, combined with the fact that "the crucial battles of the Revolution frequently disrupted the economy of industrial-urban zones," must therefore be considered a critical factor in explaining why urban workers in the Casa willingly allied with Carranza to fight against their so-called "class" allies, or peasants, in the countryside.[35] For many Mexico City workers, especially the artisans with mutualist sentiments, antagonism toward rural migrants was the flipside of a clearly urban identity, grounded in the cultural experience of successive generations of urban life in the Mexico City. This identity linked urban workers to the built environment, both buttressing their demands for urban services and reconstruction and prioritizing urban over class identities.

Efforts to defend and protect Mexico City's built environment from Zapata's attacks further served as a strong basis for unifying ideologically and occupationally disparate urban workers in the Casa around a common political project. This is suggested by an editorial in the Mexico City daily *Nueva Era*, several days after Zapatista forces approached Mexico City in one of the first serious raids on the capital after the overthrow of Porfirio Díaz:

> Aquí tenemos nuestro hogar, nuestra casa, nuestros bienes, nuestro trabajo. . . . La lucha no se entablará en la ciudad, sino en las afueras. Defender México no consiste en atrincherarse en sus edificios, construir barricadas, y trepar a las azoteas . . . , la defensa se hará allá afuera, en el campo, en los lomeríos, en las faldas de los cerros, en los caminos, y consistirá en destruir el enemigo antes de que se aproxima a la ciudad.[36]

> Here we have our families, our homes, our property, our work. . . . The struggle will not begin in the city, but in its outskirts. To defend Mexico City does not mean to entrench ourselves in its buildings, to construct barricades, and to climb roofs . . . , the defense will come from without, from the countryside, in its ridges, on its hillsides, on its roads, and it will consist of destroying the enemy before he reaches the city.

Revolutionary leaders and the local elite, in fact, often played on the anti-rural sentiments of urban workers to create virulent opposition to Zapata. In the daily papers, peasants who supported Zapata were referred to as savage hordes against whom all the city's residents should be prepared to fight.[37] At one point, President Francisco I. Madero publicly called on Mexico City's "shopkeepers, industrialists, factory owners, land owners, bankers, and all other unions and corporations, to send their employees and workers to form battalions dedicated exclusively to guarantee their honor, life, and interests in the remote case they would be threatened" by Zapata's forces.[38] Notably, among the most vocal opponents to Zapata were carpenters and cabinet-makers, mutual associations of small *comerciantes*, masons and bricklayers (*albañiles*), and plumbers, most of whom were active in the Casa.

These statements of Madero and the accounts presented in local newspapers suggest that a shared concern with protecting Mexico City and its populations may even have united workers and capitalists against rural forces. This, in turn, had implications for strategies of labor organization, which before the Revolution had generally assumed collusion between rural and urban workers against capitalists. Few in Mexico City expressed sympathy for Zapata and his "peasant followers," and they were quick to say so. One worker in the Contreras textile mill of Mexico City wrote that Zapata's "bandits" had kept his community "in a state of alarm, cost the worker his job, and damaged his home," while a letter to President Madero from another urban worker urged government forces "to hang Zapata."[39] Coupled with concerns about services and livelihood in the capital city, the growing antirural sentiment among Mexico City populations gave leaders of the Casa del Obrero Mundial good reason to enter into a tentative political alliance with Carranza, who also opposed Zapata and the rural population's political claims on the nascent revolutionary state. And the state-labor collaboration that resulted, and the urban concerns around which they were formed, were significant not just because they established the groundwork for future state-labor relations. They soon exacerbated divisions within the urban labor movement, as well. Those divisions, based on disagreements over the extent to which loyalty to the state should prevail, ultimately led to the Casa's demise and to the formation of several distinct organizations to represent workers, one of which was the ill-reputed Confederación Regional de Obreros Mexicanos (CROM).

CONFLICT OVER COLLABORATION

Why did concerns about urban life and livelihood in Mexico City help unify the labor movement at one moment and divide it at another? To answer this question, we might look more closely at distinct activities and related urban service concerns of different occupational groups represented within the Casa and the urban labor movement, and how these concerns translated into different views of the relative importance of either reconstructing the Mexico City built environment or allying with the state.

One of the first points of contention that divided the Mexico City labor movement between 1914 and 1918 was whether urban workers should ally strategically with their rural counterparts. Despite the fact that many Mexico City residents were strongly antirural, in the months before the Carranza pact was signed, several unions housed within the Casa actually did contemplate joining forces with Zapata. One of the Casa's more radical leaders, Antonio Díaz Soto y Gama, even "sensed that the Casa might not survive in urban Mexico . . . unless the rural fight was won."[40] When these propeasant forces failed to prevail with the Casa leadership and the organization joined forces with Carranza against Zapata, many of the more radical groups left the Casa altogether. This left the Casa with an even greater concentration of members concerned less about creating a national workers' movement, or about allying with peasants in the process of revolutionary state building, and more about their own trades, urban employment, and daily livelihoods. By 1915, in fact, the Casa's composition was transformed to more narrowly reflect the traditional artisan trade specializations that could be traced back to the nineteenth century. It was this slightly reconstructed Casa, whose membership shared antipeasant sentiment and a common urban identity, that was initially prepared to compromise with Carranza over housing concessions in 1915.

Yet even with this reconstructed urban-based membership, the Casa soon became increasingly polarized between artisans and mutualist organizations who "identified with an ideal which sought to preserve the small workshop and handmade products," on the one hand, and those urban factory and mill workers who had already been forced into large factories by more modernized production techniques, on the other.[41] Such internal divisions were expressed in disputes over the Casa leadership's priorities and how they should best be achieved. In debates over the appropriateness of supporting Carranza, for example, those Casa members preoccupied with proletarian struggle and establishing workers' control of large factories, like the factory and mill workers in Mexico City, felt the organization was selling its ideological purity in return for marginal concessions to better urban conditions and for limited political power within government circles. In contrast, urban artisans whose occupational activities were much less proletarianized, or whose work did not necessarily entail confrontation with large employers, were more concerned with establishing favorable services and infrastructural conditions in Mexico City; and it was these latter groups who were much more likely to believe that collaborating with the government and working through its political institutions was worthwhile.

As the Mexico City–based labor movement bickered over whether to prioritize workplace demands or urban service and reconstruction concerns, two things happened. First, the Casa began to lose its power, and more important, its legitimacy as the principal organizational vehicle for the urban labor movement, especially as it became mired in internal conflicts. Second, the government's plans to redevelop the capital were temporarily tabled, precisely because support for urban service reforms was still so controversial within the Casa, Carranza's main organizational ally. These developments worried Carranza, since they jeopardized both his long-term urban reconstruction plans and his efforts to cement his hold on the postrevolutionary state through a broad, cross-class base of political support in the capital city. As one might expect, this temporary setback and the internal conflicts it embodied also worried some in the Casa, since neither a divided rank and file, nor a politically or infrastructurally paralyzed city, boded well for the future.

In 1916, in a move that broke the stalemate, procollaboration elements headed by Luis Morones and politically linked to Carranza founded a separate federation, the Federación de Sindicatos Obreros del Distrito Federal (FSODF), to represent intellectual as well as manual workers within the

TABLE 2

Founders of the Federación de Sindicatos Obreros del Distrito Federal (FSODF); Federation of Labor Unions of the Federal District, 1916

1. Sindicato de Empleados del Comercio	Union of Commercial Employee
2. Sindicato de Peluqueros	Hairdressers Union
3. Sindicato de Carpinteros, Tallistas y Similares	Union of Carpenters, Wood Carvers and Related Trades
4. Sindicato de Plomeros	Plumbers Union
5. Sindicato de Carraujes de Alquiler	Union of Hired Coaches [taxis]
6. Sindicato de Operarios Sastres	Union of Tailoring Workers
7. Sindicato de Electricistas Mexicanas	Mexican Electricians Union
8. Sindicato de Hojalateros	Union of Sheet-Metal Workers
9. Sindicato de Empleados de Restaurantes	Restaurant Employees Union
10. Sindicato de Albañiles	Brickmasons Union
11. Sindicato de Fundidores de Piedra Artificial	Union of Artificial Stone Makers
12. Sindicato de Artes Gráficos	Graphic Arts Union
13. Sindicato de Panaderos	Bakers Union
14. Sindicato de Sastres Cortadores	Cloth-cutters Union
15. Sindicato de Moldeadores y Modelistas	Molders and Casters Union

Source: Luis Araiza, *Historia del movimiento obrero mexicano*, vol. 3 (Mexico City, 1984), 111.

Casa.[42] This new organization was just what Carranza needed: a more homogenous labor federation less concerned with proletarian rights and more supportive of the revolutionary leadership, including its urban redevelopment objectives. At its founding, the FSODF included syndicates or mutualist associations representing carpenters, plumbers, electricians, graphic artists, tinplaters, molders and casters, and masons, as well as tailors, hairdressers, bakers, confectioners, and commercial employees. Soon thereafter, the FSODF included syndicates representing small merchants, physicians, theater operators, restaurant employees, street cleaners, roadworkers, traffic operators, trolley operators, and carriage drivers, among others (see Table 2). In short, the FSODF represented those craft and artisanal workers who enjoyed greater autonomy in the labor process as well as the self-employed and commercial workers who were open to Carranza's more conservative petit bourgeois political project. But what was most significant about the FSODF was that it grouped occupations that either provided urban services—like street cleaners and traffic operators—or whose profits relied directly on a well-functioning urban environment that sustained consumer demand, like small shopkeepers, restaurant employees, hairdressers, bakers, and tailors. A large proportion of the FSODF's constituents, moreover, made their living in the building trades, an area whose expansion was fueled by the government's active efforts at reconstructing the built environment (see Table 2).

The foundation of the FSODF in 1916 opened a whole new chapter in Mexico's labor history. Because it comprised mainly urban service and trades workers, particularly those who derived their livelihood from the government's efforts to reconstruct the war-torn city and the restoration of a buoyant urban economy, the FSODF's leaders were willing to support the government and keep an open ear to some of the local business sector's principal demands. They also were willing to protect their constituents' fledgling petty trades and service activities by reviving the city's economy, at the expense of competing demands by rural workers and other laborers who cared less about preserving the urban domain and more about agricultural development or factory conditions. To take this centrist position in the postrevolutionary ideological spectrum, moreover, brought the FSODF favored government status in the urban labor movement. Within two years, this organization developed such strength and political influence that by 1918 it was able to break from the Casa completely and found an entirely new organization with much broader scope, called the Confederación Regional de Obreros Mexicanos, or CROM. Not surprisingly, the CROM maintained much of the same ideological and membership profile as the FSODF (see Table 3), which Rocío Guadarrama calls the "utopianism of the small producer."[43] It also kept its openness to collaboration with the state and clear support for reviving the urban economy, all the while distancing itself from more radical, proletarianized sectors of the urban labor movement. As such, the CROM soon became much stronger than even the FSODF had been because, by constituting its own federation as completely separate from the Casa, it no longer had to compromise with those workers still associated with the Casa, who took a different—and less collaborationist—political stance.

With the FSODF's—and then the CROM's—founding, support for urban reconstruction began to more clearly dominate the terms of negotiation between the Carranza government and the Mexico City labor movement, especially as compared to support for the rights and workplace concerns of urban laborers. And this, in turn, alienated those more proletarianized workers in the Mexico City labor movement who had remained loyal to the Casa and who were less willing to subordinate workplace demands to urban reconstruc-

TABLE 3

Initial Members of the Confederación Regional de Obreros Mexicanos (CROM); Regional Confederation of Mexican Workers, 1918

1. Sindicato de Electricistas	Electricians Union
2. Sindicato de Choferes Mexicanos*	Mexican Drivers Union*
3. Sindicato de Trabajadores de Hierro y Similares*	Union of Iron Workers and Related Trades*
4. Sindicato de Trabajadores de la Fábrica de Hilados y Tejidos de Lana San Ildefonso*	Workers Union of the "San Ildefonso" Yarns and Woolens Factory*
5. Federación de Sindicatos Obreros del Distrito Federal	Federation of Workers Unions of the Federal District
6. Sindicato de Obreros y Empleados de la Compañía de Tranvías de México, S.A.	Workers and Employees Union of the Trolley Company of Mexico, Inc.
7. Sindicato de Tráfico	Traffic Workers Union
8. Sindicato de Talleres	Repair-shop Workers Union [trolleys]
9. Unión Sindical de Empleados del Comercio y Oficinas Particulares	Office and Commercial Employees Trade Union [trolley company]
10. Sindicato de la Vía Permanente	Track Workers Union [trolley company]
11. Sindicato de Trabajadores de la Industria Lechera	Workers Union of the Dairy Industry
12. Sindicato de Médicos Homeópatas del Distrito Federal	Homeopathic Physicians Union of the Federal District
13. Alianza de Comerciantes del Mercado Pequeño	Small Merchants Alliance
14. Sindicato de Trabajadores de Limpia y Transporte	Union of Street Cleaners and Transport Workers
15. Unión de Empleados y Trabajadores de la Fábrica de Aguas Gaseosas	Workers and Employees Union of the Soft Drinks Factory

*Founding members

Source: Luis Araiza, *Historia del movimiento obrero mexicano*, vol. 4 (Mexico City, 1965), 19, 73, 32, 148.

tion priorities. These groups soon found voice in another organization, the Confederación General de Trabajadores (CGT), which immediately took on the CROM, its collaborative stances with the government, and its willingness to abandon strikes and workplace objectives (see Table 4). The CGT, like the FSODF, also emerged from Mexico City's Casa del Obrero Mundial; but unlike the FSODF and the CROM, it did not construct itself mainly as an

CHAPTER TWO

TABLE 4

Organizations Affiliated with the Confederación General de Trabajadores (CGT); General Confederation of Workers, 1921

1. Sindicato de la Fábrica La Unión	"La Unión" Factory Union
2. Sindicato de la Fábrica Al Aurrera	"La Aurrera" Factory Union
3. Sindicato de la Fábrica La Linera	"La Linera" Factory Union
4. Sindicato de la Fábrica La Trinidad	"La Trinidad" Factory Union
5. Sindicato de la Fábrica La Alpina	"La Alpina" Factory Union
6. Sindicato de la Fábrica La Hormiga	"La Hormiga" Factory Union
7. Sindicato de la Fábrica La Abeja	"La Abeja" Factory Union
8. Sindicato de la Fábrica La Magdalena	"La Magdalena" Factory Union
9. Sindicato de Trabajadores de la Compañía Telefónica Ericsson	Workers Union of the Ericsson Telephone Company
10. Talleres de la Indianilla	"La Indianilla" Workshops
11. IWW de México	IWW of Mexico
12. Federación de Jóvenes Comunistas	Young Communists Federation
13. Sindicato de Panaderos del Distrito Federal	Federal District Bakers Union
14. Local Comunista del Distrito Federal	Communist Local of the Federal District
15. Federación Local de Hilados y Tejidos	Local Federation of Textile Workers
16. Federación Local del Distrito Federal	Local Federation of the Federal District
17. Federación de Tranviarios	Trolley Workers Federation
18. Sindicato de Tráfico	Traffic Workers Union [trolley company]
19. Sindicato de Talleres	Repair-shop Workers Union [trolley company]
20. Unión de Resistencia de Obreros y Obreras del Palacio de Hierro	Resistance Union of Male and Female Workers of the "Palacio de Hierro"
21. Sindicato de Dulceros, Pasteleros y Similares	Union of Candymakers, Pastry Cooks, and Related Trades

Source: Luis Araiza, *Historia del movimiento obrero mexicano*, vol. 4 (Mexico City, 1965): 58–59, 91.

urban-based organization, despite its leadership's presence in Mexico City. Sixteen of the twenty-eight unions involved in the CGT's founding represented workers in geographic areas *other* than Mexico City, while only four openly identified themselves as representing workers or occupations in the capital.[44] The CGT, moreover, identified itself as an explicitly communist federation most concerned with factory workers and other highly proletarianized laborers; it shunned government collaboration unless workers' principled demands were met; and it proudly identified itself as *rojo*, or red, while it considered the collaborationist CROM to be *amarillo*, or yellow. Thus the more the CROM sided with the government, and supported urban service and reconstruction priorities over workplace demands, the more actively the CGT organized and the more divided the Mexico City labor movement became.

· With the CGT and the CROM distancing themselves from each other, and the Casa effectively disbanded, Mexico City saw growing labor conflicts in the late teens and early twenties, as each organization struggled to win the hearts and minds of the rank and file and control the local political turf. Much of the battle was waged around urban service provision, especially transport, not only because this issue had helped provoke the division in the first place, but also because workers employed in this sector were most torn between the two competing labor organizations and their distinct political agendas. Indeed, Mexico City's trolley workers, or *tranviarios*, were among the city's most active and divided workers in the 1910s and 1920s. Their struggles both emerged from and influenced the revolutionary leadership's efforts to redevelop Mexico City, along the way influencing the contours of local politics.

Of course, even before the 1910 Revolution, trolley workers' activism had implications for both politics and urban development in the capital, mainly because early on *tranviarios* had organized themselves in response to the growing foreign domination of the electric transport sector by a British-Canadian consortium with strong ties to German capitalists. As early as 1901, trolley workers in the Compañía de Tranvías Eléctricos in Mexico City engaged in strikes and labor actions against their foreign employers.[45] Like many caught in the euphoria of Porfirio Díaz's downfall, moreover, the *tranviarios* immediately lent their support to the new revolutionary government of Francisco I. Madero. Also, like other urban workers, many were concerned with protecting their own lives and livelihoods in the capital. In 1912, for example, "the workers of the *Compañía de Tranvías Eléctricos* in Mexico City . . . signed an accord to offer their services to President Madero, in which they asked him to name military instructors who could give them training *to protect the capital* in the event of public disorder" in the wake of peasant attacks on Mexico City (emphasis added).[46] Yet like the urban labor movement as a whole, *tranviarios* soon split among themselves over the ideological and political course the Revolution was to take, over the urban versus rural dimensions of the debate, and over the preference given to urban reconstruction.

These internal conflicts among trolley workers and between their representative union organizations carried over into the immediate postrevolutionary period, as was first clear in 1915, the same year Carranza signed the pact with the Casa. A group of *tranviarios* belonging to the Sindicato de la Federación de Empleados y Obreros de la Compañía de Tranvías supported the Casa's collaboration with Carranza and became members of the Second Red Battalion in Veracruz. But others chose to join forces with a contending revolutionary leader, Pancho Villa.[47] This latter group argued that their main political tactic should be to paralyze industry, and that in order to solve their own labor problems they should stay in Mexico City and "seize factories and workshops."[48] These initial ideological differences emerged again in 1916 when the FSODF was formed. One group of trolley workers joined the FSODF, although they withdrew only one month later and remained formally independent until 1919; another stayed loyal to the Casa. This split was later formalized in 1921, when one group of trolley workers joined the CROM while others preferred to remain "pillars" of the CGT.[49]

Internal splits among the trolley workers over the alliance with Carranza against Zapata's rural forces, and later over the affiliation with the CGT and CROM, may be partially explained by the fact that many *tranviarios* themselves were peasants with pro-Zapata sentiments who had recently migrated to the capital. Miguel Rodríguez cites archival documents showing that in a selective sample of sixteen trolley workers, eight were born in provinces and regions outside Mexico City.[50] But these splits can also be accounted for by the fact that the trolley workers were among the most occupationally heterogeneous of all the urban unions functioning during this watershed period. The trolley workers' union—like the urban labor movement in general—grouped together workers governed by different work conditions, different skill levels, and relatively incompatible postures vis-à-vis the objectives and priorities of urban service provision. As such, the trolley workers' union held within it the same tensions that gave rise to the split between the CGT and the CROM and the ideological division within the urban labor movement as a whole. Thus, the lot of trolley workers not only reflected and contributed to growing conflicts within the urban labor movement, which had implications for postrevolutionary political dynamics; it also highlights the crucial role played by urban service conflicts in the acceleration of labor repression, the establishment of state-labor collaboration, and the reconstruction of Mexico City.

URBAN TRANSPORT SERVICES AND DIVISIONS
WITHIN THE WORKING CLASS

Accounting records from the Compañía de Tranvías indicate that trolley workers were divided into two main personnel categories: workers and employees. The workers were further divided between those employed in vehicle workshops and those involved in roadway maintenance and traffic; the employees comprised accountants, billing clerks, and ticketing agents. Wage and work conditions in each of these two main categories differed greatly. Employees received between double and triple the daily salaries of shop workers, while those in traffic and roadway operations were paid somewhere in the middle range; most of those originally hired by the Compañía de Tranvías as white-collar employees were foreigners affiliated with the Canadian-based firm.[51] And unlike those workers employed in the *talleres* (workshops) where trolleys were maintained and repaired, office clerks and other employees who worked in traffic (conductors and dispatchers) had only limited supervision and were less subject to demands for manual labor.

Most scholarly accounts of the activism of *tranviarios* have paid almost no attention to these internal differences. But evidence suggests that the different political orientations and the different degrees of activism among trolley workers were rooted at least partly in these occupational differences, which ultimately provoked conflicting urban policy priorities, too. For example, electricians—who had strong political and institutional linkages to the radical electrical workers' union in Mexico City—worked mainly in the *talleres*. Thus, when the newly formed syndicate representing trolley workers agreed to join the Red Battalions and fight Zapata and other rural workers, the electricians employed in the *talleres* refused. In 1917, moreover, it was *employees* from the Compañía de Tranvías that founded a new mutualist society, intended to capture some of the original spirit of the Casa del Obrero Mundial without its syndicalist organization or rhetoric. Furthermore, a close reading of the data suggests that those involved in the more proletarianized aspects of trolley service provision, like production and maintenance of trolleys and trolley tracks (and thus those employed mainly in the *talleres*), were the ones who instigated the formation of the CGT and called the most strikes, while employees and administrators were more likely to support the CROM.[52] A general overview of which *tranviarios* joined which organization and when they did so also suggests that it was those employed in the area of traffic supervision, which included conductors and motormen, who seemed to vacillate most between these two different political orientations and labor

CHAPTER   TWO

organizations. At times conductors and motormen supported the CGT and its strike objectives as actively as did *talleristas*, but at other times they did not, throwing support to the more collaborationist, less radical, CROM.

These occupational differences and the differing patterns of political affiliation they presupposed also brought differing stances on urban redevelopment. For one thing, the work life of conductors was embedded in the daily life of the community and the general public. Because traffic operators and conductors worked the same routes and saw the same people daily, they were more attuned to the concerns of the public with respect to urban service provision. They also identified with local communities and especially felt the burden of urban chaos in Mexico City, since their popularity and prestige depended on their capacity to offer smooth and efficient transport service to these communities. Most important, perhaps, whether trolleymen (traffic operators) and conductors could actually service communities was very much contingent on the government's capacity to solve a host of other urban problems in Mexico City's built environment, such as flooding, insufficient drainage, potholes and mudheaps, and overcrowded roadways caused by street vending and animal-powered vehicles. Conductors and traffic operators, in short, were considerably more cognizant of urban problems and the need for the urban reconstruction of the capital than were maintenance and other shop workers, whose social relations and working connections with the urban public were less direct and who were more likely to define their daily work problems and political strategies around shop-floor concerns and conflicts with the company's management. These work conditions make it easy to understand why traffic operators and conductors would join other employees of the trolley company in support of the CROM, which stood behind the government and its urban policy priorities, while more proletarianized workers involved in vehicle maintenance and shop-floor activities would gravitate to the CGT.

To the extent that *tranviarios* split among themselves, however, they failed to form a unified and ideologically coherent front. This meant that chaos in the urban transport sector continued, especially as radical factions relied on labor protest to make their demands heard. These accelerating urban transport problems, in turn, gave the revolutionary leadership further incentive to control labor in Mexico City, especially in this critical sector. And this vicious circle both accelerated labor conflicts and heightened the political importance of organizations that had access to labor in the urban service sector, like the CROM. As a result, the CROM's capacity to control local services soon made it indispensable to the national political leadership, which increased its bargaining power and gave this more centrist labor organization a growing presence in national politics during the late 1910s and '20s.

That the CROM's growing power was intricately linked to its capacity to settle transport conflicts and facilitate urban service provision in Mexico City becomes clear with a closer look at labor conflicts in the urban service sector between 1916 and 1928, especially those linked to transport. Starting in May 1916, before the founding of the CROM and at a time when Carranza was still dependent on the Casa for labor support, independent trolley workers staged a strike and won a small wage boost and other minimal concessions. Trolley workers' relative success in this regard was due in part to Luis Morones's direct intervention as mediator in the state-labor negotiations.[53] However, owing partly to continued internal conflict among trolley workers over collaboration with the government on urban reconstruction efforts, and partly to a rapid decrease in the value of paper currency, which sent costs of food and other necessary items skyrocketing, trolley workers called a general strike scarcely two months later. All public utilities and public services in Mexico City came to a standstill, including trolley service. These disruptions in urban services brought a showdown between the Casa and the government; Carranza responded with direct military repression of the strikers and proclaimed the death penalty for any act of sabotage against a public utility. Sabotage was defined as "participating in strikes, organizing a strike, presiding over meetings that proposed, discussed, or approved a strike, attending such a meeting, and not leaving the meeting after its intent was clear."[54]

Given the centrality of urban transport to the process of urban reconstruction and local economic development, Carranza's authoritarian actions can be seen as intending to halt the potential chaos in Mexico City as much as to reverse the rights of workers. This was clear when, through the 1917 constitution, strikes were finally sanctioned as legal weapons (insofar as they were peaceful and "harmonized" the rights of capital and labor) *except* in the case of public services like transport. With Carranza's growing heavy-handedness toward strikers threatening their power and identity as workers, his actions broke open the divisions within the urban labor movement in general and among trolley workers in particular. His regime responded to the resurgence in labor unrest in 1917, when he became president, and in 1918, by accelerating its repressive actions against striking urban laborers. These efforts to tame the labor movement further alienated its most radical elements; yet it also convinced moderates of the need to separate themselves from the more strike-prone forces. It was in this context that Morones and his allies split from the Casa and founded the CROM in 1918.

As noted previously, after its foundation as a separate organization, the CROM used its newfound political power to consolidate its own moderately collaborationist position, especially vis-à-vis rival independent and radical unions, like the trolley workers and the CGT. Rather than pressing for accumulated demands against employers, the CROM worked most actively to undermine the political power of radical elements in the urban working class, like the CGT, who presented a challenge to labor-state collaboration and threatened Carranza's efforts to restore order in the city. The CGT not only offered an alternative institutional affiliation to the government-sanctioned CROM, it also actively initiated strikes that disrupted the national government's attempts to regularize the provision of urban transport and local economy. Striking trolley workers in Mexico City were among those that the CROM and the revolutionary leadership most wanted to control, mainly because the chaos generated by striking trolley workers posed a threat to the CROM's self-proclaimed capacity to organize workers in the service of urban reconstruction and labor peace. Accordingly, the trolley workers themselves soon became the direct target of CROM attacks.

ACHIEVING URBAN AND LABOR OBJECTIVES THROUGH CONTROL OF LOCAL POLITICS

To the chagrin of the CGT, the CROM was successful in repressing striking trolley workers and other labor unions affiliated with this "red" syndicate, not only because it worked in alliance with powerful national political leaders like Carranza, and then Obregón and Calles, but also because the CROM managed to insinuate itself into local politics in Mexico City. In 1917 Carranza introduced in the capital a legislative change that upheld the system of popular election for most local municipalities yet that gave Mexico's president the power to appoint a mayor for Mexico City as a whole, known formally as the Gobernador del Distrito Federal. With this new legislation, the most central *municipio*—or the *municipalidad de México*, where the bulk of economic activities took place and most public buildings stood—was exempted from direct popular election, and council members in that locale were to be appointed directly by the president. From the revolutionary government's point of view, one of the principal objectives of the 1917 legislative change was to overcome the deleterious effects of municipal infighting, referred to in one public document as the "continuous conflict between the District governments, the *ayuntamientos*, the courts, etc.," conflicts that hindered the development of urban infrastructure and the efficient administration of Mexico City.[55] This new legislation remedied the growing urban chaos that resulted when Madero restored the *municipios* system in 1911, by recentralizing power over urban development policy and placing it mainly in the hands of the presidentially appointed mayor and the *municipalidad de México*. One of "the principal administrative functions of the governor [or mayor] was the execution of Federal laws, the supply of public services . . . [and] the administration of public works and the police" in the capital.[56] Under the new legislation, moreover, the federal authorities and not the municipalities had the best fiscal resources, such that most of the *municipios* were not even able to cover the costs of public services.[57] Accordingly, large infrastructural projects for the Distrito Federal, selected and administered by the presidentially appointed mayor, received the lion's share of federal support, as did projects for the centrally located *municipalidad de México*.

These legislative changes in urban governance and policymaking in the capital, which echoed in many ways the urban practices of the Porfiriato, made their mark on local politics as much as on urban servicing and development. Starting in 1918, through their strong political linkages to President Carranza, CROM members attained several seats on administrative councils in Mexico City and in the *municipalidad de México*, the centermost jurisdiction of Mexico City where most commerce and services were located. By 1920, CROM founding member Celestino Gasca was appointed mayor of Mexico City (Gobernador del Distrito Federal), several CROMistas were appointed council members on the *ayuntamiento*, or city council, of the municipality of Mexico, and another high-level CROM activist headed labor policy in the Distrito Federal. As a result, by 1920 the CROM had direct access to large-scale labor contracts and huge sums of money for public works in the city, which it used to favor its own rank-and-file constituents.

With the CROM both commanding massive resources and entrenched in Mexico City politics, it could centralize control over services. It also began to cement its repressive power over the CGT, primarily because gaining political power in Mexico City gave the CROM access to the local police force and the other local agencies that helped them undermine the CGT in accordance with Carranza's wishes. This process manifested itself in several ways. In 1919, the Federal District government struck an accord with the Compañía de Tranvías to allow city police free passage on trolleys, which in turn made it easier for law enforcement officers to keep an eye on the activities of the trolley workers.[58] In 1922, the government of the Distrito Federal assumed total responsibility for traffic services in Mexico City, which had previously been provided by autonomous local councils in the different districts, or municipalities.[59] According to Luis Araiza's account of the Mexican labor movement, in fact, by this time the Mexico City government was frequently working hand in hand with the CROM and the federal government to repress the CGT.[60] In January 1923, conflict reached such a point that armed struggle broke out between CGT members, CROM sympathizers, and the Mexico City police. Thirteen CGT members and an unknown number of police and military personnel were wounded; five mounted riot police, two soldiers, and one CROM motorman were killed. A noted journalist of the period, Vito Alessio Robles, saw the Mexico City police's role in this and other labor conflicts as characteristic of the Carranza government's general strategy in dealing with the labor movement: "When workers affiliated with the CROM went on strike, soldiers and the police protected the strikers; but when workers in the CGT went on strike, the troops and the gendarmes protected the strike-breakers."[61]

Given the abuses of power that occurred once the CROM monopolized Mexico City politics, it did not take long for the CROM-CGT conflict to irreparably divide the urban labor movement and disrupt the urban environment. By 1925 "the CROM would attempt to penetrate the CGT textile workers' stronghold of San Angel-Contreras (in southern Mexico City), leading to street battles, gunfights, strikes, lockouts, and government military-police intervention on behalf of the CROM minority."[62] In response, workers belonging to the communist-led CGT continued to initiate strikes in both Mexico City and other regions, destroying tranquility in the capital and wreaking havoc on the servicing of the built environment. These strikes generally turned violent and were often directed as much against the CROM and its leadership as against employers.

With both the local and national state on its side, however, the CROM's efforts to defeat the CGT and its radical trolley worker constituents were relatively successful, at least in the short run. This occurred not only through direct labor repression, as is already well known, but also through efforts to develop new urban transport services that could take the place of trolleys. For example, it was in response to the first wave of strikes by trolley workers in 1917 that the government encouraged a move away from trolley services and toward buses and other forms of urban transport.[63] During the 1920s, with the CROM's controlling Mexico City politics, local authorities continued to finance and actively support the development of urban bus services in an effort to reduce the city's reliance on electric trolleys and thus limit the CGT's and trolley workers' bargaining power in strike actions. The drivers of this new bus fleet, not surprisingly, joined the CROM, which further cemented the repression of radical union activity in the urban transport sector. By 1922, the CROM held within its ranks the Centro Social de Choferes, the union of *transportistas* that later helped the CROM to break trolley workers' strikes by substituting buses and taxis for trolleys in Mexico City. These CROM-affiliated bus and taxi drivers were able to evoke public sympathy for their labor organization by offering transport services in areas of the city previously ignored by the Compañía de Tranvías—something they could accomplish quickly and with little capital investment because bus and taxi service required no track infrastructure.

The CROM's subsequent involvement in urban transport services not only diminished the power of the CGT and its radical trolley workers, it also helped achieve some degree of order in the built environment. In 1923, the CROM-controlled Mexico City mayor's office introduced uniform criteria for licensing transport vehicles and services. Permission was granted in 1923 for the formation of a new firm created by the Compañía de Tranvías, called the Compañía Mexicana de Omnibus, S.A., which offered bus service. The aim in granting this permission was to allow the Compañía de Tranvías management to diversify its services and further dilute the power of the *tranviarios*. The Distrito Federal government also now began to organize individual drivers to provide local transport services (*ruleteros*) in rented vehicles, precursors to the taxicab, although it made sure that CGT loyalists were barred from entry.[64] By 1924, these alternative transport services had so weakened the CGT trolley workers that the CROM was able to organize a new union, the Alianza de Obreros y Empleados de la Compañía de Tranvías de México, and bring it into the ranks of the CROM.

With the CROM waging an all-out battle against the CGT and one of its most radical unions, the trolley workers, by the mid to late 1920s trolleys began to lose their place as the principal urban transport service in Mexico City.[65] Their fate was sealed by 1925, when the Compañía de Omnibus folded and as the Compañía de Tranvías gradually withdrew its commitment to electric transport, paving the way for the unfettered rise of urban bus service. With CROM-linked officials in the Distrito Federal offering subsidized gasoline to bus operators organized by and affiliated with the CROM, bus service expanded rapidly, and urban transport conditions improved markedly. These new groups of drivers had already formed their own federation, the Alianza de Camioneros de México, within th CROM's Central de Choferes in 1919. By 1926 they had formally separated from the Central de Choferes, which grouped all manner of urban transport services, and from then on remained in their own separate union within the CROM.[66]

The fit between the new Alianza de Camioneros and the CROM was a good one: unlike *tranviarios*, who worked for the large, foreign-owned Compañía de Tranvías, bus drivers owned and drove their own vehicles. They saw themselves as self-employed businessmen, and, like many of the CROM's constituents, supported the reconstruction of Mexico City and the moderately conservative political ideology of Carranza and his successor General

Alvaro Obregón. Like many other artisans in the CROM, moreover, they also founded their own cooperatives to aid in the supply and distribution of fuel and lubricants. All these factors placed bus drivers ideologically on the side of those already organized within the CROM, whose work afforded them greater autonomy on the job, who put priority on government support of urban services, who did not share the CGT's class struggle rhetoric or its antagonism toward capital and capitalists, and who shared a common concern with reconstructing Mexico City. Indeed, the CROM's willingness to collaborate with the state was hardly a point of contention for the city's growing cadre of bus drivers; it may have been precisely the opposite, since many of them owed their livelihood to CROM-government efforts to limit trolley service and expand the urban bus industry. To the extent that the CROM-controlled government held responsibility for road repairs and the allocation of routes and permits in the capital, then, the Alianza worked eagerly and comfortably to nurture favorable relations with the CROM, with local politicians, and with their national political allies.

Because of the Alianza's openness to collaboration with both the local and national government, as well as the fact that it became the principal purveyor of urban transport services in the capital, the Alianza de Camioneros rapidly became a political force to be reckoned with during the 1920s and 1930s, first within the CROM and ultimately within the ruling party itself.[67] As a result, the CROM and the revolutionary leadership finally achieved one of their principal objectives: formal control over the provision of urban transport services. Not only did this aid in the reconstruction and urban development of the embattled capital city, it also helped political leaders control radical tendencies in the urban labor force.

THE LOCAL CHALLENGE TO NATIONAL POWER

By the 1920s, it was clear that the CROM's administrative control over transport and critical urban services catapulted it to a position of power in both local and national politics. As testimony to the CROM's role in helping the revolutionary government achieve its urban redevelopment and local political objectives with the urban labor movement, CROM leaders by 1924 held "one senatorship, one congressional seat, and a little more than half of the councilors' seats in Mexico City."[68] As of 1927, the CROM controlled both the city council of the *municipalidad de México* as well as the office of the presidentially appointed mayor, or Gobernador del Distrito Federal. By this time, moreover, CROM activists had also captured several important cabinet positions in the federal government, which of course was based in the capital city. CROMista leader Eduardo Moneda was chief of the Department of Social Services. Morones himself served as general director of Military Manufacturing Establishments, as a federal congressman, and as minister of industry, commerce, and labor under President Calles (1924–1928).

In short, many of the politicians linked to the CROM who initially started out with a power base in Mexico City were now significant players in national policymaking and politics. And conversely, those whom most scholars have treated as nationally powerful politicians in this critical period had strong roots in Mexico City politics and local, urban policy. In addition to Morones and other CROMistas just mentioned, for example, this was also true for Vincente Lombardo Toledano: he was appointed chief clerk of Mexico City, an alderman of the municipal government in Mexico City, and interim governor of the state of Puebla (a principal state bordering Mexico City), among other important posts. By the late 1920s, then, the CROM's political power was practically unprecedented, given its central location in local politics and the Mexico City–based federal bureaucracy, along with its membership of close to two million organized laborers. It even initiated its own political party during this period, the Partido Laborista Mexicano, which controlled the municipality of Mexico City starting in 1925 and which by 1928 had a serious shot at capturing national political power.[69]

Yet this was precisely the problem: the CROM's unparalleled political power, especially its capacity to wield influence both locally and nationally. Of course, the CROM's close ties with forces controlling the federal government, and its growing political power over urban services, had been just what the revolutionary leadership sought, since they aided the process of urban and economic revival and reinforced the dynamic of interdependence between the national state and moderate factions of the labor movement. Indeed, growing private sector confidence in the urban and national economy grew hand in hand with the CROM's unparalleled political power over its constituency and its attendant defeat of the strike-prone radical CGT; and with the CROM at the helm, Mexico City also experienced the first major wave of intensive urban infrastructural development since the Porfiriato. Still, the CROM's growing political power had its downside. Morones's entrenched political influence was starting to worry other factions within the revolutionary leadership, especially these who had originally envisioned a positive role for labor.

Among those most concerned about the CROM's growing political power was ex-president Alvaro Obregón, who had governed Mexico from 1920 until 1924 and by 1927 was vying to wrest control of the government from a more conservative contender, Plutarco Elías Calles, who had developed strong linkages to the CROM during his term as president (1924–1928). General Obregón had ruled Mexico with the support of a so-called populist coalition of peasants and labor, and he had long been considered a friend of labor, not only to the Casa, but also to the CROM in its early years. Yet as Morones used the CROM's growing power after 1924 to subvert many of the principal tenets of the labor movement, General Obregón began to distance himself from the CROM and its leaders. According to Rivera Castro, Obregón's 1927 decision to run for the presidency emerged largely out of his dissatisfaction with the CROM-Calles conservative partnership.[70]

In his 1928 struggle to regain the presidency, Obregón sensed that the CROM's political control over Mexico City's *municipios* and the local police gave both Morones and Calles an institutional base to challenge his candidacy. Obregón not only worried about the electoral support Morones's own political party might capture, he was concerned that, if left unchecked, continued CROMista power in Mexico City politics would further divide the labor movement. Indeed, the CROM's rivals had been in a constant battle to wrench control of the municipalities from the CROM and to create more room for independent activity and policymaking in both union affairs and local politics. These political conflicts created "near anarchy in the Distrito Federal" and prevented the government from introducing a unified administrative criterion that would apply to all the *Ayuntamientos*.[71]

With the constant conflict between the CROM and other unions, between different *municipios* where many of these ideological battles were occasionally played out, and between the Distrito Federal police and striking workers, urban service and living conditions threatened to deteriorate once again, despite the initial gains in this regard. Obregón himself went so far as to complain that "the municipal organization of the Distrito Federal ha[d] not achieved any of the objectives this form of government should, owing to the political and administrative conflicts that consistently appear with the coexistence of authorities."[72]

With chaos returning to Mexico City, pressures mounted for change, especially from those in the national revolutionary leadership who did not share Calles's conservative political profile. In an effort to restore order to the capital city and limit the CROM's capacity to damage both local politics and the national labor movement, Obregón and his political allies successfully introduced an initiative in the National Congress in July 1928 to abolish the system of popularly elected municipal rule in the nation's capital. The prescribed change placed Mexico City's governance completely under the direction of the president and his appointed mayor, and it removed all the municipal elective bodies that had been introduced back in 1911 when

Francisco I. Madero triumphed over the dictatorship of Porfirio Díaz. Whereas in 1917 only the centermost *municipalidad de México* lost the right to local democratic rule, with the 1928 proposal offered by Obregón, all the city's municipalities followed suit. Now, with democratically elected municipal government fully eliminated in the capital, popular organizations would offer the only remaining mechanisms for expressing grassroots political demands in Mexico City, although they too were weakened or under challenge after years of CROM control or repression.

Understandably, Obregón's proposed urban reform started a chain of highly significant events, not the least of which was to spur grassroots opposition to the revolutionary leadership, both local and national. Yet the proposed reform also enraged Morones, who saw it as a challenge to the local bases of his new party and his claim to national political power. A scant sixteen days after the urban reform was introduced in Mexico's Congreso de la Unión, moreover, Obregón was assassinated. In view of the clear political battle between Obregón and Morones that raged during this period, most scholars and observers have assumed that Morones was behind the killing, even though the assassination was ultimately attributed to a pro-Catholic fanatic upset at Obregón's antagonistic stance toward the Catholic Church. Whatever the true cause, after this assassination the CROM nonetheless became the target of an accelerated negative campaign, and even Calles was forced to publicly distance himself from Morones. The public attacks on the CROM provoked many of its members to abandon the federation.[73] And with the CROM in temporary disgrace, the union movement found itself in shambles, as did the revolutionary leadership. With the mobilized population in Mexico City split in multiple directions, with the national labor movement at a critical crossroads both divided institutionally and lacking its leader Obregón, with local populations clamoring for alternative mechanisms to present their demands, and with municipal governing structures abolished, Mexico's political leaders rightfully feared they would be unable to maintain political control either in the nation as a whole or in its most important locale, Mexico City. As such, the city's urban future was once again up for grabs, and with it the future of the still fragile revolutionary state.

3

MEXICO CITY GOVERNANCE

AND THE MOVE TOWARD CORPORATISM,

1929–1943

Both Obregón's assassination and the elimination of democratic elections in Mexico City threw the capital into chaos in late 1928 and early 1929. Under public attack, CROMistas no longer held the organizational authority or institutional capacity to control workers, and the urban labor movement threatened to fragment into multiple and competing organizations. While this was clearly a problem for the national political leadership, it did not bode well for Mexico City either. Without strong local or national control over unions providing urban services, and with the likelihood of a new round of strikes and independent labor actions, plans for the urban and economic development of the capital were temporarily stalled. Any backtracking on the city's return journey to prosperity could also jeopardize broad, urban popular support for the revolutionary leadership, especially that cultivated by President Calles (1924–1928), who had also developed good relations with Mexico City's commerce and business sectors.

As political leaders considered future moves, two interrelated challenges loomed large. First, the revolutionary leadership had to overcome the internal acrimony produced by Obregón's assassination and unify the sparring national political leadership. Second, and perhaps most important, both local and national politicians had to reestablish order in the servicing and administration of Mexico City. Each of these tasks required skill, especially with respect to the urban labor movement. Clearly, local labor organizations—or other segments of society for that matter—could not be allowed too much control in Mexico City, or they might unbalance national political coalitions. The CROM fiasco had made quite clear the conflicts that could result if labor organizations gained too much local power. Yet to completely eliminate labor from urban decisions would be almost impossible, since such a move could also call into question state legitimacy by underscoring the nondemocratic character of Mexico City politics. In seeking a new political strategy to negotiate this difficult terrain, Mexico's revolutionary leadership no longer sought just one set of institutional practices to achieve both urban and national objectives, as they had earlier. That is to say, rather than attempting to work primarily through Mexico City–based institutions and practices to simultaneously foster urban reconstruction and establish relations with the labor movement, after 1928 the revolutionary leadership developed both local and national political institutions to tackle the problems of urban development and national political consolidation separately. Nor did it rely only on labor-based organizations in its efforts to administer Mexico City. Rather, the revolutionary leadership established a new local structure of governance and administration in the capital, where decisions about urban policy were made by the presidentially appointed mayor in collaboration with representatives from a wide variety of social groups, not just the organized working class.

In the upcoming pages we will explore these changes in local political administration and urban policy practices in Mexico City, and consider their relationship to the formation of new national political institutions and practices. The discussion begins in 1929 with the foundation of the PNR and a newly restructured national labor movement, two developments that also set the stage for the establishment of new local political and administrative structures, primarily the Consejo Consultivo, or Consultative Council, in Mexico City. Next I examine the ways in which the creation of the Consejo both changed the dynamics of urban development decisions and produced new political conflicts over infrastructural services and administration in the capital. I then explain how a change in both the party's national practices and local policies, which occurred under the leadership of Lázaro Cárdenas, recreated urban policy conflicts in the capital and challenged the ruling party's national electoral legitimacy. I close with a discussion of the ways in which these events negatively affected both urban development policy and national politics, and how these outcomes spurred party leaders to restructure the relationship between national and local political practices once again.

FILLING THE POWER GAP IN MEXICO CITY: CORPORATISM ON THE LOCAL LEVEL

In an effort to pick up the pieces after Obregón's assassination and the public challenges to the CROM, the revolutionary leadership regrouped in order to smooth the transition to the next presidential administration. Ex-president Calles, who had strongly supported the CROM until the assassination, took the lead. Among the most significant actions taken under Calles's direction was the foundation of a new party, the Partido Nacional Revolucionário (PNR), in 1929. The decision arose from many factors, but principal among them were efforts by the revolutionary leadership to offer a new structure for political participation, to unify the highly fragmented urban labor movement, and to relink activist labor sectors to the state while at the same time avoiding the pitfalls of overly powerful organizations seen in the CROM fiasco. Brought to life under President Emilio Portes Gil (1928–1930), who in the following administration became the new party's leader, the PNR carried to power presidents Pascual Ortiz Rubio (1930–1934) and Lázaro Cárdenas (1934–1940).

That the fragmentation of the urban labor movement and the unbridled power of the CROM over Mexico City services and administration were central concerns of revolutionary leaders in establishing the PNR is suggested in the works of several scholars of the period, although none explicitly identify this dimension. Juan Felipe Leal argues that the new party was purposefully designed to "give a national coherence to the different groups of the political bureaucracy . . . and to strengthen the center position of this bureaucracy at the expense of regionalism and *localism*, which had been in command." [1] Clearly, the emphasis on localism and national coherence meant that the inordinate power of the CROM and its efforts to favor certain sectors of the urban labor movement at the expense of rural and other labor forces were still fresh in the minds of revolutionary leaders. Further evidence of the revolutionary leadership's concerns about linking labor to the state through national and not just local mechanisms could be found in the development of a new labor code. The Ley Federal de Trabajo, which was debated starting in 1929 but not enacted until several years later, provided the legal muscle to create and subsequently link a new, more unified, national labor movement to the new PNR. This labor code gave the federal government complete power to recognize unions, approve all strikes, and negotiate binding settlements with the parties concerned. In practice, the code formalized many of the relationships and activities previously undertaken by the CROM; but the difference was that now they were to apply, *de jure* to workers in all regions, locales, and organizations, and not just *de facto* in Mexico City. In this critical transition period, the PNR leadership also sought to establish an entirely new organization to represent the working classes, an institution that would replace the CROM and through which the state could manage its now legally defined relationship with labor. Given the Morones disaster, in the formulation of this new organization the party leadership was careful to avoid urban parochialism and to develop a more national orientation that would also include workers in the countryside.

As one might expect, all this was easier said than done. After a few abortive tries between 1929 and 1932, however, members of a "purged" CROM, along with the CGT and a syndicate of the workers in the Distrito Federal (the FSTDF), finally did join together into one national labor organization in 1933, first known as the Confederación General de Obreros y Campesinos Mexicanos (CGOCM), or General Confederation of Mexican Workers and Peasants. By recognizing the participation of rural workers, along with Mexico City–based workers, the PNR-sponsored CGOCM was a clear move toward a more nationally inclusive labor organization. Shortly thereafter, with a slight modification in composition to include more than a thousand unions representing a broad spectrum of activities across the nation, this labor organization changed its name to the Confederación de Trabajadores Mexicanos (CTM). The CGOCM and its organizational heir, the CTM, differed markedly from the CROM in two critical respects: They both relied on the support of the rural and provincial work force as much as on urban laborers, and they both were dominated by what we have called more proletarianized occupations, especially those that had been more likely to ally with the CGT than the CROM in the earlier years. That is, the CGOCM and the CTM primarily represented unions in large industry, mining, and railroads from all over the country, as well as several important regional organizations. Note that these were the groups that the CGT had targeted and that had been most alienated by the CROM's actions and its urban servicing and administrative priorities in Mexico City. Clearly, the new PNR had learned well. The new party's leadership was not about to reestablish the same urban-based divisions among the nation's workers as had been reflected in the CROM-CGT conflicts, and creating a truly national federation was perhaps the best way to overcome such divisions. They also were not about to lose political control over Mexico City again, and removing structures of municipal governance while incorporating urban laborers into a primarily national—rather than local—labor movement helped them accomplish that aim.

But the old CROM and many of its urban service workers, especially self-employed and small-scale artisans, as well as other Mexico City constituents, were lost in the institutional shuffle. Many bureaucrats, craftsmen, and those employed in small commerce, services, and building trades in the capital, who had supported the CROM and sustained its collaborative stances and urban service priorities, along with renters and neighborhood and professional associations, were left floating in the national political scene without organizational representation and without a local democratic structure through which to air their grievances. Starting in the late 1920s and continuing throughout the decade of the 1930s, then, social pressures from Mexico City's marginally employed urban poor and from this wide variety of middle sectors worried revolutionary leaders as much as did industrial labor and peasant struggles. While much of the growing social and political unrest in the 1930s was attributable to employment problems associated with a severe economic crisis that hit Mexico as part of the worldwide depression, it also was due to the new party's almost myopic preoccupation with industrial labor and the peasantry—preferential treatment that temporarily gave short shrift to popular and middle-class residents' demands for improved public services in the capital. In addition, the demise of the CROM and the removal of democratic political structures in the capital meant that no formal political structures existed for pressing these demands. Together, these conditions pushed Mexico City populations toward self-organization and social protest to voice their dissatisfaction.

In order to preempt opposition from the wide variety of mobilizing urban sectors, the PNR sought an alternative institutional mechanism that would take the place of democratically elected local structures and cushion the blow of their unilateral abolition. With this in mind, the party leadership established the Consejo Consultivo de la Ciudad de México, or Consultative Council of Mexico City, which was given juridical status in the 1928 Ley Orgánica del Distrito y de los Territorios Federales. The Consejo Consultivo del Departamento Central, as it was formally called, was to be a body of politically appointed representatives with the official purpose of "aiding" Mexico City's mayor in governing the capital.[2] It had no legislative power, and its representatives were handpicked by the Calles-dominated PNR leadership in conjunction with the mayor, who was himself presidentially appointed and thus beholden to the whims of the President and the national party leadership. As such, the composition and character of Mexico City's Consejo Consultivo prefigured the corporatist political system through which the Partido Revolucionario Institucional (PRI) would ultimately govern and stabilize one-party rule.

The reasons why Mexico City's Consejo Consultivo took on a corporatist character stem in large part from the ways in which resident populations in the capital were already organized. Representatives were selected who could vocalize the urban demands and redevelopment concerns of well-established organizational constituencies in the capital. Representatives also came from groups whose relatively high degree of mobilization or organization meant they could cause political problems if not incorporated into this new body. Among the Consejo's members, then, were delegates who represented property owners, renters, professionals, neighborhood associations, employees (both public and private), workers, peasants, commerce, and industry (see Table 5). Mothers' associations, or Asociaciones de Madres de la Familia, were also included in the Consejo, mainly because they had emerged as the principal voice of traditional, pro-Catholic, profamily values in Mexico City in the aftermath of the Revolution's anticlericalism and the Cristero Rebellion, a movement of fanatic Catholics who violently challenged the revolutionary leadership in 1926. Mothers' associations probably also were included because they were a well-organized core of the antiprostitution and pro-hygiene social reform movements that arose in Mexico City starting in the 1920s, especially as urban conditions deteriorated markedly in the face of growing poverty and large-scale migration of rural (mostly male) laborers to the capital.

Of the Consejo's thirteen delegates, the largest number of slots (three) was reserved for labor, while most other groups were allotted only one representative each. The disproportionate number of delegates representing *asociaciones de trabajadores*, or laborers' organizations, reflected the importance of Mexico City labor and its power within the PNR and the revolutionary leadership in 1929. The number of labor representatives may also have been meant as a concession to those Mexico City–based unions that had previously been active in the CROM but now lacked an institutional base for their political power with the abolition of municipal rule and the CROM's rapid demise. When the Calles-dominated PNR created the Consejo Consultivo in Mexico City in 1929, then, it was probably not intended just for the purposes

TABLE 5

Occupations Represented in the Consejo Consultivo del Distrito Federal (Consultative Council of the Federal District), 1929 and 1946

1929	1946
Comercio (commerce)	Comercio
Comercio en pequeño (small commerce)	Comercio en pequeño
Cámaras industriales (chambers of industries)	Cámaras industriales
Industria en pequeño (small industry)	Industria en pequeño
Profesionales (professionals)	Profesionales
Inquilinos (tenants)	Inquilinos
Propietarios* (property holders)	Bienes raices* (real estate)
Empleados públicos y privados (public and private employees)	Empleados públicos
Trabajadores** (workers)	Trabajadores**
Asociaciones de madres (mothers' associations)	
Campesinos (peasants)	

*Two representatives
**Three representatives
Sources: *Actas y Versiones del Consejo Consultivo del Distrito Federal, 1929–1930* and *Departamento del Distrito Federal: Realizaciones del Gobierno del Sr. Presidente de la República Lic. Miguel Aleman, 1946–1952* (Mexico: Talleres Gráficos de la Nación, 1952).

of fostering local involvement in policy decisions about the built environment. It also was conceived as a mechanism for the limited political participation of CROMistas, who now were relatively disempowered in the new national labor federations. This possibility is evidenced by the fact that the three labor organizations called on to send delegates to the first Consejo Consultivo were unions that had been strongly active in the CROM: the Federación de Sindicatos Obreros del Distrito Federal (FSODF), once considered the strongest labor nucleus within the CROM; the Sindicato de Redactores del la Prensa del D. F., which had the added advantage of being strategically located in the public press; and the Alianza de Camioneros de México, the union of bus drivers that had recently become powerful with the CROM's backing in struggles against the radical, CGT-affiliated *tranviarios*.[3] That most of the Consejo's labor delegates were linked to the CROM is also evidenced in the minutes of the Consejo's meetings, where the CROM's name frequently arose in the context of stances on urban policy issues taken by the labor delegates.[4]

It is also telling that many of the remaining groups or occupations allotted delegate status on the Consejo as representatives for other occupations had at one time or another also been active within the CROM, which at its height in the late 1920s included employees' organizations, street vendors, federations of *comerciantes*, neighborhood associations, renters, rural groups, and teachers as well as laborers.[5] This further suggests that the creation of the Consejo Consultivo was as much influenced by the national restructuring of the labor movement after the CROM fiasco as by the abolition of municipal democratic structures in Mexico City. With the new labor movement organizations struggling to incorporate mainly regional forces and industrial workers, to the exclusion of the Mexico City residents involved in services and artisan activities, many of the CROM's previous constituents were left without mechanisms for participation in politics—on either the local or the national level. Thus the Consejo Consultivo filled a much-needed void for those particular urban constituents, many of whom still put priority on urban redevelopment and shared little in common with the industrial laborers now incorporated into national organizational structures.

The Consejo Consultivo, however, was not necessarily intended to serve as a structure for challenging the new national labor sector's demands, just as it was not intended to accommodate only the CROM's constituents. Although this new Mexico City–based political institution may have helped counterbalance the power of Obregonista-linked industrial labor on the national political scene, it was primarily structured to serve as an arena for including previously ignored sectors in urban policymaking and for working out internal ideological differences among Callistas, CROMistas, Obregonistas, and other political factions that still existed in local and national politics. This is also clear from the decision to include peasant representatives (from more peripheral agricultural areas of the city) in this urban-based body. Recall that in 1928 and 1929 Obregonistas were still struggling to keep labor and peasant issues at the forefront of national policy, while CROMistas and Callistas sought to balance labor's interests with the demands of more liberal petit bourgeois forces, who worried that industrial labor's strength or its alliance with peasants within the ruling coalition might push Mexico down too radical a path. Political conflicts in Mexico City between these different forces could have been threatening to national politics and policy if they were not accommodated in some way or another, and the Consejo Consultivo acted as a forum for such accommodation.

Given the importance of the business sector to local prosperity and national political stability, Mexico City's industrialists and *comerciantes* were allotted two representatives each, differentiated according to size; that is, one delegate each represented large industry, large commercial establishments, small industry, and small *comerciantes*, respectively. The delegates for large commerce and large industry were members of the city's Cámara de Comercio (Chamber of Commerce) or the Cámara Industrial (Chamber of Industry); these were powerful and well-organized bodies that for years had represented the larger and more prosperous commercial firms and industries in the capital. The delegates representing *comercio en pequeño* and *industriales en pequeño* had less powerful constituencies; indeed, delegates for the former voiced the concerns of small *comerciantes*, artisans, and street vendors, groups known to have more diverse demands and a more fluid constituency than the Cámara de Comercio, while delegates for the latter represented the demands of family-run and other small workshops characteristically not active in the city's Cámara Industrial.

That small industrialists and small shopkeepers had their own representatives, separate from big industry and large commercial establishments, underscores the PNR's recognition that there were important differences between capitalists of different sizes, particularly with respect to the types of urban demands they posed, a split that would emerge once again in Mexico City in the 1950s and 1960s. It also highlights the PNR's concern with petit bourgeois sentiments in Mexico City. The new party's conscious efforts to make overtures to the liberal middle classes, who saw their influence as declining after Madero's assassination, led the party leadership to allocate special slots in the Consejo for *empleados* (employees) and *comerciantes* too. Along these same lines, the Consejo also included representatives from the city's professional associations (doctors and architects, in its first years of existence) and from organizations of local property owners, most of whom were simply homeowners and not big developers. Counted among these professionals were those who lent support to the Revolution at the outset, in its liberal Maderista incarnation, but who had been largely excluded from public discourse once labor organizations had captured the spotlight in the capital city.

With the Consejo Consultivo in place, the dynamics of urban policymaking and development in Mexico City changed markedly, especially as compared to the CROM-dominated past. Now the business of servicing and administering Mexico City was no longer controlled primarily by the urban labor movement in collaboration with the revolutionary leadership. Urban labor lost its singular, privileged position in the capital city, at least to the extent that it participated in the negotiating process side by side with a wide variety of other social groups: shopkeepers, factory owners, middle-class professionals, and property owners, to name a few. As a purely political strategy, the inclusion of so many different class forces in the Consejo broadened sympathy for the new ruling party in Mexico City. Yet because the Consejo was primarily an advisory council without jurisdictional or substantive political power, the urban policy objectives of the national party still prevailed. And it was precisely this state of affairs that made Mexico City's urban development so contentious during the 1930s. Indeed, once the Consejo Consultivo was established with such a broad class base of participation, there was not always agreement on urban policy decisions, and representatives on the Consejo fought both among themselves and with the new party leadership over several key urban policy issues, ranging from transport and housing to restrictions on store hours and selling practices.

The subject most under debate throughout the 1930s was the extent to which the national party leadership's urban development objectives would prevail over the competing demands of the Consejo's representatives. Complicating matters was the fact that only certain classes—such as industrial and commercial capital in the early years of the decade, and labor and the peasantry in the later years—had national influence or other national organizations through which to express their demands to the party leadership. Thus when they were outnumbered in the Consejo, they could always turn to national mechanisms to pressure party leaders. Those classes that had only local avenues for participation, such as artisans, shopkeepers, or middle classes, had no such recourse and they frequently lost out in urban policy conflicts. This state of affairs exacerbated urban development conflicts in the Consejo because it frequently set nationally powerful classes, or the national party leadership's urban policy objectives, at odds with those Mexico City groups who had no national organizational influence in the period. Thus, despite the fact that controversies arose over local policies, the political repercussions were in large part national, mainly because the urban policy decisions laid bare the extent to which certain classes or small groups in Mexico City wielded both local and national political power. In the conflicts that ensued, Mexico City's urban future remained uncertain.

"FUNCTIONAL DEMOCRACY"

The shifting balance of power within and between Mexico City populations and national political actors and institutions is clear with a closer look at the Consejo's deliberations. In its first few years of existence, the Consejo Consultivo served principally as a forum for public debate over provision of essential urban services in Mexico City. The demands made by delegates representing the urban bus industry against the Compañía de Tranvías, for example, generally related to the company's legal obligation to pave streets where trolley tracks were located. The fact that these questions were usually posed by the spokesman for the Alianza de Camioneros highlights the enduring character of conflicts within the urban transport industry in Mexico City, raised earlier and to which we will return in later chapters. In this period, however, transport became one of several contentious issues not so much because it laid bare divisions in the working class or between different *transportistas*, as before, but mainly because it pitted the concerns of local residents against those of transport service providers. This happened, moreover, because the Consejo was trying to fulfill two distinct functions. In addition to serving as a forum in which local populations could express demands about the built environment now that municipal self-rule was abolished, it also was a mechanism through which locally organized federations of workers, like Mexico City *transportistas*, could make labor-specific demands, now that the CROM had lost much of its legitimacy and labor organizations were being organized on a narrower occupational basis.[6]

Given its multiple functions, debates in the Consejo were frequently left unresolved. In addition, public meetings of the Consejo were frequently staged for the press and the public as a way to advocate antiforeign sentiment or other popular political opinions. Sessions were open to reporters, which was particularly useful when the Consejo wished to defend its position against citizen attacks published in the Mexico City press. Nonetheless, most discussions were substantive, and they tended to revolve around urban infrastructural concerns, related policy problems, and their possible solutions. The minutes of the Consejo suggest that the issues debated most frequently by delegates in their bimonthly public meetings were street paving, water provision, drainage, major public works, the location of neighborhood markets (*mercados*), and local taxes, in addition to housing scarcities and overall transport problems. In its first several months of existence, the urban infrastructural issues generally discussed in the Consejo were more costly than contentious, since they generally required substantial government investment in new infrastructure. Delegates rarely disagreed about the necessity of providing urban services to neighborhoods, since this was a political position almost all could support, and the Consejo's advice was nonbinding, anyway. Delegates in the new Consejo had little to lose and everything to gain by advocating approval of the demands of underserviced neighborhoods—knowing full well that the mayor and the president were left to make the difficult distribution decisions.

At least for the first several years, then, the creation of the Consejo Consultivo appeared to be a smart move on the part of the newly established PNR. Given its capacity to serve as a forum for the discussion of urban services and administration, the Consejo temporarily preempted opposition from local urban forces, which was on the rise after several years' infighting within and between the capital city's different *municipios*. In the absence of municipal democratic structures, the existence of the Consejo suggested some degree of party responsiveness and helped the PNR establish institutional linkages with a wide variety of urban populations. These linkages, in turn, became a relatively sound basis for generating local political support for the PNR's national policies, particulary those with primarily urban consequences, such as a comprehensive industrial development program, which was hovering around the corner. Still, the Consejo's success in serving as a substitute for democratic governance on the local level was not entirely unproblematic. Several meetings in the first year were devoted to counterbalancing negative public opinion and press accounts of the Consejo, its linkages to the CROM, and the fact that its members were appointed by the ruling party in cahoots with already powerful and well-institutionalized urban forces. The public and the Consejo's own members had good reasons to be skeptical. Through occasional inadvertent slips, which strangely enough were recorded in the minutes of the Consejo's deliberations, it is evident that two types of meetings of the Consejo's delegates were frequently held, a private one, presumably where major decisions were made about local issues that might be contentious, and a bimonthly public one, where delegates could sound off in a nonconflictual atmosphere in ways that appealed to their own specific constituencies.[7]

It is unclear to what extent the general public was aware of the Consejo's private deliberations but this was of little consequence because ultimately, controversy surfaced for reasons related to the Consejo's power and political structure. Many delegates were themselves becoming increasingly aware of the limits of this particular structure and its capacity to serve as a deliberative body. For example, in one meeting in early 1930, a little more than a year after the Consejo was founded, one delegate complained that delegate "alternates frequently do not correspond to the same group represented by the primary delegate, but to another group."[8] In this particular complaint, the delegate's concern was that the alternate delegate represented a CROMista union, while the primary delegate did not—something that reflected many of the members' concerns in those early years that the Consejo Consultivo might still be used by CROMistas to push their own particular objectives over those of other factions in the labor movement. In this same meeting, moreover, delegates publicly lamented the fact that the Consejo had no juridical power of its own, and that without mayoral and presidential approval, or even the presence of the mayor's or the president's personal delegates at the Consejo's official meetings, delegate representatives' recommended policies would not be implemented. From the very beginning, then, some of the Consejo's own members questioned the capacity of this corporatist-style political structure to serve as a vehicle for eliminating the overwhelming political control by well-established national political leaders and institutions.

Those most critical of the Consejo, however, were those left out of the PNR's new and relatively moderate profile, such as radical factions of the labor movement and even some of those still allied with the CROM who felt their power slipping. For example, one labor delegate who identified himself as "one of those most enamored with those institutions in the country that signify democratic advances," called all the Consejo's deliberative meetings "illegal, against the law, [and] against the rules."[9] He also used the occasion to complain that in making up the 1930 corps of delegates, the president had overridden recommendations from one of the formally franchised representative groups and had appointed instead a delegate of his own personal choice. Clearly, problems about the relationship between the party-dominated state and representative groups existed even in the thirties, before Mexico's national corporatist political structures were founded. As in later years, moreover, these criticisms frequently revolved around the issues of who, exactly, had landed in a position of representation for a particular class or constituency. It is noteworthy, nonetheless, that criticisms of the ways in which the Consejo's membership could be manipulated from above neither brought a wholesale repudiation of this local corporatist structure nor a drive to replace it with direct electoral democracy, at least from its members. Indeed, the same delegate who criticized the Consejo added that it should be lauded for its "functional democratic" character, which allowed the systematic participation of a wide variety of class and social groups.[10] The principal complaint from this and other representatives, rather, was not the absence of democratic elections in the constitution of the Consejo, but the Consejo's limited power to make urban policy.

Yet it was precisely the Consejo's "functional democracy" that became the source of serious political problems, both for the body itself and for the ruling PNR, and that truly limited local residents from having more say in urban policy. The basic problem was that this corporatist structure of participation limited the grounds for negotiation and consensus. The Consejo's functional democratic character ensured that delegates posed specific demands about their own representative groups' specific urban concerns, instead of directing their deliberations toward general policies that would aid in the overall administration or redevelopment of the city. Accordingly, when urban issues arose around which different sectors took different stances, it was difficult to agree on a policy position. Many beneficial urban policies fell by the wayside, and this frequently left delegates—and sometimes even the PNR leadership—unhappy. When one delegate (from large industry) complained that the Consejo was concerning itself with "too many specific requests," and that it instead "should be preoccupied with matters of a general character that benefit the city in general, [and] that benefit the collectivity and not a [specific] group," he ran into vocal opposition, particularly from delegates representing small industry, small commerce, and labor.[11]

With so many different class and social forces represented in one body, most of whom struggled to present their own specific urban demands, internal conflict over urban redevelopment soon riddled the Consejo. Most delegates were eager to represent their constituencies as faithfully and actively as possible, especially given past limits to local participation when the CROM malevolently dominated local politics and its own rank and file. Minutes of the meetings are peppered with policy stands preceded by statements like "as the proud delegate for small industry," or "as the honorable delegate for labor," each of which indicates delegates' self-conscious identification as representatives of specific occupations or sectors. Given the seriousness with which class or corporate identities were taken, it did not take long for delegates to disagree. Small industrialists, for example, disputed the extent of local tax breaks to be given to large industry, something that was seen as unfair to the more traditional sector of small family industries. Likewise, within the first two years of the Consejo's deliberations, small and large commerce locked horns over regulations on street vending, on selling hours and locations, and on government inspection of goods, each of which disproportionately helped or hindered Mexico City's large or small *comerciantes*.[12] In addition, labor delegates consistently found themselves at odds with delegates from both industry and commerce over work hours and worker protections introduced by the Ley Federal de Trabajo.

FROM "FUNCTIONAL DEMOCRACY" TO URBAN CONFLICT

While conflicts in the Consejo over the urban implications of the Ley Federal de Trabajo were time-consuming, they were not as divisive as they might have been precisely because this was national legislation, well-supported by nationally organized and powerful groups like the new labor federation and party leaders whose decisions ultimately decided the law's fate. Specific urban policies were quite a different matter, because they were local in scope and thus under a different legal jurisdiction. This meant that their fate was more likely to be determined in the Consejo itself, in the course of local negotiations, and with party and presidential influence brought to bear. And this, in turn, meant that the most divisive debates in the Consejo revolved around strictly urban problems, particularly those relating to land use in the city, issues that frequently pitted local residents against the party leadership. Ultimately, it was these urban redevelopment policies—particularly the issue of central city development and the role of transport in the process—that laid bare the problems with the Consejo's corporatist structure and subsequently generated a round of politically significant urban protests and grassroots dissatisfaction in the late 1930s.

One reason debate over transport and its relationship to downtown development was so divisive and politically consequential was that it involved fundamental decisions about the type of industry, commerce, services, and residential access that would exist in the capital's central areas. These decisions, in turn, had implications for the life and livelihood of almost all the Consejo's delegates and their constituents. Would large industries and commerce, necessary for the rapid economic recovery of the capital and thus the nation, successfully drive out the small, resulting in a fundamental transformation of Mexico's colonial commercial center and its surroundings? If so, would residents of the traditional center then be displaced by large public works geared toward industry and commerce, which in turn would eliminate their traditional employment activities? Where would they find alternative housing and employment, and who would pay for it? Also, would the growing demands for protecting organized labor's workplace rights adversely affect the traditional middle classes or the remainder of the city's poor, the latter of whom would then be likely to join the ranks of downtown street vendors and compete with the already large number of small commercial establishments employing the traditional middle classes?

Architects, large merchants, property owners, *transportistas*, and new urban planning professionals on the Consejo, which had just been given new powers under a 1930 Ley de Planeación General that formalized a technocratic logic in the urban planning process, argued strongly for protection and restoration of the colonial architectural beauty of downtown areas, as well as for keeping central city streets uncluttered by vendors and clear for urban transport vehicles. In contrast, small *comerciantes*, street vendors, and many renters, all of whom tended to live in old, dilapidated buildings in the center, saw this campaign as posing a serious threat to their personal livelihood. So too did many small industrial producers in family-run workshops (*talleres*) in central areas, where these small-scale enterprises relied on face-to-face contact and a local market. Accordingly, they too could not bear the costs of such urban renewal or its impact on land values. Because these small producers and local shopkeepers generally lived and worked in the same location, they were particularly concerned that urban renewal plans would move them out to peripheral areas away from local labor and markets, where they would be forced to buy or rent housing or factory space. As in many early twentieth-century Latin American cities, housing stock in Mexico City's central areas had been passed down in traditional worker-artisan families for generations. To be displaced from these locations, particularly at a time when large industry and commerce were coming to dominate the urban economy, would be a fatal blow to these small, central city businesses.

As the central city's traditional residents were quick to malign the new *técnicos* who promoted plans for urban redevelopment, conflicts over urban issues relating to both transport and downtown development accelerated within the Consejo. One ongoing debate was particularly divisive; it concerned whether street vendors would be allowed on central city streets and whether their working hours would be restricted. This issue pitted large shopkeepers against small, workers against employers, the bus drivers' union against vendors, and urban planning professionals against local residents. It also placed the PNR in an extremely difficult political position, since party leaders had to find a politically palatable way to balance plans for urban development in the capital, which it still strongly supported for its economic potential, with efforts to ensure the continued political participation and support of all the Consejo's members.

The 1930s were a particularly bad time for trying to balance these urban economic and political concerns. Deteriorating economic conditions associated with the aftermath of the 1929 world economic crisis put many out of work. In this context, *técnicos*' recommendations to restrict street vending and spend massive amounts on urban reconstruction generated serious public controversy, since petty trading was one of the few avenues open to both the unemployed and the underemployed. One delegate representing small commerce, a constituency that as just noted had a direct stake in restrictions on street vendors who counted in their potential ranks, put his opposition to technocrats and their urban renewal plans simply: "Frankly, I'm afraid of technocrats, and I'm even more afraid of offices where there are lots of technocrats."[13] Given the divisiveness and controversy over the urban renewal policies, PNR leaders feared they would be seen as being more concerned with aesthetics and redevelopment than with the concerns of the city's new class of poor if the Consejo approved such plans. Yet at the same time, because the PNR was anxious to continue restoring Mexico City's built environment and to simultaneously consolidate its support in the capital from large commerce and industry, it was felt that modernizing Mexico City's urban infrastructure would help meet both these objectives.

Achieving these goals was difficult, however, since the PNR also sought to keep the support of both labor and the middle classes. Accordingly, the party leadership was torn in different directions on many urban redevelopment issues. This was reflected in the ambiguous positions formally taken by the Consejo, particularly with respect to the nature and social composition of downtown areas. In one meeting, the Consejo's chairman, who generally voiced the PNR's priorities, argued that all necessary steps should be taken to protect the traditional character of the city, and small commerce in particular, a stance that implied restricting the growing number of poor and unsightly vendors crowding downtown streets. Yet in the same speech he also stated that the Consejo's responsibility was to provide "opportunities for poor people who honestly are looking for bread." He complained that with "14,000 dying of hunger in [Mexico] City alone," decisions about conflicts between street vendors and small shopkeepers should be made "less on aesthetics" and more on utility.[14] Walking a fine line between aesthetics and utility was awkward, but the Consejo's delegates finally voted to impose limited restrictions on street vending to help clear central city streets, ease competition with small shopkeepers, and still allow a means for the urban poor to generate some meager revenues.

Despite such skilled and conscientious efforts to balance contradictory demands, divisions and conflicts persisted over urban renewal in general and downtown areas in particular. As urban conditions deteriorated during the 1930s, new conflicts and concerns continually arose in the Consejo, pitting government planners and economists and their allies in big business against small shopkeepers and local neighborhood associations. Faced with the prospect of unsolvable conflicts, which would be politically disastrous for the still fragile PNR and which also would slow the process of urban renewal and urban policymaking, party leaders soon sought new institutional mechanisms that would bypass the crippled Consejo. In late 1933, the PNR introduced the Ley de Planificación y Zonificación del Distrito Federal. Among other things, this law called for the creation of a new Comisión de Planificación for Mexico City that would streamline urban policymaking. The new commission was to be comprised of delegates representing large industry, large commerce, and property owners, as well as bankers, the main associations of architects and civil engineers, and the federal ministers of public works, health and welfare, and the treasury. Most of these representatives supported the economic and urban restructuring that downtown development implied, while forces that opposed downtown development, like renters and small industry and commerce, were excluded from the Planning Commission, although they remained active on the city's Consejo Consultivo.[15]

This institutional separation of urban policymaking functions opened up a whole new set of political problems for the PNR, especially with its constituents in the capital. With Mexico City's small industry and commerce, renters, and laborers now excluded from major development decisions, they began to feel politically disenfranchised—as they had initially upon the 1928 abolition of municipal rule. Moreover, political exclusion from these decisions had serious economic implications for these groups, at least to the extent that the form and character of downtown areas would be affected. Accordingly, the 1933 urban administrative reform sowed seeds for the return of social unrest in the capital. This was especially the case with respect to the nonlabor delegates on the Consejo, who, in the absence of national federations (like the CTM) for participation, had no other institutional mechanism for influencing political decision making except the now emasculated Consejo Consultivo. In response to this situation, moreover, small industrialists and *comerciantes*, renters, neighborhood organizations, and even women's groups, especially in the city's central areas, began to work more closely among themselves to present their demands.[16] Because these groups were now driven outside formal political structures, which were either closed to them (like the new Planning Commission) or ever more impotent politically (like the Consejo Consultivo), they increasingly turned to urban social movements to press demands.

The resurgence of popular opposition in the capital during the last half of the 1930s highlighted several growing problems that confronted Mexico's newly founded ruling party on a national scale as well. Principal among these were the leadership's difficulties in keeping a variety of different class forces united in support of the PNR. Establishing institutional structures for their symbolic participation clearly was not sufficient. Groups had to feel that there was the possibility for policy action through those structures. Moreover, the ruling leadership had to demonstrate that traditionally powerful elites, who had controlled both local and national politics in the past, like Mexico City's big businesses and government-linked *técnicos*, did not continue to enjoy privileged access to policy and decision making at the expense of the less powerful. In the case of Mexico City's Consejo Consultivo, the PNR appeared to fail the test, especially starting in 1933 when the Planning Commission was introduced. The growing public skepticism about the party leadership's biases toward big business and technocracy brought two responses, each of which had consequences for the PNR's immediate future and for the national-level corporatist structure to be introduced within less than a decade. One (as mentioned, and to which we will return shortly) was the emergence of well-organized and vocal urban social movements, which did not reach a peak until the final years of the 1930s. The other was the reinvigoration of labor and peasant federations, as well as a strengthening of their linkages to the state.

Both labor and peasant organizations had just passed through a period of relative quiescence between 1929 and 1931, in the context of political infighting and reorganization that followed the CROM's demise. But after taking time to regroup, and while facing an economic crisis that helped mobilize their constituents, they appeared back on the urban and national political scene in ways that impacted on urban policymaking too.

Though most scholars argue that much of the reactivation of peasant and labor groups in the early to mid 1930s came in response to the conservatism of the national policies supported by the Calles-dominated PNR, it is important to remember that labor and peasant opposition to the PNR was also spurred by specific urban developments within the Consejo Consultivo in Mexico City. Indeed, when the PNR formalized the establishment of a Planning Commission filled with big-business elites and urban property owners, many of whom had been the principal supporters of Porfirio Díaz's dictatorship, labor and peasant delegates on the Consejo could see the writing on the wall with regard to the party's class and developmental priorities as well as the ideological direction the PNR planned to take. Business and commercial redevelopment was to be pursued at all costs; it was to be based on massive and costly infrastructural improvements for trade, commerce, and services; and it was to be carried out primarily in the capital city, to the exclusion of the countryside. In short, the new PNR's urban redevelopment strategy was to be undertaken at the expense of rural areas, the city's laborers, and the self- or underemployed poor who saw few outlets for industrial employment in this strategy.

CÁRDENAS'S PEASANT-LABOR PACT

In this context of clear government support for urban-based commercial development, which hauntingly echoed the Porfirian period, General Lázaro Cárdenas emerged on the political scene. He rose to power within the revolutionary leadership in late 1933 as a spokesman for labor and peasants, and he challenged the party's political and economic development practices such that he made a name for himself as Mexico's most beloved populist postrevolutionary president. Many scholars have documented the fact that Cárdenas's overall concern as president was to initiate the modernization and nationalist development of Mexico and its economy, and that he developed openly favorable policies toward both labor and the peasantry. Several unusual historical circumstances led Cárdenas to base his administration on the support of these social groups, a decision that would have direct implications for his administration's position on the urban development and reconstruction of Mexico City.

During the early 1930s, peasant demands were accelerating, having been put aside by President Calles and other revolutionary leaders in their initial efforts to foster rapid, urban-based recovery and industrialization during the 1920s. Also, by the early 1930s there was clear evidence that the world depression would continue to pummel the fragile Mexican economy for a while, bringing a rapid decline in exports, production cutbacks, and high unemployment in the nation's fledgling industries and in the countryside. With social and economic problems developing in both sectors simultaneously, the two or three years before Cárdenas's rise to the presidency were marked by a new round of labor and peasant mobilizations in the countryside, ranging from land invasions to hunger marches and demonstrations, which threatened the hegemony of the PNR and its leadership in both the city and the countryside. With the backing of much of the labor movement leadership, and with the tentative support of others who felt the PNR under Calles had abandoned revolutionary ideals and become too oriented toward elite and private sector demands for rapid urban and economic growth, Cárdenas successfully assumed national leadership. Within his first few years of taking office, Cárdenas implemented both prolabor and propeasant policies. In 1936 under Cárdenas's guidance, the PNR founded the Mexican Workers Federation, or Confederación de Trabajadores Mexicanos (CTM), which brought together the disparate federations for industrial laborers that had remained on the scene after the political demise of the CROM. In 1937 Cárdenas and the CTM signed a pact with the Mexican Communist Party and the Confederación Campesina Mexicana (the Mexican Confederation of Peasants), the latter being the precursor to the Confederación Nacional Campesina (CNC), or peasant sector of the party. These political pacts with national federations of laborers and peasants helped provide the institutional base for the Partido de la Revolución Mexicana (PRM), the party that Cárdenas created in 1938 and that replaced the PNR.

As labor and the peasantry lent their institutional support to his administration, Cárdenas fulfilled his side of the bargain. Between 1936 and 1940, he introduced some of the most radical and far-reaching reforms Mexico had yet seen. In addition to recognizing the rights of unions to exist, Cárdenas supported strikes by industrial workers for wage increases, the elimination of company unions, and collective contracts. Under Cárdenas, the industrial working class saw increases in real wages, even as the rest of the country experienced the devastating consequences of world economic crisis. In the agrarian domain, Cárdenas's actions also broke entirely new ground. As the first postrevolutionary president to actively establish strong alliances with the rural peasantry, he distributed more land to peasant families during his presidential tenure than during all previous administrations. He also introduced perhaps the most consequential innovation that Mexico was to see in the twentieth century: the legalization of collectively owned and farmed lands, known as *ejidos*.

By formally structuring the state's relationships to labor and peasants through the formation of nationally inclusive institutions linked to a ruling party, there was much less likelihood that specific labor or peasant organizations would hold undue power, as had occurred in earlier periods with the CROM. This contributed greatly to Cárdenas's success in forging a program of national development and social equality. However, this strategy also justified the government's efforts to control capital and bypass many of the urban and political concerns of non-working-class social forces, including public employees, the urban poor, and sectors of the traditional middle class like shopkeepers, doctors, and teachers, who had also felt excluded by many of the development policies of the PNR, albeit for reasons different from those of labor and peasants. Cárdenas's policies, in short, fueled a slow-burning urban opposition from both small and large industry and commerce, urban residents in local trade and services, public sector employees, and conservative elements in the military, to name a few.

What is significant for our purposes, however, is the fact that the exclusion of these particular classes and class factions had specifically urban as well as political consequences, since most of these groups were concentrated in Mexico's cities, especially its capital. Indeed, the implementation of this particular development vision meant that urban reconstruction objectives were to be subordinated to the priorities of rural development, and that the investment in Mexico City that did occur was to aid mainly labor and its industrial employment, not commerce and services. This in turn meant that with Cárdenas as president, Mexico City's middle classes and many sectors of the urban poor not only lacked national institutional mechanisms for political participation on a par with labor and the peasantry, they also lost out in urban service amenities, at least as compared to previous periods when Mexico City's urban and economic revitalization itself was considered a principal national development objective. Of course, with Mexico City's mayor beholden to the president, and with the Consejo Consultivo effectively emasculated, these groups already lacked institutional mechanisms with which to counteract the local effects of national policies. Yet with Cárdenas's ideological proclivities toward peasants and industrial laborers, the marginally employed urban poor and middle classes were in danger of being even worse off, as would be the built environment of Mexico City itself. And as the urban environment deteriorated, so the urban concerns of many of the city's residents intensified, until opposition to Cárdenas brought rising political dissatisfactions and the party's near electoral defeat.

URBAN POLICIES UNDER CÁRDENAS

Cárdenas's favoritism toward peasants and industrial workers, and his neglect of those poorly paid, frequently self-employed or nonwage workers that we define as the urban "popular" (or lower-middle) classes, are perhaps best seen in the fiscal and administrative practices introduced in the capital between 1934 and 1940. Cárdenas began his presidential administration by removing Mexico City Mayor Aaron Sáenz, an act that sparked political fires for Cárdenas among many middle-class residents, with low and moderate incomes alike, since Sáenz was known as a revolutionary loyalist with the bourgeois sensibilities that appealed to this constituency. With Sáenz out of the way, newly appointed Mayor Cosme Hinojosa began to restructure urban expenditures in accordance with the Cárdenas's national development objectives. Almost immediately, resources were shifted away from the capital city's coffers and toward the national budget, such that the latter grew faster than the former for the first time in years. Also, "the portion [of expenditures] destined for urban public works was reduced . . . [and] new social programs were introduced" that mainly benefited organized labor's workplace demands.[17] Among the latter programs were extensive investments in workers' health and education, as well as new housing for industrial laborers on newly expropriated urban lands—areas that came to be known as *colonias proletarias* (proletarian neighborhoods).[18] With these new priorities, expenditures on overall urban infrastructural services declined such that Cárdenas devoted fewer resources to water, drainage, street paving, public lighting, markets, and parks, which notably had been the principal demands of middle-class residents and various other representatives on the Consejo in previous periods.[19] Even though Cárdenas had the reputation of being populist and concerned with Mexico's disadvantaged classes, when it came to some of Mexico City's longtime residents not employed in industry and whose income also was limited, such as artisans, shopkeepers and petty traders, Cárdenas was not particularly responsive. He in fact steadfastly refused to buckle to demands by *inquilinarios* for rent control, even as he consistently responded to striking industrial workers.

Cárdenas's reluctance to support renters' demands and his neglect of basic services for general neighborhood improvement was matched by an equally quixotic stance in support of capital-intensive downtown development, albeit limited. Cárdenas's orientation toward rapid industrial development had made him surprisingly open to the demands of pro-urban-renewal forces who were pushing massive infrastructural redevelopment plans through the Planning Commission. This was underscored in a study of Mexico City's downtown zones between 1930 and 1970 that demonstrated that most of the major public works introduced in Mexico City in fact were built between 1934 and 1940, during the Cárdenas administration. These projects, whose stated intent was to "attract industrial capital," were located mainly in the central areas of the city, frequently in neighborhoods whose fate had been highly contested in the Consejo Consultivo between 1930 and 1933.[20] Cárdenas's vision of the industrial development of downtown areas was given life in the form of several new industries that located in these predominantly commercial and service areas, especially in the *delegación* of Gustavo Madero. Yet these land transformations displaced old shops and brought new workers who crowded out longtime residents, many of them renters and lower-middle-class artisans and shopkeepers, something that further served to alienate significant portions of Mexico City's population from the Cárdenas administration.

The pattern of Cárdenas's national social expenditures further confirms the class and occupational biases of his administration: the privileging of rural as opposed to urban populations, and within the latter, of industrial workers over all other urban social classes, including the middle class and non-wage-earning or self-employed poor, whom we will continue to refer to as the city's "popular classes." For example, with respect to national health expenditures, Cárdenas dictated that all "increases in the quantity [of resources] assigned to the Department of Health w[ould] be destined completely for services in the interior provinces of the Republic since Mexico City has received constant attention in health matters and the sanitary needs in the States are much more urgent."[21] As a rule, moreover, Cárdenas's largest national expenditures were devoted to irrigation or to related rural infrastructure projects for peasants, and to infrastructural projects geared toward industrial development and full employment of workers. As such, Mexico City and its non-working-class residents generally fell by the wayside. Manuel Perlo Cohen goes so far as to suggest that the policies and administrative decisions undertaken by Cárdenas were explicitly *antiurban*, at least when compared to Aaron Sáenz's practices and to those of previous administrations, which tended to favor the urban petit bourgeoisie and other urban social forces over rural ones.[22]

Because many of the capital city's residents saw Cárdenas's policies as harming their own urban trades, self-employment, and urban policy preferences in favor of the social and the service demands of the rural populations, one unfortunate by-product of Cárdenas's propeasant priorities was that during the mid-1930s Mexico City saw a reemergence of antirural sentiment that fueled many social protests in Mexico City. In an echo of debates in the revolutionary aftermath, when urban revolutionary forces struggled to gain ascendancy over Zapata's rural legions, during the mid to late 1930s residents of the capital frequently expresed vocal concerns about hordes of Indians, rural peasants, and a steady inflow of Middle Eastern immigrants—termed *judíos*—who cluttered Mexico City's streets in their search for informal sector employment. Combined with the streams of industrial laborers looking for work in the newly constructed urban factories, the burgeoning cadre of migrants were seen as destroying the traditional character of old neighborhoods, undermining the activities of small *comerciantes*, and taking jobs away from other central city residents employed in small shops and workshops. With the economic crisis reducing overall employment levels at the same time, Mexico City soon saw growing tensions between longtime residents, who tended to be direct descendants of fair-skinned Spanish conquerors and who had long dominated commerce and the urban economy, and more recent arrivals, who tended to have darker skins and distinct cultural heritages, either Middle Eastern or native Indian. One unfortunate by-product of those tensions was a renewal of conflicts over street vending and land usage in downtown areas that had first arisen in the early 1930s, but that now contained racist overtones. By the middle and later years of the decade, Mexico City housed several protofascist organizations that publicly identified themselves as the protectors of the nation's unique cultural heritage; their concerns, nonetheless, often revolved around keeping rural forces and competitive labor forces out of Mexico City. That Cárdenas, a self-proclaimed progressive, was so supportive of the peasantry probably also helped fuel this popular and middle-class support for racist ideas.

Yet Cárdenas's clear political support for peasant populations and industrial laborers was unpopular among many in Mexico City, not only because it accompanied a shift of financial resources and policies away from important sectors of the urban popular and middle classes, but also because Cárdenas's positions threw a wrench into past political and administrative practices in the capital. This was especially true with respect to the procedures of government administrators and bureaucrats, who came mainly from the urban middle classes and who in past periods had controlled most policies and decision making in the capital. Suddenly, other groups, such as peasants, who earlier had failed to influence local policymaking, were a serious force to be reckoned with. It was clear, for example, that the "expansion of ejidal property in the Distrito Federal brought peasant participation . . . in decisions about the use and control of urban lands, such that peasants became a political force with great influence in Mexico City governance."[23] And the threat of greater peasant control within the urban bureaucratic domain, especially in combination with the other developments just noted, spurred many government bureaucrats to question Cárdenas, as they felt their power and privilege shifting to activist peasants. The fact that labor unrest in Mexico City also was on the rise, owing to Cárdenas's open political stance toward the rights of industrial laborers to strike, further concerned state administrators and bureaucrats, who were beginning to worry about a radical turn in the labor movement and about the negative impact of work stoppages and labor protests on the urban and national economy. Indeed, during the mid to late 1930s it was reported that "the streets of Mexico City saw practically no tranquility . . . with demonstrations, meetings, and shouts occurring one after another agitating the souls of the urban population."[24] As a result, many residents and bureaucrats saw their work world and daily living conditions being transformed before their eyes, and many did not like what they saw.

CONFLICT BETWEEN URBAN SERVICE WORKERS AND ADMINISTRATORS

Many of the state bureaucrats expressing discontent with Cárdenas were reacting negatively to the growing laborist sentiment among state workers themselves, which also had implications for urban service provision. With Cárdenas opening both ideological and juridical avenues for more organization and activism among workers, many of those employed by the state followed similar tactics as their industrial counterparts. Labor activism among state workers produced tensions within the state bureaucracy and soon spilled over into the provision of urban services. As some state workers themselves went on strike, urban service provision and administration was fatally disrupted in several key areas, including transport, but also in other areas. This further stalled much of the city's urban reconstruction and development, exacerbated the scarcity of urban services, and equally important, called into question Cárdenas's hold on power. That urban service provision was so fundamentally altered after Cárdenas's rise to power owes directly to the strict regulation of labor in urban services imposed by previous revolutionary governments. Legislative restrictions imposed by Carranza, for example, prohibited those who worked in urban service provision from striking. By 1935, when the rest of the nation's organized laborers were enjoying Cárdenas's backing, bureaucrats, urban service workers employed by the state, and others who lacked the right to strike and who had been excluded from the national labor federation felt themselves slipping out of the political picture. They soon banded together in a larger organization that they hoped would give them as much leverage in both local and national politics as organized peasants and laborers enjoyed. Their actions were in large part inspired by the knowledge that Cárdenas's administration would be sympathetic to labor demands.

Mexico City's teachers, the street cleaners, and those employed in the water (*agua potable*) department were the catalysts of these new attempts to organize state workers. Though each of these occupations had been in separate unions for over a decade, it was not until Cárdenas came to power that they sought one larger federation to link them with other state and urban service workers and represent their unique demands. Almost immediately, these three groups were joined by workers in several key urban service and infrastructure fields also under some type of public regulation: water and sewage, parks and gardens, graphic arts (that is, newspapers), health care, communications and public works, and arms manufacturing. Shortly thereafter, in September 1936, this disparate collection of Mexico City–based workers employed in the provision of urban services and social policy founded in the Federación Nacional de Trabajadores del Estado (FNTE), or National Federation of State Workers. Upon its foundation, those employed in the state-controlled telegraph industry, street maintenance workers, postal workers, government employees in several key ministries (foreign relations, the treasury, public education, and state), as well as office employees in Mexico City government, also joined the organization.[25] The FNTE's constitution filled what many saw as a glaring gap in Mexico's still evolving political system. Since the defeat of the CROM and the political emasculation of Mexico City's Consejo Consultivo, those employed in urban services had been denied effective political mechanisms to wield power. In the administration preceding Cárdenas, they had used the PNR as the vehicle to make demands. But with the 1936 restructuring of the party under Cárdenas and its new orientation, these groups no longer dominated party politics, and they were now ready to challenge this state of affairs.

The new federation of state workers soon became so strong that when the national labor federation, or CTM, was officially sanctioned by Cárdenas in 1936, the FNTE was allowed to join as a constituent member. By 1937, the FNTE had become one of the CTM's most vocal organizations, since by this time it also represented those in the departments of labor and social services, in the judiciary, and in the national congress, most of whose employees lived and worked in Mexico City proper. The FNTE's foundation and growing activism had a paradoxical political effect, however: rather than legitimize and cement the laborist orientation of the Cárdenas administration by extending it to other workers, it set off a new round of local and national problems that would eventually undermine the president's legitimacy and his grip on national power. Partial explanations for this can be seen not only in the ways in which the organization of this segment of the urban population fundamentally altered national political dynamics both within and between the PNR and other social and class forces, but also in their urban consequences. Principally, the growing size of the public sector gave this federation of urban service employees and government bureaucrats a clear voice in national politics, which gave them the power to disrupt local servicing, and, in turn, further alienate many Mexico City residents.

Placing state workers affiliated with the FNTE into the party-led CTM initially strengthened Cárdenas's political base, by unifying all organized workers into one organization. Having on his side those who administered welfare policies and provided local infrastructural services was also a distinct political advantage for Cárdenas, because it involved these potentially dissenting forces directly in his development strategy. But once the FNTE was absorbed by the CTM, the latter became an inordinately powerful institutional force with many members enjoying direct access to powerful political figures both inside and outside the Cárdenas administration. This meant, first of all, that the precarious balance between peasants and laborers that Cárdenas had so carefully constructed was in danger of tipping; and peasant forces had reasons to be wary of an institutionally unified urban work force, given the antipeasant bias of many urban workers. In addition, the inclusion of municipal workers and bureaucrats into the CTM, via the FNTE, threatened to generate opposition from other urban forces in the capital who were still institutionally excluded from national politics. This was especially the case with urban artisans, renters' groups, and small shopkeepers, who were among the few Mexico City residents without organizational power or formal representation within the ruling party. Most critical, perhaps, the inclusion of the FNTE in the CTM generated political problems for Cárdenas with Mexico's private sector, provincial military generals, and other regional *caciques*, or political bosses. These forces feared that a strong urban alliance between state workers and industrial labor might unduly empower the working class and counterbalance regionally based demands for a more moderate, less centralized, political system with less communist influence.

Of course, these problems were not Cárdenas's only headache; Mexico's great populist leader was already treading on shaky ground in his relations with the country's private sector. His nationalist stance, in particular, had greatly worried many of the country's most powerful businessmen, at least those who owed their livelihood to trading linkages with foreign firms. Yet with the FNTE joining the CTM, and both drawing their greatest support in Mexico City, right next to the institutions of state, the urban working class now appeared more united and powerful than ever. In combination with Cárdenas's antagonistic policies toward certain sectors of business, this signaled a challenge to the power of capitalists that the private sector and its conservative allies could not let pass. A substantial number of industrialists now stepped up their opposition to Cárdenas and to the workers' movement by trying "to impose company unions, and in some cases provided financial support to such averse organizations as the fascist, paramilitary 'gold shirts,' who attacked leaders and members of CTM-controlled unions." [26] When Cárdenas carried through with threats to nationalize oil in March of 1938, all hell broke loose with the private sector. They were joined by forces within the military, many of whom were regional elites from large landowning or urban commercial families in the provinces. Because many of these forces had supported the Revolution in order to wrest power from Mexico City–based elites allied with Porfirio Díaz, both foreign and domestic, they had close ties with conservative postrevolutionary leaders, many of whom also came from the provinces. And just as some in the private sector and the radical left of the CTM each had distinct reasons to oppose the unification, so too did more conservative state administrators and workers, located primarily in the capital, who worried about losing their capacity to uphold more moderate political positions vis-à-vis newly empowered activists in their own ranks and in Mexico City, where most social policies were formulated.

In order to regain control of the deteriorating political situation, Cárdenas made a critical move. Within several days of the petroleum nationalization in 1938, he founded a new party, the Partido de la Revolución Mexicana (PRM), which was to serve as the foundation for a new political structure in Mexico. This new party institutionally incorporated disparate social and class forces such as the military and the bureaucracy, who also were upset by the nationalization, as well as labor and the peasantry. Now each of the most organized and activist sets of forces was to have its own distinct organization for representation within the party. The military sector, the newest institutional sector, included the army and the navy.[27] The peasant sector included those organized in the Confederación Campesina Mexicana, the Sindicatos Campesinos, and the Ligas de Comunidades Agrarias. The labor sector grouped those previously organized in the CTM, the CGT, the Sindicato de Mineros, the Sindicato de Electricistas, and what was left of the CROM. Most notably, urban-based administrators and service workers employed by the state were removed from the labor sector and placed within an entirely new organization called the Federación de Sindicatos de Trabajadores al Servicio del Estado (FSTSE), which was frequently referred to by Cárdenas as the bureaucratic sector, but sometimes also as the popular sector. Cárdenas occasionally called this the popular sector precisely because it was intended to accommodate those who were neither peasants nor industrial workers, strictly speaking, and thus whose class identity was somewhat ambiguous. The principal constituency of this new sector of the party, the FSTSE, not only included the workers that previously had been organized under the FNTE; it now grew to include a wider variety of state and urban service workers—still mainly from Mexico City—who had not necessarily been active or organized in the FNTE.

URBAN POPULAR AND MIDDLE CLASSES: STILL LEFT OUT

Despite the political time bought with this reform, Cárdenas continued to face ongoing problems that originated, once again, in ongoing urban service scarcities and social conflicts in Mexico City. Urban dissatisfaction threatened to disrupt the precarious balance within and between distinct class sectors that had been carefully crafted with the PRM's new institutional structure. Specifically, after the foundation of the PRM's four-tiered structure, many of Mexico City's urban poor and its traditional middle classes were even further excluded from politics and policymaking, since almost all other class and social forces in the capital now had a representative body for pressing demands, albeit a national and not a local structure. With so many government administrators, technocrats, and urban service workers now represented in the FSTSE, these remaining urban forces who had no national institutional structures at their disposal—like shopkeepers, property owners, renters' and residents' associations—were especially handicapped in their ability to push for preferred policies. Earlier, all such groups were equally represented in Mexico City's Consejo Consultivo; but this was no longer the case, as the new national party structure now gave only certain urban sectors—and not others—institutional power. In response to this change of affairs, mobilizations by Mexico City's shopkeepers, renters, and other central city residents about urban service scarcities and development of the built environment reached new heights.

Some of the first signs of a resurgence in urban popular and middle-class opposition came from the group of Mexico City–based professionals who had founded the Confederación de la Clase Media (CCM) in 1936. According to Soledad Loaeza, their intent in organizing was clear: to "protect the rights of the middle classes who felt threatened with extinction and who shunned religious or party identifications."[28] That is, the CCM's constituents did not necessarily oppose the basic principles of the Revolution, as did other more affluent or ideologically conservative middle-class sectors who supported religiously based opposition to the government and its anticlerical policies, especially during the Cristero Rebellion of the late 1920s and early 1930s. Rather, many had been strong supporters of Calles and other moderates within the PNR; one of the principal leagues within the CCM was, in fact, the Partido Anti-Reeleccionista, a liberal middle-class professional movement that emerged in opposition to the Porfiriato and that had sustained Madero's initial rise to the presidency in the aftermath of the 1910 overthrow of Porfirio Díaz. Nonetheless, by the mid-thirties, many of the CCM's middle-class constituents found themselves opposing the chaos and anarchy that resulted from what they considered Cárdenas's radical utopianism, much of it evident in Mexico City proper. Their exclusion from the labor-peasant-state worker pact pushed them to ideologically oppose Cárdenas's efforts to consolidate a strong state on the basis of a predominantly workers' party.

Equally important, however, the middle classes' dissatisfactions in the late 1930s also stemmed from Cárdenas's neglect of critical urban services and the way this impacted on them and other Mexico City residents. For example, local newspapers show that insufficient access to water consistently generated public anger among residents of the city's neighborhoods in the 1930s; when floods paralyzed Mexico City in 1939, Cárdenas's failure to improve the city's drainage system became a principal issue around which a broad spectrum of urban populations rallied some of their most forceful opposition to his regime. Problems with transport also accelerated as Cárdenas's laborist vision prevented him from keeping striking trolley workers in line.[29] Together, these conditions further spurred the self-organization of urban residents into social movements. One 1939 organization of residents that struggled against Cárdenas's classist vision of Mexican society, called the Unificación Popular del Distrito Federal, identified scarcities in public services as one of the four vital problems facing Mexico, along with the smooth operation of the economy, the administration of justice, and national defense.[30]

The rise of urban social movements after 1938 suggests that much of the growing opposition to Cárdenas came from the urban petit bourgeoisie and from what we have called Mexico City's popular sectors, or marginally employed, low-income residents including urban artisans and other self-employed workers excluded from the labor or the state worker federations. These groups were beleaguered by the chaos wrought by numerous labor strikes paralyzing the capital during the Cárdenas presidency, but they were most concerned about local service scarcities and deteriorating public services in the wake of state worker activism. Without affordable and efficient urban services to aid in the supply and demand for their goods, and without the right to strike or a national federation to help wage their demands, many of the city's artisans, small-business owners, and shopkeepers felt increasingly disenfranchised both economically and politically. Of course, rising costs, scarcities, and protests in Mexico City in the late 1930s were not exclusively Cárdenas's fault. They also were due partly to the economic crisis that accelerated dramatically during the thirties and that worsened after the 1938 petroleum nationalization. Nonetheless, many of the rising costs and service scarcities, as well as the growing social mobilization around these issues after 1938, can be traced directly to Cárdenas's policies and preferences, not only his support for the state worker federation but also his failure to implement urban service and development policies that would satisfy popular and middle classes. Combined with their exclusion from the institutional structures for political participation, these urban service scarcities drove many to the streets.

Housing and shelter struggles are cases in point, and critical ones at that. Of the few urban services that Cárdenas did implement in the capital, housing was the most visible; yet he constructed new housing almost exclusively for industrial laborers and state workers, who were members of their respective federations within the PRM. Starting in 1938, in fact, Cárdenas began what Manuel Perlo Cohen calls a "second phase" of his housing policy, when he began to initiate the construction of *colonias proletarias*, or neighborhoods for the working class on urban lands expropriated and freely given to workers.[31] Yet because these programs benefited primarily those within the state's institutional and corporatist reach, they were accompanied by a rapid acceleration of social protests and land invasions by those without access to the labor or bureaucratic federations, both the urban poor and some sectors of the non-property-owning lower-middle class. That many of those involved in the illegal land invasions—which Perlo Cohen estimates as involving 73,274 residents between 1935 and 1940[32]—were the unemployed and underemployed urban poor is evidenced in one 1938 telegram from the Federación Nacional de Inquilinarios. The organization's spokesman, while begging Cárdenas to grant legal status to lands invaded by its members, made clear that "within [its] organization exist[ed] many members without work."[33] These land invasions in the capital not only reflected the unhappiness of residents with Cárdenas's priorities; they also accelerated his political problems with established and more comfortable middle classes in the capital, many of whom owned lands that now were being invaded by the city's poorer residents. After the wave of land invasions that started in 1938, Cárdenas was flooded with written requests from organizations of property holders, both large and small, to stop the appropriation of urban lands by local populations.

Housing dissatisfactions among urban popular and middle classes in the late 1930s were also due to a booming urban land market that drove up rents, some of which can be traced partly to Cárdenas's policies, too. Though most scholars refer to rural lands when referring to Cárdenas's land reforms, much of the land expropriation undertaken during his six-year administration occurred in and around Mexico City. Of the 1,499 square kilometers of land in the Distrito Federal in 1938, Cárdenas turned more than half (821 square kilometers) into *ejidal*, or communal, lands.[34] Of course, most of this land was kept under *ejidal* control, but the expropriation and legalization of *ejidal* lands affected the urban land market nonetheless. By expropriating urban lands, returning them to collectivized control by peasant communities, and making their sale illegal, the total amount of urban land for sale in Mexico City was dramatically reduced. This brought a jump in the price of the few remaining properties under private ownership.

Evidence of the negative impact of Cárdenas's tenure on the urban land market is seen further in the skyrocketing rents of the period after he came to power: Between 1935 and 1940 alone, land prices in the Distrito Federal increased by between 50 and 200 percent.[35] Acceleration of the urban land market in the late 1930s was also due to the fact that "the limited capital that remained in the country [after massive capital flight induced by Cárdenas's nationalizations] was directed toward buying and selling urban land."[36] The 1938 annual report of the nation's commercial and industrial lobby, the Confederación de Cámaras Nacionales de Comercio y Industria (CONCA-NACOMIN) claims that Mexico City in the late 1930s saw a "blaze of building construction," mainly because land development and construction were seen as the "only secure refuges for investment," along with the production of beer, wine, liquor, and medicine.[37] And together, those two processes had a remarkable impact on Mexico City's built environment. In contrast to the previous administration, land values skyrocketed and private sector investment in development accelerated; but now, it was the market and not the state that was pushing urban development. The city's poorer and less powerful residents, accordingly, saw their urban lifestyle steadily deteriorate, even as their institutional capacity to stem these tides was disappearing even more rapidly.

FROM URBAN SOCIAL MOVEMENTS TO ELECTORAL DEFEAT

The rapid revitalization of the urban land market and the rising costs of housing that accompanied it were disastrous for Cárdenas, because they fueled a new round of political struggles over housing and shelter policy for the

CHAPTER THREE

capital, which perhaps explain why Cárdenas had to replace Mexico City's mayor twice in 1938 alone. Although the renters' movement had been simmering underneath the surface throughout the late 1920s and early 1930s, with Cárdenas on the scene the *inquilinario* movement once again accelerated. Moreover, the movement now gained widespread civilian support beyond the urban poor. Indeed, the new *inquilinario* movement was as much a movement of various sectors of the petit bourgeoisie as of the city's poor. Small business owners' and shopkeepers' low margins of profit often depended on renting affordable urban property, and their livelihood often depended on their location in central areas of Mexico City where the dynamics of the urban land market brought the city's most rapid rent increases. Hence these groups were among the most vocal advocates of rent control in Mexico City. One letter from the general secretary of the Centro de Comerciantes Mexicanos de la Merced, an organization of small merchants located in the city's principal market, urged President Cárdenas to support a hotly debated rent control law in 1938, expressing deep concern for the growing "displacement of renters who always pay their rents punctually," but who now were being displaced by speculators "of foreign nationality . . . [who] have bought houses in the commercial sector and have raised the rents of comerciantes considerably, bringing their displacement and attendant ruin."[38]

In addition to rising costs and scarcities, urban petit bourgeois support for urban social movements directed against Cárdenas was probably spurred by two other policies. One was Cárdenas's rural land reform, which drove up the costs of food sold in the city, angered small shopkeepers, who now directly felt the public antagonism to rising food prices, and even inspired some local neighborhood organizations to join small shopkeeper associations to set up food co-ops to offset the rising costs. Even the Cámara Nacional de Industria y Comercio de la Ciudad de México, which represented large industry and commerce in the capital, expressed public concern about the economy. During a four-month period in 1938 sales had dropped 80 percent in autos, 50 percent in machinery, 25 to 30 percent in clothes and shoes, and 15 to 20 percent in food, spurring the Cámara to complain that *campesinos* had "gravely obstructed channels of economic communication . . . [and] had divulged ideas destructive of the national wealth . . . without worrying about the surpluses that give life to the mercantile relations between country and city."[39]

A second policy that encouraged small shopkeepers to join the movement against Cárdenas was the introduction of the Ley de Organización de Cámaras in 1936. This law politically and economically disadvantaged small shops and enterprises, especially compared to larger businesses, by mandating a minimum size for affiliation with national lobbying organizations of industry or commerce. This legislation constituted a particularly harsh blow to small merchants who now no longer had the CROM to represent them, as they had had in earlier periods. Combined with their declining political role in Mexico City's Consejo Consultivo after the 1933 creation of the Planning Commission, many small shopkeepers felt they had few mechanisms with which to press their demands, among which rental and housing concerns were central. Thus they were quite willing to lend support to the already active and well-organized *inquilinario* movement, whose institutional power in local and national politics was also nearing extinction.

Urban popular and middle-class groups lost little time in taking to the streets. By 1939, marches and rent strikes were common occurrences in Mexico City. In one such event in late 1939, two thousand residents affiliated with the Consejo de Colonos, or Council of Neighborhoods, marched to the Mexico City mayor's office to present their demands about rent control and improvements for housing in low-income, so-called popular, neighborhoods. In another, also in 1939, masses of the urban poor initiated a land invasion of the Hacienda de los Morales, a once-lavish estate that predated the Revolution, and by so doing sparked a violent confrontation between police and *inquilinarios* struggling to claim their own lands. In response, Cárdenas forcibly dislodged the squatters; but this further convinced Mexico City's poor that Cárdenas's progressive policies were exclusionary in nature, geared only toward the industrial working class and the peasantry, and confined mainly to workplace demands.

By the late 1930s, in short, Mexico City residents had begun to question Cárdenas's political objectives, the corporatist structures upon which they were based, and their larger implications for urban development and service provision in the capital city. How could Mexico's great populist leader support urban land expropriation for peasant communities under the *ejido* system, provide housing for industrial workers and bureaucrats, and at the same time fail to provide similar benefits to other Mexico City residents, even the urban poor? A partial answer lies in an understanding of the fact that he had identified organized labor, the peasantry, and, later, state workers as his principal political bases of support, and that he had done so because he hoped to foment rapid, though regionally balanced, economic development guided by the state in partnership with highly regulated national capital. To the extent that such development required support from the prospective industrial work force, peace and agricultural productivity in the countryside, and loyalty from urban-based bureaucrats administering development programs, identifying these three groups as principal political allies made sense. Equally important, however, Mexico in the mid and late 1930s lacked the fiscal resources to provide complete social services to all sectors of the population. In balancing economic recovery and political inclusion, something had to give; and Cárdenas's vision of a class-based political franchise left very little room for the many popular and middle sectors whose class position was ambiguous and whose larger political loyalties did not necessarily lie with labor, the peasantry, or the state, even if many of their material demands were quite similar. Cárdenas's so-called populism, then, was class- and sector-specific, and this came back to haunt the ruling party in the 1940 presidential election.

Of course, growing political dissatisfaction with Cárdenas and the PRM was not purely a Mexico City—or even urban—phenomenon. Scholars have identified provincial capitalists, rural landowners, conservative elements of the provincial middle classes, and regional military *caciques* as principal bases of political opposition to Cárdenas. They also have cited Cárdenas's radical political platform as the source of his problems. Nonetheless, it is clear that a large portion of Cárdenas's overall political troubles in leading the nation and maintaining national political legitimacy lay in his inability to respond to the demand for urban services in Mexico City. Cárdenas's prolabor and propeasant policies inadvertently drove up housing and land prices, gave incentives to private developers, created chaos in urban transport service provision, and thus disadvantaged a broad spectrum of urban populations in Mexico City. The result was substantial, growing political opposition to his administration and vision of national politics. After several years of rule by Lázaro Cárdenas, many in Mexico City were clamoring for a change.

Widespread dissatisfaction expressed itself in the presidential election of 1940, perhaps Mexico's most contested national election of the twentieth century. Extensive popular—and even labor—support for the PRM's challenger, General Juan Andreu Almazán, spurred the ruling party leadership to manipulate electoral results in order to claim victory for their own presidential candidate, Manuel Ávila Camacho, who was to succeed Cárdenas as the party's standard bearer. Even with fraud, however, the PRM was forced to cede Almazán's triumph in the capital city. Almazán had run as an independent candidate for president under a moderate, albeit anticommunist, platform. Most scholars rightly note that Almazán was strongly supported by provincial opponents of the PRM, including conservative factions in the military and the so-called northern bourgeoisie located mainly in Monterrey; yet they generally fail to recognize that Almazán also relied on substantial popular support in the capital. In fact, Almazán inaugurated his national campaign in Mexico City in August 1939, and was able to generate a crowd there estimated at between 200,000 and 250,000.[40] In the election itself, Almazán not only carried Mexico City, but also gained his strongest support in the nation's two other largest cities, Monterrey and Guadalajara. Almazán's national electoral success, in short, lay in his ability to appeal to a broad variety of urban groups, many of whom had become increasingly dissatisfied with Cárdenas. Almazán advocated private property, opposed agrarian reform, and supported public housing, among other things. Each of these positions was calculated to win support from a broad range of social and class forces, mainly urban. Almazán's support of public housing programs, in particular, delighted all those in Mexico City who had struggled over housing—*inquilinarios*, artisans, and shopkeepers.

Using his campaign platform as a format for bringing urban popular and middle classes to his side, General Almazán posed a serious threat to Cárdenas and the PRM. And in a strategic move that may have sealed his electoral success, Almazán openly linked himself to Luis Morones and what was left of the CROM, an act that further solidified his political support from urban artisans, shopkeepers, and other residents who remained outside the CTM, the FSTSE, or the CNC. It is striking that the urban petit bourgeoisie's ideological affinity with the CROM long outlasted the latter organization's political hegemony. As of 1940, after the CROM had been relegated to the margins of the national labor movement, many of Mexico City's small *comerciantes* still expressed support for the CROM. They also identified themselves as preoccupied with the concerns of unemployed workers who were left out of the PRM's corporatist structures, indicating a masked antagonism toward Cárdenas and his preference toward industrial laborers. Small *comerciantes*' affinity with the CROM and their repudiation of Cárdenas's preferences for the industrial labor force are revealed in official correspondence of the Alianza de Comerciantes en Pequeño del Primer Cuadro y Puestos Aislados de la Ciudad. Their stationery proudly claims to represent workers without jobs ("Integrada por Obreros Sin Trabajo") and uses as its official motto the old CROMista slogan calling for welfare and social revolution ("Salud y Revolución Social").[41]

In addition to support from urban professionals, employees, significant numbers of state workers, and petit bourgeois forces, moreover, Almazán's candidacy even managed to split the CTM and generate support from some sectors of organized industrial labor. Despite Almazán's widespread support, in the end the PRM claimed a national electoral triumph primarily because it falsified voting results. However, as Mexico and the PRM entered a new decade under President Ávila Camacho (1940–1946), the official party's political problems were not over. Even with Almazán no longer on the scene, his popularity in Mexico City worried party leaders. The overwhelming concentration of dissatisfied urban popular and middle-class sectors in the capital threatened to disrupt national politics right at the seat of government. The

PRM's claims of a national victory had generated even further public out-cry in Mexico City: The official tally was 2,476,641 for Ávila Camacho and 15,101 for Almazán, but urban residents knew that Almazán had attracted crowds of over 200,000 in Mexico City alone. Most of the capital's citizens concluded that the PRM stole the election. In the absence of local participatory mechanisms to absorb grievances from the Mexico City population, the PRM's legitimacy was nearing bottom in the capital.

FROM INSTITUTIONALIZED URBAN MOVEMENTS
TO A NEW PARTY STRUCTURE

In order to solidify its base with disenfranchised urban forces in the aftermath of the 1940 electoral fiasco, the party leadership, under the guidance of President Ávila Camacho, scrambled to reform the party's corporatist structure with an eye toward including many of Mexico City's dissatisfied residents. Party leaders agreed to introduce new institutional changes in the corporatist system that could strengthen political linkages with dissatisfied urban popular and middle classes, particularly those who had already organized into urban social movements during the 1930s. In seeking ready and mobilizable structures through which these groups could make political demands about conditions in Mexico City, the PRM returned to practices that had already been tried starting in late 1938, in response to growing urban struggles over rising rents. At that time, when dissatisfaction with Cárdenas's four-sector PRM first surfaced, the PRM leadership had actively worked on developing stronger institutional linkages with the *inquilinario* movement by creating a Consejo de Colonos, or Neighborhood Council, which would channel renters' grievances to party leaders or government workers now organized in the bureaucratic sector of the PRM.

Between 1938 and 1939, the party continued with this approach and began to use the FSTSE, or bureaucratic sector, to develop new institutional linkages with well-established Mexico City organizations. That the FSTSE included urban administrators of local services, many of whom had already cultivated professional and political contacts with neighborhood organizations and other urban social movements, helped facilitate this process. Similarly, several months after its crushing defeat by Almazanista forces in Mexico City, in October 1940 the PRM supported the formation of the Liga de Artesanos, or Artisans' League, which served as the institutional format for channeling demands about the "social, economic, and political advancement" of artisan workers in Mexico City and the nation as a whole.[42] Yet by early 1941 it was clear that an ad hoc approach was not nearly as effective as a more co-ordinated institutional structure that could bring all these organizations, and many others that represented popular and middle-class forces in the capital, under one umbrella. In April of that year, the PRM formally established the Confederación de Organizaciones Populares (COP), which served as the co-ordinating body for a wide variety of groups in Mexico City, groups that had lacked national political mechanisms and effective local ones through which to express their demands. The COP's stated goals were to use the organiza-tion to (1) protect the masses against monopoly business speculation . . . and to keep prices of consumer goods at a just and equal level; (2) lower housing rental costs; (3) establish more hygienic housing conditions; (4) ensure sup-port for education; and (5) maintain healthy and vigorous youth.[43]

The formation of the COP was so successful in linking local groups to the PRM that by 1942 the party extended the confederation beyond the capital and used it as a model for a new national organization for urban popular and middle classes, to be called the Confederación Nacional de Organiza-ciones Populares (CNOP). The decision to go national shows, once again, as with the Consejo Consultivo's corporatist structure, how institutional re-forms introduced for the Mexico City population and local governance served as a blueprint for national political changes. This was the case not only be-cause the class diversity of Mexico City's population in many ways reflected the nation's diversity—and thus served as a good testing ground for such changes—but also because the urban dissatisfactions of the capital's popular and middle classes about local services and Cárdenas's urban development priorities presented perhaps the most pressing political problem for national political leaders. If the COP had remained a local organization, it could not really serve as an avenue for *national* political participation by these groups. To neglect their demands in this regard would be a mistake, since the political dissatisfaction of Mexico City residents in the 1940 presidential election was indeed a national political problem that required a nationwide institutional solution.

Of course, even without the creation of a national federation, the COP might have served in some way as a mechanism for local governance and political participation, and by so doing addressed some of the PRM's growing political problems. Yet party leaders also recognized that maintaining only local structures for expressing demands clearly would not solve the problem of national political participation by Mexico City's urban popular and middle classes. As a result, Mexico's national political leadership began to rethink the local-national problematic and look for alternative political structures and practices to accommodate the new tensions in Mexico City. Whereas after the CROM disaster in 1928 Mexico's political leaders saw the institutional separation of local and national political institutions as solving their problems, in 1943 they returned to a form of national-local overlap: Mexico City populations were to use national political institutions for participation and policymaking, even to address those concerns related to services in the capital. This shift in strategy was formalized in the establishment of the Confederación Nacional de Organizaciones Populares (CNOP), whose principal membership still came from organized groups in Mexico City proper.

At its birth, the CNOP became the third principal arm of the PRI, taking the place of both the military and the bureaucratic sector (FSTSE), since the constituents of each were placed within the larger, more diverse institutional structure of the CNOP. Previously the so-called popular sector of the party included only state bureaucrats and service workers (the FSTSE), who comprised only 11.6 percent of the party membership. Under the umbrella of the CNOP, however, this popular sector now included a grab bag of occupations, mainly urban-based, including artisans, small agriculturalists, small industrialists and shopkeepers, professionals, youth workers, students, groups of revolutionary women, schoolteachers, bureaucrats, agricultural cooperative members (*cooperativistas*), neighborhood organizations (*colonos*), artists, bus drivers, and the military, who together comprised 33.7 percent of the party. At its founding, the CNOP was larger than the labor sector (30.4 percent) and held almost as many members as the peasant sector (35.9 percent).[44]

The founding of the CNOP signaled a critical turning point in the postrevolutionary period, since it set the stage for a fundamentally new ideological and organizational mode of governance. Now the country was to be run by the PRM with an eye toward the concerns and demands of a wide variety of classes and social groups, from industrial laborers to the peasantry to professionals, street vendors, shopkeepers, and state workers. Starting from its first year, CNOP affiliates occupied the majority of seats in the national congress; and by 1943, the PRM was an all-inclusive corporatist political structure and Mexico's political system had finally earned its populist label. Together with peasants and laborers, the CNOP's urban popular and middle classes were seen as forming a nucleus of progressive groups who together would bring forward the revolution's objectives and prevent any return to the previous period of instability.[45] But what was unknown to party leaders was how conflictual the process of urban policymaking would become, now that Mexico City populations had a national political structure for wielding their demands.

4

BALANCING PARTY SECTORS

THROUGH URBAN ADMINISTRATION,

1944–1958

With the foundation of the Confederación Nacional de Organizaciones Populares (CNOP), Mexico City's populations once again moved to the forefront of national politics, as did several urban policies. Because the CNOP replaced the Consejo Consultivo as the main body used by Mexico City's popular and middle classes to express political demands, this local institution lost much of its utility as Mexico City populations instead used national-level mechanisms to push for urban policies. Accordingly, the influence of Mexico City populations in national political debates intensified dramatically, as did the legitimate capacity of national party leaders to make urban policies without going through purely local institutions. This was a curious state of affairs: as Mexico City populations became more directly involved in national politics through their respective corporatist federations, the national party leadership once again had maneuvering room to direct Mexico City's urban development. These institutional and political transformations produced a shift in national balances of power, economic priorities, and urban patterns and policies in the capital itself.

As Mexico City populations increasingly used the newly formed CNOP to press for rent control provisions and other policies that protected their local livelihoods, such as small-business credit guarantees and state worker protections, many other urban services and the administration of Mexico City's urban development gravitated to the hands of the party leadership, which relied on the presidentially appointed mayor to do the party's bidding. In making decisions about urban development, the party's and the president's priorities and objectives were slightly different from what they had been in earlier periods. In contrast to Cárdenas, for example, who sought to balance equally the developmental concerns of industrial labor and the peasantry, and to subordinate capital's requirements to those of labor and peasants, Mexico's new president, Ávila Camacho, turned his sights directly on urbanization-led industrial development and the capital-labor alliances necessary to sustain this strategy. Rural land reform and support for agricultural co-ops were replaced by a preoccupation with urban and industrial development at almost any cost. The political dissatisfactions of urban popular and middle classes receded into the background momentarily, not only because the newly formed CNOP bought some maneuvering space, but also because the government's plans for rapid industrial development held the tantalizing promise of urban economic growth and prosperity after a decade of crisis and instability.

Because of economies of scale and the political exigencies of the period, the bulk of this new wave of industrial development was carried out in Mexico City, to the exclusion of other cities and regions; the result was a massive infusion of state money into urban services and urban infrastructure, as well as rapid economic growth in the capital city. In addition to sustained industrial production, the capital saw extensive development of urban infrastructure, construction of numerous public buildings, and the growth of a thriving service economy intended to meet the consumption demands of a small but expanding urban middle class. Money was poured into parks and gardens, while the cultural activities of the capital's affluent linked Mexico City to Paris, New York, and Los Angeles. A budding film industry captured and glorified the changes in architectural styles, fashions, and pockets of opulence that during the forties and fifties rivaled Hollywood's best. In both life and film, Mexico City sparkled as the shining star on Mexico's horizon.

The hope among the party leadership was that this new urbanization-led industrial development strategy would produce sufficient prosperity both to expand urban employment *and* to sustain demand for local commerce and services in Mexico City. As such, the choice of urban-based industrialization and development as a priority during the early forties carried a political as much as a technocratic logic. Because the strategy obviously favored industrial workers over peasants, and Mexico City residents in particular, it suited two of the three sectors in the party whose constituencies were most vocal—the Confederación de Trabajadores Mexicanos (CTM) and the CNOP. In addition, this strategy of rapid and concentrated industrialization promised to deliver substantial quantities of material goods in a relatively short period of time. However, this strategy required sound relations with Mexico City capitalists, since their full-fledged support for rapid industrialization was essential. This, in turn, meant that the urbanization-led industrialization strategy was a fragile house of cards whose stability relied primarily on keeping both united and content these disparate class forces—capitalists, laborers, and urban popular and middle classes. Maintaining their loyalty to each other, the party, and this new developmental vision was a job that required both fiscal ingenuity and political acumen, since the collective urban demands of all these forces tended to be costly, and since their urban demands frequently contradicted each other. Together, these criteria were difficult to manage and could only be achieved with ironclad administrative control of the capital city in the hands of a strong mayor who could appease all three forces while still fostering the local economy.

Even though the underlying objectives of the urbanization-led industrialization strategy were designed to buttress the ruling party's centralized hold on national political power by establishing prosperity, the achievement of these goals was in no small part contingent on local politics and local economic development in Mexico City, since the nation's most politically and economically essential capitalists and laborers, as well as most of the nation's popular and middle classes, resided there. Given this unique state of affairs, and the capital city's even more central economic role, Mexico City's mayor soon developed overwhelming political power and decentralized authority.

The upcoming pages focus on the ways that policies affecting housing, transport, land use, and Mexico City's urban growth after 1943 slowly began to reflect the mayor's increasing local power and autonomy, even as they articulated with national political and economic objectives. I start with a discussion of the national priorities of presidents Ávila Camacho and Miguel Alemán and how their political and economic objectives translated into a national policy of urbanization-led industrialization based in Mexico City. I then demonstrate how these priorities sustained a wave of new investments in Mexico City's built environment. I then show that directing this urban and infrastructural development through only national political institutions and mechanisms became impossible over time, due to both fiscal crisis and growing local political tensions between different sectors of the urban population. The chapter concludes with a discussion of the increasingly central role played by Mexico City's mayor in resolving the fiscal crisis and balancing political conflicts in the capital, and the ways in which his growing power altered both the relationship between local and national politics and the nature and extent of urban development.

FROM OUTLYING REGIONS TO THE CENTER: THE DEVELOPMENT MIRACLE HITS THE CAPITAL

Economists look lovingly at the post-1940 period in Mexico. The nation saw a steady rise in consumption and industrial production, with Mexico City as the main beneficiary. Because most national investment and employment was concentrated in the capital, by the 1960s Mexico City was being rapidly transformed into a showcase of modernization—or so it seemed to a country facing such difficult economic and political conditions just a few decades earlier. Mexico City's industrialization and its developmental successes during this period were due largely to the changing balance of class power within the PRM that was produced when urban popular and middle classes were incorporated into national party structures in 1943 via the CNOP. Mexico's political leaders slowly turned away from the preoccupation with rural development and agrarian reform of the Cárdenas administration, and instead fostered rapid industrialization concentrated in the nation's capital, mainly by supporting the development of industries that could manufacture consumer durable goods that previously had been imported from abroad. Just as critical to the consolidation of the PRM's political power, however, and to the success of this import-substitution industrialization strategy, was the decision by the PRM leaders to institutionalize relationships with a nascent class of industrialists. In the immediate aftermath of General Almazán's challenge of 1940, party leaders felt it was necessary to link capital, industrial labor, and the state in a common developmental project in order for labor and capital to remain loyal to each other and the party. This, in turn, would help the nation steady its shaky economic future and sustain the political support of a broad range of classes.

In seeking alliances with capitalists, President Ávila Camacho could have looked anywhere, at least in principal. Yet Ávila Camacho had his eyes on Mexico City's capitalists. As such, during his administration and that of his successor Miguel Alemán, the nation's economic future and the party's overall political legitimacy continued to rest on policy decisions made in and directed toward the capital. Yet how exactly did these Mexico City capitalists maintain this pivotal position? And similarly, why were Mexico City capitalists, and not those in other regions, the privileged recipients of state aid and cooperation? These questions are critical, because this was by no means the only possible course to follow. When Mexico stood poised to embark on rapid industrial development in the early 1940s, political leaders could very well have spread industrial investments across the nation rather than concentrating them in the capital; and this would have eliminated many of the urban and political problems associated with rapid industrialization and the growing power of Mexico City's mayor, all of which wreaked havoc within the PRI in later years. Indeed, other major cities like Monterrey, Guadalajara, and Veracruz also contained the infrastructure to sustain rapid industrial development and become competing regional powers to balance the political and economic dominance of the capital. So why didn't the party-run government place its investments there?

In order to better understand the changing state and class relationships that led to Mexico City's dramatic economic growth, as well as how they influenced its pattern of urban development, we must chart the capital city's unchallenged centrality in national politics and the close relationships between revolutionary leaders and Mexico City industrialists. These close relationships were forged early on, even before the Almazán defeat, and they were cemented through the political dynamics of urban industrial location during the 1930s, which also led to the establishment of accommodating relationships between the ruling party and capitalists in Mexico City in the 1940s. But they also evolved through the course of conflict and struggle.

During the 1920s and 1930s, Mexico's political leaders often faced difficulties with businessmen who feared the Revolution's principal tenets, including the accommodating orientation toward labor and support for agrarian populations best exemplified by Obregón and Cárdenas. Most vocal among such opponents were the northern economic elites, whose power tended to depend on commerce and trading with the United States. These two activities relied heavily on agricultural and mining enterprises, which employed some of the labor movement's and peasantry's most active members. Accordingly, northern elites were much less likely to share the revolutionary leadership's preoccupation with rapid industrial development—especially as concentrated in Mexico City—or its unbridled encouragement of labor organization and benefits to rural populations. Clashes between the state and the private sector were not uncommon in this early period, and representatives of national business continually lobbied against the government's efforts to introduce new labor legislation to protect workers, arguing that the proposed law would reduce the private sector's profit-making potential.

Most important, perhaps, from early on, the nation's economic elite feared that the revolutionary government's efforts to protect workers and foment rapid and centrally planned industrial development could create a schism between Distrito Federal capitalists and those in the other states. In the 1920s, ironically, this concern seemed to be greatest among industrialists in Mexico City, who felt that their physical proximity to the governing apparatus, as well as the concentration of organized laborers in the capital, would place them at a disadvantage compared to other regions. Many Mexico City businesses opposed early labor legislation precisely because they felt that "the states would not carry out the said legislation," since they were so far away from the central government's reach; whereas in Mexico City capitalists were right under the watchful eye of the revolutionary leadership.[1] Worries about the balance of political and economic power between regions were so great that the presidency of the country's Confederación Nacional de Cámaras de Comercio rotated between those representing the major economic regions of the country: Monterrey, Mexico City, Mérida, and San Luis Potosí.[2]

By 1929, when the revolutionary leadership consolidated its position through the formation of the Partido Nacional de la Revolución (PNR), these regional conflicts became almost impossible to contain; but at this point it was the northern capitalists who had the most to lose. When the PNR proposed legislation in that same year to set a minimum wage and to limit the workday, northern economic elites headquartered in Monterrey expressed their dissatisfaction by forming their own federation, the Confederación Patronal de la Republica Mexicana (COPARMEX), refusing to participate in the Confederación Nacional de Cámaras de Comercio, which within several years renamed itself the Confederación Nacional de Cámaras de Comercio y de Industria (CONCANACOMIN), as it included within its ranks industrialists too. In addition to signaling the first irreparable regional split in the nation's private sector, the formation of a separate organization to represent the northern economic elite put the ruling party on guard. With some of the nation's most powerful elites organized in the COPARMEX and poised to fight with the CONCANACOMIN or balk at any new economic or social development policies they opposed, the PNR was forced to tread a fine line between introducing socially progressive policies, fostering national economic recovery, and keeping the private sector from erupting into irreparable conflict.

One way the party leadership could increase its leverage with northern elites and still generate prosperity was to invest even greater resources in the development of new industry in Mexico City. Not only would this reduce their political dependence on northern elites for economic recovery, it would also foster the development of a new cadre of industrialists willing to develop import-substitution activities and to accept the revolution's larger social objectives at the same time. Given the political activism and labor dissatisfaction at this time—less than a year after the abolition of municipal rule and the demise of the CROM—any strategy that both gave the PNR maneuvering room vis-à-vis capitalists in Mexico City, and allowed them to continue with labor and other social reforms, was bound to gain intraparty support. The primary emphasis given to Mexico City's industrial development over other cities or regions was, of course, also due to technocratic considerations as much as to political objectives. Agglomeration economies, Mexico City's linkages to other regions through rail and communications, the location of industrial infrastructure from the Porfirian period, the supply of small-business owners eager for the opportunity to parlay their small firms into larger enterprises, the party's more solid political control in Mexico City, and revolutionary leaders' efforts to wean themselves from the threatening actions of the more conservative northern economic elites all suggested that rapid industrial development would best be centered in the capital. Yet all the technocratic rationale in the world could not soften the fact that private sector forces in northern regions were slated to lose out. Thus, these initial efforts by the PNR to make Mexico City the nation's principal industrial center evoked even greater opposition from northern capitalists, rather than eliminating it; and this was a problem to be dealt with on both the local and national levels.

After Cárdenas came to power, for example, provincial unity eroded even faster, as private sector opposition to the government increased and regional conflicts between the nation's industrialists and *comerciantes* hit new heights. Under Cárdenas, Mexico City's capitalists prospered disproportionately, at least relative to private sector forces in other regions. There were many reasons for this, including the fact that, unlike many industrialists in the north, those in Mexico City had much less frequently relied on foreign markets for goods. When Cárdenas imposed restrictions on foreign linkages, Mexico City businesses were not hurt as directly. Yet Mexico City had other advantages, too. There was more commercial capital available for investment in industry than in most other regions, given the diversified composition of the city's commercial sector. The large concentration of population also meant that there was a ready market for consumer durable and nondurable goods, which were most easily and profitably produced in that first stage of industrialization. Accordingly, Mexico City capitalists were among the most likely to support—and profit from—the drive for industrialization initiated by Cárdenas; and their collaboration with Cárdenas, at least in this regard, helps explain his relatively open attitude toward urban renewal and downtown development in Mexico City discussed earlier.[3]

With Mexico City industrialists coming into their own under Cárdenas, the same northern capitalists who had originally opposed the idea of linking the private sector to the state now wanted to keep the national organization representing industry and commerce, the CONCANACOMIN, intact, for fear that a separate federation for industrialists might be dominated by prosperous Mexico City firms that would act to harm the northern capitalists' commercial and trading interests. In this first serious schism of 1937, when the CONCANACOMIN "forcefully expressed its fear of authorizing independent chambers to represent specialized industry," congress obliged and denied Mexico City industrialists the right to organize autonomously.[4] Northern elites' still-unparalleled power within the anti-Cárdenas, conservative revolutionary leadership, along with Cárdenas's effort to keep the private sector unified, prevented party leaders from approving of measures to institutionalize this division. However, the balance of political power within the private sector gradually shifted over the last years of the Cárdenas administration and the first years of Ávila Camacho's. Mexico City industrialists continued to gather strength while, conversely, northern elites saw their economic position and political power challenged by Cárdenas's agrarian reforms and industrial policies. When Mexico City industrialists proposed separating from the CONCANACOMIN once again in 1941, the PRM leadership was open to the change. This cleared the way for Mexico City industrialists to institutionally consolidate their own political power and to entrench themselves as central actors in the future development of the city and the nation.

LINKING MEXICO CITY CAPITALISTS TO THE PARTY

Yet why were Mexico City industrialists unsuccessful in 1937 but successful in 1941 in gaining support from the PRM for their own independent organization? The question is critical because this development cemented Mexico City's industrial centrality in the nation's political and economic future. The answer rests largely on an understanding of concurrent political developments in Mexico City and in the new party structure, especially those related to the role of the CTM and the CNOP. Political conditions in Mexico City had changed dramatically after the 1940 presidential election. The PRM was now scrambling for support from whomever it could find; President Ávila Camacho considered various strategies to generate new bases of support and solidify old ones, particularly in the capital, where Almazán had defeated him. The formation of the COP in 1941 and the CNOP in 1943 were examples of this strategy of extending the party's institutional base of support. But incorporating urban popular and middle classes into the ruling party was not enough. Now Ávila Camacho also had to appease capitalists as well as sectors of the industrial working class, primarily the CTM's constituents, some of whom had supported Almazán and others of whom thought the inclusion of middle classes signaled a move too far to the right. Of the two, capital and labor, the concerns of the industrial working class were more difficult to accommodate. Because laborers already had an institutional mechanism for participation, their support had to be revived as much through policy actions as through institutional reforms. Yet if Ávila Camacho introduced any major social reforms or new labor protections, he might alienate capitalists, many of whom were still uneasy in the aftermath of Cárdenas's nationalizations. Caught in a bind, one way Ávila Camacho could address these contradictory concerns was to bring industrialists and workers together in a common pact to foster industrial growth. To ensure the success of such a pact, given the regional conflicts that divided the nation's economic elite, Ávila Camacho grounded it geographically in the region where the economic elite was most likely to support him and where he had greatest institutional control over labor: Mexico City.

Within a year of coming to office, President Ávila Camacho initiated a program of *unidad nacional*, or national unity, to reconcile the political opposition that had coalesced around Almazán's candidacy in 1939 and 1940. The backbone of Ávila Camacho's program was a restructuring of the relationship between capital, labor, and the state in order to promote more rapid industrial development, economic growth, employment, and wage prosperity. In the development of this pact, Ávila Camacho cultivated his strongest ties with Mexico City industrialists and labor; yet in order to lay the institutional foundations for this pact, Mexico City industrialists had to be allowed to organize independently. Once this occurred, Mexico City was poised to assume an unchallenged position at the heart of the nation.

Organizational reform and the consolidation of the capital-labor-state pact did not happen immediately. They evolved in fits and starts as wildly fluctuating national and international developments between 1940 and 1945 created new conflicts within the private sector and new alliances with labor. The process began in early 1941, when Ávila Camacho introduced a new Ley de Industria de Transformación (Manufacturing Industry Law), which provided fiscal incentives for what were then considered new and necessary industries, mainly those likely to advance import substitution, like steel, paper, and glass. Mexico City industrialists reacted to the new law by seeking further organizational independence to escape from the grip of the northern elite and to take advantage of the new incentives and protection. Even though the northern-dominated CONCANACOMIN continued to radically oppose this structural change, accusing the state of trying to "divide and conquer" the private sector, the tide had turned, and both party leaders and Mexico's growing class of industrialists supported the change.[5] In late 1941, President Ávila Camacho approved a law making it possible to create a separate national federation for commerce, the Confederación de Cámaras Nacionales de Comercio (CONCANACO), which represented northern commercial and trading elites. Industry, accordingly, regrouped itself separately into the Confederación de Cámaras Industriales (CONCAMIN).

The separation of industrial and commercial firms into distinct federations gave Ávila Camacho more room in which to successfully negotiate good relations between industrialists and laborers. Free from the control of commercial and trading elites who had opposed the overly rapid development of industry and the greater tax burden that would be necessary to support this development, industrialists could articulate their concerns without having to accommodate commercial interests. In many ways, industrialists' concerns coincided with those of industrial labor: protection for national industry, government investment in industry, and social supports for the industrial labor force. As a result, in 1942 industrialists and laborers signed a Pacto Obrero, which was based on the legal principle of *tripartidismo*, or the idea of cooperation between labor, capital, and the state. The pact fulfilled both political and economic objectives. It linked two relatively antagonistic forces together in alliance with the state, and thereby limited the likelihood of strikes or labor unrest that might jeopardize the nation's industrial development.

However, the pact did not solve all of Ávila Camacho's political and economic problems. According to Brachet Márquez, starting in late 1942 it became clear that the economy was not about to take off on its own, even as World War II absorbed the attention and capital of many U.S. firms and thus fundamentally altered the United States' involvement in the Mexican economy. Indeed, "despite the obvious advantages of no longer having to compete with U.S. products, the economy suffered from the lack of imported inputs. Also, exporting scarce foodstuffs to the allies or conducting internal black market operations had become better business than strengthening the productive capacity or expanding the internal market."[6] This meant that those in either industry or commerce who fared better by trading with the United

States than by producing for the domestic market resisted the general obligations formalized in the Pacto. The success of the *tripartidismo*, so critical to economic growth and political stability, was thus in doubt almost from the beginning. In order to salvage the basic principles of the Pacto before opposition accelerated, Ávila Camacho made a critical decision in 1943: He formalized the independent organization of Mexico City industrialists involved in import-substitution, approving their institutional separation from industrialists in other regions and activities. This act not only helped produce durable relationships between labor, the state, and a growing cadre of Mexico City–based nationalist industrialists, but also set the stage for Mexico's rapid industrial takeoff in the 1940s and 1950s.

Mexico City industrialists had long been eager to form their own organization. Their willingness to formalize relationships with the Ávila Camacho administration grew out of this objective, as well as the fact that the new legislation favored the types of activities they were most likely to develop. Indeed, because Mexico City's industrialists tended to own newer and smaller firms, they had the flexibility, willingness, and incentive to jump into the nation's new import-substitution industries. Due to their location in the nation's capital, where the market for these consumer durables was greatest and where access to the government was an additional advantage, they also saw an alliance with both the state and labor as potentially beneficial. In addition, unlike the more established economic elites in other regions who had first made their mark during the Porfiriato and who had already invested capital in certain lines of production, most of these newer firms in Mexico City had little access to large financial institutions.[7] Thus they were also more willing to pursue the state's industrial priorities and devote their energies to the production of a new line of goods, since state-organized development financing and other infrastructure benefits would then be forthcoming. Equally important, many of those ready and eager to enter into state-sponsored industrial production in Mexico City were old revolutionary activists linked to the party, who resided in Mexico City precisely because of their political positions and linkages. In *The Limits to State Autonomy*, Nora Hamilton calls them "revolutionary capitalists." With the location of party institutions and governmental structures primarily in the capital—as opposed to other regions—the relationship between Mexico City industrialists and the PRM worked both ways. Party loyalists were quite willing to foster import-substitution industrialization activities because they were confident they would be on the receiving end of state developmental benefits. And the state was eager to finance economic activities of local allies who could be counted on to support the party's developmental objectives.

In institutionalizing strong relationships with industrialists in Mexico City, Ávila Camacho looked mainly to the Confederación Nacional de la Industria de Transformación, or CANACINTRA.[8] The CANACINTRA began acting informally as a federation separate from the CONCAMIN in early 1941, when the state authorized the institutional split between industrial and commercial federations. The CANACINTRA's position was very unstable in its first two years of existence, since it still had not received legal recognition as separate from the CONCAMIN. But because the CANACINTRA proved to be a loyal ally of the party during Ávila Camacho's struggles to protect labor and to harness the exploitative practices of the northern business elites between 1941 and 1943, the CANACINTRA strengthened both the economic base of its constituents and Ávila Camacho's political dependence—and thus the likelihood that it ultimately would be granted institutional independence. Evidence of its economic success is seen in the fact that after starting out with only 96 firms in 1941, the CANACINTRA grew to include 1,684 industrial firms less than a year later. Its principal members were new firms that produced consumer durables for the domestic market, as well as the steel, glass, plastic, and paper carton manufacturers that provided packaging for those consumer durables. By 1943 the CANACINTRA's rapid expansion, involvement in import-substitution industry, and loyalty to Ávila Camacho were rewarded by legal recognition of its status.

Yet full recognition of the CANACINTRA's independence did not come without some further conflict. Even before 1943, its efforts to separate from the CONCAMIN "produced various points of friction" within the private sector, pitting Mexico City's growing class of import-substitution industrialists against the commercial elites and older, export-oriented industrialists in other regions.[9] As early as 1941, when the CANACINTRA opposed a trade agreement with the United States, it generated open retaliation from northern elites in both the CONCAMIN and the CONCANACO. This further motivated the CANACINTRA to split from the larger industrial federation, however, and ally with the Ávila Camacho administration. Shortly thereafter, by 1944, the Mexico City–based CANACINTRA was considered the principal base of support for the ruling party within the private sector; it stood loyally by Ávila Camacho's side in his struggle against intransigent capitalists, in his effort to build strong relationships with labor, and his attempts to lead Mexico down the road of industrial development.

As in earlier years, the CANACINTRA's support for the PRM continued to grow as struggles with other private sector forces over critical economic and labor policy issues unfolded. In a 1942 conflict between the CTM and northern elites, the state had struggled hard to convince the CONCAMIN, the CONCANACO, and Mexico's banking federation to sign a capital-labor pact guaranteeing wages, eliminating strikes, and promoting Mexico's industrial development. The CANACINTRA was the only federation of capitalists to openly praise president Ávila Camacho's support for the CTM. In 1943, when the commercial firms in the CONCANACO opposed the government's agrarian reform policies, the CANACINTRA remained loyal to the party's agrarian objectives—which further distanced it from the other national industrial and commercial lobbies.[10] The CANACINTRA, in fact, was the only business federation to support the PRM's decision to create the CNOP in 1943, a move that was openly opposed by the CONCANACO and the CON-CAMIN.[11] And in 1944 and 1945, when the national industrial and commercial federation began to question the ideological precedent set by the state's accommodating relationship with organized labor, specifically the Confederación de Trabajadores Mexicanos (CTM), the CANACINTRA again broke ranks with other business organizations and sided with the state and labor. To most observers, then, the CANACINTRA soon "became a symbol of the industrial revolution in Mexico and the substantial state role in promoting that revolution." [12]

Due to the CANACINTRA's efforts and influence within the CONCAMIN, the latter also eventually signed the pact with the CTM, the Pacto Obrero-Industrial. Although the national association of bankers and powerful industrialists in the COPARMEX (the lobby of the northern economic elite) strongly attacked the accord between industry and workers, the pact was nonetheless widely lauded by all sectors of the PRM—CTM, CNC, and CNOP. With labor and industry allied to the state, through the party and this pact, moreover, 1945 was a critical turning point in Mexico's institutional, political, and economic history. For one thing, the pact signed in that year formalized the political role to be played by industrial capitalists in national politics, the most loyal and supportive of whom resided in Mexico City. For another, it linked dominant and subordinate class sectors in Mexico City together in political relationships that would facilitate both labor peace and urbanization-led industrial development, evidenced by the fact that the first social security policies for labor introduced under the labor-industry pact were limited to the Federal District. Most important, perhaps, this pact between the state, labor, and industrial capital in Mexico City irrevocably tied the nation's political and economic future to political and economic developments in the capital itself.

STRENGTHENING THE URBAN POLITICAL FOUNDATION
FOR MEXICO'S INDUSTRIAL DEVELOPMENT

No presidential administration better symbolizes the official party's commitment to urbanization-led industrialization than that of Miguel Alemán (1946–1952). Alemán harvested the fruits of Cárdenas's and Ávila Camacho's earlier political negotiations by presiding over the formation of the Partido Revolucionario Institucional (PRI) in 1946—the new party structure that also reflected the institutionalization of the new cross-class relationships embedded in the Pacto. Although the basic structure of the PRI paralleled that of the PRM, it was not exactly the same party. In fact, that Alemán and others were successful in pushing through a name change in 1946 suggests a subtle but significant shift in the balance of power, which is seen in the newfound political presence of Mexico City's capitalists and the participation of urban popular and middle classes within the party. With Mexico City industrialists at his side, and urban popular and middle classes incorporated into the ruling party in tandem with industrial laborers and the peasantry, Alemán came to the presidency under the most favorable political conditions for rapid economic growth since before the Porfiriato.

Given the successes of the 1945 pact between capital and labor, it is not surprising that Alemán was the first postrevolutionary president to receive wholehearted support from most of the private sector, both during the presidential campaign and after his ascent to the presidency. In fact, Alemán was the first postrevolutionary leader to campaign actively with representatives of industry—notably with Mexico City industrialists represented by the CANACINTRA.[13] From early on, then, Alemán was politically linked to Mexico City industrialists, who in turn benefited widely from his investment in massive infrastructure projects and his protectionist policies to foster their economic development. The growing cadre of industrialists with strong political links to the PRI reinforced the overlap between Mexico's private sector and postrevolutionary politicians. This explains why some scholars call these import-substitution industrialists in Mexico City the Fracción de los Cuarenta, or the Forties Faction, a label that underscores their emergence as a significant economic and political force during the Alemán period, and perhaps even why Alemán himself became actively involved in joint activities with these particular industrialists.

The 1945 pact between organized labor and Mexico City industrialists gave President Alemán political breathing room to embark on intensive, relatively conflict-free industrial development, centered mainly in the nation's capital, where his and the party's most loyal industrial allies resided. Equally important, the post-1944 disruption in trading relationships caused by World War II further helped by giving the Mexican economy and Mexico City's nascent industrialists a chance to develop and strengthen without debilitating foreign competition, which inspired optimism among many different social sectors who wished to see a new prosperity in Mexico. Of course, optimism about industrialization-led modernization was not necessarily new to Mexico during this period. The Porfirian dictatorship had based its legitimacy on that same premise; and so too had most of Mexico's political leaders in the immediate postrevolutionary period. Yet the capital-labor-state pact forged in the mid-1940s under Alemán's guidance inspired new confidence among Mexico's citizens that industrialization was both an achievable objective and the hope for Mexico's future.

In capturing the presidential candidacy, Alemán had depended on the support of relatively powerful segments of the labor movement who had consolidated their power during the Ávila Camacho administration and who continued to argue that alliances with industrial capital were necessary for economic development and the nation's potential prosperity. Among Mexico's citizenry, however, Alemán's principal political allies were the urban popular and middle classes recently incorporated into the party.[14] Soledad Loaeza even suggests that Miguel Alemán's "presidential candidacy in 1945 was confirmation of a new era for the middle classes in the nation's political life." [15] In contrast to previous leaders, Alemán was not directly linked to the military, and he held an advanced academic degree—two features that appealed directly to middle classes, many of whom also openly shared his more conservative views of economy and society. Like his predecessor Ávila Camacho, Alemán also maintained a relatively conciliatory stance toward the Catholic Church, and he soon proved to be no friend to labor, either. Some even suggest that Alemán's conservative political profile, and his strong ideological and institutional linkages to the middle classes, especially in the capital, prevented the Partido Acción Nacional (PAN), the most viable opposition party at the time, from running separate candidates in the 1946 election.[16]

Given Alemán's broad base of political support, he was in a good position to introduce relatively harsh and forcefully directed policies geared toward rapid urbanization-led industrialization. During his six years in office, Alemán elevated tariffs, applied import controls, devalued the peso, improved public services, and introduced countless other measures to raise industrial output. Not surprisingly, most of Alemán's development policies were directed toward Mexico City industrialists, not only because of his political links with them, but again because of Mexico City's unparalleled consumer market. Under Alemán's direction, the government founded its first and most comprehensive industrial park, "the Vallejo industrial complex, situated to the north of the Distrito Federal," which then grew rapidly "via government measures such as land expropriation, industrial park construction, and fiscal incentives" and which housed many of the new firms embarking on import-substitution industrialization of consumer goods represented by the CANACINTRA.[17] During Alemán's term as president, the output of Mexico City's industrial firms grew at an average rate of 9 percent per year. Under Alemán's political leadership, wages rose, employment was up, and spirits in the nation's capital were lifted to heights not reached since the previous century. From a level of 19 percent in 1930, Mexico City's proportion of national industrial employment jumped to 25 percent by 1950, and had almost doubled to 46 percent by 1960; and while in 1940 Mexico City held 8.7 percent of all manufacturing establishments, over the next two decades this rate more than tripled, reaching 29.9 percent.[18]

The government's conscious decision to promote the nation's economic growth through industrial development in Mexico City had clear implications for urban growth and infrastructural development in the capital, as well as for Alemán and his political bases in the middle and entrepreneurial classes. Rather than devoting its urban policy energies only to downtown commercial development, for example, as had been the case in the early thirties before Cárdenas, during the late forties the PRI pushed the federal government and the presidentially appointed Mexico City mayor to invest public monies in Mexico City projects that improved the built environment and facilitated both industrial and commercial development citywide. Among the top priorities in the capital were drainage, roads, and electricity services that facilitated the local production and consumption of both industrial and commercial goods. Investments in roadways extended beyond Mexico City in order to link manufacturing activities in the center to other regions of the country; but most other major infrastructural developments of the period were located in the capital. Perhaps the most politically significant investments during the Alemán period were those in the area of housing, which dominated public spending in Mexico City during the late forties and early fifties. It was through these policies that Alemán also kept labor to his—and the party's—side, at least those who resided in the capital city, the logic being that if the government was to keep labor loyal to the pact with local capitalists, it would also have to meet their demands, along with the infrastructural demands of Mexico City industrialists.

As in the immediate postrevolutionary period, housing was a major concern of the city's working classes. Owing to the minimal housing construction undertaken in the two previous decades, housing was in short supply. During the Cárdenas administration, moreover, housing construction for urban workers had played second fiddle to land regularization and other agrarian-based programs; and, in fact, Mexico had no established financial system for the production of housing during the Cárdenas period, although some construction did take place. Introduction of rent control in 1942 under Ávila Camacho (as demanded by the newly forming CNOP), and its extension by Alemán in 1947, further contributed to the paucity of investment in housing construction, as did the fact that there had been little mobilization around housing in the preceding decade. García Peralta and Perlo Cohen go so far as to claim that during the thirties and early forties, "housing did not constitute a central demand of the workers' movement, whose principal objectives were still to advance union organization and gain better salaries."[19]

In attacking the housing problem, which emerged anew in the labor movement during the late forties, President Alemán used any mechanisms he could find, primarily the newly created Instituto Mexicano de Seguro Social (IMSS) and other new programs to support the construction of single and multi-family housing. Also, between 1947 and 1950, loans for mortgages and housing granted from the General Pensions Office reached "92 million pesos—almost as much as that loaned during the previous 20 years combined."[20] Starting in 1948, moreover, two years after coming to office, Alemán further endeared himself to state workers by building special housing complexes like the Unidad Modelo, El Reloj, La Taxquena, and another in Xotepingo, with funds from the Banco Hipotecario Urbano y de Obras Públicas (Bank of Urban Mortgages and Public Works). Some of these projects housed as many as six thousand workers, and cost as much as 40 million pesos each to build.[21]

Precisely because the extension of housing and social security coverage was concentrated in urban areas, they strengthened the government's relationship to those sectors of the Mexico City labor movement willing to support the PRI in return, which in turn helped marginalize the leftist elements within and outside the CTM who had fought against continued collaboration with Alemán.[22] In many ways, this was the same strategy that had proved successful for Carranza, Calles, and even Obregón; but now, because the labor movement was more homogeneous, the recipients of these critical urban services were slightly different—and there was much more money too. Yet in addition to their general concerns with strengthening the PRI's legitimacy and its hold on political power, Alemán and the national party leadership supported public housing constrution in the capital for two other reasons. First, direct and indirect (through government credit programs) state support for Mexico City housing construction not only reduced the costs of labor that might have fallen on the private sector's shoulders, it also benefited Mexico City–based industries involved in infrastructure and construction. This aided the process of job creation, since construction was a main source of work for unskilled laborers and new rural migrants to the capital. State support of housing construction also gave a few Mexico City–based engineering firms the financial flexibility to extend their activities into other areas necessary for the nation's industrial development, including technologically sophisticated construction and urban infrastructure. Second, in the late 1940s and early 1950s the nation's rapid industrial development plans spurred inflation, and many of Alemán's allies in the private sector worried that workers would demand wage increases to match inflation rates. If workers had to secure housing and other services on the private market, especially in the costly Mexico City environment, such labor demands might accelerate even more. The preferred option for industrialists, particularly in the capital, was for the state to intervene and preempt any such problems. Given the political benefits accruing to the PRI from this strategy of housing development, the government concurred with its private sector allies.

URBAN INFRASTRUCTURAL DEVELOPMENT
AS A NATIONAL FISCAL PROBLEM

In the course of the PRI's efforts to facilitate the growth of a new class of industrial entrepreneurs in the capital, and its extensive efforts to provide housing to a specialized but growing sector of the Mexico City work force, the government financed massive amounts of new urban infrastructure between 1945 and 1955. This, in turn, meant that Mexico City's urban and infrastructural development weighed heavily on the public sector's budget. Not surprisingly, fiscal crisis loomed large by the early 1950s. Though this was in many ways a national problem, primarily because urban infrastructural development had been undertaken by the national party leadership through nationally funded institutions and programs in order to jump-start the Mexico City economy for purposes of national development, it was also a local problem for Mexico City administrators. As of 1960 the Mexico City government had "spent twice as much on ordinary administration and nearly five times as much on public works as all other municipal governments in Mexico," while the rate and prioritization of these outlays in Mexico City was much higher and more concentrated in capital-intensive projects than in comparable American cities at the time.[23] This added up to trouble.

Mexico City faced severe fiscal problems for several reasons, including the fact that its own administrative and financing arrangements had been established decades earlier to accommodate local, rather than national, requirements of economic development. That is, Mexico City's structure of governance and taxation had been established with local infrastructural demands in mind, and this legacy soon became an obstacle. When democratic rule was abolished in Mexico City in 1928, the nation's revolutionary leadership had decided that the capital city should support its own fiscal accounts, in order to politically accommodate the demands of social and class forces in other regions of the country that had originally feared that Mexico City populations would be inordinately privileged by having an appointed mayor with direct links to the president and access to national resources.[24] As a result, beginning in the 1930s Mexico City was forced to rely on local taxes to support most of its urban infrastructural expenditures. Yet the economic crisis of the 1930s also meant that the capital city had started out on very weak footing. Complicating matters, Mexico City's mayor was appointed by the president: This meant that from 1928 onward political decisions about projects and plans in Mexico City were made under pressure from the party leadership. Thus, even as the administrative structures of the capital established in earlier decades were geared toward local dynamics, after 1950 the city was under political pressure to respond to national development concerns more than to local demands or concerns of fiscal solvency. Massive construction of housing for industrial workers was a case in point.

One by-product of the contradictory political and administrative priorities was the institution of extraordinarily low tax rates on industries in Mexico City, particularly after the consolidation of the state-capital-labor pact in 1940. These low rates were introduced by federal authorities as incentives for the location and development of industry, and also because Mexico City's businesses were expected to pay both a local and a 20 percent federal tax, the former to support Mexico City's massive infrastructure and the latter to finance the government's national developmental programs.[25] However, low tax rates in the capital city meant insufficient local revenues to finance the massive urban and industrial development that the country undertook after 1940. Accordingly, the Mexico City government continually relied on subsidies and public debt to support local infrastructural expenditures. Between 1940 and 1955, accumulation of this burden contributed to the city's steadily weakening fiscal position, until Mexico City's fiscal solvency stood in an inverse relationship to the extent of its urban infrastructural development. By the early 1950s, it had reached a point where most of the city's urban infrastructural expenditures had to be financed with public debt rather than tax revenues.[26]

As one would expect, this had serious implications for both urban and national economic conditions and for both local and national governmental capacity to continue with these urban infrastructural projects. Inflation was stimulated by the growing public debt borne by the local and national government to facilitate infrastructural development in Mexico City. Direct subsidies to industry that also characterized the period further fueled the inflationary spiral. This, in turn, wreaked havoc on Mexico's import-substitution strategy, which hurt Mexico City industrialists by reducing local buying power and pushing up the costs of imported capital goods so necessary for new manufacturing industries. Adding fuel to the fire, social pressures to keep industrial wages high—and thus keep intact the state-capital-labor pact that sustained industrial growth—further exacerbated inflationary pressures, as did changing international conditions. As costs of other basic goods skyrocketed, the national government at first attempted to keep the support of urban labor by implementing even more new urban housing programs, located mainly in the capital, of course. The preferred strategy was to keep wages low and to have the state compensate for economic decline by providing housing and other critical urban infrastructural services. Yet this meant more—not less—government spending, and thus greater inflationary pressure. As the federal government printed money throughout the early 1950s to meet both growing social and political demands, and to shoulder the financial burden of infrastructural and housing investment in Mexico City, inflation burned out of control, and all regions, not just Mexico City, suffered.

The situation demanded policy changes. Alemán's successor, President Adolfo Ruiz Cortines, first attempted to deal with these growing fiscal problems by selectively cutting social spending. This policy was intended to control inflationary pressures, but it also cut into the public services in Mexico City that had made the capital-labor pact so successful. Organized labor failed to rally behind the cuts and waged a series of critical strikes in Mexico City in 1953 and 1954. The decision to cut infrastructural expenditures was not very popular among Mexico City's industrialists either, many of whom had come to rely on sustained government investment to keep the economy buoyant. By mid-1954, it was clear that the government had to take another course. A strong concern with industrial labor prevented Ruiz Cortines from continuing to sacrifice housing and other social expenditures, particularly in Mexico City, where organized labor was strongest. Yet the fiscal situation in both Mexico City and the nation was slowly slipping out of control. By the end of the year, Ruiz Cortines reversed himself on spending cuts and poured money into urban housing again, much of it in Mexico City. In 1954, for example, Ruiz Cortines established the Institución Nacional de la Vivienda (National Housing

Institute) and the Fondo de Habitaciones Populares (Popular Housing Fund), which functioned within the Banco Nacional de Obras y Servicios Públicos (National Bank for Public Works and Services). Predictably, however, this further weakened the government's fiscal solvency, and bankers and other creditors began to put pressure on the government to devalue the peso, which it did.

Unfortunately for the PRI, the 1954 devaluation brought a sharper rise in consumer prices than did inflation, as producers and retailers readjusted their prices to parallel the jump in import costs. Mexico City populations were hit hard, creating new dissatisfactions among both labor and industrialists in the capital, where most industrialists relied on foreign imports of capital goods for their consumer durables–producing factories. The devaluation also alienated the city's popular and middle classes, who found themselves continually squeezed between the demands of capital and labor and excluded by most of the government housing programs, which were targeted at industrial workers. With the PRI caught in the middle of competing demands between labor and capital, on the one hand, and the city's urban popular and middle classes, on the other, questions about the provision and administration of urban services in the capital city came to the forefront of national policy and politics once again. As growing fiscal problems limited the room for infrastructural maneuvering, tensions arose with regard to housing, urban transport, and urban land use, each of which was critical to both the city's industrial producers and consumers, but which required massive amounts of money. At this juncture, the Departmento del Distrito Federal (DDF), or the Mexico City mayor's office, moved to center stage. Mexico City's mayor was in the most strategic position to balance these competing local and national fiscal priorities, the growing inter- and intraclass tensions, and renewed signs of political dissatisfaction with the PRI on the part of Mexico City's industrialists, laborers, and urban popular and middle classes. Of course, managing both politics and the economy in Mexico City required real political skill; yet it was the PRI's fortune to have Ernesto P. Uruchurtu at the helm, sailing a tight ship that kept the party afloat in an urban sea of broad-based popularity.

MEXICO CITY'S MAYOR TAKES CHARGE

Ernesto P. Uruchurtu governed Mexico City for an unprecedented fourteen years, or almost three full terms, starting in 1952. Uruchurtu, the first and last Mexico City mayor in postrevolutionary times to serve more than one consecutive term, left his mark on Mexican politics and development in countless ways. Uruchurtu's impact was due in no small part to the fact that he came to the mayorship at a time when the nation's capital was experiencing fundamental social and spatial transformations spurred by its new identity as a burgeoning industrial metropolis, which by the late 1960s would be filled with large factories and multinational headquarters bursting its infrastructural seams. Accordingly, Uruchurtu's urban service and administrative practices, particularly those relating to housing and transport, held the potential to either still or accelerate Mexico City's urban growth, and by affecting the city's social and spatial character at the same time, they could also influence the course the PRI and the national economy might take as well.

Uruchurtu's steady rise to national political prominence began in 1945, when he served as a principal organizer of Miguel Alemán's presidential campaign. When Alemán captured the presidency, he appointed Uruchurtu as secretary-general of the newly founded PRI, a position that Uruchurtu held for only a short time before Alemán appointed him to the powerful post of Subsecretary of Gobernación. By the end of the Alemán administration, Uruchurtu had become Secretary of Gobernación, one of Mexico's most powerful national cabinet posts. Given his strong ties to Alemán and his visible presence in the Alemán cabinet, most analysts considered Uruchurtu an undisputed member of Alemán's political team within the ruling party.[27] Alemán and Uruchurtu's personal relationship began in preparatory school and was politically cemented over the years as Uruchurtu gained positions as a magistrate of the State Supreme Court, president of the Regional Committee of the PNR, secretary-general of the PRI, Subsecretary of Gobernación, and ultimately, Secretary of Gobernación before being appointed mayor of Mexico City in 1952.

Uruchurtu also made a name for himself during the thirties and forties, fighting *coyotes* (persons trafficking in illegal goods) and protecting Mexico's borders from foreigners and illegal entrants—both Guatemalans and other Central Americans who entered the country in flight from rural poverty or political repression, and a growing number of Jewish immigrants fleeing from pogroms in Europe. His ardent commitment to nationalist causes, which at times brought charges of xenophobic and fascist leanings, may have come from his earlier judgeship in the U.S.-Mexico border town of Nogales, where he served as immigration gatekeeper. Yet his concern with foreigners and contraband also reflected his growing preoccupation with several critical urban problems and his support for the ideological concerns of many small shopkeepers, issues that would require his attention as mayor of Mexico City. Uruchurtu's antagonism toward illegal immigrants and so-called *coyotes* often manifested itself as opposition to all non-native Mexicans and even to darker-skinned rural migrants; and it was these groups who over the years had become a growing presence in Mexico City's small-scale service and commercial sector.[28] In identifying the so-called foreign element as encroaching on the social space and economic livelihood of Mexico City's longtime residents, especially those in center city neighborhoods, Uruchurtu made clear his political and ideological linkages with the large number of Mexico City residents employed in small commerce and services—most of whom still lived and worked in Mexico City's central areas as recently as the 1960s, as Susan Eckstein has so carefully documented. This ideological orientation toward Mexico City's more traditional petit bourgeois sector not only gave Uruchurtu several key qualifications to move from Gobernación into Mexico City's mayorship in 1952, it also was perfectly consistent with one other important biographical fact about Uruchurtu: He had served as the campaign manager for General Almazán in Sonora during the 1940 presidential election. Thus from the beginning, Uruchurtu was known to be politically allied to the more conservative forces within the PRI, particularly those with an elective affinity to smaller industrialists, urban petit bourgeois forces, and traditional middle classes who populated Mexico City and who had thrown support to Almazán in 1940, as discussed earlier.

In addition to the fact that he maintained strong relationships with outgoing president Miguel Alemán, Uruchurtu's ideological proclivities and his receptiveness to the city's petit bourgeoisie and their urban concerns were perhaps his principal qualification for being mayor. That these were essential for any mayoral candidate is suggested by the fact that one of the most contentious public issues in Mexico City from 1950 to 1952, immediately before Uruchurtu was appointed mayor, was a massive urban redevelopment plan for the downtown, promoted by large developers and approved by Mexico City's Comisión de Planificación (but opposed by small industrialists, shopkeepers, and other residents of central city areas). According to documents produced for the Planning Commission, the plan's principal objective was "to resolve the problem of transit in order to revive land values, which recently had depreciated dramatically." When this plan brought a visible public outcry from central city residents and shopkeepers, and when the press jumped into the fray, then-mayor Fernando Casas Alemán (no relation to Miguel Alemán) saw a rapid decline in popularity. With this urban development conflict capturing local political debate, in 1952 the PRI turned its energies toward finding a mayor who could regain the trust of the capital's central city populations, mainly nonwage artisans, shopkeepers, and vendors, as well as lower-rung government employees, who comprised the city's popular and lower-middle classes. This was increasingly necessary as these groups felt ever more excluded by President Alemán's open support of industrial development and housing construction for workers. Indeed, Mexico City's older residential neighborhoods in downtown areas, where the largest concentration of these populations resided, were being rapidly transformed by pressures for land valorization and by the location of larger industries within the city's borders. And Mexico City's Planning Commission had been storming ahead with redevelopment plans, even though they were somewhat constrained by the persistence of rent control regulations. It was between 1940 and 1950, in fact, that transformations in downtown road infrastructure—coupled with the practice of subdividing large homes surviving from the colonial era—dispersed some of the central city's longtime residents.[29] So when most of the new public housing projects built by President Alemán were located outside the city's traditional center and reserved for the CTM's constituents, central city artisans, shopkeepers, small producers, and low-level government employees felt even more neglected.

Evidence of growing political dissatisfaction from these groups emerged in the 1952 elections for congress in Mexico City. Support for PRI candidates hit a new low of 49.01 percent, even as the party's national average was 74.31 percent (see Appendix C). This was a drop of almost 12 percentage points from the 1949 election, before the urban redevelopment plan enraged urban residents. With the party's popularity below 50 percent in the capital, the PRI leadership was further convinced that it needed a mayor who could bring these disenfranchised forces back into the political fold. Both the PRI and Mexico City residents saw Uruchurtu's rise to the mayorship as offering a potential respite from past practices, which were so clearly embedded in the party's national political orientation toward organized labor, local industrialists, and land developers.

Uruchurtu did not disappoint. When he stepped into the mayor's job in late 1952, one of his first acts was to table the central city redevelopment proposal indefinitely, an act that underscored his willingness to appease the city's more traditional popular and middle-class residents. And given the PRI's almost myopic orientation during the 1940s and early 1950s toward organized labor and its urban infrastructural needs, especially housing, it is not surprising that residents of Mexico City's traditional neighborhoods were pleased with someone like Uruchurtu. Many were optimistic that he would protect them against further urban development and displacement caused by the city's continued growth, and that he would place their own housing and urban service demands on the agenda.

GOVERNING FOR THE TRADITIONAL MIDDLE CLASSES

Uruchurtu's appointment as mayor was a critical political move on the part of the PRI. He brought back to Mexico City governance the voices of those less powerful residents whose capacity to influence urban policy had been slowly undermined over the years: first by the abolition of municipal rule in 1928; next by the formation of the Comisión de Planificación, which emasculated the Consejo Consultivo in Mexico City during the thirties; and last by the growing capacity of the CTM and locally based industrial capital to use national political institutions to control urban policy and service investments in the capital during the forties and fifties. Of course, the formation of the CNOP in 1943 had been intended to provide a format for these very same urban popular and middle classes to make political demands. But the diversity of occupations and organizations within the CNOP frequently prevented it from functioning coherently in this regard. With groups as diverse as bus drivers, shopkeepers, teachers, doctors, and state bureaucrats interspersed with groups of residents organized on the neighborhood level all in one organization, it was difficult for the CNOP leadership to come to a singular forceful position on the urban demands of Mexico City residents. Frequently, the CNOP's bureaucratic constituents determined the organization's political agenda, since they were its largest single constituency. Moreover, this was a national organization, after all, which in early years prevented it from taking on too many of the specific urban policy concerns of the local constituents.

Accordingly, when it came to wielding political power in the ruling party's national policymaking process, the CNOP could not hold a candle to the CTM. The largest and most powerful group within the CNOP still consisted of state workers, many of whose urban housing demands were starting to be met by new housing construction built under the auspices of IMSS and other federal programs. But with Uruchurtu in the Mexico City mayor's office, many of those urban residents that fell outside the labor sector's reach now had a politically powerful advocate and an alternative, locally based political structure for pressing their concerns and demands. Uruchurtu's appointment, in short, helped the PRI achieve its commitment to balancing the concerns of capital, labor, and the popular and middle classes, although this balance required a mix of local and national political structures. By making sure that he kept his eye most open to the city's middle classes, low and moderate income alike, Uruchurtu's reign as mayor nicely complemented the party's national commitment to industrial capital and labor.

Once in office, Uruchurtu introduced a whole new approach to Mexico City governance. This was particularly the case in comparison to the city's previous mayors, many of whom developed questionable reputations as advocates for big capital, while also enriching themselves through support of massive urban land redevelopment projects. Uruchurtu broke this mold in several ways. First, he immediately introduced a tone of morality into public discourse that appealed to the more conservative and traditional values of the city's middle sectors. His public statements proclaimed an intent to "moralize the city" and rid its central areas of elements and institutions that threatened the nation's health—from prostitutes and street vendors to cantinas and cabarets.[30] Of course, such arguments were not completely novel, having emerged with vigor throughout the 1920s and early 1930s as the social composition of downtown areas changed dramatically. Because the city held larger and larger numbers of unemployed migrants and working men—many of them single—who consumed those "immoral" services, such arguments had long been floating in private discourse. But they had not been central concerns of Mexico City mayors, at least since 1928, nor had they been publicly discussed with such vigor since the 1910s and early 1920s, when moral corruption was a principal theme of postrevolutionary urban administrators. By reviving these concerns about public decency and morality in the fifties, Uruchurtu gained a reputation for being outspoken and unencumbered by past party practices. Most important perhaps, he appealed directly to the sentiments of many of the city's middle classes, who tended to be more traditional in social customs and religious practices and whose moral concerns had not been openly addressed by the PRI for some time.

Second, rather than devoting attention to massive urban reconstruction and major infrastructural developments demanded by financiers and land developers, or large-scale housing projects demanded by the organized labor sector, as had his immediate predecessor Casas Alemán, Uruchurtu focused most of his administrative attention on urban service concerns, particularly the concerns of those populations residing in the center where pressures for land redevelopment were greatest. In one of his first public statements as mayor, Uruchurtu identified his major objectives as regularizing and restricting street vending in central areas (*primer cuadro*, or first quadrant) and improving local transit. In discussing these objectives, along with his plans to reduce the scarcity of water, clean the city's streets and neighborhoods, eliminate flooding, and increase police protection, Uruchurtu made special note of his plans to build new markets for small *comerciantes* from central city areas and to introduce new transport policies and bus routes to facilitate circulation on downtown streets—something he intended to accomplish without widening roads or creating construction problems for local residents. Uruchurtu also pushed hard and successfully for the continuation of rent control regulations—which benefited mainly downtown residents in older housing stock, as well as local *comerciantes* and small businesses—despite the desires of developers to shed this restrictive shackle on downtown land use. In fact, during Uruchurtu's term as mayor, the city's Planning Commission, which long had been dominated by big business and landowning representatives, and which had forcefully advocated downtown development and land valorization since its inception in 1933, was convened only twice in fourteen years.[31]

Over his two and a half terms in office, Mayor Uruchurtu's orientation toward the urban service demands of traditional middle classes and central city residents remained relatively fixed. Most of the housing developments built during his tenure were apartments for the middle classes. He devoted substantial resources to beautifying Mexico City, mainly by developing parks, flower gardens, and picturesque boulevards that appealed to middle-class families who, as noted, tended to live in more central areas of the city, which included Colonia Roma and Colonia Condesa, where many of the beautification projects were concentrated. Uruchurtu also allocated massive public funds to drainage projects to protect against the disastrous floods Mexico City had been facing for decades, another urban service concern that had peaked in the late thirties with the growing opposition to Cárdenas. Uruchurtu's efforts to put these two urban service issues on the policy agenda, which had been neglected in the rush to build housing for the working classes, truly endeared him to many of the city's longtime residents. Furthermore, Uruchurtu was credited with regularizing urban transport by placing urban bus services under the restrictive guidance of a joint public-private regulating body known as the Unión de Permisionarios. This stance was perhaps his most controversial, and as we will see in upcoming chapters, it ultimately determined Uruchurtu's fate.

Given his openness to expanding Mexico's urban service provisions to indulge many of the luxury demands of many of the city's middle-class residents, it may seem surprising that Uruchurtu was also extraordinarily well known for his tight fiscal hand, especially during his first term in office (1952–1958), when Mexico's economy was weakening and the country experienced two currency devaluations. During his terms as mayor, however, Uruchurtu helped the PRI maintain the nation's economic solvency by keeping the capital city's fiscal house in order. In fact, Uruchurtu was arguably the most fiscally responsible politician Mexico has known in the past half century, at least in the mayor's office. His successes in this regard endeared him to the party leadership, which sought a tight fiscal ship in order to reduce inflation and thus keep both industrial labor and capital on their side.

BALANCING MEXICO CITY'S BUDGET

Uruchurtu's fiscal successes in Mexico City were all the more noteworthy because he faced an almost impossible task. As noted earlier, the PRI had further reduced the tax burden on the industrialists located in the Mexico City area during the administration of Miguel Alemán. While these regulations were successful in giving Mexico City industrialists incentives, they made the Mexico City mayor's job more difficult, because such regulations had the net effect of reducing the Distrito Federal's revenue base. In addition to the changed restrictions, demographic changes and economic pressures also altered the Distrito Federal's revenues and expenditures. Massive rural migration to Mexico City during the forties and early fifties had raised "the concentration of low income groups in the core of the city and led to increased welfare and public expenditures," which in turn led to declining property values, "as wealthier families departed to the periphery."[32] The Distrito Federal's fiscal vulnerability was furthered by the growing relocation of industry outside its boundaries in the late fifties and early sixties, as several of the most successful and rapidly growing import-substitution industries sought to take advantage of open spaces and cheaper land. This was particularly the case among the larger, internationally linked firms like Nestlé, Pfizer, General Motors, and Volkswagen, many of which moved to the outskirts of the metropolitan area far beyond the boundaries of the Distrito Federal.[33]

The movement of some of Mexico City's larger and more successful import-substitution industrialists outside of the Distrito Federal boundaries is important for more than just fiscal reasons; these changes also significantly altered Uruchurtu's political constituency and thus affected the ways in which he could achieve fiscal solvency. Because Uruchurtu's jurisdiction was the Distrito Federal, or Mexico City proper, and not the whole metropolitan area, he directed his policies and political energies toward those industrialists who remained within the formal juridical confines of the capital city. These tended to be small and medium-sized industrialists, for whom central locations and access to the consumer market were more important than the tax savings gained in the process of such a major relocation. In contrast, the tax savings that came with locating outside the Distrito Federal—at least as compared to increased transport costs for both employees and products—were more important to larger industrialists with larger production capacities, and for that reason they tended to relocate outside the city. To the extent that small and medium-sized industrialists and shopkeepers remained in the Distrito Federal, while larger industries relocated, Uruchurtu had greater incentive to use urban service and administrative policy to protect the city's so-called middle sectors, which included these groups. This also meant that Uruchurtu continued to foster strong working relationships with the CANACINTRA, which increasingly represented this particular constituency of smaller, Mexico City–based industrialists.

Owing to his priorities while mayor and his initial political linkages with Alemán, Uruchurtu and the CANACINTRA soon became great allies. They took almost identical positions on major urban policy issues during the fifties and early sixties, including a call for limiting urban growth and encouraging decentralization.[34] They also shared a strong nationalist orientation that was seen in public calls for restrictions on both foreigners and foreign capital. Uruchurtu relied heavily on the CANACINTRA's counsel, and he appointed its members to his own Consejo de Planeación Económica y Social en el Distrito Federal, a new advisory body he created to consider Mexico City's problems, especially urban congestion, now that the CNOP concerned itself primarily with national problems. Uruchurtu's good political relationship with the CANACINTRA seems to support the conclusions of many political observers who have identified Uruchurtu as allied mainly with economically dominant groups and industrialists within the Distrito Federal. Yet few have noted that some of the more politically vocal industrialists in Mexico City during the late fifties and early sixties were smaller industrialists and entrepreneurs who had started their manufacturing activities in the thirties and forties. They tended to be affiliated with the CANACINTRA, and not the organizations representing larger industries nationwide, like the CONCAMIN. These smaller industrialists generally posed demands very different from those of larger ones, who were increasingly involved in capital goods production, were often directly connected with international capital, and who relied on their own banking institutions for credit.

Although the urban dispersion of larger industries outside the city's formal boundaries may have helped solidify the CANACINTRA's and Uruchurtu's linkages with each other and with other small and medium-sized industrialists producing consumer durables in the capital, they did not eliminate the city's fiscal problems. Much of the industrial labor force still resided inside the city's boundaries, and they required social and infrastructural expenditures. Moreover, the smaller industrial firms that remained in the Distrito Federal provided only a modest revenue base. Uruchurtu overcame this handicap by restructuring the Distrito Federal bureaucracy in order to enhance revenue collection. In addition to encouraging fiscal solvency, this act further linked many Mexico City bureaucrats directly to the mayor and created networks within which Uruchurtu could cultivate his own team of political allies. These reforms and the alliances they generated helped Uruchurtu maintain Mexico City's fiscal solvency. From 1952 to 1963, the Distrito Federal's revenues increased nearly five times in current prices and over three times in real terms; and these revenues came not from an increase in tax rates but from an expanded tax base and improved administration by Uruchurtu himself.[35] This dramatic change in Mexico City's fiscal position sheds light on why many felt Uruchurtu worked miracles: He came to Mexico City with a budget of barely 300 million pesos and outstanding debt obligations of more than 270 million pesos from previous administrations, but by 1964, Uruchurtu was overseeing a budget of 1.4 billion pesos, having given the city more than 190 billion pesos worth of infrastructure without relying on any external debt.[36] In perhaps the most comprehensive study of the Distrito Federal's role in financing urban development, Oliver Oldman and his colleagues note that under Uruchurtu (between 1953 and 1966) Mexico City "generated substantial budget *surpluses* . . . despite government expenditures which expanded at a rate of 130 percent compounded annually."[37]

Uruchurtu's fiscally conservative approach to urban governance and his orientation toward the city's middle classes and local industry paid off in personal political capital. Throughout his administration, he received public accolades from residents and local industrialists alike. They cited his capacity to manage transport and other critical urban services, his honesty, and his economic efficiency. As early as 1957, at the end of his first term, Uruchurtu's popularity was practically unparalleled. One newspaper editorial noted that "the consensus of the *capitalinos* unanimously declares Lic. Ernesto P. Uruchurtu as one of the best—if not the best—mayors of Mexico City."[38] Another columnist labeled Uruchurtu "a superior governor [whose] supporters and enemies alike recognize the public works introduced by him for the city and its inhabitants."[39] The presiding spokesman for Mexico City's Centro Patronal, an organization of employers, said of Uruchurtu: "This is the first time we make note of the fact that a governor has exceeded his obliged duties."[40] And in September 1957, the Mexico City daily *El Universal* printed a letter to the editor summing up Uruchurtu's mayoral term with the words "veni, vidi, vici." A month later the paper awarded him their medal of merit, granted to a public official for the first time ever.

FROM ASSET TO POTENTIAL LIABILITY IN SIX SHORT YEARS

By the end of his first term in office, Uruchurtu had accomplished the unimaginable, at least in terms of buttressing support for the PRI in Mexico City. In the 1955 Mexico City elections for congress, the PRI's support rose to 56 percent from a low of 49 percent upon Uruchurtu's arrival in 1952; and by 1958, after six years with Uruchurtu as mayor, Mexico City support for the PRI hit a (still) unprecedented 68.59 percent (see Appendix C). Despite these triumphs, however, Uruchurtu's administration was not entirely unproblematic. Some of the policies he introduced started a slow-burning opposition from other segments of the urban population, and this in turn began to create new problems for the PRI. Perhaps the most critical—and ultimately the most controversial—of Uruchurtu's proposed policies was to limit the population growth of the city, a stance he hoped would help him achieve fiscal solvency in the Distrito Federal. Uruchurtu's concern about restricting Mexico City's rapid growth was evident almost from the beginning of his administration. As early as mid-1954, around the time of the peso's devaluation, Uruchurtu made public statements about the importance of "pre-planning the growth and provisioning of [Mexico City]," a strategy that was expected to include "avoiding the disordered and indefinite growth of the capital."[41] Strictly speaking, controlling Mexico City's growth and maintaining fiscal solvency were not so controversial as the policy by which Uruchurtu attempted to achieve these objectives: the imposition of strict limits on the expansion of new squatter settlements and housing developments in the Distrito Federal.

Of course, Uruchurtu could do nothing to stop the hoards of rural inmigrants that burst the city's infrastructural seams during the 1950s. But he could, and did, create obstacles to their permanent settlement in the city, particularly in new areas where city expenditures on drainage, roads, electricity, and land regularization would be legally required. Wayne Cornelius, for example, notes that Uruchurtu's administration was perhaps best known for "prohibiting the subdivision of land for low-income housing, acting immediately to evict squatters from invaded land and denying tenure rights and basic common services to most existing *colonias* formed through squatter invasions."[42] Uruchurtu's often heartless actions against squatters and other low-income population settlements can be understood as a product of his dual concerns with maintaining a middle-class base of political support and achieving fiscal solvency in order to help local industrialists and the national economy. Together these distinct political and economic objectives helped produce his antiurban growth orientation. Because regulations stipulated that all new developments *had* to be supplied with essential services, Uruchurtu saw the restriction of land developments as one of the simplest means of avoiding such expenditures, thereby leaving scarce resources for projects demanded by the middle class and small industrialists or *comerciantes*. Such restriction on settlement also rid the city of the eyesore of underserviced and overcrowded squatter areas, which both complemented the beautification strategy Uruchurtu employed to appeal to middle-class sectors and helped him retain the character, charm, and manageability of Mexico City that they so desired.

By removing urban blight, moreover, Uruchurtu felt he could keep middle sectors content with the city and thereby prevent their dispersion to suburban residential areas outside his jurisdiction, which in turn meant the Distrito Federal would not lose its property tax revenues. Uruchurtu also worried that low-income rural migrants and squatters, crowding into central areas of the Distrito Federal in search of employment, were driving middle-class families with fiscal resources away from the increasingly chaotic and overcrowded capital. The dispersion of central city firms and local residents outside the Distrito Federal was of particular concern to Uruchurtu because property taxes were the principal source of local revenues and because tax rates on industry were kept low to facilitate profitability. Additionally, Uruchurtu's restrictions on new housing developments and urban squatting also helped keep land speculation under control. This capped the costs of housing and rent in the Distrito Federal, another issue that greatly concerned middle classes, who up to that point had not received the subsidies and state-built housing reserved for the city's industrial working class. In short, Uruchurtu had relatively good fiscal and political reasons to limit urban growth and forcibly remove squatters and the urban poor.[43]

After taking his positions on squatting, urban growth, and downtown development, Uruchurtu was so popular with Mexico City's middle classes that his name was proposed by the right-wing PAN as their prospective candidate for the 1958 presidential elections, which he declined.[44] Uruchurtu's traditionally conservative political views and his orientation toward middle classes and small businesses fitted well within the PAN, which was working to cultivate support among urban middle-class voters. It did not take long, however, for Uruchurtu's antiurban growth orientation, his conservative profile, and his specialized attention to downtown *comerciantes*, small businesses, and other traditional sectors of the middle class to alienate several politically and economically powerful groups in Mexico City that also were critical to the PRI's political success. By the late fifties, for example, developers began to question Uruchurtu's reluctance to eliminate rent control or approve new subdivisions. Their concern was matched by a growing cadre of businessmen and industrialists who sought to invest in tourism and commercial redevelopment in downtown Mexico City. Also, Uruchurtu's restrictions on new settlements and housing developments threatened to alienate those within the CTM who advocated the construction of more *colonias proletarias* for the city's still-growing class of industrial laborers. Thus, as Uruchurtu's popularity with the middle class increased, so did the harshness of his actions; and this frequently brought urban policy stances that were incompatible with those held by several of the PRI's most powerful supporters in the private sector and in organized labor.

Equally important, Uruchurtu's orientation toward central city shopkeepers, small factory owners, and other traditional sectors of the middle class threatened to create serious divisions within the CNOP itself. The increasing likelihood of a schism within the CNOP was thus due to a combination of demographic changes and spatial transformations, both of which were exacerbated by several aspects of Uruchurtu's approach to the built environment and his urban policy orientations. As Mexico City had grown by attracting rural migrants to work in the expanding industrial sector, the number of those employed in street vending and irregular services (generally known as the informal sector) had also grown. As noted earlier, Mexico City had long hosted marginal populations in the informal sector, especially during the thirties, when the world economic crisis and international migration accelerated. Yet most scholars have traced the exorbitant growth of Mexico's informal sector in the fifties to a different set of causes: the fact that industrial jobs (or those in the formal sector) were insufficient to absorb the masses of impoverished rural migrants coming to the capital city to seek work and a better future. This was, indeed, a vicious chain of events that was fueled by the government's preference for industrial over agricultural development and for the overwhelming dominance of the capital city.

Uruchurtu's policies could do very little to stop this flow, but ironically, they did channel it in ways that exacerbated many of the city's urban problems. In previous years, the first stop of these new migrants had been the center city. But Uruchurtu's relatively successful efforts to preserve the urban core for middle-class families and other longtime residents, in part through restrictions on vending in central city streets, made this increasingly difficult. Thus, starting in the fifties and sixties, the city's central areas did not absorb the same number of new migrants as the more peripheral areas. And because Uruchurtu's policies tended to discourage migrants' location downtown, they were pushed outward, which resulted in the spatial expansion of the metropolitan areas. Yet even as he kept them from central areas, Uruchurtu refused to approve or regularize their settlement in the more peripheral areas of the city. Indeed, his efforts to protect small shopkeepers drove him to actively patrol the city streets for petty traders and vendors who cluttered downtown areas or competed with local businesses. Many were "cleaned" from the streets, forcibly evicted for selling without appropriate licenses or credentials. Uruchurtu's policies thus pitted the informally employed urban poor against the traditional middle class.

Yet both sets of groups were members of the CNOP; and therein lay most of Uruchurtu's troubles. Soon, the growth in the numbers of informal sector workers, and their organization into neighborhood federations to demand urban services denied by Uruchurtu, made them perhaps the most active and vocal constituency in the CNOP. By dividing the CNOP and by making urban middle classes aware that their demands and concerns differed from those of others in the same party sector, Uruchurtu's actions in support of the traditional middle classes held the potential to challenge the party's legitimacy as a representative of the urban poor, especially the nonwage working poor without access to the party's labor federation, even as they gave testament to the fact that Mexican politics—and the CNOP in particular—did not function equally for all.

To complicate matters, several other of Uruchurtu's urban policy actions threatened to dramatically alter the balance of power within the corporatist political system as a whole, and they also began to catch up with him by the late fifties. For example, Uruchurtu used his position as mayor to practically eliminate the Comisión de Planificación and revive the almost defunct Consejo Consultivo. By publicly reviving the Consejo's role as a mechanism to "obtain the public's collaboration in [Mexico City's] governance," Uruchurtu in some ways created a shadow CNOP that could bring traditional sectors of the urban middle class directly to his side.[45] At the same time, by limiting the political access of the Comisión de Planificación in Mexico City, Uruchurtu managed to institutionally preclude powerful real estate developers from policy decisions in Mexico City, leaving them few other mechanisms within the PRI-dominated state through which to make demands or represent their own special interests and urban service concerns in the nation's capital. By wielding control over urban policies and administrative expenditures for such an extended period, moreover, Uruchurtu also developed his own team of bureaucrats in the local government. This threatened to wreak further havoc in the CNOP's functioning as a national political organization representing all state bureaucrats, national and local alike. Uruchurtu developed particularly strong linkages with low-level city employees organized in the Sindicato Único de Trabajadores del Gobierno del Distrito Federal (SUTGDF), for whom he built parks, installed kindergarten facilities, modernized clinics, and created special stores with clothing, furniture, and "other indispensable household goods" sold at restricted prices adjusted to the "buying power" of city employees' salaries. He gained their absolute trust and support, moreover, with "promotions, payment of thoughtful and just salaries, and satisfactory resolution of other small problems."[46]

With his strong hand, then, Uruchurtu's tenure as mayor solved some problems for the PRI by keeping some key sectors of the middle class in the political fold, primarily shopkeepers, merchants, small industrialists, and mid- or lower-level government employees, particularly those employed in the Distrito Federal agencies. But it also created others, mainly by laying the groundwork for growing political tensions between classes and within the incorporated political system itself. By 1958, these tensions hit a new peak. Uruchurtu and his antiurban growth allies began to lock horns with forces both within and outside the PRI who did not share his urban vision or his political objectives. At stake, moreover, was more than just the growth and composition of Mexico City.

PHOTOS 1, 2, 3: In the first decades of the twentieth century, Mexico City showed little sign of the bustle that was to come. Photos courtesy of the Archivo General de la Nación Mexicana, Colección Propiedad Artística y Literaria.

1 Calle Tacuba, one of the city's principal downtown shopping streets, 1909.

2 Avenida Juárez, with a view to the nation's new legislative palace, under construction, 1922.

3 Paseo de la Reforma, then and now the capital's most elegant boulevard, 1922.

PHOTOS 4, 5, 6: The 1930s saw steady urban growth, underscoring the importance of efficient transport services in the capital. Photos courtesy of the Archivo General de la Nación Mexicana, Colección Díaz, Delgado, y García.

4 The Plaza de la Constitución (Zocalo), downtown Mexico City, circa 1930.

5 Mexico City's bus drivers' association, La Alianza de Camioneros, 1933.

6 La Alianza de Camioneros, 1933.

PHOTOS 7, 8, 9: By the 1940s downtown Mexico City served as the magnet for all facets of public life.

7 Public demonstration clogging a central thoroughfare, circa 1940. Courtesy of the Archivo General de la Nación Mexicana, Colección Díaz, Delgado, y García.

8 Strolling on Calle Tacuba, circa 1940. Courtesy of the Archivo General de la Nación Mexicana, Colección Díaz, Delgado, y García.

9 Traffic jam, downtown Mexico City, 1944. Courtesy of *El Universal* (Mexico City daily).

PHOTOS 10, 11, 12: As the city grew, so did demands for roadway and drainage infrastructure, priorities of Mexico City's most popular mayor, Ernesto Uruchurtu.

10 Streetcleaning vehicles poised for inspection, 1947. Courtesy of the Archivo General de la Nación Mexicana, Colección Díaz, Delgado, y García.

11 A 1951 storm disabling downtown streets. Courtesy of the Archivo General de la Nación Mexicana, Colección Díaz, Delgado, y García.

12 Mayor Uruchurtu visiting a public works site. Courtesy of *El Universal* (Mexico City daily).

PHOTOS 13, 14, 15: Despite pressures otherwise, the tranquil middle-class character of many downtown areas endured for decades. Photos by Hector Garcia.

13 Families strolling across the Alameda Park, circa 1950.

14 Construction of the Torre Latinoamericana, Mexico City's first skyscraper, circa 1950.

15 Lower middle-class housing, downtown Mexico City, 1967.

5

THE PRI AT THE CROSSROADS:

URBAN CONFLICT SPLITS THE

PARTY, 1958–1966

Ernesto Uruchurtu's six years as mayor of Mexico City may have occasioned misgivings from urban squatters and land developers, but these concerns were not enough to turn the national party leadership against him, at least not immediately. When PRI candidate Adolfo López Mateos took office as Mexico's new president in 1958, Uruchurtu was reappointed Mexico City's mayor for a second term. The PRI's decision to keep Uruchurtu in office was no doubt rooted in his overwhelming success in balancing the Mexico City budget, making the city run more efficiently than ever, and sustaining popularity with critical sectors of the public and local industry, especially the CANACINTRA and urban middle classes. Uruchurtu had accomplished the near impossible: administering Mexico City in such a way as to keep national political leaders, nationally powerful classes, and local forces happy all at the same time. The PRI was so happy with Uruchurtu that they, like the PAN, even seriously considered him as the party's candidate for the presidency before López Mateos was finally selected. In addition to the successes noted in the last chapter, one particularly pressing reason the PRI returned Uruchurtu to the mayorship was his success in the area of urban transport, which was key to the smooth and efficient expansion of the city. As discussed earlier, Mexico's political leaders had long viewed the capital city's growth, economic prosperity, and political stability as tied to urban transport and to the local government's efforts to streamline its delivery. Uruchurtu recognized this, and paid serious attention to urban transport problems and policy starting early in his fourteen years as mayor.

The problems Uruchurtu faced in the 1950s, however, were much more complex than those faced by Mexico's political leaders in the 1910s and 1920s. By 1950, the Distrito Federal was more than seven times the size it was in 1920; and from 1940 to 1960 alone, it had nearly tripled in size. By the 1950s, Mexico's urban transport sector also was much more diverse and competitive than in earlier years, with a well-developed bus industry existing alongside electric trolley service. This made Uruchurtu's administrative requisites in the area of transport even more difficult, but he was well prepared for the task. His foresight and special skills in politically accommodating providers of urban transport gave him maneuvering room to successfully administer and service Mexico City. Yet the political relationships he forged in this and other areas also limited the nature and scope of his urban policy priorities during the fifties and early sixties. As such, Uruchurtu's political alliances, many of which revolved around his relationships to the urban bus industry in particular, made their mark on the city's spatial development during the period. By so doing, moreover, they also generated political opposition from sources within and outside the party, both local and national, who did not share the same plans for Mexico City's future growth.

Ultimately, these disagreements over the city's growth and spatial development critically wounded the PRI and created intraparty conflicts that spilled over into subsequent administrations and affected both urban and national development policy. The upcoming pages trace the source of these conflicts and controversies to the differing local and national objectives of Mexico City's mayor and Mexico's president. I identify their divergent positions on urban growth and its relationship to national development as grounded in the differing social and class coalitions within which each leader was embedded, as well as in the differing party resources, obligations, and institutional linkages at their disposal. I also show how the unequal distribution of these class coalitions and institutional linkages and resources both fueled these conflicts and helped determine their outcomes in both local and national domains.

POSITIONING THE ALIANZA IN POWER

Starting in December 1952, his first month in office, Uruchurtu was careful to make urban transport services one of his top priorities, even though his most immediate concern was a new drainage infrastructure that would help alleviate the yearly floods that paralyzed Mexico City. By 1955, Uruchurtu had canceled all contracts with foreign firms providing trolley services, a move that was intended to put a significant proportion of urban transport provision directly under his charge. Given his ideological affinity with small firms, and his almost xenophobic commitment to nationalist ideals, it is logical that he targeted foreign-owned trolleys for government takeover rather than urban bus services, which were completely under Mexican ownership. Once the Compañía de Tranvías was nationalized, a new agency under the administration of Mexico City's mayor was created to provide and absorb the costs of trolley service: the Sistema del Transporte Eléctrico del Distrito Federal. Yet trolley service was not cheap. In addition to the expenditures associated with public expropriation and the high costs of maintenance and track extension, new trolleys had to be purchased from abroad, where they were manufactured. At a time when the peso's value was plummeting, and when Uruchurtu sought to maintain fiscal solvency, this presented no small obstacle. With the 1955 devaluation inflating total costs, Uruchurtu found himself trying to balance the city's scarce fiscal resources, urban transport necessities, and the public goal of providing mass transit services.

Uruchurtu developed a two-pronged approach to public transportation. He continued with trolley service, since an extensive network of trolley tracks still served some of the most critical central areas of the city. At the same time, he became more directly involved in regulating privately owned buses and taxis, which offered their services to newly populated areas of the city beyond the reach of existing trolley tracks. Although relatively successful, this dual approach was not conflict-free. In 1955, when Uruchurtu introduced new regulations for urban bus services, he was barraged with complaints from organizations of bus drivers regarding the imposition of fines and restrictions on routes. Among the most vocal *transportistas* in the 1950s were those within the Alianza de Camioneros, the private organization of bus drivers and bus owners that had formed in the 1920s for the purpose of breaking the trolley worker strikes. The Alianza had steadily gained power over the years, due to its support from government officials concerned with urban services, the declining strength of the trolley workers' union, and the emergence of the CNOP, which gave bus drivers an institutional format for participating directly in party politics. That the Alianza was used by the PRI to bus party supporters to official rallies and to the polls during election periods also contributed to its growing political influence, since its services in this regard were essential. By the 1950s, the Alianza de Camioneros was one of the most powerful lobbies in Mexico City.

The Alianza also buttressed its political influence with its growing economic strength, which began decades earlier when it received direct subsidies for fuel under the CROM's initiative during the 1920s. Its economic power continued throughout the 1930s as the Alianza was able to fight for its own interests in Mexico City's Consejo Consultivo, where it had secured representative status. During the 1930s and 1940s, moreover, the Alianza formed production and distribution cooperatives that helped its members secure parts and gasoline at reduced cost. The Alianza de Camioneros, in fact, was one of the first organizations to take advantage of the 1929 law on co-ops introduced by General Obregón immediately before his assassination; and the Alianza's successes as a production and distribution co-op set it on a path of rapid economic expansion that made the urban bus industry one of the most economically and politically powerful industries in Mexico City before 1945, at least outside the consumer goods production sector. On this strong footing, the Alianza continued to strengthen its economic position. During the mid to late 1940s, it developed supply linkages with the automobile industry, which at the time was rapidly becoming one of the most successful manufacturing industries in Mexico. In 1949 the Alianza signed an agreement with General Motors to supply parts for the Alianza's fleets of buses.[1] Even more important, the Alianza used its privileged position in the capital to monopolize control of interstate transport routes, many of which passed through Mexico City because of the capital city's centrality in the national economy. Through its growing control over interstate transport routes, by the late forties and early fifties the Alianza entered into two other highly lucrative industries in Mexico: tourism and cargo trucking. As such, its economic centrality to the nation's economic takeoff was almost unparalleled.

It is not surprising, then, that by the mid-1950s the Alianza already wielded a significant degree of influence in Mexican politics, both locally and nationally. As one of the CNOP's most powerful members, this group of "owner-workers" exemplified the middle-class successes the CNOP's founders advocated. Its high visibility and economic power also meant that the Alianza had been able to permanently secure several of the congressional deputyships and senatorships allocated by the CNOP to its most critical members at every election.[2] One Alianza member stated it succinctly when he said that the "bus owners union is a political organization. We have struggled to maintain a political presence; even though at times it was an anonymous presence it was always active in national politics. We are politicians and we have achieved, thanks to our organization, important posts in national politics."[3]

Yet the Alianza's growing political power also had its costs. Most notably, the Alianza's growing strength, combined with Uruchurtu's restrictions on routes and service delivery starting in 1955, exacerbated competition among bus drivers and produced serious political infighting within the urban transport industry as a whole, which included taxis, *ruleteos* (an earlier form of *pesero*, or taxi on a fixed route), and various other forms of vehicle transport, such as bus drivers not represented by the Alianza. Divisions within the Alianza had existed for years, owing to the competition for private routes and other factors. That some bus companies developed direct linkages to national (as opposed to foreign) producers of bus equipment, for example, was a source of controversy between different lines, as was the fact that some companies gave employees a greater role in management decisions.[4] These nascent conflicts between different bus operators intensified in 1957, when Uruchurtu began imposing restrictions on services that favored some lines over others.[5] The accelerating internal conflict within the urban bus industry translated into more fragmented routes and more chaotic transport service, as increasing numbers of vehicles scrambled to capture the commuter market. The unstructured routes and competition for prime locations also meant that central areas of the city, also known as the *primer cuadro* (first quadrant), had more bus routes than necessary, since this area held higher population densities and fewer residents with cars. By the early sixties, in fact, sixty-five of the ninety-one bus lines—and 4,000 of the city's 5,600 buses—traveled to the city's first quadrant.[6] In addition to producing chaos on the city's streets, one of the unfortunate consequences of these unstructured routes and competition for prime locations was a lengthening of total commuting time for daily passengers, since routes were indirect, if not circuitous, in order to maximize passenger counts.

In 1958, in order to deal with growing urban transport chaos, Mayor Uruchurtu took a decisive step toward restructuring the urban transport industry. He created the Unión de Permisionarios de Transportes de Pasajeros en Camiones y Autobuses en el Distrito Federal. The Unión de Permisionarios was a new governing body composed of representatives from the Distrito Federal and from the Alianza de Camioneros, and its principal duty was to regulate bus fares, routes, and operations. One of Uruchurtu's main objectives was to minimize competition among bus owners and thus instill order in urban transport conditions. By "rationalizing" route structures and limiting the money spent by bus riders in these chaotic commuting conditions, Uruchurtu also hoped to satisfy the city's residents, many of whom commuted daily on public transit. This was as much a concern for the city's employers as its residents, since workers' arrival times were unpredictable and the buying power of their salaries was increasingly eroded by rising fares and by the costs of riding numerous buses to reach their final destinations (this occurred frequently because many bus drivers were still independent operators, owning one or two buses at most, each of which had a distinct route).

The creation of the Unión de Permisionarios and the regulations that accompanied it brought more efficient and affordable bus service to Mexico City, and Uruchurtu received praise for reducing urban transport chaos in the capital. One commentator noted that with the introduction of the Unión de Permisionarios, the "ancient struggles among bus owners that had created anarchy in public services" were eliminated and transport conditions in the Distrito Federal were improved by 40 or 50 percent.[7] Uruchurtu's already considerable popularity was further enhanced by this policy, and it probably helps explain why—a scant few months later—he was reappointed as mayor. Yet the creation of the Unión de Permisionarios also had its downside, because it institutionalized the unparalleled political strength of the Alianza de Camioneros.

Several factors explain why the creation of the Unión de Permisionarios gave the Alianza unparalleled bargaining power. First, of course, was the fact that it now became a principal institutional player in behind-the-scenes negotiations over urban policy in Mexico City. Yet just as important was the fact that this move helped concentrate firms and capital under the umbrella of the Alianza. For example, fare and route regulations gave almost all bus drivers incentives to organize within the Alianza and remain loyal to its leadership, even those who in the past had competed with the Alianza for routes and riders, since membership in the Alianza seemed to be the best way to bargain successfully with authorities. Moreover, standardized fare regulations themselves reduced intra-industry competition and conflict. And as service became more regularized, the Alianza could claim more bargaining power with the mayor's office, which in turn further enhanced the Alianza's political strength and monopoly control over bus transport. By the late fifties the benefits were undeniable, as the Alianza became known for its capacity to concentrate capital and decision-making power in a few hands.

Like many of his political predecessors in the 1910s and 1920s who also sought to control urban transport conditions in Mexico City in order to achieve political and economic objectives, Mayor Uruchurtu's alliances with the Alianza de Camioneros helped him establish order on the streets of Mexico City, which was a high priority for residents, businesses, and party leaders, all of whom worried that services were not keeping up with the city's enormous growth and expansion. But in some ways, Uruchurtu created a monster in the process. Even though the creation of the Unión de Permisionarios brought him kudos from capital, labor, and the middle classes, the Alianza's growing institutional power in the Distrito Federal after 1958 produced new political problems for Mayor Uruchurtu. These problems involved some of his original political supporters and some of his longtime enemies. Yet Uruchurtu's troubles were due to more than the mere fact that the Alianza had inordinate political power and powerful access to the mayor to push for their own specialized demands. They also had to do with the changing social and spatial conditions in Mexico City, which increasingly pitted different groups against each other. Shifting urban transport priorities, in particular, tended to exacerbate these growing tensions and conflicts, each of which had serious implications for future trajectories of urban development in the capital.

POLITICAL GRIDLOCK OVER DOWNTOWN DEVELOPMENT

The Mayor's political problems and the growing tensions between social and class groups within Mexico City first rose to the surface in 1958 during discussion of an urban renewal proposal backed by prodevelopment forces from the Mexico City Planning Commission. The renovation was strongly supported by the Alianza and Uruchurtu. Its stated intent was to widen several of the busiest streets in the *primer cuadro*, notably Calle Tacuba and Calle Guatemala, in order to improve circulation in the central city.[8] Both the content and timing of the proposal suggest a political bargain struck by the Alianza and Uruchurtu: In exchange for concessions to the city on fare and route structures, the city offered to invest in roadway improvements. Infrastructural improvements on central city streets would facilitate vehicle mobility and the reduction of private maintenance costs, both of which had long been principal concerns of the Alianza's membership. One way that bus drivers could more easily turn a profit, especially now that the 1957 legislation so strictly regulated fares, was to complete many trips in a short period of time. Wider and well-paved streets would aid in this objective while reducing overall maintenance costs, which were greater when buses traveled on narrow, potholed surfaces. Since central city streets like Tacuba and Guatemala were both the most populated and most traveled by buses, they were a priority for roadway improvements. A second principal objective of the 1958 proposal was to "directly link the city's commercial center, its businesses, and offices" to more peripheral parts of the city to the east and west.[9] This attracted support for the proposed widening project from several large department stores and commercial establishments in the central city, which would profit from increased access to their enterprises.

Even though this proposal shared several of the principal components of a failed urban redevelopment project of 1951, it now gained support from increasingly successful large *comerciantes* in the city's center who had previously opposed such plans. This was partly due to the fact that the 1958 plan was much less comprehensive and thus less destructive than the 1951 proposal that had created such public outcry and sealed the political future of then-mayor Casas Alemán. Indeed, the 1958 proposal sought to widen only two major streets, while the 1951 proposal had been a large-scale plan for downtown redevelopment that affected almost all principal streets in the first quadrant and extended into other areas immediately surrounding the center. Yet the *comerciantes'* support for the plan is also explained partly by changes in the nature and structure of the urban economy. Many of the larger downtown *comerciantes* expressed concerns about "competition produced by the urban subcenters that sprouted up in recent years."[10] Some of these new shopping areas, especially on Avenida Insurgentes, were beginning to threaten the traditional commercial dominance of central areas because transport access was so much easier. While streets like Insurgentes offered plenty of parking spaces and relatively smooth access from numerous points in the city, conditions on central city avenues were the opposite. Streets were narrow, no parking was available, and intersections were blocked by street vendors whose ranks were swelled by steady streams of rural migrants. The fact that central streets were flooded with street vendors, or *tianguis*, also meant that central city *comerciantes* were being hurt by both blocked consumer access and stiff competition from unregulated vendors planted in front of their doors.

It appears that the larger *comerciantes*, organized within the city's powerful Cámara de Comercio (Chamber of Commerce), were most hurt by the development of new commercial subcenters, and they lent the most vocal support to the redevelopment project. According to documents gathered by Victor Manuel Villegas, they joined ranks with the property owners and real estate developers who had argued for the redevelopment plan since as early as 1951. Opposing the project were smaller and more specialized *comerciantes* in the first quadrant, who sold such products as bakery goods, shoes, paper products, fabrics, and dry goods. Of course, the residents and shopkeepers on the two streets slated for widening also opposed the project, because of the disruption they feared it would produce. Yet because the central city's smaller merchants catered mainly to local residents, they were less concerned about competition from new subcenters and vehicle access, since most of their customers arrived on foot. These smaller merchants were also more likely than large *comerciantes* to both reside in and rent their commercial spaces and thus they were also more concerned about the local effects of downtown redevelopment. Joining in opposition to the project were those who sought to facilitate the tourist industry and a growing cadre of historic preservationists, who feared the destruction of irreplaceable colonial buildings and the diminution of the city's charm if central city streets were widened. Mexico City would become, in one urbanist's words, "a replica of Houston, Dallas, or any other Texas city."[11]

Given this strong opposition to the project, Mayor Uruchurtu was caught in a difficult position. Downtown development was as politically divisive— if not more so—as it had been in the early thirties when the Planning Commission was created, or in 1952 when Uruchurtu's predecessor lost his job by promoting large-scale downtown development. Yet now the repercussions for the national economy and national political power were perhaps even greater. Uruchurtu knew the street-widening plan would appease the Alianza and larger *comerciantes*; and he considered these to be stable allies with much political and economic power. The critical role they played in service provision and in the local economy made him reluctant to alienate them or to lose their support. Uruchurtu also saw the plan as fiscally sound: He thought the project would revitalize central city commerce and valorize central city properties enough to generate more tax revenues. Nonetheless, smaller *comerciantes* and central city residents were starting to complain that Uruchurtu was abandoning his initial antidevelopment stance. They publicly claimed that Uruchurtu had promised them in 1954 that no urban redevelopment of central city areas would ever occur under his administration.[12] Thus, if Uruchurtu carried through with this new street-widening project, he would embarrass himself politically and jeopardize these critical supporters, many of whom relied on him in the absence of other local mechanisms for political participation in urban policymaking. Moreover, any decision on the project threatened to throw open the nascent divisions between *comerciantes* of different sizes and destroy the unity of one of the mayor's most critical political bases.

The involvement of historic preservationists and spokesmen for the tourist industry who opposed the demolition of historic buildings and colonial monuments in downtown areas also made the plan politically problematic for Uruchurtu. Tourism was just beginning to blossom in Mexico, taking its place as Mexico's number one earner of foreign exchange. The number of hotels, motels, and tourist boardinghouses had increased dramatically, with the supply of rooms doubling between 1954 and 1962, and with more than one-third of them located in the Distrito Federal.[13] It was in 1955, moreover, that the national government began promoting tourism and that the industry's principal lobby, the Confederación Nacional de Asociaciones de Hoteleros, was founded. If Uruchurtu carried through with the proposed project, he risked alienating powerful promoters of Mexico's growing tourist industry, of which the Alianza was one. Promoters of tourism were not inconsequential forces for the mayor to reckon with. The chief of the Departamento de Turismo, a national agency, had become publicly involved in opposing the project, suggesting that the conflict over the widening of Tacuba and Guatemala was beginning to take on national dimensions.[14] Moreover, ex-president Miguel Alemán and several other powerful Mexico City industrialists, considered members of the *Fracción de los Cuarenta*, were among the nation's most prominent investors in tourism, which in this early period was still concentrated mainly in and around Mexico City. In addition to Alemán, the names that were starting to emerge in this still nascent industry included Antonio Ruiz Galindo, founder of Grupo DESC, and Alberto Pani, who served several terms as finance minister of Mexico and who owned the Hotel Reforma in Mexico City. Because Uruchurtu still concerned himself with maintaining good political relationships with both local industrialists and Alemán (a mentor and a powerful force of conservatism within the PRI, with whom Uruchurtu still shared many ideological objectives), the mayor found it difficult to forcefully push through the project against their objections. The fact that tourism generated much taxable revenue for the city also convinced Uruchurtu of the validity of the opposition to the widening plan. After what one journalist characterized as two years of "social, political, and urban tension," Uruchurtu finally dropped the project in early 1960—with surprisingly little public fanfare, according to press accounts—and stated his intention to leave the roadway infrastructure of the area "as is."[15]

Master politician that he was, however, Uruchurtu still attempted to appease the conflicting urban forces and rationalize transport at the same time. But instead of widening the streets, he introduced new regulations that rid Tacuba and several other central city areas of all street vendors and *tianguis*.[16] This move was one of the few available to him if he wished to facilitate bus transport on central city streets without disturbing existing buildings or residential and commercial patterns.

Although these actions would cause him serious problems in the future with the poorest of the poor—and with their advocates within the PRI—

they sufficed for now to restore Uruchurtu's popularity. Meanwhile, Mayor Uruchurtu reorganized the Oficina de Mercados and ordered the construction of new markets in more distant areas that could house the smaller and less profitable *comerciantes*, thereby leaving the space and the incentive for larger *comerciantes* to work on redeveloping the attractiveness of the much-maligned central city areas. In the nine years between 1958 and 1967, in fact, Uruchurtu was reported to have built a new market every month; his administration was credited with the construction of such important markets as La Merced, La Viga, Jamaica, La Lagunilla, and San Juan.[17]

Uruchurtu's new restrictions on street vendors and his support for the construction of new local markets were urban policy solutions that would win the approval of several of his longtime constituents: *comerciantes*, both large and small, central city residents, and now the urban bus industry. Of all the forces pushing the Tacuba widening project, it was only real estate speculators whose demands for a more substantive central city redevelopment plan remained unmet. Yet despite his skills in forging this compromise, Uruchurtu's decision to table the central city redevelopment project and to introduce new urban policies to clear the streets and relocate smaller *comerciantes* neither ended all his political troubles nor fully resolved the issues of central city development. Changes in the local and national economy continued to generate support for changes in downtown land use and transport access in the late fifties and early sixties. Mexico City continued to grow, downtown streets became more populated, and large *comerciantes* saw their position slipping even more. Real estate developers soon began to lobby for new redevelopment plans, local residents continued to oppose them, and Uruchurtu found it increasingly difficult to balance different class and urban interests as the city's population grew by leaps and bounds. As a consequence, what loomed on the horizon was something far more threatening: a proposal to develop a subway for downtown Mexico City.

FROM STREET WIDENING TO UNDERGROUND SUBWAY

Unlike the proposed Tacuba widening, the new plan for a subway that captured developers' attention in 1960 was not formally initiated by Uruchurtu, but rather by one of Mexico's most powerful and accomplished engineering conglomerates, the Mexico City–based Ingenieros Civiles Asociados (ICA).[18] The proposal for a subway appeared to be a long shot. Back in 1952, engineers and urban planners had toyed with the idea of building an underground transport system in Mexico City, but had questioned, and all but discarded,

Downtown Mexico City

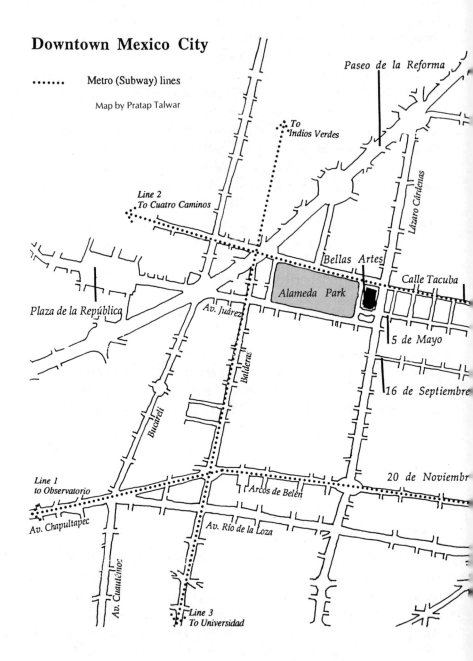

.... Metro (Subway) lines

Map by Pratap Talwar

Paseo de la Reforma

To Indios Verdes

Line 2
To Cuatro Caminos

Lázaro Cárdenas

Bellas Artes

Calle Tacuba

Alameda Park

Plaza de la República

Av. Juárez

5 de Mayo

Balderas

16 de Septiembre

Bucareli

Line 1
to Observatorio

20 de Noviembr

Arcos de Belén

Av. Chapultapec

Av. Río de la Loza

Av. Cuauhtémoc

Line 3
To Universidad

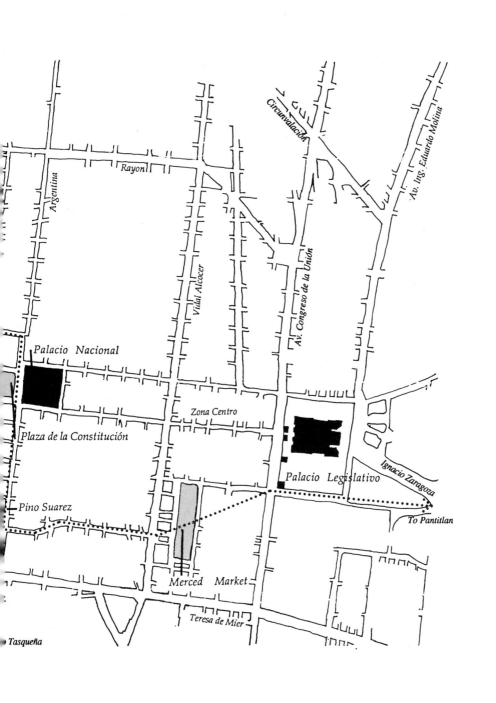

Rayon

Argentina

Vidal Alcocer

Circunvalación

Av. Congreso de la Unión

Av. Ing. Eduardo Molina

Palacio Nacional

Zona Centro

Plaza de la Constitución

Palacio Legislativo

Ignacio Zaragoza

Pino Suarez

To Pantitlan

Merced Market

Teresa de Mier

Tasqueña

its utility. The feasibility of subway construction was determined unlikely not only because Mexico City's subsoil was so precarious, given its high water content, but also because the technology—which would have to be imported—was inordinately expensive. Technicians at ICA were not daunted by such considerations. In 1958, the same year the Tacuba widening controversy developed, ICA initiated a project to review the world's subway systems and to consider development of a mass rapid transit system for Mexico City. By early 1960, when the street-widening plan was gasping its last breath, ICA stood poised and ready to sell Mexico City's mayor on the idea. The company's position as the most experienced engineering and construction firm in Mexico ensured that the subway project would be taken seriously by many in both government and the private sector. Indeed, ICA's stellar reputation lent it no small amount of political capital in promoting the subway project and bringing allies to its side. So too did the fact that its employees had made clear inroads in government agencies contracting major infrastructural works. Many members of ICA, in fact, became high government officials; and there have been many others who, according to ICA's founder Bernardo Quintana, "have held positions of less visibility but of much utility" in agencies charged with administering urban and national infrastructure.[19] Thus if any local firm could push through a plan for developing and constructing a subway in Mexico City, it was ICA.

The firm's desire to surpass technological frontiers within the subsoil engineering field and highlight its own skills and expertise partially explains ICA's strong support for the project. Many of Mexico's engineers had doubted that a subway could ever be built in Mexico City, an active earthquake zone with high water content, so for ICA to successfully pull off the subway project would—and in fact did—bring admiration from the international engineering community. However, as one savvy commentator noted, "man is not necessarily interested in undertaking everything that is technically possible," and thus it was "not the technical possibility or impossibility of excavating a network of underground tunnels in the city" that determined ICA's decision to study and ultimately propose the METRO project.[20] Rather, ICA was smart enough to see that many powerful forces supported efforts to redevelop downtown and to facilitate urban transport access to central areas. The company also recognized that two of the major obstacles to past redevelopment plans (both the 1951 and 1958 projects) had been the threatened destruction of old buildings and the threat of massive displacement of the city center's residents. If a redevelopment plan could proceed without destruction of Mexico City's historic facades and without displacement of its most prominent commercial enterprises, the chances for successful implementation were much greater.

A subway seemed to cover all the bases. Because it would be constructed underground, it would boost land values and bring smooth access to central city enterprises without destroying buildings. In the words of one Mexican urbanist who supported the project, moreover, it would aid in transforming the center into "a commercial and banking zone of the highest value and in displacing 'dirty commerce' and second class offices and commercial establishments now housed in buildings in the center."[21] This new metropolitan subway system, to be known as the METRO, would be the "first step [in] remodeling the old commercial center of the city,"[22] because the subway would link outlying areas to central ones much more efficiently than would other modes of transport. It would also help Mexico City achieve what was then considered a principal objective: the "simultaneous decentralization and revitalization of [the] old center[s]."[23] Many of the METRO's supporters hoped it would help restructure old and so-called inefficient patterns of land usage, and transform the city's center into an area of high-density usage. With the markedly higher land values the subway was expected to generate, the small-scale shops and factories of the center would be forced to relocate. Developers then hoped to replace them with larger commercial and banking enterprises willing to pay higher rents in order to secure centralized access to surrounding areas, access that would be facilitated by mass rapid transit linking surrounding areas to the center. The increased land values would also help push longtime residents out of central areas, thereby allowing the demolition of low-density residential buildings and their replacement by high-rises, facilitating greater density downtown.

Yet ICA was not necessarily the innocent bystander in proposing what it argued to be a technological solution to the growing controversy over central city redevelopment that had dominated Uruchurtu's policy docket during the fifties.[24] In fact, much of ICA's desire—and political capacity—to push through the subway project was traceable to its own economic interests. The subway project held the potential to be a gold mine for ICA, given its status as a huge vertically integrated conglomerate comprising multiple divisions that conceivably would undertake construction, electromechanical installation, track laying, and civil works for the subway.[25] The engineering firm was not a disinterested party when it came to land valorization and urban redevelopment for Mexico City, either. Even though ICA was founded as a construction firm, it quickly expanded and diversified to include both heavy equipment production and the promotion and management of multiple investments in residential and industrial developments. Its direct involvement with real estate began scarcely a year after its inception and the receipt of its first major construction contract in the late forties. Since the fifties, ICA's own banking institution, the Banco del Atlántico, had been Mexico City's most prominent participant in real estate development.[26] It should be no surprise that the president of the Cámara de Comercio, which so actively promoted central city redevelopment in the late fifties and early sixties and which came out strongly in support of the widening of Tacuba and Guatemala, was Carlos Abedrop Dávila, a prominent member of ICA.[27] In fact, many of ICA's activities were considered innovative in the real estate and urban development fields: ICA promoted and constructed Mexico's first satellite city (Ciudad Satélite), located on a highway circling Mexico City and linking downtown areas to the nearby state of Mexico. The company was also "the initial promoter of condominiums" in Mexico and developer of "diverse residential suburbs and creat[or] of numerous industrial parks" in various areas within and surrounding Mexico City.[28] By the mid-sixties, in fact, ICA was beginning to locate condominiums in prime real estate sections of both Mexico City and the provinces, including Reforma-Manchester, Colon, and Satélite, and the Costero in Acapulco, to name a few. Some of its best-known real estate developments include Navarte, an upper-middle-class residential development in a south-central area of the state of Mexico, Taxqueña, and Tlatelolco.

OPPOSITION FROM URUCHURTU

With ICA's prominence and power, as well as its skillful timing and project conceptualization, many thought that the subway was a foregone conclusion. Yet Mayor Uruchurtu was far from convinced that Mexico City should construct an underground rapid transit system. For close to six years, until November 1966, Uruchurtu successfully kept debate over the subway off the Distrito Federal policy docket and out of sight, even as ICA and other powerful political forces struggled hard to introduce the project. That Uruchurtu opposed the subway project so vehemently, and was relatively successful in doing so, is striking on two counts. First, big-city mayors rarely oppose massive infrastructural projects like subways because of all the attention and glory they generally bring. The fact that Uruchurtu was so strongly opposed to the METRO project calls into question that long-standing logic and suggests that something much more complex than his own fame was behind Uruchurtu's stance on the subway. Second, and more critical for our understanding of local and national political tensions and changes in Mexico during the late fifties and early sixties, Uruchurtu successfully kept the METRO project off the Distrito Federal policy docket even after Mexico's president, Gustavo Díaz Ordaz (1964–1970), identified himself as a principal proponent of the METRO and publicly announced his full support for the project. This sequence of events challenges scholars' arguments that Mexico's system of "presidentialism" gives the president almost total control over major policy decisions; it also calls into question well-worn arguments that the policy concerns of big capital generally prevail in Mexico. Conversely, it suggests that those who opposed the METRO, like Uruchurtu, had a powerful political basis for derailing the project.

So why did Uruchurtu oppose the subway, and why was he able to hold out so long against the wishes of Mexico's president? The answer lies in a recognition of the significance of the METRO project for Mexico City's built environment, for its future growth, and for the political balance between the city's residents so carefully nurtured by Uruchurtu. The METRO threatened to blow apart the working coalition of downtown residents, small industrialists, bus drivers, and shopkeepers that acted as Uruchurtu's principal political base of support and upon whom the party had depended for past political successes. By transforming the character of the city, and privileging certain political coalitions and class factions over others, the METRO project held the potential to destroy the precarious balance that Uruchurtu had so skillfully managed in Mexico City. This in turn threatened to make Mexico City politically unmanageable, an outcome that could have devastating repercussions for both Uruchurtu and national politics.

From Uruchurtu's vantage point, the METRO would unbalance the Mexico City governing coalition and affect its spatial future in several ways. First, it was obvious to Uruchurtu that mass rapid transit would directly challenge the livelihood of the urban bus industry, with whom he had worked closely over the previous fourteen years. The METRO would eat into the ridership that the Alianza de Camioneros depended upon for its livelihood, and the proposed location would prevent bus owners from routing their buses into central areas. This would be a mortal blow to the Alianza, since it was by traversing central city streets that the urban bus industry maximized its passenger loads and total revenues. If the project was implemented and private buses had to compete with government-provided subway service, moreover, the political monopoly the Alianza and its top leaders held over transport conditions might also be in question.

This is not to say that Uruchurtu's opposition to the subway project owed solely to his ties with the Alianza, even though the bus monopoly was on record as opposing the subway.[29] Indeed, Uruchurtu's earlier acts to municipalize trolleys and to extend trolley services demonstrated that he was perfectly capable of implementing new transport policies that negatively affected the urban bus industry—in some limited way—when he felt they were necessary. In the case of the METRO, however, Uruchurtu was not convinced that such actions were necessary or that the capital needed a subway. Mexico City already had an extensive network of trolleys that was still operating and that linked several critical peripheral areas to the center. Equally important, the Alianza de Camioneros already provided comprehensive urban transport services, and because buses were privately owned, these services cost the city hardly a penny. This meant that the Distrito Federal did not have to spend scarce resources earmarked for other critical urban infrastructural necessities on public transport provision.

Cost, in fact, was one of Uruchurtu's primary concerns in opposing the METRO, and for good reason. Since it would have to be publicly provided with enormous government investments in infrastructure and technology, the METRO would be a huge drain on the city's budget, which Uruchurtu had worked so skillfully to balance. Estimates presented in the official feasibility report produced by ICA indicate that even with substantial amounts of foreign lending, estimated to be almost 1.5 billion pesos, the proposed costs to be borne by the Distrito Federal for construction of the METRO would be 900 million pesos (almost three-quarters of the 1,400-million-pesos yearly budget of the Distrito Federal in 1964); and yearly maintenance and operation costs were expected to reach close to 136 million pesos.

Given these projections, in fact, Uruchurtu usually couched his opposition to the project in financial terms. As early as 1962, when the subway was not yet being discussed publicly, Uruchurtu made a veiled reference to the inordinate costs of mass rapid transit and boasted publicly that he would not leave "a single cent" of debt on the Distrito Federal's books at the end of his term.[30] Several months later, Uruchurtu openly underscored his opposition, once again, in direct response to an offer by the director of Paris's municipal transport agency to send French technicians from the Paris Metro—ostensibly to "determine whether it was feasible to construct an underground train in Mexico City."[31]

As pressure for the project mounted, Uruchurtu held firm and continued to argue that the costs of the proposed subway made it unrealizable.[32] Even after the French ambassador publicly claimed that "a consortium of [French] industrialists and investors [was] ready to channel the necessary money" for a subway to Mexico City, Uruchurtu still refused to budge, arguing that foreign borrowing would be especially disastrous to the city's fiscal solvency.[33] To add weight to his argument, Uruchurtu claimed that the METRO would not necessarily improve transport conditions, at least in an amount equal to these overwhelming costs; and to bring this point home to the city's citizens,

Uruchurtu frequently insisted that the subway's presence would raise the costs of daily transport.[34]

To the extent that Uruchurtu saw the subway's capacity to speed the length of daily commutes as being outweighed by its enormous costs, he really had very little reason to support the project. The only remaining advantage of the METRO would have been its contribution to downtown development and its potential to facilitate rapid and dispersed urban growth; yet these features hardly brought Uruchurtu to the side of subway proponents. As most of his past actions indicated, Uruchurtu was generally unsympathetic toward downtown redevelopment, given his strong political connections with small businesses, *comerciantes*, and middle-class residents in central areas who for years had fought against such urban renewal projects. Even before the METRO project was a possibility, Uruchurtu had publicly expressed concern about Mexico City's rapid and uncontrolled urban growth. By the time the METRO project was presented as a serious possibility, Uruchurtu's opposition was even more vehement.

In chronicling the most serious problems of Mexico City in 1963, and why a subway was a disastrous alternative, Uruchurtu decried the city's "gigantismo metropolitano" and "macrocefalia capitalina," and openly lamented the monstrosity that his beloved Mexico City had become.[35] Uruchurtu saw the subway project as facilitating what he called an unfortunate madness, and as siphoning needed resources away from more pressing social problems. His preferred policy stance, at least in public accounts, was to invest those massive resources in rural areas, so that the masses of rural-urban migrants would not fuel the city's demographic explosion. Like many of the city's residents, Uruchurtu blamed the streaming masses of poor uneducated migrants—many of them of Indian heritage—for the physical and social destruction of the city. To limit urban growth, either by keeping these migrants in rural areas or by preventing their permanent settlement in the city, would be to keep Mexico City as the glorious old middle-class city that he remembered.

FIGHTING AGAINST UNCONTROLLED URBAN GROWTH: THE TIES THAT BIND

Uruchurtu's concerns about rapid urban growth were much more than the backdrop for his opposition to the METRO, however. They were the common thread that united his political supporters and that lent coherence to most of his urban policy stances, from opposition to land regularization to restrictions on street vending to rejection of the METRO project. The urban bus industry, for example, feared that rapid urban growth would reduce their profit-making potential. As the city grew outward, it became difficult for bus companies to offer service that was both profitable and comprehensive enough to meet the Unión de Permisionarios' demands for low-cost yet extensive public service. The more dispersed the population settlements, the less likely that maximum ridership rates on buses could be assured, since the volume of passengers declined in peripheral areas. It was through packing passengers into crowded vehicles that the bus companies maintained their profit margins. If the average daily trip was longer and more treacherous, as would be the case if populations settled in underserviced areas in the periphery, companies would have to devote greater revenues to maintenance. Of course, lower passenger density rates and additional maintenanc.; costs could be recouped with a rise in fares; yet both the Unión de Permisionarios and the public struggled to keep fares low, and Uruchurtu willingly obliged, given his constituency. Accordingly, urban growth would tip the delicate balance that Uruchurtu and the Alianza had negotiated over the efficient and affordable provision of urban transport. And if the city burst beyond its formal bounds, the Alianza would lose its monopoly control over urban transport in the capital. Unlimited urban growth meant that bus companies in the state of Mexico (which surrounds the Distrito Federal) might have an entry into urban transport service provision, because greater and greater numbers of passenger trips would originate there. This was of particularly great concern to the Alianza because it had long been under attack by bus companies in the state of Mexico and other surrounding regions who hoped to break into the Distrito Federal market, but had been blocked by the Alianza's growing political power and ability to monopolize urban transport services.

To complicate matters, both Uruchurtu and the Alianza feared that to push beyond the city's formal bounds would be to open a Pandora's box of political problems that neither wished to confront. In addition to the jurisdictional struggles that were bound to emerge in the process of regulating cross-boundary transport, intersectoral struggles within the PRI would be pushed to the surface. For years, the labor sector (CTM) had tried to organize bus drivers in the state of Mexico in order to challenge the questionable labor practices and monopoly rule of the Alianza, which was affiliated with the popular middle-class sector (CNOP). To give bus drivers from the state of Mexico an entrée into Mexico City transport would be to fan this low-grade fire of CTM-CNOP tensions into a full blaze.

Many of the city's urban middle classes also had good reasons to be wary of the subway project and the urban growth and redevelopment it presupposed.

Any urban growth facilitated by the subway was expected to manifest itself in both dispersion and densification; thus it would negatively affect housing costs, commuting times, and land usage. If people and housing were forced to the periphery by rising land prices in downtown areas near subway lines, both resident and government concerns about automobile traffic would increase. All residents, of course, would be affected in one way or another by longer journeys to work and by rising shelter costs associated with a reheated urban land market. Yet the middle classes had a particular worry in addition to these general concerns: Urban growth challenged their historical patterns of location in the more central areas of the city; thus they faced a change in lifestyle that had a social as well as spatial meaning. Today, of course, it is difficult to consider the problems of central city Mexico as problems of the middle class. Our images of downtown streets and central city barrios like Tepito, studied by Susan Eckstein in *The Poverty of Revolution*, hardly suggest a middle-class lifestyle, especially to the foreign eye. People crowd into small units with crumbling walls and the most rudimentary of water and drainage infrastructure, downtown streets are filled with vendors and the urban poor, and residential subdivisions in far southern and northern areas are home to many of the city's professionals, bureaucrats, and white-collar office employees. But in the fifties and sixties, shopping areas near the central plaza and older residential sections less than a few miles away, like Colonia Roma and Colonia Condesa, had a different feel and identity, and the economic base and class structure of Mexico City was such that these old, downtown neighborhoods were indeed the residence for much of the city's traditional middle classes, such as small businessmen, shopkeepers, government employees, and clerical and service workers. Today, of course, we might consider owners of small shops and firms in these central areas, whose profits are clearly marginal, as the lower middle class or even the urban poor. But in earlier decades, these groups were relatively privileged compared to new migrants, industrial workers, and many others, and they proudly saw themselves as constituting the social and cultural middle-class foundation of Mexican society.

The growth of the capital during the forties and fifties had already made it difficult for many of the city's traditional middle classes to live in central areas, especially as the property market put pressure on many to convert large houses into offices and commercial holdings. According to Oliver Oldman and his colleagues, massive rural migration to the capital had raised the concentration of low-income groups in the core city and led to increased welfare and public expenditures.[36] Central areas of the city were invaded by the poorest of the poor, who lived in subdivided houses now called *tugurios* and who frequently resorted to street vending and other informal sector livelihoods. The middle class, accordingly, found densities rising, local conditions deteriorating, and their neighborhoods changing rapidly before their eyes, the unwanted fruit of the PRI's earlier successes in forging the capital-labor-state alliance in Mexico City. As such, downtown residents worried that continued urban growth would destroy the social fabric of their community and their cultural identity even more than had already occurred. And the subway project in particular, by transforming downtown land usage and extending the city in space, further threatened to speed that process.

Uruchurtu tried to deal with many of the urban middle classes' concerns in this regard by placing restrictions on street vendors and by politically supporting the construction of a few selected housing estates for middle classes in central areas (like the Nonoalco-Tlatelolco housing project, which was completed in 1964). Some of the traditional character of the city in fact, was saved by his efforts; and as recently as 1965 more than 60 percent of the residents of Mexico City's *primer cuadro* also worked there, in government offices, shops, and commerce.[37] Yet Uruchurtu could not stem the tide enough to fully eliminate middle-class concerns. Given the scarcity of vacant land downtown, most new housing for middle classes tended to be in subdivisions outside central areas, away from relatives and essential services, and away from the bustling life and fond memories of *el centro*. Clearly, the greatest problems facing the city's traditional middle classes were the metropolitan area's rapid urban growth, its steady stream of rural-urban migration, and their impact on daily life in the city's core.

In seeking to accommodate middle-class concerns about the city's growth and character, Uruchurtu turned to one other critical political base, Mexico City's small and medium-sized industrialists, who rounded out a loosely defined petit bourgeois coalition of forces against urban growth in general and the METRO in particular. By the late 1950s, local industrialists also had begun to express public concern about the city's transformation. Rising rents in central city areas and decades of urban growth changed the character of Mexico City. Small family firms and light industrial workshops were bought out by big landowners, and downtown areas became the home of several modern buildings as well as "new types of businesses, primarily large department stores . . . and banking institutions."[38] This turnover in ownership and land use put pressures on traditional industries (*talleres* and *fábricas pequeñas*) to move out to more peripheral locations. By transforming the residential structure of the central city, it also made it increasingly difficult for these smaller factories and workshops to survive if they did stay, since they relied on local labor— often even family members and neighbors—for production. These small and medium-sized industrialists were concerned about urban growth and the land use transformations it wrought, a position that is clear in the statements of the CANACINTRA, the Mexico City–based organization that represented them. As early as 1958, the CANACINTRA published a position paper on the need for controlling growth in the Distrito Federal. The CANACINTRA's leaders called for an "industrial location policy that would modify the tendency of geographic concentration" in Mexico City, that would not "displace or close established industries" there, and would continue to prioritize local labor absorption and production of consumer goods over capital-intensive or exporting industries.[39] And as the CANACINTRA argued for strict regulations on new industrial location in the capital, as well as for active efforts to implement industrial decentralization, Uruchurtu willingly complied. As late as 1964, the CANACINTRA and Uruchurtu publicly "agreed that not one more industry should be established in the [Distrito Federal]."[40]

In the growing controversy over the subway project, then, positions taken reflected political alliances loosely formed around the issue of urban growth. In one corner, arguing the subway's fiscal inappropriateness, extravagance, and disruptive potential, stood Mayor Uruchurtu and his allies: the urban bus industry, small industrialists and shopkeepers, and many of the city's traditional middle classes. In the other corner, the ICA loomed large, armed with confidence, foreign financing, and ideologically compelling arguments about bringing Mexico City into the ranks of the world's most modern cities by facilitating its growth and high-rise development. In the first rounds, who would triumph and why was not apparent, and the significance of the fight remained obscure. But as the controversy dragged on throughout the first half of the 1960s, the conflict took on greater meaning, not only because it lasted so long, but because new forces and changing economic conditions altered the nature and terms of the conflict. Cheering on the fight was a class of large capitalists whose activities depended on urban growth and redevelopment, joined by powerful party leaders willing to challenge Uruchurtu's antigrowth stance and single-handed control of the capital city. On the other side of the ring, however, even greater numbers of the city's middle classes lent support to the underdog, Uruchurtu.

If we analyze different positions on the METRO project and the different actors involved in the early and mid sixties, it becomes clear that the controversy over the METRO was not just any old conflict over urban transport policy. It was a struggle over Mexico City's character, over the place and power of middle classes in local and national politics, and over the urban and industrial future of the nation. Whether Mexico City would continue on a path of rapid and uncontrolled urban growth depended largely on its capacity to expand in space and on the possibilities for central city land use transformation, both of which would be facilitated by the introduction of mass rapid transit. And whether or not Mexico City continued to grow had implications for the balance of social and class power within the incorporated political system, particularly if metropolitan growth continued to swell the ranks of the urban popular sectors. Accordingly, the METRO project was at the center of a struggle over the nature and direction of politics and the economy, both local and national.

If Mexico City's downtown areas were transformed and if the city expanded, shopkeepers, small industrialists, and many of the city's traditional middle classes could lose their livelihoods. They also would be faced with clear evidence that their political demands played second fiddle to those of big developers, large industrialists, and tourist promoters who supported the subway. On the other hand, if the political will of these petit bourgeois and middle-class sectors prevailed, and the METRO project was cast aside, Mexico City would be more apt to keep its old colonial character: crowded streets, low-density use of central city lands, and a mixture of small shops and residences in downtown's prime areas. Valorization of the land market would not occur, and real estate developers and finance capitalists would be forced to seek other outlets for investment besides the built environment of Mexico City. Either option had direct implications for the sectoral composition and nature of both the local and national economy, as well as for the functioning of the incorporated political system.

To the extent that the METRO project embodied both political and economic concerns, its proposal split the PRI and pitted capitalist against capitalist and middle classes against others in ways that had not been seen in Mexico before. The METRO project, in short, presented the ruling party with a series of difficult questions that it had managed to avoid during the previous two decades when the euphoria of rapid industrial growth and the promise of local prosperity prevailed. Would Mexico move from a postcolonial economy based on services and the activities of small-scale capitalists to a "modern" one run by large industrialists and finance capitalists? Would Mexico's incorporated system offer avenues of political participation for traditional sectors of the middle class, or would their political demands be secondary to those of big capital, or even labor? Would the central government continue to dominate Mexico City decision making, or would local constituencies and political actors be allowed political participation in the determination of their own futures?

MEXICO'S ECONOMY IN THE EARLY 1960S:
THE CITY AS A GROWTH MACHINE

To understand the controversy over the city and the subway, as well as the conflicts between local officials and the national government, we must look at stabilizing development and other macroeconomic policies introduced to fuel the national economy. By the early 1960s, economic changes associated with the introduction of stabilizing development in 1955 had begun to create serious divisions among Mexico's industrial capitalists on the basis of size, activity, and location. Stabilizing development, as national macroeconomic policy, relied primarily on financial intermediation to finance growth; and one of the prime beneficiaries of this development strategy, to the disadvantage of other sectors, was the banking sector. The expansion of the financial sector was accompanied by an accelerated economic concentration, as groups linked to financial institutions began to dominate more sectors of the economy, while other groups weakened accordingly.[41] As a result, large internationally linked firms with access to their own financial institutions prospered, while smaller industrial firms that were not linked to financial institutions became increasingly disadvantaged.

These macroeconomic changes were manifest in spatial organization as well. As larger, internationally linked firms prospered, they diversified activities and grew in size. As a result, starting in the late fifties and early sixties, industries accelerated their flight from the jurisdictional confines of the Distrito Federal in search of new locations where land for industrial plant expansion was available.[42] This meant that their urban concerns and demands differed increasingly from smaller firms remaining in Mexico City, who relied on local services and a local labor force to maintain profitability. Different-sized firms were not simply differentially located in space. Their relationships to space also differed. Smaller industrial firms rented—and much less frequently, owned—the land they used for productive activities. When small shops and firms owned their own property, it was generally for use value, not exchange value. Yet larger capitalists, particularly those connected with financial capital, often used space to generate profits, too. They either rented out choice central locations or speculated in real estate. They located their own plants in entirely different areas of the metropolitan region. The result was a growing antagonism between industrialists and capitalists who profited from land speculation in the capital and those smaller industrialists and shopkeepers who were hurt by it.

Accelerated investment in land and real estate development occurred because increased capital liquidity associated with the expansion of the banking sector meant that new sources for investment had to be found. This was particularly the case as problems with the internal market and international competitiveness made many activities in the highly protected national manufacturing sector unattractive for new investment. In contrast, property development was a safe bet. Clark Reynolds argues elsewhere that macroeconomic policies introduced in the late fifties and early sixties were a principal determinant of excessive urban concentration. He supports this claim by showing that investment in land speculation and development in Mexico City increased dramatically after the introduction of stabilizing development.[43] His statements are well corroborated by the independent findings of other scholars. Oliver Oldman found that by the early sixties, the "real estate market acted as a partial substitute for weak capital markets . . . [with] the immediate result . . . an upsurge of real estate speculation."[44] In the five-year period immediately after stabilizing development was introduced (1958–1963), commercial rents in Mexico City rose approximately 200 to 300 percent.[45] And the activities of several other principal industrial groups in Mexico support the contention that large industries tended to invest heavily in real estate development during the early sixties. According to Marta Schteingart Kaplan, who has conducted extensive research on the subject, Grupo DESC, Grupo Industria y Comercio, and Grupo Banamex were among the most prominent industrial firms that poured massive monies into real estate speculation, in addition to ICA's own Banco del Atlántico. She also identifies Grupo VISA, which in the early 1960s was still part of Grupo Cuauhtémoc-Hylsa, and Grupo Bancomer as heavily involved in real estate development.[46]

These economic developments had political as well as spatial consequences. Business lobbying organizations changed their character as larger industrial firms became more involved in real estate development and cultivated more open relationships with foreign investors. The CONCAMIN had become increasingly identified with the grand bourgeoisie "allied with foreign capital" and with bankers and large commerce.[47] In contrast, smaller industrial firms without banking institutions or international connections continued to turn to the CANACINTRA, which was strongly allied to Uruchurtu. Thus, the fact that in the early sixties the CANACINTRA began to argue vehemently against excessive foreign penetration of the economy and supported the state's role as a "substitute for foreign capital" is largely attributable to changing macroeconomic conditions, which further compelled small industrialists to join with Uruchurtu and sustain the antiurban growth stance. Political differences between industries of different sizes were exacerbated by the fact that smaller firms had little political clout on their own, and thus they became more dependent on political organizations like the CANACINTRA to protect their interests in the urban domain. Larger firms were much more politically autonomous, mainly because they tended to participate in large *grupos*, or huge conglomerates, that moved massive amounts of capital and sometimes controlled entire sectors. Because of their interlocking relationships, larger firms also relied on an entire network of business organizations allied with each other, specifically the CONCAMIN, the CONCANACO, and the Asociación de Banqueros Mexicanos (ABM).

Both of these factors gave larger industrial firms and their lobbying organizations, like the CONCAMIN and even the ABM, increased political influence with the ruling party leadership. The CANACINTRA, in contrast, now found its privileged political status and unparalleled political power in jeopardy. The result: The CANACINTRA and its constituents placed even greater faith in Uruchurtu and his capacity to control urban development policy in Mexico City, one of the few domains in which they still held sway.

The growing tensions between industries of different sizes made serious political waves within the PRI in the debate over which presidential candidate would follow López Mateos in 1964. The outcome of this election would not only determine Mexico City's developmental future; it was also expected to determine the political power of these competing factions of industrialists, which had clear implications for Mexico City's future. Bertha Lerner and Susana Ralsky argue that Miguel Alemán staked a claim in this conflict from early on. Still considered a spokesman for more nationalist industrialists, Alemán supported Antonio Ortíz Mena for president. Ortíz Mena was best known then as the originator of the stabilizing development strategy. Alemán believed that, as president, Ortíz Mena would maintain a balance among industrialists of all sizes, protect Mexican industry against excessive foreign competition, and continue the state's role in financing industrial development without overly privileging large firms and their speculative practices.

Despite Alemán's unparalleled power within the PRI, the position he and Ortíz Mena represented was neither desired nor accepted by everyone. Larger, internationally linked industrialists were developing access to their own resources, either from abroad or in their own financial institutions, and they sought greater liberalization of the Mexican economy and less protection of smaller, unproductive industries. They neither shared Alemán's development priorities nor his support of Ortíz Mena. In the conflict that ensued, Gustavo Díaz Ordaz emerged as the presidential candidate most connected to these financial and internationally linked sectors of industrialists.[48] In turn, Díaz Ordaz carried the banner of a more "modern" and internationalist Mexico. He called for a break from past practices of protectionism on behalf of inefficient and uncompetitive firms, sought support for Mexico's banking sector and its strongest industries, and proposed a new modern infrastructure—mainly urban—to propel Mexico into the twenty-first century.

With two candidates representing different positions on Mexico's future, each backed by political supporters wielding substantial political power, the party was divided. One way to appease both factions was to ensure that both policy positions were represented in the new cabinet. Thus, although Díaz Ordaz successfully captured the presidential nomination, Uruchurtu was re-appointed as mayor for yet a third term, in what most saw as a concession to Alemán's allies. Yet with different ideological and class-based factions of the ruling party in control of the urban and national domains, the PRI was in for rocky times. The Mexico City subway project, which had been causing political tensions between Uruchurtu and developers ever since its proposal in 1962, quickly rose to the surface as both the source and the symbol of this growing intraparty conflict. With both Uruchurtu and Díaz Ordaz identifying the METRO as critical to their political bases and developmentalist vision, the battle had begun; and though the project was a purely "local" one with direct implications for the city's urban development, the stakes and the players were clearly national.

THE MAYOR AND THE PRESIDENT AT LOGGERHEADS

As the new administration began, Uruchurtu's opposition to the METRO and his ability to push that position through control of the mayor's office very quickly became Díaz Ordaz's cross to bear. One of the first projects that Díaz Ordaz publicly supported was the METRO. His position was grounded not only in his strong personal and political ties to ICA,[49] but also in the exigencies of the moment. When he assumed the presidency in December 1964, Díaz Ordaz was under pressure from land developers and tourism promoters to move forward with the METRO project, especially after Mexico signed a contract in 1964 to host the 1968 Olympics. Many argued that the METRO would help ensure the Olympics' success, elevate Mexico's international prestige, and showcase the capital city as a tourist destination. A modern subway project would facilitate urban transport for visitors to the city's downtown tourist sites; equally important, when cameras were focused on the Olympic Games, the world would see that Mexico, the first developing country ever to host the Olympics, deserved the honor. Indeed, with a gleaming new METRO, Mexico's capital city could justifiably be considered among the ranks of the world's greatest cities—a claim made in ICA's feasibility report for the subway. Equally important, Díaz Ordaz's position on the METRO was grounded in strong national support for urban growth and redevelopment, which both he and his political allies saw as important for the national economy. Yet Uruchurtu still stood firm in his opposition to the project; and when behind-the-scenes negotiations did not end the stalemate, the battle went public.

The first sign of open antagonism between Díaz Ordaz and Uruchurtu came in January 1965, scarcely a month after entering office, when the new president started what one newspaper commentator called an "unjustly aggressive campaign [against Uruchurtu], carried out by certain others within the Distrito Federal itself, in the banks and in the corridors of the Chamber of Deputies, as well as in the public sphere and through the writings of journalists." [50] Throughout the first several months of 1965, Díaz Ordaz released public statements about the necessity of the METRO for the Olympics, and he publicly blamed Uruchurtu for urban problems that might ruin the Olympic Games. In one such announcement, Díaz Ordaz stated that a subway was necessary to ensure the smooth operation of the Olympics and that "Uruchurtu . . . would be responsible for the role that Mexico would play in the Olympic Games." [51] By tying chaotic transport conditions to the Olympics' success or failure, and by identifying Uruchurtu as responsible for both, Díaz Ordaz tried to cultivate the seeds of public opposition to Uruchurtu and his anti-METRO stance. He gambled that even Uruchurtu's middle-class supporters would be unwilling to support a mayor who might disgrace Mexico when world attention was fixed on the Olympics.

Díaz Ordaz took no chances with public opinion. By September 1965, Díaz Ordaz was publicly blaming Uruchurtu for all the city's current maladies, including the rising cost of meat in the city, urban poverty in numerous neighborhoods circling the capital, delays in urban transport, the housing shortage facing city residents, and even the failure of Mexico's national soccer team. Díaz Ordaz's intent, in short, was to make Uruchurtu "the object of a most vicious political campaign . . . directed at deteriorating his prestige and popularity." [52] Felling Uruchurtu was not easy, given the popular mayor's as yet untarnished reputation as one of Mexico City's most accomplished public servants. Yet the more obstinately Uruchurtu opposed the METRO project, the greater the stakes for Díaz Ordaz, and the more he struggled. If Uruchurtu's intransigence continued unabated, the starting date of the project would be delayed, and this would mean an irreparable loss of political and public support for the METRO, since many of the arguments for the project revolved around its importance to the 1968 Olympics. So when Uruchurtu refused to budge, even after several months of leaks to the press about the mayor's bullheadedness, Díaz Ordaz began to rally support for his position within the party and the private sector.

The first signs of war appeared in July 1965, when one popular periodical claimed that "it was thought and is rumored with insistence that there was a distancing between Mayor Uruchurtu and the Deputies of the Distrito Federal."[53] In August 1965, Uruchurtu was openly "censure[d] by real estate developers . . . and public functionaries."[54] As a result, the mayor's problems quickly multiplied. Scarcely three months later, in November 1965, leftist and rightist opposition groups within Congress took advantage of Uruchurtu's struggle with Díaz Ordaz and powerful private sector forces in the capital to introduce an initiative to reestablish a municipal form of government in the Distrito Federal. The stated objective was to reverse the decision made by the PRI back in 1928, when national political leaders saw the elimination of democratic practices as the only way to control labor politics and urban development in the capital. The issue of municipal political reform was a compelling one for opposition forces. The chance to reintroduce democratic structures for mayoral elections and direct political participation would give many opposition groups a chance to have their voices heard on the local level for the first time in decades. Yet there was much more to the initiative than the electoral and organizing concerns of Mexico's opposition. Political observers at the time suggested that one goal of this initiative was to give a mutilating blow to Uruchurtu by creating federal limitations on the power of the mayor.[55]

Of course, this preliminary, albeit unsuccessful, attempt within the Cámara de Diputados to revive democratic municipal rule can be attributed to several factors besides the opportunities raised by Díaz Ordaz's well-acknowledged fight with Uruchurtu, primarily the changing balance of power between the PRI and opposition parties. The 1964 Cámara de Diputados was the first in Mexico's postrevolutionary history to have seats juridically allotted to opposition parties. With their newfound status, opposition groups wanted their voices heard, and Uruchurtu's growing and almost total political control of Mexico City emerged as a rallying point for these still underdeveloped parties. From the point of view of these new congressional actors, there were as many good reasons to challenge Uruchurtu as to call for municipal rule. The leftist opposition forces that now held parliamentary seats, like the Partido Popular Socialista (PPS) and the Partido Auténtico de la Revolución Mexicana (PARM), tended to represent the urban poor and other marginal sectors of the population, and as such had frequently criticized Uruchurtu and his urban policy stances. Many left-leaning deputies representing the PPS and the PARM were displeased with the mayor's general approach to squatters and his reluctance to install basic urban services in the city's peripheral areas and new settlements, where most of the disadvantaged sectors of the urban population lived. These particular members of Congress were also antagonized by Uruchurtu's blatant ties to local industrialists, albeit smaller ones, and his orientation toward the middle classes. Expenditures on fountains, parks, massive flower gardens, and other special projects for the city's middle classes, while the city's poor were without housing and basic services, galvanized their antagonism to Uruchurtu's administration.

Support for municipal reform in 1965 came not only from the left, however. The right-wing opposition party, the Partido Acción Nacional (PAN), jointly sponsored the initiative for municipal reform. The PAN was not necessarily antagonistic to the ideological content of Uruchurtu's policies or to the man himself, whom they had sought as a presidential candidate in 1958. But the issue of political decentralization had long been one of the three main planks in the PAN platform. Thus, on this issue the PAN joined with the left and Díaz Ordaz in order to gain some political power of their own. The party calculated that if municipal elections were allowed, Mexico City's large population of disenfranchised urban middle classes might actually bring in a PAN mayor.

Despite broad-based support, or perhaps because of it, the initiative for municipal reform failed to win approval from most of the PRI congressmen. Many within the PRI calculated that despite its value in weakening Uruchurtu, reintroducing a municipal form of government would have set the stage for other political parties to challenge the PRI in Mexico City, particularly the PAN. It would also give life to new institutional structures for political participation that could compete with the CNOP. The PRI was not ready to accept such challenges to its corporatist structure, particularly in the country's largest and most important city.

Nonetheless, the municipal reform challenge was important for several reasons. First, it allowed Díaz Ordaz to test the depth of support and opposition to Uruchurtu. Second, it showed Díaz Ordaz that he could use the initiatives of the PAN and the PPS to destroy and discredit Uruchurtu.[56] That is, Díaz Ordaz learned that under certain circumstances he could unify right- and left-wing support in his struggle against a fellow party member, in this case, Uruchurtu. Last and most important, it demonstrated to Díaz Ordaz that he needed the political support of more centrist deputies in order to bring Uruchurtu's resignation: Far left or far right opposition forces, alone, would not do.

But how to pull the rest of the party into the struggle with Uruchurtu over the METRO and urban growth, especially its ideologically centrist constituents, many of whom were strongly behind the mayor? Clearly, Díaz Ordaz had to break Uruchurtu's reputation as Mexico City's finest mayor, the man who tamed the perilous urban monster, while at the same time repudiating his negative position on the METRO. And the best way to do that was to challenge Uruchurtu in precisely the domain where he had appeared strongest: urban transport. If urban bus transport was thrown into chaos, not only would it challenge Uruchurtu's claim that the METRO was a wasteful, unnecessary expense for Mexico City, it also might weaken middle classes' and small industrialists' support for Uruchurtu. And starting in July 1965, Díaz Ordaz was presented with a golden opportunity to pull this off, as the city was paralyzed by a series of bus strikes.

During the summer of 1965, bus drivers had started to protest the low wages and deteriorating working conditions they increasingly faced as the city expanded. Bus drivers also protested against the monopoly power of the Alianza, its unabashed support by the Unión de Permisionarios, and the corruption of the leadership in the bus drivers' union, which often worked against the interests of the bus drivers themselves. By November 1965, after several months of revolt, over 1,700 buses had staged a work shutdown.[57] Strikes among urban bus drivers continued during the fall of 1965 and through the first six months of 1966, growing in strength and magnitude. By early 1966, the urban transport system Uruchurtu had so carefully crafted and managed was thrown into near-chaos, and his reputation began to suffer accordingly. Of course, given the validity of bus drivers' grievances, the strikes and their disastrous consequences for Uruchurtu cannot be attributed fully to President Díaz Ordaz. Indeed, evidence that grievances were heartfelt, and not merely fabricated by Díaz Ordaz's allies in the PRI in order to undermine Uruchurtu, is seen in the fact that the first bus strikes in mid-1965 were started by more radical and independent union leaders, and not by the PRI-controlled union leaders. Nonetheless, government complicity in fomenting this labor unrest is indicated by the fact that the bus drivers' strikes were allowed to continue for so long, as well as by press accounts from the period; moreover, it cannot be totally accidental that the rash of bus strikes hitting Mexico City in late 1965 and 1966 coincided directly with Díaz Ordaz's efforts to introduce the subway, his campaign against Uruchurtu, and the latter's obstinacy and public statements opposing the METRO. This was just the time that the president's allies in the Cámara de Diputados began to criticize Uruchurtu publicly. Most significantly, perhaps, before this time bus strikes had been almost nonexistent, due to the strong control of organized bus drivers by Joaquin del Olmo of the Federation of Workers of the Distrito Federal (FTDF), a branch of the government-controlled CTM. This relative calm within the bus industry in Mexico City had, in fact, been one of the reasons that Uruchurtu had been able to strike an accord with bus owners, since the bargaining power of both

C H A P T E R   F I V E

was contingent upon the ability to ensure smooth urban bus service. That this calmness was disrupted—and supported by the CTM for the first time in years—suggests a government complicity in the growing urban labor unrest among bus drivers. After all, grievances were not new. Conditions and salaries for bus drivers had been deteriorating for years, and were just as bad before the summer of 1965 as after.

The steady spread of these bus strikes, then, can also be traced partly to Díaz Ordaz's capacity to use judicial prerogative and the government-controlled CTM to sustain them. Indeed, even though the CTM was slow to support the striking independent unions, the fact that the CTM did not publicly interfere with the independent bus drivers' union's calls for strikes also indicates a level of tolerance rarely evidenced by the CTM and the ruling party leadership. Up to that period, this party-controlled confederation had generally squelched independent union activity. But in 1965, "organizations that traditionally were considered antagonistic in the struggle for power by this [independent] union participated together, for the first time".[58] Authorities ultimately judged the strikes on bus lines under the control of the Distrito Federal illegal, but did not condemn the strikes on other lines under federal control.[59] This fact underscores the extent of conflict over these strikes between Uruchurtu—whose political power rested in Mexico City jurisdictions—and Díaz Ordaz, who as president had greater control over the federal domain. Moreover, shortly after Joaquín del Olmo's purported "loss of control" over the bus drivers' union, Díaz Ordaz used his federal power to appoint him a federal deputy.

Of course, the fact that independent unions were aware of the conflict between Díaz Ordaz and Uruchurtu over transport further helps to explain the emergence and severity of these strikes in Mexico City. Independent unions saw intraparty conflict over the METRO as an opportunity to better their own conditions, since it gave them the opportunity to call for municipalization of bus transport. If the METRO was to be publicly provided, why not other forms of transport? At a minimum, the independent unions hoped these strikes would increase their bargaining power with the monopolistic Alianza de Camioneros or the Unión de Permisionarios, since their now-demonstrated capacity to disrupt urban transport might give Uruchurtu and the Alianza more incentive to accommodate their grievances and demands. Nonetheless, because the Alianza held fast to its position of not bowing to the bus strikers and because Uruchurtu supported them, the bus strikes continued.

Its corrupt origins notwithstanding, the power struggle among striking bus drivers, national authorities encouraging and legalizing the strikes, and the Unión de Permisionarios supporting the Alianza was politically costly and, in the long run, speeded Uruchurtu's demise. First, with months of sporadic strikes by bus employees, the first bus lines to buckle due to economic losses were the small and medium lines, fleets with fewer buses and shorter routes.[60] The smaller lines had long held grievances against the larger lines, whose owners were often the top leadership of the Alianza. Now they had a real reason to actively confront the Alianza, since the latter's rigidity in facing the striking bus drivers had weakened its control. By mid-1966, in fact, several representatives of small and medium-sized bus lines broke ranks with the Alianza and came out with a public statement supporting the METRO.[61] This was a devastating blow to the legitimacy of Uruchurtu's anti-METRO stance. This support for the METRO project from owners of smaller bus lines was due to several factors. First, the approval of the METRO project might bring about the end of the government-sanctioned bus strikes, which hurt smaller lines most. Second, if government authorities could introduce the METRO, the power of the few large lines that dominated the Alianza might diminish, which in turn would give smaller owners more latitude to press their demands. Third, these small and medium-sized bus lines could take advantage of the assured transport demand resulting from bus routes structured to feed the METRO, if the project were approved. At a minimum, they could hardly lose with a METRO in place, since the large owners already monopolized the best routes. Clearly, it was the monopoly owners within the Alianza, and not the smaller lines, who had the most to fear from the METRO's introduction; and the latter lent their support with surprising ease.

URUCHURTU'S POLITICAL DEMISE

As the strikes progressed, Uruchurtu saw his political position weaken, and so too his capacity to push forward his vision of restricted urban growth. His diminished power stemmed not only from his own previous efforts to provide and administer urban transport, but also from the capital and labor dynamics of urban transport and the ways in which the incorporated political system exacerbated tensions within and between these two aspects of the problem. As noted earlier, Uruchurtu had solidified his political support in Mexico City among urban middle classes through his control over the provision and administration of urban services, particularly transport provided by the Alianza de Camioneros. Yet his actions in this regard—particularly the formation of the Unión de Permisionarios—contributed to the concentration of ownership and capital in the urban transport sector. This, in turn, exacerbated the conflicts between bus firms of different sizes that threw into question the anti-

C H A P T E R   F I V E

METRO stance that had emerged from his orientation toward urban middle classes and the Alianza de Camioneros.

Díaz Ordaz seized the moment, skillfully; and by so doing wrought a strange reversal of fortune. During the 1910s and 1920s, the government had used labor leaders in the government-controlled CROM to break strikes among urban transport workers—then mainly *tranviarios*—and support instead the development of urban bus services in the hands of private owners. Their objective had been to subordinate urban labor activists to the state and create the conditions for smooth and efficient urban transport services. Now the tables were completely turned. The federal government used its control over the labor sector to support striking transport workers, but in order to fight against the mayor and the urban bus industry. And this time, their principal objective was to destroy the mayor's capacity to administer the urban domain smoothly and efficiently. What was similar in both periods, however, was the desire of federal authorities to control local politics—and local labor activism—for their own specifically national purposes.

With transport chaos hitting Mexico City from mid-1965 all the way through 1966, and with Uruchurtu unable to support the argument that bus service was the solution to Mexico City's transport problems, Uruchurtu's stand on the METRO became a legitimate basis for Díaz Ordaz's challenge to him as mayor. As early as November 1965, Uruchurtu made serious efforts to restore his shattered prestige by publicly announcing last-minute plans to restructure and reorder urban transport conditions. His plans included the introduction of new routes of *camionetas peseros*, or minibuses. But the transport improvements offered by Uruchurtu were not enough to counter pro-METRO forces, who were gaining legitimacy and power with their claims about the subway's technological potential to resolve the city's urban transport chaos. In the face of a plan for a modern network of underground trains claiming to move thousands in minutes, minibuses hardly generated enthusiasm. The population's increasingly negative image of the Alianza de Camioneros, moreover, cast doubt on Uruchurtu's statements that bus transport could be improved. Much of the public felt that overcrowded inner-city transportation and the unsafe operation and maintenance of buses were the direct result of the Alianza's greed. With horror stories about its antilabor practices emerging in the publicity surrounding the strikes, the Alianza's image was further tarnished. Many residents thought that Uruchurtu's new plans would only serve the Alianza's interests and perpetuate the same conditions anyway. Even the director of transit in the Distrito Federal, General Gustavo Larriva, was pushed to publicly acknowledge that Uruchurtu's plans to introduce *pese-*

ros, or collective taxis, to address the growing urban transport problems, most probably would not affect the interests of the bus lines that had existed over the years.[62]

Last, Uruchurtu's piecemeal attempts to address public concern about transport chaos with minor policy modifications held little currency in the face of the upcoming Olympics. As the government-sanctioned bus strikes continued, Díaz Ordaz's campaign against Uruchurtu centered around the city's chaotic transport conditions and how they could destroy the operation and success of the games. With bus strikes already casting a pall on the mayor's popularity in the Distrito Federal, this would serve as the last straw for Uruchurtu.

By late summer of 1966 Uruchurtu's days were numbered. To the extent that he was losing the administrative capacity to keep the city running smoothly, Uruchurtu's political support from middle classes—who had cared most about such issues in the past—was in serious question. With previously loyal political supporters no longer willing to lend unconditional support, Uruchurtu was unable to sustain either his anti-METRO position or his hold on the Mexico City mayorship, particularly given the strength and vigor with which Díaz Ordaz and his prodevelopment opponents challenged this stance. By early fall, after fourteen years of loyal service to the PRI and to Mexico City, Uruchurtu was out: The Cámara de Diputados forced the mayor's dismissal. Uruchurtu's resignation came after a vote of censure in the CNOP-dominated Cámara de Diputados, provoked by the razing of a squatter settlement on the southern rim of the Distrito Federal, known as Colonia Santa Ursula (in an area known as the Ajusco), on September 12, 1966. Within a week of the forced resignation, President Díaz Ordaz appointed a new mayor, Alfonso Corona del Rosal, a good friend and strong political ally who had served in his cabinet as secretary of national properties. With the change in mayors, public works and preparations for the Olympics were immediately accelerated, and with much public fanfare. Scarcely one week after filling Uruchurtu's position, new mayor Corona del Rosal publicly announced that the Distrito Federal would formally accept the METRO as a project for consideration. By early spring 1967, construction work began on the subway, and in 1969 the first line opened.

But this was not the end of the myriad conflicts that underlay the METRO controversy. Soon it was clear that the PRI's sabotage of Uruchurtu, the mayor's forced removal, and the implementation of the METRO would come at a considerable price. For one thing, the city's rapid growth was assured. Residents would see urban problems and service scarcities accelerate accordingly; and the PRI would see a dramatic rise in the cost of meeting the city's service and infrastructural needs. Second, after Uruchurtu's startling budgetary successes, urban fiscal crisis was once again a serious concern, and with it, a national fiscal crisis. Equally important, out of the ashes of Uruchurtu's demise and the triumph of pro-urban growth forces several new political problems emerged, not the least of which was rural unrest, as Díaz Ordaz's preoccupation with the urban development of the capital city reminded the peasant sector that they had been largely excluded from Mexico's development miracle and from major decision making. Another was the irreversible disaffection of Mexico City's traditional middle classes, who felt abandoned without Uruchurtu and whose demands and concerns held little sway in Díaz Ordaz's developmental vision. Still another was a clear political imbalance within the higher echelons of the PRI between the different sizes and sectors of capital. With Uruchurtu out, Alemán's faction of import-substituting industrialists, and the nation's smaller manufacturers, lost out to bankers and foreign-linked firms in the ongoing battle to wield power. And because the conflicts between different factions of capital were so intricately linked to differing positions on urban growth, as were the concerns of the ever more disenfranchised middle classes and the complaints of rural peasants, the local-national tensions that originally emerged in the METRO conflict and over urban growth were about to haunt the PRI once again.

6

RETHINKING MEXICO CITY'S

ROLE IN NATIONAL DEVELOPMENT,

1966–1973

To scholars and laymen alike, 1968 was a watershed year in Mexico's political history. Protesting students were massacred by government troops at the Tlatelolco housing complex in October of that year, an act that stunned citizens, party activists, and foreign observers while generating a wave of grassroots unrest and political dissatisfaction that continued throughout the 1970s and beyond. Many saw this event as signaling a turn toward authoritarian rule; and some observers even suggest that Mexico never truly recovered from the legitimation crisis produced by the Tlatelolco massacres. At minimum, the writings of almost all recent analysts of Mexico reflect the historic significance of the year 1968 in Mexico's political development.

As they highlight the events at Tlatelolco as a critical turning point in Mexico's political history, scholars tend to focus on state-society conflicts emerging at this watershed moment and how they led to a steady delegitimation of one-party rule starting in 1968 and continuing through the 1970s. Yet we now know that other equally serious problems were afoot within the party, and that the PRI was facing these internal problems well *before* 1968. Indeed, conflicts existed within the higher echelons of the PRI, within and between different institutional sectors of the party, and between local and national politicians, all of which suggest an already troubled political apparatus. We also know that many of the internal party conflicts and popular dissatisfactions of the time revolved around urban service scarcities and policy concerns in Mexico City, especially those related to transport and growth. As such, many of the political tensions of the sixties period were not necessarily spurred by a general dissatisfaction with one-party rule or accelerating capital-labor conflicts, as scholars have suggested.[1] Rather, a good portion of the PRI's political problems were sector-specific: Not all social and class sectors shared the same antagonism toward the ruling leadership, and most notably, capital-labor tensions were hardly as worrisome to the PRI as were urban conflicts. This, in no small part, derived from the fact that the labor sector of the party functioned as a representative vehicle for labor's workplace demands more coherently and legitimately than the CNOP functioned as a representative vehicle for urban demands. It was precisely this problem, in fact, that made the policymaking efficacy and personal popularity of the mayor so fundamental to the overall legitimacy of the political system.

Precisely because many of the PRI's problems in the late 1960s lay in conflict and controversy over Mexico City's urban development, especially the control and administration of urban services in the capital, the party leadership was confronted with a serious dilemma that it had not yet had to face: whether to continue nurturing Mexico City's urban growth and whether to do so under the auspices of local or national control. These questions were especially difficult for the party leadership to answer because different class and social forces, both within and outside the party, took different positions. Complicating matters was the fact that some groups cared more about larger class concerns, or their capacity to participate in national versus local decision making, than about the issue of urban growth itself. For some, urban growth and the government's position on it were merely masks for other political and economic concerns, many of them national in character; for others, the local dynamics of urban development were precisely what was at stake.

In this complex terrain, conflicts over growth and urban development decisions, and their resolution, unbalanced the complementarity of local and national decision making so well crafted in earlier periods, especially during Uruchurtu's administration. Before 1966, with Uruchurtu at the helm, boundaries were clear; Mexico City's mayor used local institutions and urban policies to accommodate traditional middle classes and small industrialists, while national party structures and institutions acted on behalf of industrial labor, bureaucrats, and as time passed, the urban poor. After 1966, however, the whole system was turned on its head as Mexico City's new mayor, Corona del Rosal, began to run the capital with an eye to the demands of nationally powerful groups whose local political and urban concerns were very different from those of Mexico City's middle classes and local industrialists, who previously had captured the attention of Mexico City politicians, especially Uruchurtu.

The issues at stake, and the shift in affairs in pre- and post-1966 periods, are clearer with a closer look at the machinations used to oust Uruchurtu and reverse his policy on the METRO. As noted in the last chapter, support for Uruchurtu and opposition to the METRO project and unlimited urban growth were not widespread, but concentrated in the traditional middle classes and several other groups formally organized within the CNOP, including those that provided urban services, such as the Alianza de Camioneros. Because of the class-basis of these supporters and opponents of Uruchurtu, then, the controversy over his urban policy positions quickly transformed itself into institutional tensions between the CNOP and the CTM that burst beyond manageability in the years after Uruchurtu's forced dismissal. Conflicts over urban growth and land use policies—and the METRO in particular—not only reflected growing intraparty sectoral tensions and middle-class dissatisfactions; they also contributed to the PRI's growing political crisis during the 1960s, including the 1968 upheaval. Given the nature of the issues at stake with the subway project, in fact, Uruchurtu's forced resignation involved much more than replacing one mayor with another, or prioritizing one urban policy over another. It also meant repudiating certain classes, their vision of the city, and their institutional capacities to push their positions. These dynamics are perhaps best seen in the event that spurred the forced resignation and that set the tone for Uruchurtu's successor: the bulldozing of a squatter settlement in southern Mexico City.

In the upcoming pages I identify the forces involved in the bulldozing of 1966 that brought Uruchurtu's downfall, as well as the responses of certain party members and class actors (especially the CNOP leadership, its rank and file, and the CTM). I examine their positions on urban growth in contrast to the unique local and class alliance of forces that emerged in support of Uruchurtu, highlighting the ways in which each involved national political leaders and institutions. After tracing Uruchurtu's dismissal and the METRO's fate to these local-national tensions, I examine their impact on Mexico City's subsequent mayors and on the succeeding presidential administration of Luis Echeverría. Among other issues, I trace Echeverría's nationalist development policies, his urban and administrative reforms, and a subsequent national political crisis to his efforts to coordinate mayoral and presidential initiatives, recatalyze the CNOP, and hence reduce the local-national tensions exacerbated by the Díaz Ordaz administration's handling of Uruchurtu and the METRO project during the sixties.

BRINGING SQUATTERS AND THE CNOP
INTO INTRAPARTY CONFLICT

On September 12, 1966, Mexico City residents woke to the news of a squatter settlement bulldozing in the city's southern periphery, an area known as the Ajusco. According to newspaper accounts, Mayor Uruchurtu had ordered the razing of a low-income settlement of three hundred families who illegally occupied lands in the Ajusco's Colonia Santa Ursula. The original foundation of this squatter settlement dated back ten years, although many of its residents had arrived more recently. Like many other low-income squatter communities in the metropolitan area, Santa Ursula served as a refuge for the growing number of urban poor who could neither afford rents nor locate available housing in more central areas of the city. Securing access to affordable housing had become increasingly difficult over the sixties, not only because the city's population was growing so rapidly, but also because Uruchurtu had been relatively successful in regulating land redevelopment and imposing restrictions on new housing construction. With demand high and supply down, rents were continually on the rise and thus residents frequently turned to illegal settlements like Santa Ursula to solve their housing problems. Because Santa Ursula's residents were so poor, however, the bulldozing captured public attention and outrage; and within a day party leaders had used this event as a basis for forcing Uruchurtu's resignation as mayor.

In considering more carefully what led to the forced resignation, it is perhaps telling that the merits or debits of Uruchurtu's general position on urban growth did not enter into the public debate, which focused mainly on his actions against urban squatters. But Uruchurtu's opposition to urban growth as well as his position on the METRO were lurking beneath. Given Uruchurtu's intransigence in servicing low-income settlements and providing new permits for urban land development, in fact, Díaz Ordaz and his pro-urban growth allies may have considered it poetic justice that the bulldozing of a squatter settlement was the basis for the public campaign against the mayor that brought his removal. Squatting was often encouraged by real estate developers to start the process of land regularization, and this had been the case in Santa Ursula. When attention focused on Uruchurtu for evicting squatters with a bulldozer, public discussion centered around its impact on the city's poor; but equally under contention were issues of urban land speculation and dispersed urban growth.

That the bulldozing was no more than the proximate cause of Uruchurtu's dismissal is made evident by the fact that this razing of Santa Ursula was not the first such action Uruchurtu had taken to forcibly remove illegal settlers. Another had occurred as recently as November 1965. Uruchurtu, moreover, was by no means the only public official to have cleared squatters by force: Police evictions of residents from illegal lands had been undertaken by mayors and other national politicians in practically every administration since the PRI came to power, and they would continue to occur in subsequent years. Accordingly, most political observers agree that the controversy over the bulldozing of Santa Ursula was "fabricated in order to create an adverse situation which would oblige [Uruchurtu] to resign." Berta Lerner and Susana Ralsky have claimed, in fact, that this particular bulldozing was used to obscure another more serious problem: Uruchurtu's "incompatibility, both personal and in terms of his political team, with President Díaz Ordaz." Others have agreed: One newspaper account noted that while on the surface the furor over the bulldozing was "a frontal attack on legality, in its origins it was a game of dirty pool."[2] The bulldozing, in short, was almost universally considered a pretext fabricated by President Díaz Ordaz.

Knowing that the bulldozing was meant to generate political opposition to Uruchurtu among the urban poor, and to legitimize his forced removal, helps explain why the Santa Ursula eviction was presented to the public the way it was, and how it was discussed in Congress. Newspaper accounts note that members of the PRI and the CNOP-controlled Congress "happened" to be on hand at the bulldozing, which occurred before sunrise. Also present were the subchief of police of the Distrito Federal, residents of the settlement, members of the press and photographers, and several tractors, which were first referred to as bulldozers by congressmen in the Cámara de Diputados. Once public discussion began, the event was almost immediately labeled a "bulldozing," and from that point on Uruchurtu was frequently referred to as the bulldozer mayor in accounts of his tenure. The evidence is clear, however, that Mexico's Congress also rose to the occasion of the carefully orchestrated scandal in order to add fuel to a slow-burning fire of opposition to Uruchurtu.

When Díaz Ordaz's spokesmen introduced a motion to censure Uruchurtu in the Cámara de Diputados a day after the bulldozing, hundreds of squatters were brought into the gallery to set the stage, and photos and copies of press accounts were distributed widely by members of the PRI. Diputado Enrique Ramírez y Ramírez, who offered the motion, purportedly represented leftist elements within the CNOP—which at that time were taken to include squatters. In his diatribe against Uruchurtu in the Chamber of Deputies Ramírez y Ramírez shouted, "Bulldozers against homes, no! Public works without human and social sentiment, never!" while the gallery audience responded in kind.[3] One journalist characterized the events that day as "a pathetic and demagogic tragicomedy admirably organized and directed, with the enthusiastic involvement of all the parties of the 'opposition,' by PRI Diputado Alfonso Martínez Domínguez, leader of the legislative group and man of confidence of the Díaz Ordaz regime."[4]

Alfonso Martínez Domínguez's involvement in Uruchurtu's forced resignation is significant for several reasons, one of which was the fact that it implicated the CNOP leadership in the conflict. It was no secret in high political circles that there was a long-standing competition between Uruchurtu and the CNOP, of which Martínez Domínguez was a powerful and active member.[5] Ex-mayor Octavio Sentíes attributed this partly to the fact that groups in the Distrito Federal often played the CNOP and the mayor's office off against each other: When Uruchurtu did not respond to street vendors, for example, they headed straight for the CNOP. If the CNOP did not accommodate the demands of central city shopkeepers, they turned to Uruchurtu.[6] The competition also could be attributed to the fact that Uruchurtu wanted urban groups to negotiate with him rather than the CNOP, given his position as mayor and his desire to keep tight reins on developments in the city. Uruchurtu's political fortunes thus had serious implications for the CNOP, and its principal spokesman Martínez Domínguez. If Uruchurtu remained as mayor and continued to impose restrictions on urban growth and low-income settlements, the CNOP would face political problems with squatters, who comprised a growing and increasingly vocal constituency in this organization. Yet if Uruchurtu were removed, other urban middle classes who opposed unrestricted urban growth would lose their principal political advocate within the incorporated political system. Either way, one principal urban political constituency might be lost to the party.

In many ways, Martínez Domínguez's participation in the Santa Ursula controversy had a clear institutional logic: It both emerged from, and exacerbated conflicts within, the CNOP over that institution's limited role in urban politics. And the CNOP leadership had just as many reasons as Díaz

Ordaz to oust Uruchurtu. Although the CNOP was still dominated by state workers who quickly controlled the sector after its establishment in 1943 (and who comprised the largest single federation within that organization and with whom Martínez Domínguez had his strongest ties), it had been struggling to represent the poor as well since the early 1960s. In order to maintain its institutional legitimacy as a participatory vehicle for squatters and the urban poor, the CNOP leadership was willing to join Díaz Ordaz's efforts to remove Uruchurtu, who had been no friend of these groups with his urban policies. Tensions between the CNOP and Uruchurtu over the urban poor, especially as seen in the controversy over the September bulldozing, exemplify the ways in which national-level political institutions, like the CNOP, often encouraged conflicts between local populations for larger political purposes. Yet the Santa Ursula event also underscores the fact that there were both organizational and urban developmental reasons for state workers and squatters within the CNOP to form alliances in the early and mid 1960s. In exchange for securing urban services and maintaining claims to illegal lands, for example, the urban poor frequently supported the party and its corporatist structures, which in the case of squatters meant bureaucrats dominating the CNOP leadership. Because traditional middle-class concerns shaped Uruchurtu's urban service priorities and antidevelopment stance, moreover, the mayor continued to alienate these unemployed and underemployed urban poor who often lived in peripheral squatter settlements. As a result, these populations had even greater incentive to turn to bureaucrats in the CNOP and bypass the mayor's office.

STRANGE BEDFELLOWS? NATIONAL LABOR FEDERATIONS AND BIG CAPITAL UNITED AGAINST URUCHURTU'S URBAN VISION

The support and active participation of squatters in the September 1966 effort to force Uruchurtu's dismissal was absolutely critical to its success. This was so not only because the urban poor helped push the CNOP leadership to join Díaz Ordaz and act against the mayor, but also because they brought forces associated with the labor sector—and leftist elements outside the party leadership—to actively work for the mayor's resignation, too. Both the labor sector and the more left-leaning deputies, within and outside the PRI, sided with President Díaz Ordaz against Uruchurtu, even though Díaz Ordaz was known for his ties to elites linked to foreign capital and land speculation as well as for repressing democratic reforms through authoritarian actions. So why would labor and leftist deputies ally with Díaz Ordaz rather than with Mayor Uruchurtu, whose connections to the nationalist Alemán made him less open to international capital and extravagant urban development measures? And what does that tell us about the relationships between class identity and politics, or the limits to popular support for certain urban development strategies?

The Partido Auténtico de la Revolución (PARM) and the Partido Popular Socialista (PPS) had long opposed Uruchurtu's actions against squatters, as noted in an earlier chapter. The bulldozing of Santa Ursula was no exception. Progressive or left-leaning parties considered Uruchurtu a political conservative with allegiance to petit bourgeois sectors of society who ignored the rights and concerns of the city's impoverished residents in his efforts to serve the city's middle classes and smaller-scale nationalist industries. Moreover, Uruchurtu opposed a modern and sophisticated form of transport that promoters claimed would make a real difference in the cost and comfort of the arduous daily commute of most Mexico City workers, even as he lent his political support to the exploitative and corrupt Alianza de Camioneros. Thus it is no surprise that Uruchurtu was not well loved for his stance on the METRO and urban growth, among other things, by leftist and other opposition forces outside the PRI. In contrast, Díaz Ordaz's pro-METRO and developmentalist stances found sympathetic ears in these parties, as shown by their efforts to orchestrate Uruchurtu's defeat.

Had Uruchurtu been able to rely on support from congressmen representing the CTM, he would have been able to counterbalance the opposition from the mainstream CNOP leadership and other independent parties and political forces. This did not happen, and starting in early 1965, when the controversy with Díaz Ordaz started brewing, public support for Uruchurtu from CTM spokesmen began to diminish. In the immediate aftermath of the bulldozing, moreover, the CTM leadership and three of the labor movement's most powerful syndicates (the FTDF, or federation of Distrito Federal workers, the Sindicato Mexicano de Electristas, and the Federacion Obrera Revolucionaria) were among the first outside the Congress to publicly call for Uruchurtu's dismissal.[7] The CTM's support for Díaz Ordaz, in particular, and its opposition to Uruchurtu, did not necessarily lie in any direct sympathy for squatters, of course. Many local organizations of squatters identified more with the CTM's main institutional rival, the CNOP. However, by the early 1960s portions of Mexico City's industrial working class had begun to organize at the neighborhood level, which made much of the labor movement leadership, in the CTM and other federations, more open to the new urban social movements that were emerging within squatter areas. Also, the fact that

Uruchurtu favored middle classes over many other social forces in the capital city made much of the labor movement's constituency wary of him and of his frequently hard-hearted positions on urban services.

Yet even these factors were probably not as important as the fact that Uruchurtu so openly presented himself as beholden to forces that restricted the rights of labor, namely the Alianza de Camioneros. The CTM, in particular, saw Uruchurtu's allegiance to and protection of the Alianza during the wave of bus strikes in 1965 and 1966 as undermining the demands of urban transport workers and challenging the basic principles of labor activism. A long-bitter relationship with the Alianza further explains why the CTM would be so antagonistic to Uruchurtu. As early as 1936, after censuring the Alianza for its antilabor stances in a conflict waged by bus drivers on the Mexico-Atzcapotzalco line, the CTM had proposed to "initiate a campaign against the bus monopoly represented by the Alianza de Camioneros."[8] A year later, the CTM leadership started to organize workers in bus lines then controlled by the Alianza, particularly those who sought to create their own worker cooperatives. In fact, it was precisely because the Alianza repudiated the CTM's efforts to organize its bus drivers that the urban bus industry was so quick to join the CNOP at its founding in 1943. Early on, this institutional split over the appropriate sectoral affiliation for urban bus drivers defined subsequent relations between the CTM and the urban bus industry, which were never resolved and thus resurfaced during the METRO-Uruchurtu controversy. As one of the most prosperous and best-organized businesses in the CNOP, and in Mexico City, in fact, the Alianza had been able to ensure that many bus drivers on its own lines in Mexico City would also be organized within the CNOP, even as bus drivers in states outside the Distrito Federal were organized within the CTM. Accordingly, the CNOP and the CTM struggled over the hearts and minds of transport workers throughout the 1950s and early 1960s until their rivalry bubbled over in 1966 in the conflict over Uruchurtu and the METRO. Before 1965, of course, Uruchurtu had been able to weather the antagonism between the Alianza and the CTM. But a year's worth of ongoing strikes and labor actions from Mexico City bus drivers pushed many in the leftist parties to repudiate Uruchurtu. As a result, the CTM leadership sided with Díaz Ordaz and his pro-urban growth allies, who dangled the possibility of publicly provided transport services as a way to break the power of the Alianza.

It is somewhat ironic that the long-standing controversy between the CTM and the Alianza had its origins in the efforts made by party politicians, like Uruchurtu, to balance demands for efficient urban services with workplace demands from the providers of those services. In order to ensure that urban transport conditions would be under control, the ruling party leadership and local administrators in Mexico City, especially its mayor, had encouraged the organization and facilitated the development of the Alianza de Camioneros, even when it meant undermining striking transport workers. Yet precisely because this pitted transport workers against owners of bus lines, it created problems within the PRI's structure of incorporation, since it helped pit the CNOP against the CTM. The bus strikes that characterized Uruchurtu's last year in office, along with his stance on the METRO, brought these institutional and class-based tensions to the surface. In many ways, these tensions recalled those that characterized the late 1910s and 1920s, when demands from labor organizations were pitted against urban transport service goals in Mexico City. Like Obregón and Calles, Uruchurtu's principal concern was to facilitate urban transport in the capital and keep the city running smoothly and efficiently. Yet like the *tranviarios* of earlier decades, the CTM was primarily concerned with strengthening organizational unity among urban transport workers during 1965–1966; and it was not above supporting the introduction of the METRO to break the power of the Alianza if it would make it easier to bring all urban transport workers into the CTM. These two objectives— labor unity and smooth urban administration—appeared incompatible, and by the early 1960s the stakes were much higher and the issues more divisive.

With the CTM willing to join the CNOP leadership in calling for Uruchurtu's removal, and with left-wing parties outside the PRI concurring, there was no way Uruchurtu could remain in office. The PAN also joined in voting for the censure, hoping to capture the disenfranchised middle classes who had remained loyal to Uruchurtu to the end. According to one commentator, then, Uruchurtu's forced resignation was an event almost unparalleled in Mexico's history: It had united all the parties of the opposition together with the PRI.[9]

AS LABOR AND CAPITAL UNITE, THE CNOP DIVIDES

Though the bulldozer controversy and calls for Uruchurtu's resignation managed to unite the high-level CNOP leadership with the CTM, squatters with bureaucrats and laborers, and opposition parties with the PRI, it did not unite all critical social forces in opposition to the mayor. In fact, the Díaz Ordaz–Uruchurtu controversy and the mayor's forced resignation exacerbated a growing split among urban populations, especially those formally incorporated into the CNOP. One rift was between state employees—who increasingly allied with the urban poor in the CNOP and who dominated the organization's leadership—and other traditional sectors of the middle class, who remained the organization's rank and file. A second was between those traditional middle classes who had turned to Uruchurtu in the past for political leadership, and those who now remained loyal and active participants in the CNOP. The roots of these intraclass, intra-institutional splits were not just urban, of course; yet conflicts among those urban residents who felt ignored by the CTM and the CNOP leadership lay at the foundation of these growing divisions, and the Díaz Ordaz–Uruchurtu controversy threatened to blow it all apart.

The first visible signs that middle classes formally represented by the CNOP would not remain politically united behind the PRI leadership came in the late 1950s, when state workers openly distanced themselves from the rest of the CNOP's urban middle-class constituents. Although the CNOP had been founded to accommodate the urban policy concerns of Mexico City residents who were excluded from the party's labor and peasant sectors, these objectives never made it to the forefront of the organization's national political agenda. As state involvement in the country's rapid urban and economic development grew during the forties and fifties, the numbers employed in the public sector increased accordingly. As a result, the federation of state workers (FSTSE) solidified its dominant political position within the CNOP and the PRI, pushing the urban concerns of its remaining urban popular and middle-class constituents to the back burner. To accommodate its growing centrality within the CNOP, the FSTSE also began to clamor for the same degree of political power and comparable social programs as the labor sector, which had managed to keep its privileged political position because industrialization remained a national priority. This was first clear in 1959, when the FSTSE was able to push the PRI to expand social security benefits for state workers through the establishment of the Instituto de Seguro Social Para Trabajadores en Servicio al Estado (ISSTSE). This program formalized benefits for state workers at a level already offered to industrial workers organized in the CTM.

As beneficial as this was for state workers, the effect was to exclude other middle classes and the non-wage-earning urban poor from such benefits, since the program was administered through the ISSTSE and not the CNOP. This meant that traditional middle classes had greater reason to turn to Uruchurtu to address their concerns, especially those urban problems that fell under his jurisdiction. This is not to say that populations organized within the FSTSE did not look to Mayor Uruchurtu for political leadership or for special attention, too. Uruchurtu's administrative control over Mexico City afforded him the power to respond to some of the most pressing demands of these Mexico City–based public sector state workers. Many members of the FSTSE were directly employed by the Distrito Federal to provide social and urban services in the capital, and most lived in Mexico City proper, because of the concentration of federal agencies there. Since most government buildings were located in the city's central areas, moreover, a large proportion of state workers lived in neighborhoods circling the city's traditional center, where Uruchurtu developed his policymaking energies and where he was known to have some of his strongest political support. Many public employees preferred to be within a short distance from work, and both Uruchurtu and the federal government had responded to their demands by building much of the housing for state workers within a radius of a few miles of the city center. The Tlatelolco housing project for middle-class government workers was built a few kilometers from the *zócalo*, or central government plaza, with state workers in mind.

Nonetheless, because the FSTSE had direct access to the PRI leadership and to new social programs for serving the demands of its constituents after 1959, the CNOP's role changed accordingly. This change had implications for the relationships within and between its constituents, who sought other ways to express their demands. First, the urban development priorities of many of the CNOP's popular and middle-class residents were put on the organization's back burner, particularly as the leadership of the bureaucratic sector concerned itself more with workplace demands and national political concerns (like mobilizing electoral support) than urban services. According to one of the sector's initial participants, the CNOP was in fact hardly active at all during this time, at least relative to later periods.[10] Second, the FSTSE itself experienced a growing split between its leadership and its rank-and-file membership. As leaders of the state workers' federation solidified their political positions in national decision making by pursuing careers as congressmen or senators and becoming upwardly mobile in high-level government agencies, the local, urban concerns of the rank and file were increasingly left to Mexico City's mayor.

Uruchurtu responded skillfully by organizing many of these urban constituencies as his political base, especially shopkeepers, small businesses (including the urban bus industry), and other city center residents, as discussed earlier. He made it quite clear that he did not want the CNOP leadership too involved in his own activities, which further exacerbated the tensions between the CNOP leadership and its urban rank and file. It is hardly surprising, then, that we see Uruchurtu stepping into the battle over downtown development on the side of these urban forces in the late fifties, at around the same time the transformations in the CNOP's structure began to seriously disenfranchise them.

In addition to these changes in the CNOP, which had emerged by the early 1960s, several other events exacerbated the tensions within the CNOP—and between Díaz Ordaz and Uruchurtu—over the divided political loyalties of the city's middle classes. First, in early 1965, during the first months of Díaz Ordaz's presidential administration, Mexico City doctors initiated a national strike. Doctors made concrete demands about wages and working conditions and also loudly expressed their anger at the PRI's irrational and coercive way of grouping unions in party structures, which mixed professional and trade groupings within the CNOP and thus "limit[ed doctors'] ability to present their interests."[11] Many doctors, moreover, were state employees, working in public hospitals or in state-sponsored social security programs. Precisely because of their position in the CNOP's state worker federation, with strict syndical regulation and low pay, many doctors also felt that the so-called proletarianization of their profession was cutting into the social and economic privileges they had enjoyed previously, just at a time when expectations for Mexico's modernization and development were rising. The doctors' strikes, in short, brought to the surface doctors' concerns about their declining middle-class status as well as their feelings that the nation's middle classes were bearing much of the cost of rapid industrialization. As working classes continued to receive more extensive social programs—as in the public hospitals—the workplace demands of these middle-class health providers were being placed on the back burner.

Ideologically, Mexico City's doctors found common ground with Uruchurtu, and the mayor was quick to turn this into political capital. Even as Díaz Ordaz remained intransigent about doctors' demands, Uruchurtu "ordered the elaboration of a proposal for individual work contracts for doctors that would be operated under the jurisdiction of the Distrito Federal."[12] The doctors' strike in Mexico City and Uruchurtu's response to it underscore the CNOP's divisions and Uruchurtu's role in exacerbating these tensions, in two ways. First, by offering to sign individual contracts with the doctors in his own jurisdiction, Uruchurtu used the institutional power of the Distrito Federal mayor's office, and his popularity among urban middle classes, in order to work against the wishes of President Díaz Ordaz. Second, by offering a solution outside the structures of the CNOP or the PRI, Uruchurtu underscored the incapacity of the PRI's representative structures to accommodate Mexico City's middle classes—an issue also highlighted by Uruchurtu's orientation toward the urban demands of middle classes and his opposition to the METRO project.

At around the same time that the doctors' strike hit the city, two additional challenges to the PRI erupted, both of which further pulled several urban middle-class sectors away from the CNOP and toward Uruchurtu, much to Díaz Ordaz's chagrin. One was a student strike at the National University, also located in Mexico City, during which Díaz Ordaz refused to capitulate to student demands, only to be humiliated by a defiantly independent Uruchurtu who publicly offered to establish a Distrito Federal university separate from the National University in order to fulfill student demands.[13] The other was a movement within the PRI itself, headed by the party's new president, Carlos Madrazo, along with reformist forces within the CNOP, to open new channels for political participation among middle classes and other sectors of the population who were feeling politically disenfranchised by the hierarchical structures of the existing organizations. Both of these developments exacerbated internal divisions within the PRI and the CNOP and called attention to the party's institutional incapacity to meet the demands of Mexico's traditional middle classes, two conditions that lent urgency to the Uruchurtu–Díaz Ordaz policy conflicts.

The university strike began in the law school, home to many frustrated middle-class students who, according to Rafael Segovia, were especially sensitive about their uncertain futures.[14] Less favoritism toward students hooked into the PRI's old-boy network at the university was a principal demand; there were also calls for a less restrictive admissions policy. The fundamental political reforms proposed by Carlos Madrazo also called into question old-boy networks within the PRI in general and the CNOP in particular, as well as the political system's ability to address the concerns of middle classes. One proposal was a call for more popular participation in the PRI's preselection of candidates for deputies and governors. Of course, Madrazo's efforts to structure more democratic participation into the PRI on the local level were supported by many citizens, not least by those in the labor sector who also struggled against the top-down hierarchy of the CTM. Madrazo's plans for reform, moreover, were national—and not just local—in scope. But political observers have suggested that Madrazo's proposal was largely geared toward the PRI's traditional and more politically moderate middle classes in Mexico City, whose capacity to participate in national politics through the CNOP had never reached the levels of the other sectors.[15] Particularly with the changing power of the FSTSE after 1959, the CNOP's remaining middle-class members increasingly decided that this organization was unable to respond adequately to the political concerns of Mexico City's middle-class residents. Madrazo's 1965–1966 reform efforts catered to these middle classes who still remained formally loyal to the ruling party but who clamored for greater political participation.

The reforms proposed by Madrazo underscored a crucial dimension of the conflict also brewing between Díaz Ordaz and Uruchurtu: the incapacity of the PRI's nationally constituted, corporatist political structures to adequately deal with local politics and problems. According to Jacqueline Peschard, in fact, Madrazo was the first president of the PRI to try "to democratize the party from below, that is to say, on the basis of municipal committees"; while Madrazo himself had argued that the "local council [*ayuntamiento*] is the cradle and refuge of public liberty."[16] To the extent that both Madrazo and Uruchurtu looked to the locality and catered to the urban middle classes not well represented by the CNOP leadership, their positions underscored growing divisions within the CNOP. And precisely because their appeals about municipal power and local politics threatened to lay bare the party's national biases, and thus unbalance the precarious stability between the institutionalized sectors the PRI had so carefully nurtured over the years, Díaz Ordaz worried about the continued presence of both Madrazo and Uruchurtu. Their support from middle classes threatened to grant each sufficient power to block the objectives of national party leaders—in both the CNOP and the CTM—and other Díaz Ordaz loyalists. In the case of Uruchurtu, the possibility that middle classes might secure more political autonomy on the local level also had implications for the METRO and the urban growth strategies over which they all were struggling. Madrazo, meanwhile, was also challenging Díaz Ordaz's capacity to control national politics on the local level, especially in Mexico City, precisely where many of the president's policy positions were under question.

Not surprisingly, then, Díaz Ordaz's responses to Madrazo, Uruchurtu, and striking students were almost identical. As we already know, Uruchurtu was forced to resign in 1966, the same year that Díaz Ordaz fired both Madrazo and the rector of the National University.[17] All three acts raised serious questions about both Díaz Ordaz's and the PRI leadership's capacity to accommodate alternative political visions or to respond to traditional middle-class demands that prioritized local over national institutions and concerns. Still, of all three acts, Díaz Ordaz's heavy-handedness with Uruchurtu had perhaps the most lasting implications. Why? Even with middle-class support, students still existed on the fringe of corporatist politics, and their actions alone did not threaten the incorporated system as a whole. Madrazo's challenge and the political response to his dismissal were much more damaging in this regard. Yet even with proposals for greater democratization within the party temporarily sidetracked, there still existed sufficient mechanisms for some political participation within the labor and peasant sectors of the corporatist system to keep Madrazo's ouster from fatally damaging party politics, even though these mechanisms were highly controlled. Uruchurtu's forced dismissal from Mexico City, however, left little to counterbalance its effect, since there existed no sufficient outlets for local political participation that could even symbolically suggest an openness to residents' urban concerns, especially those posed by the middle classes. As such, Uruchurtu's dismissal opened the party's political floodgates, and a tidal wave of problems ensued.

THE POLITICAL AFTERSHOCK: A STEADY DECLINE
IN URBAN MIDDLE-CLASS SUPPORT

Uruchurtu's forced removal in 1966 signaled to many middle-class residents that their urban demands about squatters, downtown development, transport, and land use might henceforth go unheard, not to mention their general political concerns about the growing power of capital, labor, and an overly bureaucratized state in national party politics. The response to the bulldozing at Santa Ursula had demonstrated that, if anything, the party's leaders were most open to the demands of squatters and state workers, and that the CNOP leadership itself was more willing to work in alliance with big developers than with the middle-class rank and file. Equally important, when Díaz Ordaz loyalist Alfonso Corono del Rosal replaced Uruchurtu in October 1966, urban policy changes in Mexico City were introduced almost immediately. Because they were both visible and disastrous, especially with respect to the subway and the city's continued urban growth, Uruchurtu's absence hung over the city. The biggest of the urban policy changes that followed Uruchurtu's dismissal was an immediate turnabout in favor of the METRO project. The subway's promoters wanted to see it operating in time for the tourists and foreign journalists who would flood the capital during the 1968 Olympics, so the costly production schedule was accelerated under Uruchurtu's successor, Corona del Rosal. This decision marked the beginning of an extended period of chaos, particularly in the city's center, where construction and underground digging for the subway disrupted the activities of merchants and local residents from 1966 until 1970. Because the METRO was expected to boost the urban land market, real estate also became a prime investment opportunity, since developers were particularly eager to improve land that had remained idle for so long under Uruchurtu's restrictions on property development and urban growth.[18] But the new plans for developing *fincas muertas*, or abandoned lots, "facilitated the process of land speculation" and served as a basis for "transform[ing] the city center to one of commercial, financial, and tourist" land uses.[19] Downtown Mexico City also saw a rapid growth in tourist activities, highlighted by the opening of the Camino Real Hotel in 1968, which displaced some local residents and further changed the area's character.

Over the long term, these policies were even more disastrous: They fed the urban monster that Uruchurtu had tried so hard to tame. With Díaz Ordaz now unfettered in pushing through his pro-urban development priorities, the city continued to grow rapidly, and conditions deteriorated. Moreover, increased rural-urban migration, created by the rural stagnation and impoverishment associated with stabilizing development and spurred by the new administration's public openness to squatters, brought hundreds of immigrants to Mexico City daily. All these circumstances produced greater dissatisfaction among the city's traditional middle classes, who along with Uruchurtu had long opposed sustained rural-urban migration. Both these developments negatively impacted the party's support among Mexico City residents, not only middle classes, but also the urban poor. Although the president and his allies in the CNOP presented themselves as friends of urban squatters when they used them to oust Uruchurtu in the 1966 bulldozing, Díaz Ordaz quickly ignored squatters' demands once his plan succeeded.[20] Urban growth and redevelopment, not the urban poor, were the president's priorities; and this betrayal was clear almost immediately. As a result, squatters and other sectors of the urban poor continued to mobilize for urban services, even more so after 1966 than before, precisely because the developmentalist biases of Mayor Corona del Rosal and the triumphant Díaz Ordaz administration left their demands unmet.

The increasing mobilization of the poor fueled the vicious cycle of opposition to Díaz Ordaz and the PRI because it pushed the city's traditional middle classes to further distance themselves from the CNOP, which they now saw as an organization through which the PRI would deal primarily with the hordes of squatters descending upon the city. Together, the growing protests and political dissatisfactions on the part of squatters and urban popular and middle classes underscored what one analyst called "the incompetence [of the Díaz Ordaz administration] to confront the problems of a huge city."[21] Middle-class concerns about deteriorating urban conditions and the growing presence of squatters in Mexico City were only one source of the PRI's new political problems. Middle classes also began to question the continued dominance of state workers in the CNOP in the aftermath of Uruchurtu's defeat. In what could be seen as a reward for remaining loyal to the president during his struggles, Díaz Ordaz approved the establishment of the Congreso del Trabajo in 1966, a new organization that grouped state workers with CTM representatives in a new coordinating body charged with setting major social and developmental policy within the PRI.[22] With the largest and most powerful of the CNOP's constituents—government workers and teachers— now active members in another formal organization with direct policymaking potential, the CNOP came to be considered little more than a symbolic body by the late 1960s. As a result, the more traditional middle-class constituents of the CNOP were now institutionally excluded from major policy debates, which now occurred mainly in the Congreso del Trabajo. So too were many of the city's urban popular classes like squatters, street vendors, and informal sector workers organized as *colonos*, who remained organized within the CNOP but whose capacity to wield power also declined with Díaz Ordaz's clear favoritism toward big capital. With an unsympathetic mayor and the CNOP effectively disempowered, many of the city's nonwage urban poor and middle classes were increasingly excluded from politics and decision making.

Many of these new problems and the growing opposition to Díaz Ordaz and the ruling party were reflected in changing electoral patterns. Starting in 1970, the PRI's electoral support dropped dramatically in Mexico City. After hitting a peak level of support ranging from 64 to 69 percent during Uruchurtu's term, electoral support fell 20 percent (or 10 points) to 55.41 percent in 1970. This compares to an 80 percent support rate nationally. Moreover, according to Mario Ojeda, close to 80 percent of the Mexico City population voted in local elections in 1960; yet by the 1967 local elections the figure had dropped to 64.5 percent, and to 59.7 percent by the 1970 national elections.[23] These electoral results support the conclusion that Uruchurtu's abrupt demise and replacement by Alfonso Corona del Rosal resulted in growing urban dissatisfaction with the PRI. It is not surprising, then, that urban middle classes and students, both of whom Uruchurtu had tried to bring to his side in 1965 and 1966, joined together in the months preceding and following the Tlatelolco protests in 1968 to challenge the party and its leaders. Nor is it surprising that some of the most visible signs of dissatisfaction and social unrest during the 1968 protests revolved around Díaz Ordaz's imperviousness to urban poverty and unemployment alongside his devotion to lavish urban renewal development schemes, land speculation, and the Olympics.[24]

Membership figures in the CNOP provide further evidence of the PRI's declining legitimacy among the urban poor and middle classes after Uruchurtu's dismissal. While in 1958 the CNOP still accounted for 33.23 percent of the PRI's membership, a proportion that had remained stable since its founding in 1943, by the end of 1969 the CNOP's proportional membership had dropped to 24 percent.[25] Again, this reflects declining political support from the rank and file, not a change in the political power of the CNOP leadership, which was still controlled by state workers. Indeed, in 1967, at the height of Díaz Ordaz's power, the CNOP still dominated the Congress with 55 percent of congressional seats, up substantially from the 37 percent figure for 1943, when the CNOP was founded.

With discontent among Mexico City's urban popular and middle classes at new heights during the 1969–1970 presidential campaign period, Mexico's PRI faced new difficulties. Many of Mexico City's urban popular and middle classes felt repudiated by the CNOP leadership, which allied with Díaz Ordaz against Uruchurtu in the struggle over the subway and Mexico City's future. Their unhappiness with urban policies was matched by discontent with national policies, which they saw as inextricably linked to Díaz Ordaz's plans for Mexico City. The same developmentalist president who pursued lavish urban infrastructural development at the expense of local populations, and who ordered striking students shot so they would not disrupt the Olympics, had eliminated their favorite local politician and heated the Mexican economy to a point of crisis. The elimination of Uruchurtu meant that fiscal austerity would no longer prevail; and with the triumph of Díaz Ordaz's progrowth allies, Mexico indeed saw an inflationary spiral that cut urban popular and middle-class buying power to a degree not seen since the last serious economic crisis of the mid-1950s. According to Leopoldo Solís, moreover, inflationary problems came to a head in 1968, following the massive government borrowing and spending for the Olympics.[26]

Among those most visibly upset with these inflationary developments were smaller industries in Mexico City producing for the local market, most of whom were still represented by the CANACINTRA, who had found fault with Díaz Ordaz after his dismissal of their ally Uruchurtu. Of course, inflation and balance-of-payments problems hurt all import-substituting industrialists, not just smaller ones who generally allied with the middle class and who already opposed Díaz Ordaz, mainly because the capital goods import component in the production process was still so high. Inflationary problems hurt residents in the outlying regions, too, not just in Mexico City. Yet because inflation and balance-of-payments problems reduced local buying power, these economic trends disproportionately hurt small and medium-sized industries producing for the domestic market. This meant primarily Mexico City industries and their local consumers. Mexico City's small industrialists relied much more heavily on local demand, mainly for the consumer durables they produced, than did large internationally linked firms or firms in peripheral regions of the country.[27] Because small industrialists and other traditional businesses had already seen their political power deteriorate with Uruchurtu out of the mayor's office, moreover, they were quick to join in the chorus of opposition to Díaz Ordaz and the development policies he had advocated.

Making matters worse for the PRI, some of those who had benefited from President Díaz Ordaz's urban and economic policies, and thus had supported him in his struggle against Uruchurtu, also started to feel the pinch. For example, as a result of the strategy of stabilizing development that Díaz Ordaz so wholeheartedly supported, the late 1960s saw the growth of capital-intensive industries and increasing income polarization, both of which hurt the organized labor sector, which still drew the largest concentration of its affiliates from Mexico City.[28] Many industrial workers whose sectoral leaders had joined Díaz Ordaz in opposition to Uruchurtu now faced the prospect of unemployment, especially as jobs in small and medium-sized industries increasingly disappeared due to growing international competition and steady inflation. Some of this dissatisfaction from the organized working class was evidenced by the increasing numbers of workers participating in the movement for independent unions in the late 1960s.[29] Yet the PRI also faced growing rebellion and unrest in the countryside, and this too was in no small part a product of Díaz Ordaz's urban policy priorities. Economic conditions had deteriorated rapidly in rural areas in the wake of Díaz Ordaz's clear preference toward rapid urban and industrial growth.

ECHEVERRÍA TRIES TO RECONNECT THE URBAN AND NATIONAL DOMAINS

With all these problems bubbling to the surface at the time the party convened to select a presidential successor to Díaz Ordaz, the PRI leadership felt that some demonstration of change or accommodation was warranted. There was little consensus, however, on exactly how fundamental or far-reaching these changes should be. The changing balance of economic power between capitalists of different sizes and in different activities made it even more difficult to agree on the new course of economic development to be taken, since each group had so much to lose if a new direction was taken. One way out of the stalemate was to rally around a compromise candidate who could address the concerns of different perspectives without falling completely into one camp or the other. One such candidate was Luis Echeverría. Much to his advantage, Echeverría was not clearly identified with any clear political tendency in the party, at least according to Berta Lerner and Susana Ralsky.[30] His young age was expected to both distance him from the old-guard conservatives who were associated with the Díaz Ordaz administration and bring him support from youths and middle-class professionals, who longed for a change in the PRI's old-style politics. Still, because Echeverría took public responsibility for the student massacres at Tlatelolco when he was Secretaria de Gobernación for Díaz Ordaz, he had a certain legitimacy in the eyes of the pro-urban growth, ideologically conservative forces in the PRI tied to Díaz Ordaz, who were not about to support a candidate who would totally undermine their economic and political strength or objectives. Because Echeverría had married into a liberal family, and his brother-in-law was jailed in the railroad workers' conflict, more radical segments of the PRI identified him as having the potential to be ideologically open to their concerns.

Luis Echeverría was chosen precisely because he was not fully wedded to any one team or well-articulated strategy, and when he was named presidential candidate, his general mandate was to respond to the dissatisfactions and demands of various political and economic groups that had expressed growing dissatisfaction with the PRI. Generally speaking, Echeverría used a new macroeconomic development policy to achieve this objective. He called his approach Desarrollo Compartido, or shared development. Shared development sought growth through redistribution, and it presupposed a reactivation of interventionist measures by the state and strong support for national industry. Those familiar with Mexico know that there are countless studies of the social and political logic that gave rise to Echeverría's strategy of shared development and that determined his inability to successfully pull it off. In this regard, Echeverría is probably the most chronicled Mexican president since Lázaro Cárdenas. These scholars tend to analyze shared development, its redistributive components, and its eventual "failure" as owing to Echeverría's efforts to respond to the demands of an increasingly independent labor movement, to restore legitimacy to the more youthful populations in Mexico (especially the students mobilized in the wake of Tlatelolco), and to reintegrate rural populations into the corporatist political structure. Further, most claim that this particular combination of objectives gave rise to a peculiarly populist development strategy that was economically unsound.

In identifying labor and the peasantry as the social bases of Echeverría's populism, however, scholars tend to make the same mistake as do most analysts of the Cárdenas period. They ignore the nonwage urban poor, or popular, and middle classes. In doing so they fail to take into account the conflicts within and between the CNOP and other sectors in Mexico City, or the controversy between Uruchurtu and Díaz Ordaz over urban growth and development, and how both these factors influenced Echeverría's development strategy. They also fail to acknowledge how urban concerns united all these disparate social and class groups together behind Echeverría and his hybrid strategy known as shared development. These concerns, however, were not lost on Echeverría. Early on, the poor, working, and middle-class populations, and especially their urban problems, claimed special attention in his campaign.

In a June 1970 campaign speech Echeverría laid out his colors when he claimed to be "deeply worried about the rapid growth of [Mexico] City. . . .

The most acute scarcities in the capital," he cried, were "generated by the excessive urban accumulation . . . and it is essential that the city does not grow larger than its capacity [if we are to] offer remunerative work opportunities and the possibility of a dignified, harmonious, sane and just existence."[31] Echeverría showed particular awareness that in order to achieve political and economic successes, he would have to look beyond organized labor and the urban poor to attain the support of dissenting and institutionally marginalized populations in Mexico City, not only the middle classes, but also smaller-scale industrialists. He also sought to use urban issues as a basis for rallying confidence among those groups who had been disenfranchised by the Díaz Ordaz administration's urban and national policies. Shared development was the ideological and policy vehicle he used to do so.

A closer look at the principal components of his shared development strategy, which called for redistribution with growth, makes clear Echeverría's concerns about urban growth in Mexico City as much as national development, and his preoccupation with issues of urban political participation in Mexico City as much as overall income distribution and economic growth. For example, Echeverría advocated social, spatial, and sectoral redistribution, in order to redress urban inequalities. Spatial redistribution was to be accomplished at the national level through the conscious attempt to decentralize industrial development, which had been concentrated mainly in Mexico City, as well as with a renewed emphasis on the country's deprived zones, particularly stagnating agricultural areas. During his presidential campaign, Echeverría noted that even though in previous periods industrial concentration had been beneficial, owing to the economies of scale that it could generate, "at present, far from benefitting [Mexico], it has brought with it migration of great numbers of rural inhabitants who now form belts of misery around these areas."[32] Echeverría often used this claim to justify a call for more equitable spatial distribution of services on the community level, including better provision of housing, drainage, and public health services.

The new president's heightened attention to urban problems, and income and spatial redistribution in particular, was clearly aimed at restoring confidence among Mexico City populations, who had complained increasingly during the 1960s about uncontrolled urban growth and the lack of urban services. This not only meant those traditional middle classes who feared displacement in the wake of Díaz Ordaz's post-1966 urban redevelopments and pro-urban growth stance; it also included squatters and other poor urban groups who suffered with the resurgence of real estate development in the periphery, where they had settled. In addition, it was also intended to appeal to more independent sectors of the organized labor movement who were increasingly organizing their constituencies at the neighborhood level as overall urban conditions deteriorated and as squatting became an activity of choice even for wage-earning populations. By gearing his urban policies as much toward the capital city's poorest groups as toward its traditional middle classes and labor, Echeverría tried to create a strong and relatively broad alliance of support. There was also an urban logic to Echeverría's advocacy of sectoral redistribution in the industrial sphere, though it has frequently been ignored by scholars preoccupied with Echeverría's efforts to foster balanced economic growth. For example, Echeverría's calls for sectoral redistribution were often accompanied by support for Mexico City industry rather than real estate and financial services, and—within this general schema—for national as opposed to international capital.[33]

If these issues are placed in the context of the spatial location of national industries as well as industrialists' initial political loyalties to Uruchurtu, their urban dimensions cannot be ignored. Indeed, most of the smaller and more nationalist industrialists aided by Echeverría's nationalist development policies were located in the Mexico City metropolitan area. They were members of CANACINTRA, and had been facing rocky times with Uruchurtu's forced departure and Díaz Ordaz's support for investment capitalists and internationally linked industry. It is hardly surprising, then, that Echeverría relied heavily on these Mexico City industrialists for political support. Leopoldo Solís argues that "it certainly was not a coincidence that the [presidential] campaign ended with a meeting about industrialization in Naucalpan [an industrial zone in the Mexico City metropolitan area] before the powerful association of local manufacturers where, in his final speech of the campaign, the candidate underlined the important role of nationalistic industrialists in a healthy and growing economy, independent of foreign domination." [34]

Echeverría's spatial and sectoral redistribution policies, which were geared in no small part toward the demands of Mexico City residents, were matched by efforts to introduce administrative reforms and changes in established political practices in the capital. Echeverría's strong efforts to push agricultural development can also be seen as having an urban as much as a rural logic, since they were intended to reduce deteriorating rural conditions and peasant unrest in the countryside, which sent streams of poor peasants to Mexico City. On the administrative level, Echeverría called for greater coordination of public and private investment decisions in Mexico City, where the administrative practices of the previous presidential administration had intensified urban chaos. Many of the desired political and administrative changes were exemplified in a call for an *apertura democrática*, or "democratic opening," which Echeverría claimed as an equally important component of his overall development strategy. Also falling into the category of a democratic opening were Echeverría's efforts to encourage the formation and political participation of independent trade unions, who had been struggling against the CTM leader, Fidel Velázquez, who had so strongly allied with Díaz Ordaz in the last several years.

Echeverría's efforts to create more political space for union dissidents are generally perceived as a response to the demands of Mexico's industrial working class. Though true, this is too narrow a view. Echeverría's *apertura democrática* was also a call for increased political participation of all popular and middle classes in governance, in much the same way that Carlos Madrazo had intended in 1965. Like Madrazo before him, Echeverría sought to counter the declining legitimacy of the CNOP, which was losing support from many of the city's traditional middle classes and non-wage-earning popular sectors. While Madrazo had tried and failed to reactivate the CNOP's traditional rank and file with a reform of the electoral primaries, Echeverría took different steps, which were more successful. One was to lower the voting age as well as the minimum age for election of congressmen and senators. Echeverría hoped this would expand both his electoral support and CNOP membership, which was the formal mechanism through which youth groups participated in politics. Another was to refocus CNOP activities on the demands and concerns of the urban poor and middle-class groups of all incomes and occupations, whose participation had been minimal in previous years, given the organization's domination by bureaucrats. Among the groups most actively targeted, in addition to youth, were women, artisans, shopkeepers, small industrialists, nonsalaried workers, and middle-class professionals. As a third way of reactivating the CNOP's legitimacy, Echeverría actively recruited into his administration younger, middle-class political activists who were not directly linked to the CNOP's old-guard bureaucrats, and who would serve as mediators between them and the newly restored base of constituents in the CNOP.

In short, in implementing shared development Echeverría hoped to restore a balance between local and national priorities, both political and economic. That is, he sought to establish mechanisms and policies that would address the needs of Mexico City populations, especially students, the urban poor, middle classes, and national industrialists, yet that would also cater to demands by the organized labor movement and pro-urban growth forces still allied to Díaz Ordaz. Furthermore, he sought to reduce expenditures on highly capital-intensive urban projects, even as he prioritized less costly urban service concerns of Mexico City populations and the economic development of new regions.

Of all these goals, the fiscal and urban administrative ones were the first to cause problems. This becomes clear with a close look at the specific cost-cutting policies Echeverría implemented during his first year in office. In order to set a stable economic base upon which to implement shared development, early on Echeverría quickly imposed dramatic constraints on all public spending and restructured procedures and administrative practices for doing so. Upon taking office, Echeverría delayed approval of public sector budgets for the departments of public works, communications and transport, and water resources. Economically speaking, the overall intent was to reduce spiraling inflation and a negative trade balance that had accompanied the massive spending programs undertaken by Díaz Ordaz for downtown urban renewal and other major infrastructural projects, like the subway, in the late sixties.[35] Next, Echeverría restructured administrative practices in Mexico City in an effort to curtail spending and broaden political participation. Perhaps the most significant legislative change he introduced in this regard was in the Ley Orgánica del Departamento del Distrito Federal. Announced within weeks of his inauguration, Echeverría sought to quickly build grassroots support by constructing a direct line of communication between the neighborhoods and the Distrito Federal government and bypassing the old-guard networks. The nucleus of this new system of political participation was the *junta*, or community organization. Each of the sixteen electoral *delegaciones* of the Distrito Federal would now have a *junta de vecinos*, or neighborhood council, whose elected leader would serve on a consultative council to the Mexico City mayor. What this new political structure did, effectively, was to restore incentives for the urban poor and middle classes to participate politically, and within this general mandate, to articulate urban policy demands.

Three months into office, in March 1971, Echeverría introduced yet a third provocative reform: the Ley del Tribunal de lo Contencioso Administrativo del Distrito Federal. According to administration spokesmen, this new law would give a greater political voice to residents of the capital "whose capacity to protest has been minimal, disgracefully, and who have had few means to express dissatisfaction."[36] The reform was to help democratize life in the Distrito Federal, by establishing a tribunal process through which residents could challenge fines or other alleged violations of rules and regulations imposed by government administrators or agents. This democratic reform, moreover, like Echeverría's other urban administrative reforms, created another means of challenging bureaucratic decision making on the local level. It was followed by one last administrative change, a radical reform in government purchasing procedures, which also posed a similar challenge. According to Judith Adler Hellman, "Under previous administrations the practice was for each government dependency and agency to receive its budget and then decide on its purchases for itself," which at best meant "government departments and ministries [were] powerful and arbitrary kingdoms with little coordination between each other."[37] Yet Echeverría completely changed this process, establishing a new system of planning that mandated greater coordination between urban and national development policy and between local and national bureaucrats.

Yet rather than eliminating the PRI's political problems, these new policies and administrative changes introduced by Echeverría accomplished almost the opposite: they generated new problems within the party, and between it and the Mexican citizenry, both those with urban and those with national concerns. First of all, Echeverría's public spending cuts posed a problem for private sector forces with concerns about the national economy who had allied with Díaz Ordaz and Martínez Domínguez in earlier conflicts over Mexico City policy. They also undermined the strength of nationally powerful old-guard politicians in the public bureaucracy, most of whom were members of the FSTSE and the CNOP, and politically linked to Martínez Domínguez. These politicians had created and sustained their political and economic power within national party structures by controlling and allocating fiscal resources, both local and national. They wielded most of their power in Mexico City, since it was home to most of the nation's bureaucrats, and saw cutbacks in spending as a direct threat to their own political power. Yet it was not just cuts in spending that hurt the old guard. By offering alternative local structures of participation to the CNOP's rank and file, and by substantially altering local bureaucratic control over Mexico City resources and local administrators' abilities to grant favors in the Distrito Federal, Echeverría greatly undermined the political and discretionary power of those old-guard politicians specifically linked to pro-urban growth forces. Even though Echeverría's reforms were designed to revitalize the existing CNOP structure with local populations, they threatened the modus operandi of the CNOP as a national organization, at least to the extent that it institutionalized a way for the rank and file to make specifically urban demands independent of the organization's old-guard leaders, their bureaucratic allies, and their national-level political objectives.

Unfortunately for the president, these were critical errors. The crux of the problem was that the urban legislative changes and the new local and national spending practices introduced by Echeverría challenged the capacity of these forces to use the expansion and administration of Mexico City as a basis for accumulating political and economic power. As early as mid-1971, tensions between Echeverría, old-guard bureaucrats in the CNOP, and progrowth forces grew into what was considered "in all senses of the word, a political crisis unprecedented in [contemporary] Mexican history."[38] The political actors and economic elites who saw Echeverría's urban and national reforms as a threat to their power began to openly challenge the president. Díaz Ordaz loyalist Alfonso Martínez Domínguez led the political attack on their behalf, armed with the institutions and resources of the Mexico City mayor's office.

That Martínez Domínguez even held the post of Mexico City mayor reflects the peculiarities of the political transition from the Díaz Ordaz to the Echeverría administrations. Like a true compromise candidate, Echeverría's initial platform had incorporated the concerns of many different sectors, as noted earlier. But when Lázaro Cárdenas died during the campaign, the PRI was left without its most prominent nationalist spokesman and principal champion for peasant rights. As the campaign unfolded, Echeverría felt compelled to take on Cárdenas's old positions and thus to harden his agrarian reform position, his nationalist orientation, and his opposition to the urban redevelopment policies of the past administration that had pushed growth at the expense of equitable development. This stance on urban and national development, however, began to make several powerful interest groups linked to Díaz Ordaz quite uneasy. Miguel Basañez goes so far as to claim that Martínez Domínguez, who was still president of the PRI, and who saw eye to eye with many in the pro-urban growth faction, advised Díaz Ordaz to "retire" Echeverría's candidacy in the midst of the presidential campaign.[39] Facing opposition within the party even before he took office, Echeverría sought to compromise and bring these dissenting groups into his cabinet as a sign of goodwill and allegiance to his predecessor, Díaz Ordaz, who after all had been instrumental in his appointment. In the spirit of compromise that gave rise to his nomination, Echeverría named several old Díaz Ordaz allies to high-level cabinet positions. Among these appointments was Martínez Domínguez, who became Mexico City mayor in January 1971.

As soon as Martínez Domínguez assumed Mexico City's mayorship, he stormed ahead with the same forceful approach to urban governance and urban reconstruction seen under Alfonso Corona del Rosal, who had replaced Uruchurtu. Given the level of urban mobilization and the signs of presidential support for grassroots participation in urban policymaking with Echeverría as president, Martínez Domínguez was even less open than his predecessor to voices in Mexico City that might have challenged his urban growth plans.

This attitude became apparent upon taking office, when he refused to allow Mexico City's Consejo Consultivo to participate in urban governance. The Consejo's president, Bartolo Sanabria González, publicly lamented that the Consejo Consultivo had become virtually inoperable, and that during his limited term as mayor, Martínez Domínguez had never once called a meeting of the Consejo.[40] Given this approach to governance and urban policy in the capital, almost immediately Martínez Domínguez's appointment as mayor became a serious political problem for Echeverría. Few were surprised, then, when a public battle broke out in June 1971. The pretext for the battle was Martínez Domínguez's use of force against protesting students in Mexico City. But underlying the tensions, which ultimately resulted in Martínez Domínguez's forced dismissal, was something far more serious. Again, it appeared that symbolic issues would be used as the scapegoat for conflict between president and mayor over who maintained power and administrative control in Mexico City.

Echeverría's battle with Martínez Domínguez was not over one particular protest incident. Rather, what was under contention was Martínez Domínguez's institutional capacity to push a certain developmentalist position in the nation's most critical political and economic locale, Mexico City, of which urban redevelopment, and even attitudes toward urban protest, were a critical part. Put another way, what was at stake in the Echeverría–Martínez Domínguez controversy was which faction of the party was to control politics and policy in the capital city, and with whose objectives in mind. The event that brought these issues to the surface and signaled Mayor Martínez Domínguez's challenge to Echeverría took place on June 14, 1971, when, in Echeverría's absence from Mexico City, the mayor was involved in instigating a violent confrontation between striking students and what was meant to look like the Echeverría administration. Under Martínez Domínguez's orders, Mexico City police stood back while a paramilitary force attacked a group of demonstrating students at the Monumento de la Revolución. In later accounts, it was determined that the paramilitary force, known as Los Halcones (the Falcons), was politically linked to Martínez Domínguez. There were also reports that members of the Mexico City police department, who were under the mayor's command, actually participated in the attack along with the Halcones.[41]

By staging an attack on students in the name of the Echeverría administration, Martínez Domínguez and his allies sought to remind students of Echeverría's role in the 1968 Tlatelolco student massacres and thereby resuscitate a repressive and antidemocratic image of the president. The mayor's actions were intended as much more than a case of violent mudslinging: The attack on students was also intended to demonstrate to the president that

Martínez Domínguez had the institutional apparatus and political support for wielding independent power in Mexico City, certainly enough to seriously obstruct Echeverría's urban reform program at least. The lesson was not lost on observers of the incident: "President Echeverría, who came to power with a commitment to reform the government apparatus and redirect Mexico's economy domestically and internationally . . . [learned] that his capacity to transform the economy depends on his political power."[42] The Halcones incident, then, also was intended to stall Echeverría's intended efforts to reform urban administration and raise grassroots support among rank-and-file constitutents of the CNOP. Although they were not the only CNOP constitutents alienated by the Díaz Ordaz administration, students had been among the most vocal and active. Their support was critical to Echeverría's ability to create a political base strong enough to make him independent of Díaz Ordaz and his pro-urban growth allies, and Echeverría had targeted their support both in and outside the CNOP during the campaign and these first months in office. Thus Martínez Domínguez's involvement in the attack, which stirred outrage among students, in part displayed the old CNOP leadership's opposition to political change within their sector, as well as their and other part members' worries that, with student support, Echeverría might put together a broad enough political alliance to implement shared development and its controversial spatial, sectoral, and social components.

Given what was at stake in terms of his own political bases, Echeverría refused to let the Martínez Domínguez challenge pass. He responded vehemently to the mayor and other public and private sector challengers by publicly chastising what he labeled the "foreign interests and reactionaries who instigated the massacre" of students. To Mexican political observers, this was an oblique reference to "old-guard diazordistas, the armed forces, and other encrusted interests" in the private sector.[43] Echeverría, moreover, used this opportunity to demand Martínez Domínguez's resignation, along with that of the head of the PRI's executive committee, the chief of Mexico City police, and several others involved in the action against students.

ANOTHER STANDOFF IN MEXICO CITY?

In pushing through Martínez Domínguez's resignation from the Mexico City mayorship, President Echeverría's actions paralleled those of his immediate predecessor, Díaz Ordaz, who had seen Uruchurtu's independent control in the Distrito Federal as an obstacle to implementing desired policies as well, although the tables were turned somewhat in terms of each participant's position on urban growth and administration. Echeverría, like Uruchurtu, sought to limit Mexico City growth, while Díaz Ordaz and Martínez Domínguez pursued a growth-oriented developmentalist vision. Yet unlike Uruchurtu, Echeverría sought greater inclusion of the urban poor and working classes in his approach to urban administration, a stance that Díaz Ordaz and Martínez Domínguez were not fully committed to but exploited anyway in order to force Uruchurtu's resignation. Yet in the 1971 mayoral-presidential conflict, controlling Mexico City was even more critical for Echeverría than it had been for Díaz Ordaz. Why? Because urban, political, and economic developments during the 1950s and 1960s, especially between 1966 and 1970, after Uruchurtu's dismissal, had linked the CTM and the CNOP leadership to pro-urban growth forces, and had split the CNOP leadership from the rank and file. Without CTM and CNOP leadership supporting Echeverría's urban policy and political objectives, the president was forced to rely largely on institutional structures and practices in the Distrito Federal to make policy and generate political support, instead of the party's incorporated sectors. This stood in stark contrast to Díaz Ordaz, who could—and did—rely on the CNOP and CTM leadership to do his bidding with Mexico City populations. Accordingly, the extent to which Mexico's president—and the PRI leadership as a whole—could still influence urban policy in the capital rested on the president's ability to hold sway over decisions made in the Mexico City mayor's office.

With Martínez Domínguez out of the way, it at first appeared that many of President Echeverría's political problems would be solved and that he would have full control in the capital city. After June 1971, the president was able to make some fundamental changes in urban policy in the capital that reflected his developmental priorities rather than those of Martínez Domínguez and his pro-urban-growth allies. One of the most noteworthy examples was the administration's new position on the subway. The METRO project, in fact, had been another focal point of conflict between Mayor Martínez Domínguez and the president. Thus, Echeverría's changing positions on the policy, both before and after Martínez Domínguez's removal, reflected the balance of power between urban reformers and progrowth forces. Throughout the presidential campaign, for example, Echeverría had been reluctant to support the METRO project, though he noted that traffic congestion in the capital was a major problem. Echeverría made it clear that he was worried about the METRO's enormous costs, its high import value, and its contribution to foreign indebtedness. However, as soon as Martínez Domínguez assumed the mayoralty, there were behind-the-scenes pressures to continue the project. For example, in press accounts of Echeverría's cabinet appointments and upcoming policies and activities, the new word was that "for the next six years the Departamento del Distrito Federal should be continuing with the METRO."[44]

The problem, of course, was that the METRO project so strongly pushed by Martínez Domínguez was inconsistent with the program of shared development. To invest so much in Mexico's largest city, especially through extension of the METRO, would reinforce urban growth and the infrastructural neglect of smaller cities and rural areas, which Echeverría had vowed to develop more equitably in order to counterbalance Mexico City's dominance. Since all the subway technology was produced in France, the METRO would require substantial foreign imports, which Echeverría had pledged to reduce during his term. Finally, beyond the general problems of foreign borrowing and importing, the subway had limited potential to generate export earnings or increase employment, two additional objectives of the shared development strategy. Thus Martínez Domínguez and Echeverría found themselves in a situation similar to that of Uruchurtu and Díaz Ordaz, with horns locked over rapid mass transit in Mexico City. Just a few months before his dismissal, Mayor Martínez Domínguez noted publicly that he was not able to extend the METRO network as he wished, precisely because there "were some in support and others opposed."[45]

With Martínez Domínguez out of the mayor's office, urban policies changed dramatically. Echeverría publicly committed his administration to bus transport, highway development, and other surface transport improvements. Moreover, urban transport policies under Echeverría after 1971, as under Uruchurtu, clearly benefited the urban bus industry through such measures as shortened routes, increased fares, concentrated bus lines, and major expenditures on surface construction of existing roadways. Proposals pushed by Martínez Domínguez to produce an extensive network of subway tracks in the metropolitan area were also scrapped; and from 1971 to 1976 no new construction on the subway network was undertaken, except for a few months in late 1971 and early 1972 to complete the lines already initiated under Díaz Ordaz. The METRO network remained more or less the same length during the entire Echeverría administration, with money spent only on operation and maintenance of the existing system. All these policy decisions stood in clear opposition to the urban policy agenda of the Díaz Ordaz administration, which had made the METRO a priority, built close to forty kilometers of track in three years, and expected to see the network grow under Martínez Domínguez's mayorship.

That Echeverría was able to end expansion of the METRO after 1971 was a demonstration of his renewed ability to set the urban policy agenda in Mexico

City. But this observation raises several important questions about his administration and about the relationship between urban and national development policy. Why did an administration that was known to be a relatively progressive and populist one, characterized by the introduction of many urban, economic, and political reforms and a serious commitment to greater state intervention, shun a public transport system (the METRO) and support a private service (buses) instead? Why did a president known for nationalist economic policies give priority to surface over underground transport for the capital city, a decision that many claim clearly benefited the U.S.-dominated automobile industry in Mexico? Why did a president who called for increased technological innovation and efficiency oppose the modern and sophisticated METRO technology and instead support polluting and energy-inefficient buses? And why did this progressive and so-called populist administration take a position on the METRO identical to that of Ernesto Uruchurtu, considered to be one of the PRI's more conservative and backward-looking politicians?

These questions about Echeverría's position on the METRO highlight several popular yet competing views of the logic of Mexican politics and policy. One possible explanation that is frequently heard in Mexico is "projectitis," a term referring to a public figure's preoccupation with a particular project as a way to raise his or her reputation. Since the METRO was considered Díaz Ordaz's pet project, some in Mexico argue that Echeverría shunned the subway project mainly to distance himself from the previous presidential administration. Others have concentrated on corruption within the political system as an explanatory factor, and have portrayed both Echeverría and Octavio Sentíes, Martínez Domínguez's successor as mayor, as allies of the urban bus industry who would personally profit from favoring surface transport over the METRO. Sentíes was the corporate lawyer for the Alianza de Camioneros and thus had clear political ties to the bus industry. Finally, there are those who make the less cynical and more technical argument that the Echeverría administration simply did not have the resources required to continue the subway project. Each of these views clearly holds a kernel of truth; but each also reflects an incomplete and overly simplistic view of the Mexican political system, thus leaving much to be explained about Echeverría's decision to halt the subway. For example, if "projectitis" was the problem, why would Echeverría continue some of Díaz Ordaz's urban projects, like peripheral highway development, but not others, such as the METRO? If lack of resources was the principal issue, how and why was it decided to cut funding for the METRO, but increase support for other urban and national projects? And if desire for personal gain explains the demise of the METRO, why did Echeverría and his newly appointed mayor Sentíes vacillate on their position on the subway project? Moreover, why would Sentíes and the urban bus industry not have been able to extract "rents" from service delivery with greater subway expansion? Mexico City, after all, was nearing the size of the world's largest city in 1970. There was little likelihood that track extension could ever meet the population's growth and transport demands, and thus bus transport was still—and would continue to be—quite necessary.

Arguments about corruption and personal gain for Mayor Sentíes and his clients, the Alianza, are not as hard to dismiss as the issue of Sentíes's appointment, so let us begin there. The reason why Sentíes became the new mayor offers insight not only into the fate of Mexico City's METRO but also into Echeverría's efforts to link local and national development priorities. Indeed, the ouster of Martínez Domínguez and his replacement by Sentíes enabled Echeverría to achieve some of the stated objectives of shared development, especially but not exclusively those aimed at Mexico City. However, the appointment of Sentíes and the changes in urban development policy this wrought also exacerbated intraparty conflicts, generated widespread urban political mobilization, and contributed to an urban and national fiscal crisis. So why did Echeverría put Sentíes in the mayorship, and what does that say about the impact of urban development conflicts on the PRI and about the relationship between urban and national developments under Echeverría?

AN ALLY AND *TRANSPORTISTA* TAKES CHARGE

Echeverría's appointment of Octavio Sentíes as mayor of Mexico City came in the midst of forceful challenges to the president's urban vision by Alfonso Martínez Domínguez and his progrowth allies in mid-1971. In the context of open conflict before and after the Halcones incident, Echeverría knew that placing a close political ally in the mayorship was an absolute necessity, especially one who shared his overall developmental objectives and who could effectively administer Mexico City at the same time. Octavio Sentíes was the perfect candidate. He was a longtime member of the CNOP who might help the president establish close ties with the CNOP's rank and file, and possibly even some of its old-guard leadership. Sentíes's credentials as a lawyer also would serve him well in administering the new legislative changes being introduced in the Distrito Federal. Moreover, as noted earlier, Sentíes made his professional and political name as a corporate lawyer for the Alianza de Camioneros specializing in urban transport law. This meant that his inclusion on Echeverría's governing team also brought the active political support of the Alianza and its founder and undisputed leader, Rubén Figueroa Figueroa.

Besides offering full control over the provision of urban services in Mexico City, Figueroa and the Alianza de Camioneros had long been advocates of nationalist industrial development in Mexico. As early as the late 1950s and early 1960s, Figueroa led a group of bus line operators who called for the Mexicanization of the bus industry, demanding Mexican control of the transport industry and use of locally produced bus equipment whenever possible. Despite his reputation as a corrupt and ruthless businessman and politician, Figueroa was considered a powerful "reform-minded" member of the PRI, at least in terms of his antagonism to the pro-foreign-capital elements that had emerged in the last administration and, as such, was considered one of the best-known Echeverristas in national politics.[46]

With Figueroa's personal and corporate ally Sentíes in control of Mexico City, Echeverría could cast a wide net for political support that included many beyond the urban bus industry. The president could also count on the smooth and efficient transport servicing of the capital city. This would not only aid Echeverría's attempt to seriously address urban problems, which after all was a principal campaign promise; it would also be an absolute necessity if the METRO was not to be extended, since buses were the principal alternative to mass rapid transit. Thus, even though many observers argue that it was Sentíes's appointment as mayor that explains Echeverría's rejection of subway extensions and support for surface transport, the logic works just as well the other way around. That is, once Echeverría decided to shun the METRO project and introduce a new urban development vision in the capital, a decision that was determined both by his national development objectives, his political conflicts with Martínez Domínguez's forces, and his opposition to unlimited urban growth, it was absolutely necessary that he appoint a mayor who could guarantee control in Mexico City and who could ensure that other means of urban transport would be well provided. Enter Sentíes.

As the urban voice for Echeverría in Mexico City, Mayor Sentíes was an outspoken and unequivocal supporter of the president's urban priorities. Upon taking office in mid-1971, Sentíes made it clear in his public statements that he would back Echeverría's urban reforms and reject the urban policies of his predecessor, Martínez Domínguez. In a meeting with CANACINTRA representatives early in his term, Sentíes declared that "the era of sumptuous and unnecessary works is over," and that it was time to make "social benefits the priority" for Mexico City residents.[47] He announced a totally new program of public works and took the occasion to state that METRO construction would not continue.[48] In outlining urban policies, moreover, Sentíes frequently underscored the differences between his urban objectives and those of Díaz Ordaz, particularly with regard to the METRO. The new mayor claimed that his concerns were not to "achieve a monumental work in the Distrito Federal to perpetuate his [own] name"; but rather, to work "tirelessly for the benefit of the most needy classes by channeling the largest quantity of the Distrito Federal's resources to public works in the *colonias proletarias* and in the 'belts of misery'" that surrounded the city.[49] And as he laid out his strategies, Sentíes was careful to identify urban growth as the source of the city's current problems, and to link rapid growth to the scarcity of public services in the capital.

In distinguishing his urban objectives from those of the previous administration, Sentíes explicitly targeted the disenfranchised urban groups that had initially supported Uruchurtu and opposed Díaz Ordaz. These were also the groups that Echeverría hoped to accommodate with shared development. In early July 1971, for example, Sentíes proclaimed that his administration would not only seek "the humanization of public services," it would also grant greater "opportunities to youth for the promotion of their physical and intellectual development"; implement a "profound regeneration of municipal services," which would include efforts to build schools, markets, and popular housing; and actively work on administrative decentralization in the capital, by revitalizing the "linkages between government and citizen in the 16 *delegaciones*" of the city.[50] In short, Sentíes and Echeverría sought to rebuild the confidence and participation of the urban poor and middle classes in the provision and administration of the capital's public services.

The change in orientation in the Distrito Federal was intended to be, in Sentíes's own words, "a true urban revolution."[51] In political terms, this meant a legitimization of one-party rule by reinvigorating the CNOP and extending its appeal among the urban poor and middle classes. This probably explains why Sentíes directed much of his rhetoric and policy toward the groups that were formally represented by the CNOP—but who had been upstaged by squatters after Uruchurtu's departure—like street vendors and small *comerciantes* who populated downtown areas. Sentíes in fact decreed selective modifications in the labor codes in order to expand the hours of Mexico City shopkeepers, and announced a new plan to employ *comerciantes ambulantes* in "dignified, useful and more rewarding activities."[52] Thus, even as Sentíes and Echeverría took on the antiurban growth stance of Uruchurtu, they did so in a way that balanced the demands and concerns of street vendors and other informal sector workers along with those of small shopkeepers and other more established central city residents.

In addition to structuring policies around the concrete concerns of specific occupations and groups, Sentíes worked hard to link the interests of the middle classes with those of the urban poor and thus overcome the schisms within the CNOP. For example, in an August 1971 public meeting Sentíes called on Mexico's "cultured and technically skilled" middle classes to increase their sensibility to social problems of the city's poor.[53] In November, Sentíes enjoined, with some success, local industrialists in the CANACINTRA to work both with him and other urban groups to solve the city's problems. In a public statement heralding a new "stage of co-responsibility in attitude with respect to serving this grand City," the CANACINTRA pledged to keep the capital "the city of palaces, but a city of palaces where the poor can also enter."[54]

The key component in Echeverría's and Sentíes's urban revolution, however was the *junta de vecinos* system. Despite the great friction this system initially generated between Echeverría and groups allied with Martínez Domínguez in early 1971, when it was first announced, Mayor Sentíes made the *junta* the primary vehicle through which urban popular and middle classes could present their demands to Sentíes and, through him, to Echeverría. The *junta* also served as an important symbol of Echeverría's ability and desire to respond to urban groups who had been unable to push their demands through other formal political structures, especially through the CNOP, after Uruchurtu's dismissal. In his first public interview as mayor, Sentíes "called for collaboration from all the inhabitants of the Distrito Federal on projects to be undertaken, and he spoke of the *vecino* [resident], who had the capacity to raise his understanding and personal knowledge of government works" by participating.[55] Within a week of taking office, Sentíes formalized this commitment to citizen participation by presenting the city's new plan to administer public services and restructure urban governance through the *junta de vecinos* system. As in other pronouncements and plans made by Sentíes and numerous public spokesmen during the Echeverría administration, problems associated with rapid urban growth figured into the development and justification of the proposed plan. Sentíes characterized the reform of urban governance as especially critical because it would enable the city to deal with the "violent growth" it had suffered, and with the extraordinary problems that the "insensitivity or lack of attention" to this urban growth had produced.[56]

In addition to the decentralization of decision making, this *junta de vecinos* was expected to address Echeverría's concerns about reviving political legitimacy among urban populations. Since plans about schools, housing, and buildings were to be passed through the new *junta* system, local residents could again feel that they had a voice in decisions affecting them. Hopes were high, moreover, that these changes would bring political benefits to the PRI as a whole. Sentíes believed that the new system would help the *delegaciones* function more responsively to those who lived in their respective jurisdictions. That is, even though the new *junta de vecino* system would bypass the CNOP,

Sentíes and Echeverría still thought the new system would buttress the PRI's legitimacy because the *delegaciones* would be the principal territorial unit for electing senators and congressmen.

THE URBAN REVOLUTION STALLED

With Sentíes as mayor of Mexico City, it looked as though Echeverría might achieve his shared development objectives, especially their urban dimensions. He was able to introduce a series of administrative changes in urban and national development policies, some of which had already been legislated but were difficult to implement with Martínez Domínguez in office. He was able to halt the METRO project and carry out a massive industrial decentralization plan, which established industrial parks in other regions of the country, and he promoted development in several other critical regions far from the nation's overpopulated center and closer to the coast and borders. Still, far from solving the political problems that had reached a peak during the Díaz Ordaz–Martínez Domínguez period, the Sentíes-Echeverría team and the urban policy reforms they introduced revived old conflicts and created several new ones, especially those that touched on the ability of previously powerful forces to push urban redevelopment and growth policies. Among those most affected by the shift in orientation after Sentíes became mayor were ICA and its cadre of engineers and planning technicians, who had sought and successfully gained control over much of Mexico City decision making under Díaz Ordaz. The changes in urban administrative practices introduced by Echeverría gave Sentíes more power over local contracts; and it is no surprise that he selected firms whose leadership was likely to share his perspective on urban development. Yet, as a consequence, ICA and other technocrats pushing the urban growth and redevelopment vision were either politically or economically shut out. It was public knowledge that ICA's public contracts for infrastructure projects in the Distrito Federal declined dramatically while Sentíes was in office.[57] Even according to its own accounting documents, ICA's share of contracts with the Distrito Federal dropped from sixteen during the Díaz Ordaz administration to two under Echeverría.[58] In value, this was a dramatic decline: ICA's revenues from these contracts with the Distrito Federal fell from 809,701,000 pesos during the Díaz Ordaz period to less than one-tenth that amount, 69,055,000 pesos, under Echeverría.[59]

At issue for ICA and other pro-urban redevelopment forces during the 1971–1976 period were not only the personal losses by urban development contractors, but also the myriad agencies Echeverría assembled to administer the new programs. These new agencies complicated bureaucratic procedures rather than streamlining them, and undermined many of Echeverría's efficiency principles. This, in turn, did little to smooth his relationship with old-guard bureaucrats who were already unhappy with their loss of control over urban policy and administration in Mexico City. As the antagonism mounted, Echeverría and Sentíes had little recourse but to compromise many of their objectives, specifically their positions on public spending, the subway project, and urban political reform. By January 1972, scarcely six months after Martínez Domínguez's dismissal, there was evidence that Echeverría was in for sustained conflict with CNOPista bureaucrats and other urban administrators over his urban revolution, and that he needed to back off.

Even with the strong support of Mayor Sentíes, Echeverría's program was generating opposition among Mexico City's government employees. In January, for example, representatives from the Sindicato Unico de Trabajadores del Gobierno del Distrito Federal (SUTGDF), a union of government employees in the capital, visited Sentíes and pleaded with him to protect their positions as civil servants. As noted earlier, much of the SUTGDF membership who had supported Uruchurtu were generally pleased that Mayor Sentíes was implementing many of their original urban policy priorities. Yet the threat of conflict now hung over this organization. While the SUTGDF leadership expressed a desire to remain "enthusiastic about work and disposed to respond to the political dynamics of the Primer Magistrado de la República [Echeverría]," the divisions were serious enough to warrant a public call for "unity" within the rank and file.[60] And as before, what concerned these bureaucrats were changes in the administration of urban services. Among other things, the decentralization of urban decision making and the successful implementation of the *junta de vecinos* system of neighborhood councils was starting to limit the autonomy and prerogatives of the city's bureaucracies.

The impact of the new *junta* system on past urban policymaking practices was clear in several ways. For one, shopkeepers and *comerciantes* now bypassed city agencies and presented their concerns and demands directly to the mayor. Many of these demands ran counter to the urban policy practices around which local bureaucrats had built their small empires and around which powerful urban forces had come to dominate urban policy. In February 1972, for example, the Central Revolucionaria de Comerciantes e Industriales en Pequeño met with Sentíes and presented a list of demands, including requests for the construction of clinics and assistance centers for their constituents, technical assistance in establishing a commercial distribution system, creation of new supply centers, and removal of *vendedores ambulantes* from their zones of principal activity. Not since Uruchurtu was removed from office had these groups appeared to have such direct—or at least public—access to the mayor. To the dismay of local bureaucrats, Mayor Sentíes not only let the Central Revolucionara into his office, he acceded to their demands. Sentíes's urban policies and administrative reforms also relegitimized the practice of local demand making by groups with little power or connections within the CNOP, and by doing so limited the less-than-legal privileges of the bureaucrats. For many civil servants, administering and regulating the services offered by local residents with little political power in the party had been one of the principal ways of securing extra income through bribes. City inhabitants had long complained about the corruption of local administrators and their great appetite for payoffs, a situation that had played a part in the drive to restructure urban decision making in the first place. These complaints frequently came from the rank and file of the CNOP, whom Echeverría hoped to accommodate: shopkeepers, street vendors, and other *comerciantes* who were subject to health regulations and restrictions on working hours.

Successes in this regard, however, were not without cost. Facing declining power and autonomy, bureaucratic opposition increased and hindered Echeverría's program of shared development. And an important consequence of vocal and sustained bureaucratic opposition to his urban revolution, in fact, was that Echeverría was never in a strong enough political position to give "teeth"—in Alan Gilbert and Peter Ward's words—to most of his urban reforms, especially the *junta de vecinos* system.[61] That is, opposition from local bureaucrats was so strong that the *junta* system never materialized as more than a symbolic reform in the structure of urban participation. In assessing the reasons why the *junta de vecinos* reform remained largely symbolic, scholars like Gilbert and Ward tend to focus on its hierarchic character. The *junta* could consult with the city government, but had no direct power over decision making. Furthermore, the *junta* worked through the *delegación*, a territorial unit of electoral participation controlled by the PRI. In identifying these factors, then, scholars have generally considered Echeverría's introduction of the *junta* system as disingenuous. To put it mildly, most observers considered this system a typical example of state manipulation of popular sentiments with no real reformist intent.

This interpretation is compelling, and few would doubt that Echeverría intended to reshape the entire system of political participation in Mexico City, particularly in a way that could threaten the PRI's political hegemony. Nor is it difficult to understand Echeverría's caution, given that he took office at a time of great citizen unrest and mobilization. But these explanations ignore the conflicts and political problems that Echeverría faced from fellow party members and other state actors, particularly local bureaucrats in the Distrito

Federal, all of whom worried about the extent and nature of the urban reforms embodied in the *junta de vecinos* system. That is, prevailing explanations miss important contextual factors by tending to assume a homogenous and all-powerful state apparatus, one fully in control of reforms and both willing and able to pull off such a manipulative gesture.

If we instead consider the urban political problems and bureaucratic opposition Echeverría suffered in the first years of his administration, we can understand why the *junta* structure was not endowed with more substantive power. To introduce this new system in Mexico City *and* to endow it with full powers would have irreparably split the CNOP and alienated progrowth forces to the point of a full-blown political confrontation with Echeverría. Indeed, to fully empower Mexico City neighborhoods would have called into question the existing corporatist structure, which relied on national political institutions like the CNOP and CTM to represent political concerns and demands of local populations. Thus it may be argued that the *junta* system was not given teeth, so to speak, due to contention within the state itself about urban political reform and the role of national political actors and institutions in local policymaking, not because it was a Machiavellian effort to co-opt the populace. This assessment becomes credible if we take into account that the *junta* system from the beginning was clearly contingent on political conditions. The *junta de vecinos* was not even semioperational until Sentíes became mayor; and the system, set up to work through the electoral *delegaciones* and established neighborhood organizations, also was susceptible to control by the CNOP. Many of the *junta* representatives were drawn from the same organizations that the CNOP had dominated for years. With Martínez Domínguez and other progrowth and bureaucratic forces controlling the CNOP and its patron-client linkages, it is no surprise that the *junta* did not act more forcefully than it did.

For our purposes, however, exactly why the *junta* system did not serve as a viable alternative for local political participation is not nearly as telling as what its so-called toothlessness meant for Echeverría and for urban development policy in Mexico City. Echeverría's inability to truly empower and vitalize the *junta de vecinos* system, whatever the causes, spurred him to cultivate his own patron-client relationships to offset those still controlled by antagonistic bureaucrats and CNOP leadership; these connections would ultimately impact both urban policy and national politics in Mexico. Between mid-1971 and 1973, Echeverría established several new, semiautonomous agencies charged with the implementation of urban policies, primarily those related to land tenancy, housing, and other policies that required substantial state intervention and that were considered relatively radical. Among the best known were the Procuraduría de Colonias Populares (PCP), the Fondo Nacional de la Vivienda, the Fondo Nacional de Habitación Popular (FONAHPO), the Fideicomiso de Desarrollo Urbano del Distrito Federal (FIDEURBE), and the Instituto del Fondo Nacional de la Vivienda para los Trabajadores (INFONA-VIT). Some of these new agencies functioned through the Distrito Federal, like the PCP, and others through the federal government, like FIDEURBE and INFONAVIT; yet their objectives were almost identical: to offer institutional mechanisms for primarily urban populations to wield demands about critical local services, especially housing.

Again, Alan Gilbert and Peter Ward see the establishment of these agencies as a product of Echeverría's efforts to co-opt politics while presenting an image of openness. They argue that these new agencies for housing and urban infrastructural development were intended "to generate close contact with existing leaders and to attend to their demands." They also claim that Echeverría "kept 'open house' to *barrio* residents and their petitions, responding personally to any crisis that threatened to cause major civic disruption [in order to supplant his] power to modify agency programmes and to develop a wide patronage network." [62] Yet, clearly, Echeverría's concerns signified something more than self-aggrandizement or political megalomania. He used these new agencies and networks to build an institutional framework for strong relations with local communities; and this occurred precisely because the *junta* structure had failed to provide such a relationship.

THE PARADOX OF URBAN REFORM

Like many of the early 1971 reforms in urban administration and in political practices, Echeverría's later efforts also initiated a new round of conflict. This cycle of reform and conflict, in fact, marked Echeverría's entire term in office, alternately advancing and limiting his administration's efforts to modify the course of political and economic development in Mexico City and the nation as a whole. This situation was not simply due to Echeverría's personal and political obstinacy in implementing shared development, or even to his opponents' concerted efforts to protect their own domains of profit making or bureaucratic control. It can also be traced to the ways in which class and urban concerns did and did not articulate within the existing national corporatist structures of the PRI. Political structures of incorporation established in the 1930s and early 1940s were founded and organized around class identities. Yet by the 1960s and early 1970s, urban problems had risen to the forefront of political debate as much as workplace and other purely class-specific concerns. Because urban problems and urban administrative concerns frequently split both classes and the organizational structures of political incorporation, especially the CNOP, the PRI itself became ever more divided and unable to reach consensus. And among the issues that divided the PRI at this time, those related to the servicing and administration of Mexico City were paramount, especially questions about which urban services were to be provided in the capital, with whose interests at heart, and with how much grassroots participation.

Echeverría's answers to those questions, as revealed in the establishment of the *junta de vecinos* and several other political and administrative reforms, gave support to some factions within the party while antagonizing others. Yet because there was no consensus, and because both sides in the debate counted on equally widespread and strong support from a variety of forces, the conflict continued throughout the Echeverría administration. That both the president and the mayor were unified in their position on urban services and participation—unlike during the Díaz Ordaz administration, when Uruchurtu took an opposite line—explains why the conflict continued unabated, despite strong opposition from other quarters in the party, and why no one set of forces triumphed fully, as occurred in the blow-up between Díaz Ordaz and Uruchurtu. Yet paradoxically, it was precisely because the conflict continued unabated within the party that Echeverría worked so hard to introduce new urban institutional reforms. The existing political structures of incorporation both fed the conflict and deepened the stalemate, because of the disarticulation between urban and class concerns evident in the 1960s and early 1970s. It was therefore even more necessary for Echeverría to create new political structures and mechanisms with jurisdiction in the capital city to help push through his reforms.

By 1971, old structures like the CNOP were split and its leaders were unable to take a firm position within the party; the Mexico City bureaucracy was too well entrenched and self-protective to allow changes that might undermine its own gains and position. Although the institutional reforms Echeverría introduced between 1971 and 1973 were intended to facilitate the processes of urban governance, they only deepened the trenches of intraparty conflict and thus created greater obstacles to governance. This occurred because many of Echeverría's administrative changes provided organizational bases to challenge the progrowth position, which further angered and mobilized his opponents. Echeverría's urban reforms also threatened to alter—if not undermine—the political structures and practices upon which the PRI had based so many years of stable rule. Most notably, the creation of the *junta de vecinos* structure in 1971 and the appointment of Sentíes that same year shifted the locus of decision making about some of the most principal concerns of the CNOP's constituents away from this national political organization and onto the local level. As such, Echeverría's urban reforms challenged the rationale for the three class-based structures of political participation that comprised the party, by threatening to make one of these institutions, the CNOP, almost obsolete.

As if this were not enough to generate concern within the PRI, many of Echeverría's administrative reforms also pitted the urban poor and traditional middle classes against each other, in both political and institutional terms, resulting in an array of different institutional mechanisms through which urban populations could—and were required to—make demands. This was especially apparent starting in 1972 and 1973, when Echeverría established a series of new independent agencies to address urban problems. As noted earlier, many of these agencies, like the FIDEURBE and INFONAVIT, were established precisely because the CNOP's top-down control over local bureaucrats and neighborhood associations had prevented the *junta de vecinos* from operating as planned and had prevented much of the CNOP membership itself from willingly complying with many of Echeverría's plans in Mexico City. As a consequence, after 1973 there existed several competing mechanisms, each of which struggled for the hearts and minds of urban populations and each of which allowed different groups to wield demands. With the establishment of independent agencies linked directly to the presidency, some low-income communities bypassed the party and headed directly for the federal state apparatus, even as others already linked to the CNOP through urban *caciques* did not.[63]

The *junta de vecinos* structure, at least as envisioned by Echeverría, nevertheless remained relatively untapped as an independent political mechanism, since what did exist of that system was limited in scope by the actions of old-guard CNOPistas. As Alan Gilbert and Peter Ward note, before Echeverría "most [community] leaders had sought patrons within the party; now they aimed to ally themselves with the heads of government agencies."[64] Accordingly, the establishment of the *junta* system further added to political and institutional fragmentation of local structures for political participation, rather than remedying this problem. Traditional middle classes like shopkeepers and small industrialists frequently found it lacking and thus were motivated to turn to yet another bureaucratic forum for making demands—in this case, the mayor's office. Because traditional middle classes frequently were less concerned about housing than other urban service policies, they had little incentive to use Echeverría's semiautonomous agencies to address the urban housing and property rights concerns of low-income populations like squatters. Sentíes and the Departamento del Distrito Federal provided an open ear for many of their complaints; and Sentíes's ties to urban service providers like the Alianza de Camioneros reinforced his image as institutionally responsible for accommodating urban service demands outside the housing arena. This left the old-guard bureaucrats and other public sector workers in the CNOP without much to do, now that the urban poor used semiautonomous agencies and the traditional middle classes went directly to the mayor.

With reduced rank-and-file support, the old-guard CNOP leadership worried even more about the loss of institutional power, and thus fueled the vicious cycle of political conflict. The CNOP leadership struggled to hold the line against Echeverría and his planned urban reforms in order to protect their institutional autonomy. In response to this retrenchment, Echeverría rapidly mobilized a new cadre of professionals and technocrats to infiltrate the CNOP and keep it loyal to his own urban objectives, but this hardened the intransigence of the old guard. This was first seen as early as November 1971, when groups of militant and progressive *profesionales* and *técnicos* held their first meeting under the auspices of the CNOP.[65] In contrast to CNOP meetings in earlier periods, the participants were young architects, planners, engineers, and sociologists, many of whom had been participants in the sixties student movements and who were now employed in the semiautonomous agencies Echeverría was in the process of establishing. With their involvement, the old-guard leadership's fears about declining political power over the CNOP were realized less than a year later. In November 1972, the CNOP's initial secretary-general, C. Julio Bobadilla Peña, was replaced by Oscar Flores Tapia, a man who was closely linked to progressive youthful factions and who was expected to be more amenable to Echeverría's political and economic objectives. And with the change in leadership in the CNOP, tensions between different factions of state workers also hit the surface, further fragmenting the CNOP internally.

Younger, highly educated, and more progressive professionals and technocrats recruited by Echeverría struggled over both urban and national policy with old-guard state workers, many of whom had arrived at their positions in the bureaucracy through years of service to the party's founding leaders. Those entering the bureaucracy for the first time, under Echeverría's patronage, shared few of the old-guard's concerns about the loss of power and well-established patron-client networks that were expected to result from Echeverría's policy reforms. Yet this made old-guard bureaucrats and progrowth forces that had earlier used this organization to push their perspective even more anxious to hold their own against Echeverría. Their first recourse was to fight from within the organization itself. But soon, old-guard bureaucrats allied with progrowth forces began to look outside the CNOP for ways to challenge the president, and they often relied on private sector spokesmen to do the dirty work. This was clear by late 1972 and it continued through 1973, when Echeverría faced a new wave of outspoken political opposition from large industrial groups who, during the Díaz Ordaz administration, had allied with Martínez Domínguez and other pro-urban-growth forces. Combined with the mounting tensions within the CNOP and a turbulent economic forecast after the international collapse of the gold standard, private sector opposition and preliminary evidence of capital flight gave Echeverría pause for the first time in his administration. By 1975, he began to recognize the potentially fatal political and economic effects of his insistence on pursuing the principal components of shared development, both in Mexico City and in the nation as a whole.

Stuck in the center of a growing controversy, Echeverría found himself with two principal problems. First, it was clear that if private sector forces were angry enough, they could seriously disrupt both the urban and national economy by accelerating capital flight. To the extent that this could counteract any positive developmental aspects of shared development, it would undermine Echeverría's original intentions. Second and equally important, it was increasingly clear that conflict and fragmentation within and between the CNOP and other state agencies entrusted with urban development policy were producing disastrous political results. To the extent that inter- and intra-agency tensions also began to severely limit his capacity to implement shared development in an efficient and administratively coherent fashion, Echeverría was prepared to compromise in order to keep conflict to a minimum.

PHOTOS 16, 17, 18, 19: With downtown areas retaining their traditional character, the city's burgeoning population pushed outward rather than upward, and transport became key to the city's vitality.

16 Trolleys, buses, trucks, and cars compete for access to Calle Bucareli, circa 1960. By Hector Garcia.

17 A program of central arteries (*ejes viales*) built in the early 1970s speeded travel within the city limits. By Hector Garcia.

18 Mexico City's subway, built in 1967, moves millions of commuters from central areas to the city's perimeter. Courtesy of *El Universal* (Mexico City daily).

19 By 1990, the city of palaces was transformed into a network of roadways. Courtesy of *El Universal*.

PHOTOS 20, 21, 22: Poorer populations tended to settle on the outskirts of the capital, where services were scarce, daily commutes tortuously long, and political activism high.

20 "Lost city" (*ciudad perdida*) on the edge of the metropolitan area, where residents live on illegal and underserviced lands, foregoing basic necessities like roads, piped water, and proper drainage. Courtesy of *El Universal* (Mexico City daily).

21 Illegal settlers taking advantage of free access to rail lines. Courtesy of *El Universal*.

22 Residents of a *colonia popular* from the city's outskirts flood the Zocalo to demand schooling and land rights, 1971. Courtesy of the Archivo General de la Nación Mexicana, Colección Hermanos Mayo.

PHOTOS 23, 24, 25: With the metropolitan area nearing 18 million, downtown districts were not immune to the effects of uncontrolled urban growth. Photos courtesy of *El Universal* (Mexico City daily).

23 Street vendors clog a downtown historic district, 1993.

24 Battling vehicles and crowds, daily commuters face chaos as they emerge from the Balderas subway station, 1992.

25 Traffic slows to a crawl on Calle Corregidora, across from the national legislature, as commuters, vendors, and cargo trucks conduct their daily business.

PHOTOS 26, 27, 28: With the exception of its lone skyscraper, the physical character of the downtown area has changed little over the past seven decades; yet population growth and unmanaged sprawl have destroyed its ambiance and set dangerous limits on the city's future.

26 Panorama, Mexico City, 1922. Courtesy of the Archivo General de la Nación Mexicana, Colección Propiedad Artística y Literaria.

27 Mexico City's lone skyscraper, Torre Latinoamericana, 1992. By Francisco Mata Rosas.

28 Avenida Madero at the base of the monument to Revolution, 1992. By Francisco Mata Rosas.

7

FROM URBAN TO NATIONAL

FISCAL CRISIS, 1973–1982

During his first three years in office Luis Echeverría attempted what no other postrevolutionary president had dared: to unlink the servicing and administration of Mexico City from traditional institutions of national politics and to foster the balanced macroeconomic development of the nation as a whole, rather than focusing most federal resources and programs primarily on Mexico City. In addition to establishing new local structures of political participation in the capital, he actively supported the economic growth of other cities by investing scarce national resources in regional development initiatives. This is not to say that through this spatial shift in gears Echeverría sought to completely transform the class and developmental bases of Mexican politics as practiced by Díaz Ordaz and in other presidential administrations, as scholars like Miguel Basañez suggest when they label his administration as a populist break from the immediate past, more in tune with pre-1940 Mexico.[1] In Echeverría's vision, there was ample room for the capital/labor and peasant pacts of the earlier period. However, in the process of institutionally separating the urban and national domains, and empowering populations in the former, Echeverría widened his governing pact to include—though not necessarily prioritize—the urban poor and middle classes with relatively little political power on the national level. Accordingly, Echeverría's administration must be understood not as challenging the formal class basis of past ways of doing politics in Mexico, since technically all classes were still institutionally represented in national party politics, but as challenging the class balance and urban-national articulations in past practices.

The viability of this strategy lay in Echeverría's capacity to efficiently and distinctively administer both the urban and national domains. His choice of Sentíes as mayor of Mexico City was intended to aid in this objective, and it did. In terms of tightly administering the capital city and keeping a lid on the intervention of national political actors in urban development affairs, Sentíes and Echeverría were a relatively successful team. The national economy, however, was an entirely different story. By 1973, national and international economic conditions were such that Echeverría's efforts to redirect macroeconomic development away from Mexico City–based import-substitution industrialization, and to implement a balanced, regionally based export-substitution policy, faced grave obstacles. The country's currency was rapidly weakening against the U.S. dollar, inflation was rising slowly but steadily, and the nation's largest bankers and capitalists—many of whose activities were still located in the Mexico City metropolitan area—were starting to seriously question the administration. And it was in the context of these macroeconomic weaknesses in the national domain that Echeverría's urban-based reforms ran into new troubles. Part of this problem resulted from the historical relationship between the two domains, of course. If the national economy weakened, so too did the urban economy, owing to the concentration of national investments there. But because the relationship was more than reciprocal, the impact of national economic troubles was even more seriously felt in Mexico City. That is, once regional and other national economic activities began to hit the skids, Echeverría faced even more pressure from his antagonists to foster urban-based economic activities, like real estate and urban infrastructural development, in order to counterbalance those losses and generate profit and prosperity in one of the domains where gains could still be easily made. These national economic concerns, moreover, brought many in the private sector and the party itself to challenge Echeverría's efforts to establish greater political autonomy in the servicing and administration of Mexico City.

These developments put Echeverría in a curious bind. With many urban administrative reforms already in place, and Sentíes at the helm in Mexico City, the president had embarked on a plan for change in urban politics and policymaking that could not easily be abandoned. Yet by 1973 and 1974, he was facing even greater pressure to discard his controversial approach to the urban and national economy. In his efforts to strike a compromise that would cede some concessions to various opposition forces, Echeverría modified several of his urban policy positions, especially those policies affecting urban land use and urban growth, including the subway project. The end result, unfortunately, was disastrous for Echeverría, the party, and the macroeconomy: a mix of urban policies with ambiguous content and negative urban service implications, especially in transport. Combined with barely functional structures of local participation, this state of affairs generated serious political dissatisfactions among the city's residents and fiscal problems for both the city and the nation that helped propel Mexico into a fiscal and political crisis in 1975 and 1976.

Although the consequences of Echeverría's compromises in the urban domain after 1973 were not fully apparent until his departure from office in 1976, his successor, José López Portillo, bore the political brunt of these problems. By taking a similar and ill-fated compromise approach, López Portillo faced urban dissatisfaction and fiscal problems that grew into an economic and political crisis of unprecedented proportions. Within five years of Echeverría's departure, in 1981, Mexico found itself facing one of the world's worst debt crises; and the PRI would be struggling to hold onto power, especially in Mexico City, where grassroots opposition was reaching new heights. Mexico City's METRO project played an especially significant role in these developments by increasing both the city's and the nation's foreign debt; and as the city faced its own fiscal crisis during López Portillo's term, Mexico City Mayor Carlos Hank González restructured urban administration in order to adapt to the changed fiscal environment of the city and country. Nonetheless, by 1982 urban political dissatisfaction about transport, infrastructural services, and Mexico City's growing unmanageability translated into widespread mobilization and swelling dissatisfaction with the myriad competing urban political institutions that were introduced in the course of delinking local and national politics and addressing the fiscal consequences.

With foreign debt obligations out of control at the same time, governing officials on both the local and national levels had little room to maneuver, at least within the existing institutional constraints of one-party corporatist politics. Mexico City's authorities, however, were faced with the most serious fiscal, institutional, and political constraints. This condition not only prevented them from responding to the growing urban service demands of the capital city's residents; it also fueled resident political dissatisfaction with local government and one-party rule. In the upcoming pages I chart the origins and effects of the growing political dissatisfactions with the ruling party among Mexico City populations between 1973 and 1982. I link this phenomenon to deteriorating fiscal conditions and trace both these developments to the political reforms and urban policy stances introduced in Mexico City by Mayor Sentíes and his successor, Hank González. Central to this analysis are each mayor's efforts to guarantee his respective presidential administration both the political and administrative scope to fulfill both urban development priorities and national political and macroeconomic objectives. Also critical are the contradictory and ambiguous urban policies that emerged from these efforts to integrate urban and national objectives in the face of declining fiscal resources and the reduced power of existing institutions.

URBAN TRANSPORT AND THE PRESSURE TO COMPROMISE

When both macroeconomic and political problems loomed large in late 1972 and early 1973, Luis Echeverría saw the expediency of appeasing the growing chorus of critics who threatened to further delegitimize his already contentious administration. Various factors pushed Echeverría to reconsider several of his urban policy positions. For one thing, specific urban policies, except for those mandated by the constitution, could be changed relatively rapidly without causing irreparable harm to the fundamental institutional structures and practices of Echeverría's national program of shared development. For another, unlike currency valuations or wage rates, urban servicing decisions could be modified through simple bureaucratic directives, without creating far-reaching political or economic instability. Thus they were a good terrain for negotiation and compromise. Last, Echeverría still depended on good administrative relations with Mexico City Mayor Sentíes, who could accept modifications in specific policies without seeing a threat to the entire urban vision or his commitment to urban reform. The same could not be said for Echeverría's relationships with most other national cabinet ministers, several of whom had already resigned or been replaced because of their dissatisfaction with the president's policies or their attempts to carve out autonomous policy niches.

Among the urban policies Echeverría attempted to modify in order to silence his increasingly vocal critics, the METRO was one of the most obvious candidates for reform. By reversing himself on opposition to the METRO, Echeverría hoped to generate support from bankers, financiers, real estate developers, and other pro-urban-growth forces who sought a jump start in the local economy to compensate for the sluggish national scene. The METRO, moreover, was a high-profile policy as much as it was a controversial one; thus any reforms in this policy were likely to generate public kudos for Echeverría from his antagonists. Accordingly, by late 1972 Echeverría began to openly renege on his opposition to the METRO project. That Echeverría altered his stance on the METRO for the sake of political compromise is especially clear with a look at the timing and nature of the myriad changes he sanctioned vis-à-vis the subway project between 1972 and 1975. Starting in February 1972, before the weakening national economy seriously plagued the Echeverría administration, opposition to the METRO was still firm. Mayor Sentíes publicly questioned the viability of the METRO, stating that the Departamento del Distrito Federal had no plans to extend the METRO.[2] Scarcely seven months later, however, as conflicts within the CNOP over bureaucratic autonomy rose to the surface and private sector forces opened a public campaign against Echeverría in order to turn around the macroeconomy, Sentíes reversed his administration's position.

The administration's position on the METRO remained inconsistent, however, shifting as political conditions dictated. On August 22, 1972, Mayor Sentíes announced that the METRO network would be extended to more than double its length: The city would add fifty-three kilometers of track to the existing thirty-eight in operation, and construction would likely begin later that same year. Within six months, the plans for the full fifty-three kilometers of track extension were scrapped before new construction began, due to fiscal obstacles, although even then the tentative recommitment to mass rapid transit was not fully dropped. Then, in 1973, the administration decided to manufacture one of the key elements of the mass system: the subway cars themselves. Starting in late 1973, even as plans for track extension were stalled, Echeverría gave the go-ahead for construction of manufacturing facilities to produce rolling stock for the subway in the state-owned Ciudad Sahagún industrial complex. By mid-1974 agreements were signed with French technicians, and the production lines started rolling.

Though not always readily apparent, the administration's vacillation on the METRO extension as well as the plans to "Mexicanize" subway production were driven by changing macroeconomic conditions as much as by brewing political conflicts within the CNOP. For example, the talk of new track extensions coincided with Echeverría's late 1972 plan to use government expenditures to help revive high growth rates and to placate bureaucrats whose political power had been curtailed by his initial decision to dramatically reduce public spending. Between 1972 and 1973 alone, federal expenditures rose 41 percent.[3] The METRO was a prime candidate for expenditures, because ICA technicians and other METRO proponents were eagerly waiting in the wings with a fully developed plan that could be implemented almost immediately.[4] Greater investment in the costly METRO project was also expected to counterbalance the banking sector's concerns about Echeverría's earlier austerity measures and their national fiscal consequences. According to Leopoldo Solís, a rapid increase in public spending was of particular interest to bankers and financiers in mid and late 1972 because they were facing an oversupply of capital in their lending institutions; this excess capital had been accumulating in Mexican banks since the late sixties, as a result of the stabilizing development strategy's financial measures.[5] Public spending on the METRO would absorb this uninvested capital and, at the same time, fuel the real estate market by increasing urban land valuation.

This is not to say that Echeverría totally ignored his own shared development policy preferences in favor of the METRO and increased expenditures on other urban projects. In late 1972 and early 1973 the Echeverría government also began investing heavily in tourist infrastructure, mainly in coastal areas, while several medium-sized industrial cities received greater attention and massive investment too.[6] In keeping with decentralization objectives, moreover, those towns and cities most heavily subsidized were located outside the capital, generally in peripheral regions of the country. As a result of Echeverría's efforts in these areas in fact, between 1970 and 1980 Mexico's census registered the appearance of eighty new cities (population 5,000 or greater), an increase of almost 40 percent, which brought the total number of urban localities to 258.[7] Yet despite his desire to keep the initial commitment to industrial decentralization embedded in shared development, Echeverría felt pressure to compromise with respect to his position on urban policy and servicing in Mexico City, and he did so by altering his stand on the METRO project.

Echeverría further modified his position, from one of subway track extension to one of manufacture, largely because of the macroeconomic problems he faced. Once Echeverría started a new round of public spending in late 1972, in the spirit of political compromise, it soon became clear that something had to give with all of these new and expensive projects. Echeverría's political capitulation, for example, had necessitated a rapid increase in the money supply, and the peso's value plummeted. According to the *Quarterly Eco-*

nomic Review of Mexico, by July 1973 inflation had reached such heights that government–private sector relations had "soured," even though the same publication reported "smiles again in the private sector" scarcely three months earlier.[8] At first, Echeverría tried to implement a business tax to finance the increase in public spending. Yet progrowth forces in the private sector balked loudly at the prospect of a tax increase. Many considered it a threatening portent of greater state control over the economy and the private sector, and a move that would cut directly into their profits.[9] Unable to tax business, and facing political pressures over inflation from the private sector, as well as from working and middle classes, Echeverría had to turn to another strategy. Somehow inflation must be stopped; but spending must remain high without raising taxes.

In traversing this circumscribed political and economic terrain, Echeverría again struck a path of compromise that had direct implications for his urban policy stances. As revealed in the 1974 federal budget, three interrelated national objectives guided Echeverría's policy shift after 1973. One was a desire to reintroduce austerity, albeit only partially. Thus many major public works projects were stopped and bureaucratic salaries were once again cut back, since by 1974 many were put under temporary contract in order to achieve, in Echeverría's words, more efficient control of public expenditures.[10] A second objective was to concentrate public spending on projects that reflected or reinforced consensus, especially on those projects that somehow fit private sector demands, Echeverría's own shared development plans, and the social and political concerns of his most loyal bases of political power. The third and last objective that molded Echeverría's compromise and his new national strategy was a preference for borrowing abroad to finance special projects. With nationwide political opposition to tax increases, this was seen as the most viable alternative to the inflationary route of printing money.

In the context of these three national priorities the Echeverría administration's position on the METRO changed to one of stock production rather than track extension. This shift was first clear in January 1974, when Sentíes reversed his 1972 plans to build 53 kilometers of track, and announced that only 12.7 kilometers would be laid. Also in early 1974, Echeverría approved the pending proposal to Mexicanize the manufacture of rolling stock for the METRO, initiating a production schedule that would deliver 345 cars by 1976. Both plans—minimal track extension and the Mexicanization of rolling stock production—relied almost exclusively on French credits. This new stance on the METRO, like the post-1974 compromise strategy on public spending in general that generated it, seemed to cover all the bases. It was a moderate concession to progrowth forces who had argued for subway extension. Even though the plans for track extension were drastically slashed, the Mexicanization project suggested some possibilities for the future beyond Sentíes and Echeverría, which appeased progrowth forces. The Mexicanization project had its own benefits as well. The government's commitment to invest resources in a new production plant in one of the country's new industrial cities, Ciudad Sahagún, was expected to bolster the national economy and generate employment. It would also involve both foreign and national firms, public and private; and because it was based on foreign credits, it would not use scarce public monies.

Both symbolically and substantively, the Mexicanization plan introduced in 1974 demonstrated Echeverría's efforts to strike a compromise between the myriad pro- and antiurban growth forces that had strongly supported or opposed the state-interventionist and nationalist components of shared development. Equally important, by coupling the Mexicanization plan with a refusal to build an overly extensive new network, Echeverría was able to hold onto his critical ally Sentíes and his supporters both in the Alianza de Camioneros and in Mexico City who opposed redevelopment or urban growth and whose loyalty in those difficult times was especially crucial. In the context of the competing political and economic demands, then, the compromise position on the METRO appeared to be a relatively logical and skillful one. Until late 1975 and early 1976, at least, it appeared to give him the political space to balance pro- and antiurban growth factions within and outside the party and thus to keep the PRI's legitimacy relatively intact. Owing largely to his urban policies, despite opposition from far-right and far-left forces in society, Echeverría still commanded support from powerful social and class forces within the party. In addition to his new stance on the METRO, he continued to construct massive amounts of workers' housing in the capital in order to keep labor unions happy; he expanded the technocratization of urban and national planning, in order to employ and incorporate younger middle-class professionals into state activities; and he introduced a policy of urban land regularization that aided some of Mexico City's poorest residents.

Yet Echeverría's attempts to appease labor, the urban poor, professional middle classes, and bankers and big capitalists all at the same time had several fatal flaws, nonetheless. One problem with Echeverría's new urban policies was that they laid the groundwork for urban and national fiscal insolvency. This fiscal crisis first appeared in Mexico City; but given the capital's centrality to the national economy, and the nature of the urban expenditures that underlay the crisis, Mexico City's urban fiscal crisis affected the entire nation. A second weakness in Echeverría's post-1974 policies was their inherent inconsistency with respect to urban growth and urban services. Echeverría was strong in balancing the concerns of different producers, especially in transport, but weak in meeting urban service demands and stemming the urban growth that prevailed. A third problem stemmed from the second and was as devastating for Echeverría as the first: the fact that the urban political and administrative reforms in the capital generated a movement toward self-organization among Mexico City's populations, who soon began to challenge the party for neglecting or inadequately providing urban services. In short, Echeverría's efforts to balance pro- and antiurban growth factions through urban and administrative policy reforms led him to introduce inconsistent and ambiguous—if not contradictory—urban policies.

URBAN SUCCESSES AND FAILURES
IN THE ATTEMPT TO COMPROMISE

An examination of the METRO policy after 1974 reveals the disastrous political and fiscal consequences of Echeverría's efforts to walk both a pro- and antiurban growth line. First, the decision to extend the METRO network and manufacture rolling stock in Mexico contributed heavily to the nation's foreign indebtedness, and the costs weighed as heavily on Mexico City as they did on the nation's current account balance (see Table 6). Of course, Echeverría's new METRO policy cannot alone be blamed for the rising foreign debt, nor for the urban problems and political conflict that beset Mexico in the late 1970s and early 1980s. The administration's policy shifts on urban transportation, however, were highly visible, politically controversial, and economically shortsighted. Moreover, changing positions on the subway and other related urban policies brought increased chaos to urban service provision and created tensions within the party and between the PRI and Mexico City's mobilized citizenry, two developments that placed the party in a difficult position in the late 1980s. Thus Echeverría's compromise on the METRO can be seen as both reflecting and contributing to the fundamental weaknesses of his administration.

One reason that Echeverría's post-1974 compromise on the METRO was so disastrous, both fiscally and politically speaking, was that the Mexicanization of rolling stock production for the METRO was an inordinately expensive proposition. Though the original objective was to bolster confidence in the productive capacity of the national economy, the costs of the technology, patents, and foreign management assistance completely drained Mexico's budget and saddled the government with millions in foreign and domestic debt. Even with Mexicanization of critical parts of the rolling stock,

TABLE 6

Operation Costs of Mexico City's METRO, 1973–1980 (thousands of pesos)

	1973	1974	1975	1976	1977	1978	1979	1980
COST								
Cost of Operation (technical)	304,953	359,338	500,753	706,676	992,290	1,117,932	1,408,286	2,016,688
Cost of Administration	95,221	141,661	204,847	338,847	401,352	644,133	783,050	1,104,821
Cost of Financing[a]	409,706	487,423	458,291	494,146	665,371	40,224[c]	87,757[c]	118,008[c]
Total Cost	809,880	988,422	1,163,891	1,539,669	2,059,013	1,802,289	2,279,093	3,239,517
INCOME								
Income from Ridership	448,375	501,016	565,078	657,284	655,528	851,863	1,022,570	1,182,507
Federal Subsidy	—	—	—	—	900,000[b]	912,000	1,095,000	1,676,600
Total Income	448,375	501,016	565,078	657,284	1,555,528	1,763,863	2,117,570	2,859,107
NET LOSS	361,505	487,406	598,813	882,385	503,485	38,426	161,523	380,410
Without Subsidy	361,505	487,406	598,813	882,385	1,403,485	950,426	1,256,523	2,057,010

% Increase of Net Loss, 1973–1980 (without subsidy): 469%[c]

% Increase in operational and administrative costs, 1973–1980: 680%[c]

[a]This category primarily represents interest payments for the construction and financing of the METRO.

[b]In 1977 the government began subsidizing the operation of the METRO.

[c]In 1978 the federal government began to directly subsidize the debt repayments of the METRO. Hence the reported cost of financing, and the net loss from that year on, do not accurately reflect the magnitude of the losses.

Source: Cuenta Pública del Departamento del Distrito Federal, 1973; 1974; 1975; 1977; 1978; 1979; 1980 (Mexico City: Departamento del Distrito Federal).

less than 50 percent of the value of subway production originated in Mexico; and according to one ICA engineer, it would have cost the government *less* to import subway cars than to manufacture them.[11] Also, the decision to produce subway cars in Mexico did little to generate exports; and there were few forward and backward linkages between rolling stock production and other manufacturing processes. The fiscal problems brought on by local manufacture of rolling stock, however, owed to more than the net costs of manufacture. The patent, technology, and capital for the production process were primarily French and thus contributed directly to Mexico's foreign debt.[12]

Again, to highlight these fiscal consequences is not to argue that Echeverría's decision to manufacture subway cars in Mexico City was the only determinant of the acceleration in foreign borrowing in Mexico between 1974 and 1976. The government borrowed heavily for other industrial projects, and to meet foreign obligations incurred by the Díaz Ordaz administration, principally the costs of technology and debt repayment for the original METRO plan. Nonetheless, undertaking national production of subway cars was much more expensive than continuing with full opposition to the METRO, a stance Echeverría had originally held and one that precluded both track extension and national manufacture. Moreover, Echeverría's decision to produce subway cars in Mexico was not only economically unsound, it also created new political problems. With plans for national manufacture in the works, subway proponents now had reason to push for further track extensions, since the costly decision to produce more rolling stock could be considered irrational if more tracks were not installed as well.[13] And with the possibility of track extensions now much more likely, new conflicts emerged between ICA engineers and Mayor Sentíes over the right mix of subway and bus incentives.

Naturally the controversy between Sentíes and subway proponents also revolved around the extent to which the interests of the Alianza de Camioneros should continue to dictate urban transport policy. Some of these issues were temporarily resolved in 1975 when the Alianza agreed to consolidate its eighty-six bus lines into twenty separate ones, each of which was structured to complement extended METRO services. On the surface, this agreement suited both parties, subway and bus promoters. Yet as a compromise stance, it was just as problematic, in terms of urban development and political controversy, since it sharpened the contradictions of Echeverría's urban strategy and highlighted the principal political flaws of shared development. Why? Because this compromise benefited only urban transport producers—the Alianza de Camioneros and rolling stock manufacturers (mainly ICA and the state-owned Constructora Nacional del Coches de Ferrocarril)—and left urban service consumers high and dry.

The problems with the bus line restructuring compromise became clear after 1975, when urban transport and related problems accelerated in the capital precisely because of the new urban policies hammered out in the compromise between bus and subway proponents. For example, in exchange for the Alianza's agreement to restructure routes, the government subsidized a switch to diesel motors, which used less expensive gas but polluted more. In this deal, bus drivers' routes were restructured to reduce the average number of kilometers traveled from 29.5 to 14.5, even though they were permitted a bus fare hike. In addition, a rise in bus tariffs authorized for the new units created an incentive for bus owners to buy a new type of bus that was manufactured in Mexico, with more Mexican components.[14] The upshot of all this was that transport producers gained and consumers lost. Now Mexico City residents paid more for shorter routes, which added to the total cost of daily commuting; pollution was exacerbated; and, adding insult to injury, residents indirectly suffered the consequences of foreign debt and budgetary deficits associated with the manufacture of subway cars and the construction of the network.

Not only were daily commuting costs higher, but after a six-year moratorium on track extension and after on-again, off-again austerity cuts in transport, service did not markedly improve in any substantial way. This was particularly true of the METRO services, though the assessment rings true for various urban services. For example, because the Echeverría administration failed to commit to an extended subway service that might fully serve the city's millions, and instead kept the same thirty-odd kilometers of central city track, conditions on the METRO deteriorated rapidly during his administration. By 1977, when Echeverría left office, saturation of the subway's three lines had reached a point of crisis.[15] Not only did this endanger passengers, but power losses resulting from an overload of passengers often disabled the entire system and resulted in complete transportation chaos. In typical tongue-in-cheek fashion, taxi drivers jokingly referred to the METRO as Mexico City's greatest bargain: It was the only place in the capital to get a steambath and massage for just one peso. Such claustrophobic conditions, however, were not always humorous. Passenger panic was frequent, with physical injury often the outcome; sexual molestation occurred all too frequently. One particularly gruesome case of public sexual attack in a crowded subway car in the late 1970s prompted the authorities to authorize separate cars for women and children during rush hours. The use of cars segregated by sex and age slightly eased the discomfort for women and children, but armed guards' efforts to pack males into even scarcer space generated a perpetual tone of violence in the underground stations.

Urban transport problems were not due solely to Echeverría's reluctance to extend the subway network. Another critical factor, which further highlights the contradictions inherent in the compromise, was the decision to route all of the city's bus passengers to the three central city subway lines. This served both bus drivers and the subway authorities: Buses would complement, rather than compete with, subway service, and the METRO would generate enough ridership revenues to justify the project's enormous costs.[16] The latter was especially important because the METRO had originally been promoted as a mode of transport for the city's working classes, and thus there were clear political limits to how much could be charged. Yet this meant that the only way to raise revenues was to increase ridership rates. The results were appalling. In addition to overcrowding, daily commutes were long. Residents who lived and worked in the periphery of the city were forced to take buses that routed them from the periphery to the center, then take the METRO, and then travel back out again to the periphery by bus. Of course, commuting time was considerably shorter for those white-collar employees journeying to offices, government buildings, banks, and corporate headquarters located in the central city near the new subway lines. These fortunate few could make it to work with a single subway ride, or no more than one bus and subway ride. Nonetheless, this pattern of commuting was exceptional. Departamento del Distrito Federal documents indicate that as recently as 1981, 97.5 percent of those who used the METRO took multiple transport modes daily. This, in turn, raised the cost of living for the capital's residents. Riders were forced to buy a new ticket on each transport mode; there were no transfers or multi-mode tickets because buses were still privately owned and each line operated as an independent profit-making unit. Between 1966 and 1976, the proportion of family income spent on transport increased from 9.45 to 13.48 percent. With that jump, transport went from the third-largest family income expense in 1968 to the second-largest in 1977, edging out housing, and following only food and beverages.[17]

This convoluted transportation system pushed commuting time to new heights, and Mexico City residents were highly aware of this fact. One article on transport in Mexico City noted that among "the penalties that their fascination with the urban illusion impose[d] on those who live in the capital, transport is surely the most cruel, most constant, and most unjust. Thus, every day we see the cruel paradox of thousands of workers who cross the entire metropolitan area, changing their mode of transport several times, spending as much as four and five hours to get from their homes in Ciudad Netzahualcoyotl to the factories of Naucalpan, Tlalnepantla, and Vallejo."[18] Paradoxically, many of those middle-class residents working downtown, for whom the METRO network was most convenient, refused to take the subway because internal conditions were treacherous or because they identified the subway as the working classes' mode of transport. The disdain and fear middle-class commuters felt for the METRO reinforced their already well-established habit of taking taxis or driving their own cars. Thus while the city's streets became gridlocked by the growth in automobile traffic, the subway also became ever more crowded, due to the force-feeding into it of the city's peripheral residents, who would not have been riding the central city subway if the direct bus routes linking peripheral home and work destinations had not been eliminated. The result was a particularly quixotic state of affairs: low-income, peripheral residents who worked in factories on the outskirts of the city used the central city subway, while middle-class residents whose employment destination was the central city shunned the subway and drove cars or took taxis instead.

The impact of these illogical urban transport conditions and commuting patterns is clear when looking at vehicle usage statistics. In the ten-year period from 1970 to 1980, the number of automobiles in the Distrito Federal tripled, from approximately one-half million to one and a half million. Because the number of buses on the streets increased by fewer than five thousand in the same period of time—and because the METRO network was not extended much either—the ratio of residents to vehicles in Mexico City dropped almost half in the decade welcoming the subway, from 9.7 in 1970 to 4.7 in 1980.[19] Thus, after the subway's introduction there were *more* vehicles on the street, relative to population size, rather than fewer. With the rapid acceleration of automobile usage by Mexico City's middle classes, moreover, levels of pollution also soared. This was due not only to the increase in absolute numbers of vehicles, but also to what transport engineers call intense traffic, a situation in which cars that are forced to move slowly due to congestion pollute more heavily. And as pollution in the city increased and downtown areas became less accessible, residents began to abandon the city for the suburbs in increasing numbers, a pressure that further added to the city's outward growth.

But would the myriad urban problems that emerged in Mexico City during the 1970s have been avoided if Echeverría had not compromised on the subway and instead had introduced a more "correct" policy stance on urban transport? Maybe not. Even if buses had not been fed into the METRO, overcrowding the subways, the middle-class residents would likely have continued to prefer private over collective transport. Nor would extending the METRO network have made a difference, unless authorities could somehow have more effectively controlled or eliminated the low-income METRO users that scared away many middle-class riders. Moreover, if the METRO project had been halted completely, but land speculation and population dispersal had continued, bus services might not have been sufficient to solve the city's transport servicing demands either. Thus urban growth, urban transport chaos, and pollution in Mexico City might have continued—though maybe not at the same pace—if Echeverría had been more committed to mass rapid transit. In order to stem these problems, Echeverría would have had to place constraints on investment, land use, location, and transport. He would also have made many enemies. Probably the last authority capable of doing all that was Uruchurtu; but with his forced dismissal and the introduction of infrastructure for mass rapid transit, it seemed pretty clear that Mexico had passed the point of no return in terms of its technological capacity to control urban growth.

Yet what is important for our purposes is not just Echeverría's inability to control urban growth or urban problems once the decision was made in the late sixties to continue on this path, or even his failure to be more successful in this regard, but rather the nature of the choices he made about urban policy, the political constraints that determined these choices, the ways they were interpreted both within and outside the party, and the ways they affected corporatist politics both locally and nationally. At the heart of Echeverría's compromising position were a series of conflicts and controversies within and between the party and economically powerful forces that made it difficult for Echeverría to successfully unlink urban and national policymaking and at the same time seriously address the city's urban service problems. All decisions about Mexico City's administration and servicing were simultaneously embedded in questions about the national economy and local balances of power within and between the state and the various classes. In the absence of political space or local opportunities to appease all sets of forces and achieve national economic goals as well, Echeverría's response was an ambiguous set of compromising policies that ultimately failed to solve problems in either the political or economic domains, in Mexico City or the nation.

Echeverría's ambiguous urban policy stances were not confined only to transport, either. Given the difficult obstacles he faced in balancing urban and national priorities and constraints, both political and economic, he also produced contradictory policies in several other policy arenas. For example, according to Gilbert and Ward, the Echeverría administration displayed an inconsistent attitude in housing and land use policy in the capital, too. They argue that Echeverría took an ambiguous—if not contradictory—stance toward the expansion of low-income settlements. "New regulatory agencies and [restrictive] legislation on human settlements went hand-in-hand with the emergence of a large number of new settlements—mostly *ejidal* subdivisions and invasions."[20] That is, at the same time Echeverría both restricted and encouraged densification of urban land use in the capital. Moreover, through the Ley General de Asentamientos Humanos introduced a few months before the end of his term, Echeverría attempted to walk the fine line of compromise with respect to administration of the urban domain, as well. This new law governing land settlement sought to give the government power to expropriate land for housing, to limit real estate speculation, and to formalize popular participation in municipal governance. Yet at the same time, the law was designed to give life to a more efficient system of planning that would both empower local technocrats and facilitate the servicing and extension of private property ownership.

The land settlement law turned out to be as disastrous politically for Echeverría as the METRO policy was financially, though again this was not clear until the final days of his administration. What Echeverría set out to do with this juridical reform was to codify the changes in urban governance and political participation that he had been seeking since the beginning of his administration, and at the same time to protect the rights of squatters and the urban poor. However, private sector resistance forced Echeverría to weaken key elements of this law. As with his new position on the subway, Echeverría's compromise on the land settlement law invited criticism, especially from the left, but also from urban residents who felt Echeverría had not carried out the substantive urban changes promised during his campaign and first years in office. Indeed, some critics claimed that the revamped law's true intentions were to obscure the state's capacity to control the population—rather than allow for real grassroots participation and change in the arena of urban services and urban governance.[21] This assessment prevailed despite the fact that the Ley General de Asentamientos Humanos institutionalized fundamental transformations in the power of the state and the community to regulate private land investment, and despite the fact that most organizations representative of banks and big capital criticized it too.

The public response to this law, coupled with the deteriorating urban transport conditions, sealed Echeverría's fate by spurring a large-scale questioning of his strategy of urban governance and national development. By the end of his term, many of the urban poor were beginning to think that Echeverría had ignored their concerns under pressure from bankers and industrialists, even as bankers and industrialists felt that he showed too many populist sympathies. From two different sides, Echeverría was seen as an opportunist who let political ties—rather than policy coherency—dictate his agenda. Most of this growing dissatisfaction, moreover, was concentrated in the capital. This is perhaps clearest from voting statistics for 1976, which show a clear difference in local and nationwide support for the government. In the elections of that year, while the PRI received a little over 80 percent of the vote nationally, its support in Mexico City barely topped 55 percent (see Appendix C).

THE POLITICS OF AMBIGUOUS URBAN POLICIES

Echeverría may have been fortunate that he did not have to face the most serious consequences of his many ambiguous and compromising urban policy positions, but his presidential successor, José López Portillo, was not so lucky. For this new president, the most striking negative consequence of Echeverría's efforts to forge a compromise between competing interests was Mexico's first peso devaluation since the 1950s, which was implemented in 1976 immediately before López Portillo took office. The International Monetary Fund (IMF) had pressured Mexico to devalue its currency in order to counteract the disastrous effects of its accelerating foreign debt, which grew partly as a result of expenditures on both urban development and regional industrialization. Echeverría complied with the devaluations, many claim, in order to spare his friend and political ally López Portillo the negative political consequences of this unpopular action so early in his administration (1976–1982). But President López Portillo could not be spared the negative economic consequences of Echeverría's policies: substantial foreign debt and a sizable current account deficit showing signs of massive capital flight and limited exports, albeit relatively stable imports. Capital flight was partly due to general concern about the recent transfer of power and to uncertainty about the direction of the economy after the 1976 peso devaluation. It was also a result of growing private sector fears that López Portillo would continue Echeverría's ambiguous and populist policies.

Yet just as important as the precarious economic situation in 1977, López Portillo had to address the increasing fragmentation of local structures of political participation, the crumbling urban environment, and growing urban social movements, all of which were also partly traceable to Echeverría's compromises. Alan Gilbert and Peter Ward report that President López Portillo began his adminstration with the objective of "overcom[ing] some of the problems posed by the previous government's failure to improve servicing levels" in Mexico City.[22] They also argue that López Portillo found himself needing to increase the tax base both to finance major public works and to contribute toward the Federal District's massive external debt. Both these problems were as difficult to accommodate as the nation's currency and balance-of-payments crisis. Finding new revenues to finance urban expenditures through either taxation or austerity cuts was difficult, given the nation's weak economic position and IMF stabilization plans. After 1976 it was even harder, because residents in the capital city had become highly organized in the face of the chaotic and inconsistent urban policy positions of the previous administration. To the extent that Mexico City residents continued to make demands for more urban services, not fewer, López Portillo had to find resources to cover both past debt and future projects.

López Portillo's problems with the insistent demands of a highly mobilized urban population owed in no small part to the urban political reforms introduced by his predecessor, Echeverría. Indeed, even though Echeverría's intent had been to offer new structures of political participation that would link the capital's residents to the local state, eliminate grassroots dissatisfaction, and thus legitimize the political system with urban populations, his administrative changes produced almost the opposite effect. With the *delegado* system in place alongside the CNOP, and several programs running out of the mayor's office, fragmented and often competing urban political structures in Mexico City both exacerbated intraparty conflicts over urban issues and helped set the stage for further disenfranchisement of urban populations, since there was no single—let alone unified—organization within the party for either channeling or accommodating the urban demands of Mexico City residents. Indeed, urban forces working within only one of the three structures now had even less strength to command party responsiveness. Moreover, with the fragmentation of mechanisms for urban participation, Echeverría's administration left a growing cynicism among Mexico City's residents. This cynicism deepened as Echeverría appeared as only a weak challenge to powerful and conservative forces in the party, many of whom continued to dominate the CNOP. With many of Mexico City's residents abandoning hope that the PRI would ever address their urban concerns, their enthusiasm for formal political participation in both city and national politics declined, and they began to see the CNOP as a controlled structure for co-opting and regulating urban populations instead of a mechanism for effectively channeling grievances and facilitating political participation.

Just as important, Echeverría's urban reforms actually increased incentives for Mexico City populations to mobilize against the state around urban issues. Because the *junta de vecinos* system he instituted gave residents both a rationale and a formal structure for presenting urban demands, neighborhoods began organizing with greater intensity. Urban social movements in Mexico City, in fact, gathered intense strength during the first years of the Echeverría administration and then accelerated during that of López Portillo. From 1976 to 1979 most particularly, urban residents acted on their cynicism and joined independent and autonomous urban organizations that would by-pass the CNOP and represent their demands directly to the mayor's office through new administrative structures controlled by federal agencies. Urban social movements grew rapidly throughout the 1970s with the participation of populations who, in previous decades, had channeled demands within the CNOP, not only the urban poor, squatters, and renters but also *comerciantes* and *transportistas*.[23] Now these same populations were likely to rely on urban social movements, instead of the CNOP, to press demands about such issues as public housing, transport, roads, water, and urban renewal. By the late 1970s, Mexico City had become a city of highly mobilized and well-organized urban residents who were ready to seriously challenge the PRI's urban policies and priorities; and among their principal concerns were the scarcity and high cost of urban services.

The city's growing urban social movements continued to pressure López Portillo to increase government expenditures on services and social programs in the capital. These demands were extensive and difficult to ignore, especially since they spoke to the heart of the city's most serious problems. Among the issues that urban social movements focused on most actively were land regularization and transport. The former demand resulted partly from Echeverría's 1976 implementation of the Ley General de Asentamientos Humanos, which spurred squatters and other illegal or informal settlers to demand land tenancy and the infrastructural services that generally accompanied regularization, like roads, water, and electricity. Demands for transport could also be traced to Echeverría's policies, though more to his failures than to his successes. Thus, calls for more adequate transport services, including the municipalization of all buses and related transport services, became one of the principal urban platforms of Mexico City's opposition parties during the 1976 election and thereafter.[24] After an administration of favoritism toward the Alianza, urban transport services were considered one of the city's principal urban problems, sparking as much controversy and mobilization as housing. By the late 1970s and early 1980s, in fact, Mexico City saw a rash of bus hijackings by residents to demonstrate their dissatisfaction with urban transport services and the corrupt Alianza. Residents frequently demanded that the city take bus lines away from the Alianza and that it nationalize bus transport and extend the METRO lines. These demands, which were quickly adopted by opposition parties, not only caused ripples in the CNOP, where the Alianza was still quite powerful; they also required huge government expenditures.

López Portillo's political problems were not confined to urban social movements and their demands for urban public expenditures. The new president was also under pressure to please middle classes and progrowth forces within the party. While Echeverría had come to the presidency with a plan to build a coalition of urban poor, working, and middle classes to counterbalance progrowth forces, López Portillo was under party pressure to simultaneously keep these groups plus private sector forces loyal to the party. Echeverría, too, had been compelled to worry about private sector support. But in 1970, he had the advantage of following Díaz Ordaz, who had assured big businesses and their progrowth allies that the PRI was strongly committed to protecting their interests. López Portillo found no such margin for error. He followed a president whose allegiance to progrowth forces—like large industrialists and real estate developers—had been called into question early on, and who, at best, had responded to their concerns only under pressure and with compromise rather than capitulation. Accordingly, from the very beginning López Portillo had to search for common ground among the myriad competing class forces. Making this task more difficult, Echeverría had split any potential coalition wide open, with policies that encouraged conflict between factions within the CNOP, between bureaucratic leaders and the rank and file, and between producers and consumers of urban services. This was the case not only with the administrative reforms that limited the power of old-guard bureaucrats; it was also the case with the city's traditional middle classes. Many of those forces were unhappy with urban transport chaos, with the fact that Echeverría's housing was directed mainly at industrial workers or for the urban poor, and with the land regularization policies that they felt encouraged squatting or lawlessness. With these urban service and administrative changes as his legacy, López Portillo faced more intraparty division and deeper private sector hostility than Echeverría had at the start of his term in 1970.

Amidst this political storm, López Portillo found himself under pressure to please all contending forces, and he proceeded to leap from one expensive program to another, each intending to satisfy a different class or faction. With the concentration of urban problems and activated social movements in the capital, this was most apparent in Mexico City, where public expenditures on all manner of projects skyrocketed in response to growing political dissatisfaction with urban services, and to the dissatisfaction of pro-urban growth forces with development policy. As a result, by early 1980 Mexico City was sinking into a fiscal quagmire, and it appeared that it would soon pull the rest of the nation down with it. With López Portillo in the presidency, in fact, even more so than with Echeverría, it began to look as if all of Uruchurtu's worst fears would be realized. Mexico City had become a gigantic monster: unlivable, unmanageable, and fiscally parasitic. Its depressing profile and uncertain future was a harsh portent of the disastrous decade of crisis that Mexico would face during the 1980s. Mexico City's fiscal crisis went hand in hand with the nation's deteriorating economic situation; this in turn fueled the vicious cycle of demands on both the local and federal governments to continue investing in Mexico City in order to offset the local effects of the crisis.

But why did López Portillo continue with a compromise strategy that was fiscally disastrous and that fueled the nation's 1981 debt crisis? Given the weakness in the current account balance and growing foreign obligations, some scholars suggest that the severe economic crisis Mexico suffered starting in 1981 and lasting throughout López Portillo's administration was inevitable, resulting from foreign banking institutions' increased lending to Latin American countries in the late 1970s to compensate for dollar-denominated losses in Eurocurrency markets. However, several factors indicate that the debilitating economic crisis hitting Mexico in the early eighties was not necessarily a foregone conclusion. For one thing, within one month of his inauguration, President López Portillo announced the discovery of massive oil reserves. In an international environment of scarce and highly priced oil, this was a godsend, placing López Portillo in a position to reap the dividends of the large, direct state investments in export and basic industries made by Echeverría. Oil and state investment income would enable the government to begin repaying foreign debts accumulated during the Echeverría and Díaz Ordaz administrations, to restore the current account balance, and to provide external resources for domestic production, which would limit the government's need to sustain an overvalued peso. This income, moreover, would generate confidence among bankers and large industrialists. For another, since the Echeverría administration had already shouldered the political burden for devaluing the peso, López Portillo was in a position to take advantage of the devaluation's positive impact on the export sector without facing the political opposition of the national industrialists most dependent on imports, who had been directly hurt when the devaluation caused the costs of imported production components to skyrocket. Yet even with these two positive conditions, López Portillo followed the same path of foreign indebtedness and current account imbalances blazed by the two previous administrations.

Again we turn to the urban domain, and the articulation of Mexico City and national priorities, to understand why this was so. López Portillo employed what can be called a "petroleum-led" development strategy: a rapid expansion of public spending fueled by oil revenues. Much of this expenditure was used both to promote urban growth in Mexico City *and* to develop new and extensive community projects in rural regions. Moreover, López Portillo supported Mexico City's cadre of smaller-sized nationalist industrialists even as he benefited large, foreign-linked industrial conglomerates and regionally-based capitalists in agriculture by opening the economy to the world market. He also responded to the urban service demands of *all* the capital's residents, not only low-income and middle classes, but also to urban service producers as much as consumers. In short, López Portillo neither subordinated urban policies to national development objectives, as did Mexico's presidents from Ávila Camacho up to Díaz Ordaz; nor did he try to integrate urban and national priorities into one coherent and complementary strategy, as Echeverría had attempted with shared development. Rather, López Portillo treated both urban and national development as distinct and equally worthy objectives whose direction was to be determined in the course of demands presented by forces concerned with either Mexico City or the national economy, respectively. Moreover, within this general framework, rather than prioritizing the urban policy preferences of certain classes over others, as had been the case with previous presidents, he sought to address the urban needs of all. While following this inclusive strategy may have been politically expedient, it was fiscally disastrous, even with oil reserves available. Why? Not only were López Portillo's dual orientations toward city and countryside, national industry and international capital, and competing social classes obviously contradictory,[25] they were fundamentally dangerous for the national economy.

The problem was not just the total amount of spending this strategy would require, but also the fact that oil revenues were available only in theory, not in reality, at least at that early stage. While logic generally holds that increasing exports helps balance current account deficits, and thus reduces the long-term risk of foreign borrowing, this was not necessarily the case with a policy built around oil exports. López Portillo's efforts to rapidly develop the oil sector were not without cost. Because massive oil deposits were newly discovered, and as yet relatively unexploited, Mexico spent as much money on imports to develop refineries and extract the oil as was generated by oil exports. Lance Taylor estimates that oil-related imports and exports during the López Portillo administration were nearly equal in value, resulting in little net gain from the oil sector. Moreover, the international oil market was quite shaky in the late 1970s, and relying principally on oil exports placed Mexico's economy in a highly vulnerable position. To rush into expanded oil production and establish oil as the economy's foundation, was risky. One looming danger was the sheer macroeconomic weakness of the approach. Mortgaging a country's future on one commodity has never been a stable or predictable strategy, as we have learned from the history of one-crop-exporting developing countries. Nor has borrowing so extensively, even if the commodity used to generate foreign exchange is among the world's most coveted. So when the price of oil dropped unexpectedly in 1981, the bottom fell out of López Portillo's compromise development strategy. Unfortunately for López Portillo and the PRI, however, the nation's fiscal crisis hit Mexico City early and hard, and this was where conditions began to deteriorate most rapidly.

THE URBAN FOUNDATIONS OF THE DEBT CRISIS

Mexico City's involvement in the impending crisis should not have been surprising, given the direction and character of urban policies introduced under López Portillo and his appointed mayor, Carlos Hank González. One institutional legacy Echeverría left López Portillo was increased incentive for urban populations to struggle more actively for their specific urban demands; and given this heightened activism among urban populations, as early as 1976 López Portillo was aware that policies and practices in the capital could make or break the party's legitimacy. Thus, he wanted someone at the helm in the capital who would work well with a wide variety of social and class groups. Upon assuming the presidency, he named as mayor Carlos Hank González, a former teacher with good political connections within both the party hierarchy and the CNOP. Having just served as governor of the state of Mexico, Hank González also enjoyed relatively good political relations with low-income urban constituents of the PRI, particularly those who settled in the poor communities in that state, which borders the Distrito Federal. He had developed strong links to the private sector too, owing to his family's involvement in one of Mexico's largest industrial conglomerates. In fact, during his administration as governor of the largest state surrounding the capital city, a growing number of large industries had sprouted in the state of Mexico, and despite the usual tensions accompanying industrial expansion, Hank González had been able to remain on friendly terms with both organized labor and corporate leadership. Hank González thus was considered a politically astute spokesman for pro-urban-growth forces. Because the state of Mexico had long absorbed much of Mexico City's excess population, Hank González supported the expansion of the metropolitan area. As early as 1969, he had helped establish the Instituto AURIS, a government-sponsored organization charged with developing plans for integrating Mexico City with the surrounding state of Mexico. And his personal connections reinforced this commitment to urban growth and transport's role in the process: His family was involved in transport equipment production, through its own firm and its ties with both Grupo ICA and Volkswagen, and it soon became common knowledge that construction firms under his directorship undertook construction for the METRO and for a wide variety of public works in the capital.

These private gains reinforced his commitment to a pro-urban-growth and redevelopment stance.

Some political observers have suggested that López Portillo had little choice but to appoint Hank González as mayor, due to tension between pro-urban-growth forces and López Portillo's own political mentor, Echeverría, which forced López Portillo to take a compromising stance on Mexico City. This interpretation is lent some credence by the fact that López Portillo and Hank González did not always see eye to eye on urban or development policy. For example, López Portillo frequently refused to release federal funds for Hank González's urban projects, including some of the METRO extensions. This was particularly significant because it drove Hank González to private creditors—both national and international—to fund Mexico City's urban redevelopment policies, which further weakened the city's and the nation's fiscal position. Yet in considering Hank González's personal and political history, it also can be argued that López Portillo chose Hank González for mayor because he could negotiate with a wide range of urban forces, not just the progrowth forces in general and the CNOP leadership in particular, both of whom earlier had allied with Díaz Ordaz, but also with the urban poor and working classes Echeverría had tried to accommodate. Thus the marriage between López Portillo and Hank González was an uneasy but workable compromise that balanced the political pressures of a variety of forces and that fit nicely with López Portillo's national objectives.

A general overview of urban policies between 1976 and 1982, particularly those related to transport, gives evidence of Hank González's efforts as mayor to address the concerns of a wide variety of social and class groups in the capital, as well as of the negative consequences for the city's fiscal solvency. During his term as mayor, for example, two new subway lines were built and 37 kilometers of subway tracks were installed. This practically doubled the existing network, which jumped from a total of 41.3 kilometers in 1976 (only 1.7 were added under the entire Echeverría administration) to 78.2 kilometers. The decision to extend the subway network was considered a principal plank in the platform of the Programa General de Gobierno del Distrito Federal, which was written by party policymakers with Hank González's tacit approval, under the auspices of the Centro de Estudios Politicos, Economicos, y Sociales del Distrito Federal, in 1976. In a public announcement, the government committed itself to the rapid construction of 45 kilometers of METRO. Because this move was openly supported and then implemented by Hank González, the METRO's extension soon came to be identified with the new mayor. He frequently praised the project as the spinal column of the mass transit system and was considered one of the strongest public advocates for the extension of the system.

Yet strong support for the METRO did not mean that surface transport was neglected. Even though Hank González publicly declared that his principal goal was the continued extension of the METRO, he also undertook a massive reconstruction of the city's streets to facilitate automobile transport. These newly widened streets, known as *ejes viales*, created a grid of major thoroughfares that crossed the entire metropolitan area and that made both automobile and bus transport much more efficient. Moreover, in 1981 under Hank González and López Portillo, the urban bus industry was municipalized. That is, the Alianza's lines within the Distrito Federal were turned over to the Mexico City government and replaced by the Ruta 100 public bus service, which traversed the entire city. The Alianza had fought municipalization; but with the recommitment to the METRO now beyond question, the Alianza's future control over urban transport in the capital was in jeopardy. There seemed little point in fighting Hank González, López Portillo, ICA, and the public, all of whom saw the METRO as the future of the ever-expanding city and who argued for municipalization. The Alianza did not fare too badly in the deal, either, since they maintained control over their interstate lines, including those linking the state of Mexico to the Distrito Federal. Now that the city's continued growth was a fait accompli, the Alianza leadership was perfectly willing to give up the shorter routes within the city boundaries and concentrate on the longer. In some ways, in fact, the municipalization was a political godsend, given the public's heightened antagonism about urban transport conditions and the attendant—albeit unspoken—limits placed on fare increases.

Hank González's urban policies were intended to cast a broad net, as was clear with his multifaceted stance on urban transport. This strategy was further revealed in his reorganization of the Mexico City department of transportation. During Hank González's term as mayor, the department split into two separate, semiautonomous dependencies, COVITUR-Transporte and COVITUR-Vialidad. COVITUR-Vialidad was charged with making decisions about major urban infrastructure, including highway construction, street repair, and roadway extensions. COVITUR-Transporte was to concentrate on routing traffic and coordinating transport modes. By dividing the capital's department of transportation this way, there was less likelihood for political conflict between infrastructure producers and urban transport consumers. There was also a greater possibility that specific progrowth forces, particularly those represented by ICA engineers and architects, but also those linked to Hank González's own construction and manufacturing firms, would hold bureaucratic dominion over issues of special importance to them (like capital-intensive urban infrastructure), which they did through access to COVITUR-Vialidad, without running into conflict from those whose objective was more efficient urban transport service provision.

Just as administration and provision of urban transport services were restructured to cater to the concerns of both residents and various industrialists and urban developers during Hank González's term, so too the new mayor's land and housing policy were calculated to please disparate social and class forces. Under Hank González's administration, for example, new policies were introduced to extend and improve the efficiency of drainage and water supply, street paving, and electricity provision. These acts were intended to meet the high expectations of residents—raised but not met by the Echeverría administration—the demands of land developers, and the redevelopment priorities of urban financiers. For example, Hank González "implemented a systematic programme of [land] regularization," which gave low-income populations opportunities to purchase land in existing settlements, but which also accelerated the real estate market, particularly in the outskirts of the city.[26] In short, even as Hank González continued an Uruchurtu-like opposition to land invasions and other unauthorized settlements within the city's boundaries, he also remained a strong advocate of providing low-cost land for settlement outside the Distrito Federal. Moreover, his "servicing policies ha[d] not acted significantly to restrain or control the expansion of low-income settlements."[27] That is, while helping real estate developers they also catered to the needs of those low-income populations that Echeverría had tried to accommodate with his anti-urban-growth orientation.

The question arises, though, as to why Mexico City saw such a contradictory mix of policies in the late seventies and early eighties, particularly since the fiscal consequences were so obvious and disastrous. Had officials not learned from Echeverría's experience? Some, like Alan Gilbert and Peter Ward, have argued that there was a logic of bureaucratic efficiency and hierarchical power that explains this outcome. They suggest that changes made under López Portillo and his mayor Hank González actually streamlined bureaucratic decision making while at the same time ensuring that Mexico City officials held firm control over policy decisions that they personally favored. They cite as evidence Hank González's tendency to introduce costly urban infrastructure policies, like the METRO and the *ejes viales*, which benefited him politically, sustained his own construction firms, and aided his pro-urban growth allies. Yet there is an alternative explanation for Hank González's mix of urban policies, one that depends less on Hank González's personal proclivities and more on an understanding of the political logic of new urban institutional structures he introduced, how they interfaced with older, nationally constituted structures, and how they operated in the context of the fiscal constraints and obligations facing Mexico City authorities. With a focus on these competing local and national priorities and structures, as well as their diverse class and political constituents, we have a better understanding of the ambitious and costly mix of urban policies implemented under Hank González.

Paradoxically, some of the roots of the overspending lay in political responses to earlier austerity measures. In the final months of the Echeverría administration, the IMF dictated that the government devalue the peso and follow a stabilization plan. As noted earlier, this was an absolute necessity if Mexico was to receive funds to compensate for the massive capital flight and the surge in external debt that came with the devaluation, since money was owed in dollars, not in pesos. As was customary, the IMF's stabilization plan called for a reduction in public expenditures and protectionist measures, and thus it was not overly popular. Not only did many state bureaucrats and national industrialists oppose the stabilization plan, citizens were calling for greater social expenditures, and workers feared the plan's restrictions on wage increases. Given the high level of organization among Mexico City residents, demands for increased urban service expenditures in the capital topped the list of grievances. Amid this clamor from urban social movements in the capital, López Portillo and Hank González saw it as expedient to recognize or empower the various participatory structures that Echeverría had initially established; meaning it was the empowerment of local structures in Mexico City in the previous administration that contributed as much as to the mix of expansionary urban development policies as anything else.

Starting in 1977, for example, one of Hank González's first acts as mayor was to attempt to give the *junta de vecinos* structure "teeth" by imbuing it with greater legitimacy and powers. Throughout Hank González's term as mayor, in fact, local neighborhood organizations were encouraged to "report and advise on settlement servicing, to participate in civic functions, and to comment on housing, social services, and administration." [28] At the same time, however, Hank González turned to local *delegados*, who were party members appointed by the mayor to serve as representatives in Mexico City, to provide input on decisions about street paving, street lighting, water, and drainage provision. The effect was to set up a "shadow" *junta* structure, based on the *delegados* system, with greater powers and more direct ties to the mayor, while still keeping intact the original *junta* system—which was more identified with low-income populations first mobilized under Echeverría.

With these institutional changes in Mexico City governance, demands generated within the *junta* system were now to be channeled directly through the *delegados*, who first screened requests and then went to the mayor with neighborhood demands. The purpose of this new structure was to offer new urban groups and old party activists their own format for making service demands. This included not only urban middle classes, but also *transportistas* and others with a specific urban agenda who sought to pressure the mayor directly and show that power within the *junta* structure was negligible. Of course, Mayor Hank González still controlled major resources and decisions, and powerful lobbies promoting major infrastructural projects—like ICA— had greater chances for success because they dealt directly with the mayor. Nonetheless, the structure of urban participation and decision making under Hank González was such that outcomes tended to reflect the conflicting priorities of various urban groups, rather than the priorities of only one or the other. This is revealed by Peter Ward's description of how the system operated: The *delegados* "were left to draw up priorities for servicing the communities in their areas and to submit plans annually to the Federal District central departments. In this way, the city mayor continued to control resources but created a method for determining servicing priorities which deflected attention away from himself and the new president [López Portillo], and towards his appointees, the *delegados*." [29]

At least initially, these changes in the nature and functioning of local structures of politics gave both Hank González and López Portillo maneuvering room to administer Mexico City, as well as to accommodate urban demands from others beside low-income residents who had used the *junta* system. As such, these reforms structured new possibilities for greater participation in urban politics from a broad spectrum of classes and social forces, an issue of high priority for the PRI as it faced declining electoral support in the capital, growing urban social movements, and a concern among pro-urban-growth forces that their input in infrastructure policy had been on the decline in the preceding administration. Yet these changes also brought a more complex network of mechanisms for expressing demands about urban policy in Mexico City, which in turn laid the groundwork for urban fiscal crisis because it brought pressures to rapidly accelerate urban expenditures on a wide variety of projects and policies geared toward a multiplicity of urban policy preferences, some of which were competing. Within a few scant years, then, the reforms that had been intended as political appeasement for Mexico City populations drove the city—and then the nation and the ruling party—into even more serious difficulties.

FROM POLITICAL EMPOWERMENT TO FISCAL CRISIS

The growing fiscal crisis in the capital caught many local officials off guard. Indeed, by politically empowering new local structures of participation in Mexico City, it had not necessarily been Hank González's intent to lay the foundation for urban fiscal crisis. He had been careful to see that political reforms in Mexico City would not immediately translate into greater expenditures, which were openly discouraged under the IMF stabilization plan of 1977–1978. One way the mayor tried to ensure this outcome was to change the way delegates were elected and the manner in which demands were processed in the *junta* system. Hank González restructured the *junta* system so that only formally elected *junta* presidents would be recognized by Mexico City authorities, an act that also appealed to the grassroots movements clamoring for greater political input by making local elections especially important. At the same time, despite his reliance on the *delegados* structure, Hank González also worked hard to ensure that all urban policy decisions after 1976 were "taken in collaboration with the *junta* so that negotiation and competition between *barrios* effectively shift[ed] responsibility away from the *delegado* and the central agencies and place[d] the onus on the local neighbourhoods to sort out their problems."[30] What this meant, in short, was that local neighborhoods would compete with each other for very scarce resources. As Gilbert and Ward put it, "The central issue [became] one of how to divide the cake rather than how much cake is put on the table."[31] As such, Hank González probably assumed he could keep local expenditures under control, at least enough to limit spending on citizen demands and maintain a healthy budget for expenditures on the METRO and minor roadway improvements demanded by his pro-urban-growth allies.

This political strategy worked relatively well in 1977–1978, when IMF stabilization policies put a damper on public spending. After 1978 and 1979, however, the rapid development of the oil sector freed new resources for public spending, which made it increasingly difficult for Mayor Hank González to ignore or restrict demands for local expenditures. Since oil was nationalized, its income ran directly to the state, which meant that different groups could legitimately make demands on the López Portillo government for greater urban expenditures, even when the mayor thwarted their demands. Given López Portillo's own concerns with carrying through Echeverría's commitment to the urban poor, this was a frequent course of events. In order to keep Mexico City populations within his own local political domain, after 1979

Hank González gave the *juntas* "larger . . . budgets and they were left to draw up priorities for servicing the communities in their areas and to submit plans and cost estimates to the Federal District for special projects."[32] Making matters worse, after the 1979 boom in the oil sector, progrowth forces placing pressure on the party through their national lobbies and with their strong ties to Hank González were also in a position to pose unconstrained and ambitious urban demands, for the first time in years. For example, when spending began again, the bulk of it went to large capital projects in Mexico City, especially those favored by ICA and other progrowth forces such as the METRO and *ejes viales*.

As just noted, the growth of expenditures on big projects in Mexico City was partly due to the political and economic strength that these progrowth forces wielded over local governance. When Hank González became mayor, architects and engineers from ICA and from the mayor's own construction firm once again entered Mexico City administration, through COVITUR-Vialidad and other agencies, and pushed for large-scale infrastructural projects. Another reason that Mayor Hank González spent more on large infrastructure than on neighborhood services was that progrowth forces had greater access to his office than did the grassroots organizations using the *delegado* system. Owing to Hank González's institutional reforms in 1977, in fact, demands from popular groups had to travel through two channels, the *junta* system and *delegados*, while decisions about larger infrastructural projects and about citywide services went directly to the mayor's office. All this meant that economically powerful progrowth forces were more able to push for their urban projects even after stabilization constraints were removed in 1978. And push they did. One of the best examples was Hank González's project of *ejes viales*. This massive plan to realign Mexico City's major streets in a grid pattern cost millions of dollars and displaced close to twenty-five thousand families. But it also helped achieve what many developers and progrowth forces wanted: a resurgence of urban infrastructural development leading to a renovated and efficient city. The demands of individual neighborhoods, in contrast, were frequently lost in the shuffle, except of course when they agreed among themselves or with progrowth forces.

This dynamic also played itself out in Hank González's stance on the METRO. Given the urban transport problems produced during the Echeverría administration, extending the METRO network was a project that aided progrowth developers and financiers while still appealing to some communities. Now that the central network was already built and buses forcefed into it, further extensions to the METRO network were seen as beneficial to many of the city's residents, and many local communities lent support to the project. As such, it was much less controversial and more popular than were the *ejes viales*. Yet like the roadway improvements, the continued expansion of the subway network was intended primarily to reinvigorate the local land market, which had experienced a crisis in 1976 with Echeverría's Ley de Asentamientos Humanos, and to extend the functional boundaries of the metropolitan area.

However politically expedient Hank González's support for the METRO and the *ejes viales* may have been, these policies were fiscally disastrous in the long run, much more so than Echeverría's Mexicanization project, which at least added to the nation's industrial infrastructure. After track extensions undertaken by Hank González between 1978 and 1981, the subway's costs to the Mexico City budget, alone, were four times greater than the combined costs of providing drainage, drinking water, and health services for the entire Distrito Federal population, which was over nine million people.[33] Consider, moreover, that the subway was transporting only 13.4 percent of the city's commuting population at the time, and that its costs to the Distrito Federal budget were calculated only on the basis of operating and administrative expenditures. Under an agreement between Hank González and López Portillo in 1977, the federal government had agreed to absorb the subway's original debt repayment costs and also granted a yearly subsidy (which reached 1,676,600 pesos by 1980). Federal assistance to the METRO was necessary because the subway clearly could not pay for itself. The net losses of the system increased from 61 million to over 2 billion pesos between 1973 and 1980, an increase of 469 percent. By 1982, revenue from operations accounted for just one-tenth of the per person costs of operating the subway.

One reason the METRO was so costly to operate and needed such a massive subsidy was that its fare was still kept artificially low, despite the 1976 devaluation. Until 1985, in fact, Mexico City's METRO was the lowest-priced subway in the world, costing less than one cent (in 1985 exchange rates) for an unlimited ride on the system. This was due in part to the fear that the public would not quietly accept a fare hike, especially when the high costs and limited availability of other urban services were so controversial. Yet this reasoning, although politically laudable for various reasons, was economically harmful, mainly because the subway system utilized an expensive technology that required huge investments in track infrastructure and whose import component cost was inordinately high. There was no way around it: Hank González's revival of the METRO project was fiscally devastating, especially in combination with massive expenditures for surface transport embodied in the *ejes viales*. As of 1981, the subway had become the largest debt-producing item on the Mexico City budget.[34] It drew scarce and much-needed resources away from other critical services, it contributed to the city's increasing indebtedness, and it reinforced the city's dependence on the federal government for subsidization. At the same time, it contributed to the city's uncontrolled growth by extending ever farther out into peripheral areas of the metropolitan region. This state of affairs in turn helped lay the groundwork for a national debt crisis, especially as Hank González continued to support massive urban expenditures for the ever-expanding city, even when there were fewer local and national revenues to support these policies. According to Patricio Iglesias, by 1983 Mexico City was increasing its expenditures at a rate of close to three times its population growth since 1970, even while its ordinary income in that period (that is, nondebt sources of public finance) declined, in real terms, at an approximate rate of 2.47 percent annually.[35]

Of course, Mexico City's steadily deteriorating fiscal situation during Hank González's term was due to declining revenues as much as to increasing expenditures on costly capital projects like the METRO and the *ejes viales*. During the 1970s, many larger industries had moved to small towns in the far outskirts of the Mexico City metropolitan area, like Puebla (Hank González's hometown) or Querétaro; while others had relocated in northern border areas under incentives offered in the *maquiladora* programs, through which large (frequently foreign) firms were encouraged to move the assembly stage of the production process to designated areas where wage rates were low and regulations minimal. Smaller firms stayed in the capital, where they comprised an ever-greater proportion of the local tax base. Because these small firms were revenue-poor, between 1970 and 1980 Mexico City began to lose independent sources for self-financing. While in 1970 Mexico City still financed 60.26 percent of its budget from tax revenues, the figure dropped to 22.14 percent in 1980, and by 1982, at the end of Hank González's term as mayor, it fell to 9.66 percent.[36] Also, between 1975 and 1980, under Hank González, the proportion of total revenues coming from taxes on production and commerce in Mexico City fell from 23.6 percent to 8.8 percent.[37]

It was precisely the city's deteriorating fiscal health that made the mayor's decision to continue with the METRO and other capital-intensive transport infrastructure even more devastating than it had been in earlier administrations. Balancing the budget would have been difficult enough if the city had covered only the costs of basic urban services for the growing metropolis. But with the political pressures to meet multiple demands for land regularization, servicing, and continued growth, the decision to fully support the METRO's extension and other programs that facilitated the city's growth pushed an already stumbling Mexico City into a fiscal pit. Complicating matters, given the inordinate costs of these services in general, and the METRO in particular, Hank González was forced to seek external resources—both federal and international—to continue with the subway project, actions that further weakened both the city's and the nation's fiscal position.

The nation's own precarious economic situation fueled this vicious circle of decline. As the value of the peso declined steadily between 1978 and 1980, due to rising inflation associated with both growing public expenditures and rapid development of the oil industry, Hank González was unable to rely on national government subsidies and was thus forced to devote substantially larger proportions of the capital's own limited resources to foreign debt repayment. Naturally, this debt weakened Mexico City's fiscal position and reduced Mexico's credit rating as a whole. When the peso's value fell by over 500 percent in the course of just a few weeks in 1981, under IMF pressure for devaluation, and as the price of oil dropped unexpectedly, both the city's and the nation's unsteady fiscal profiles became chaotic as the dollar-denominated costs of debt repayment soared beyond reach. Mexico City's fiscal demise, unbeknownst to most outside observers who viewed only the national accounts, was stunningly fast. While Mexico City's external debt in 1970 constituted scarcely 15 percent of the total budget, by 1979 it had jumped to 28.3 percent, and by 1981 to 44 percent.[38] The acceleration in urban expenditures over the late seventies not only weakened Mexico City's fiscal position, then, it also contributed considerably to the nation's external indebtedness.

The political consequences of these fiscal developments were just as devastating. When the 1981 fall in oil prices brought debt crisis and forced the government to impose a rigid austerity plan, Mexico City's budget was one of the first to feel the effects. Federal subsidies to the capital were cut immediately, and so too were many of the urban policies introduced by Hank González in his first five years of office. Local service provision began to be slashed dramatically, although money continued to be poured into the subway. In response to cuts or rate increases in such necessities as electricity, water, and bus transport, urban opposition to the PRI again reared its menacing head—especially in the face of continued support for more conspicuous and lavish projects like the METRO. It was in some ways a replay of 1969, yet now urban residents had one clear alternative for mobilization: a citywide network of urban social movements. Because the money for neighborhood projects immediately dried up, making the *junta* system lose its already questionable utility, residents were quick to turn to local organizations that were poised to make direct demands on the mayor or the president, bypassing established local or national structures for participation. The acceleration of urban social movements in Mexico City was so rapid after 1981 that a new organizational structure developed to coordinate the activities of these neighborhood-based groups, called the Coordinadora Nacional de Movimientos Urbanos Populares (CONAMUP). This popularly constituted coordinating organization came to challenge both Hank González's and López Portillo's urban policies, and even to inject national political debates over one-party hegemony and the foreign debt into the discussions. In 1982, CONAMUP sponsored a National Forum Against Scarcity and Austerity, using this format to establish linkages between urban poor organized on the neighborhood level and disenfranchised labor organizations.[39] With such challenges coming from new, urban-based political organizations acting outside the party's formal political structures, the PRI leadership saw a rocky road ahead, especially in the upcoming 1982 national elections for president.

The party was in a particularly critical bind because the organization it had long used to mobilize much of the urban population for electoral purposes, the CNOP, was nearing total inoperability. Even though Echeverría and Sentíes had intended the *junta* structure to revitalize the CNOP, Hank González had approached both the CNOP and the *junta* system with quite a different objective, and by so doing had weakened the PRI's power with Mexico City populations even further. Indeed, Hank González had used the *junta* system as an institutional replacement for the CNOP, at least in terms of urban demand making, even as he allowed his own politically appointed *delegados* as much power—if not more—as the *junta* representatives. The result was that during the López Portillo administration the CNOP lost even more of its power, at least with respect to mobilizing the urban poor, nonwage workers in the informal sector, and middle classes either around certain urban policies or in support of the party. Alan Gilbert and Peter Ward cogently summarize the consequences of Hank González's restructuring of the *junta* system: "The effect [had] been to depoliticize demand making and to significantly reduce the myriad opportunities that the PRI and other parties previously held for popular 'mobilization.' The overall effect of the change [was] that the influence of the PRI [was] held in greater check than ever before."[40]

It did not take long for local political leaders in the capital city to recognize the extent of the damage, too. By the early eighties, the PRI had little influence over allocation of services, and the people were therefore skeptical about the promises made to them by deputies and PRI militants at election times. Not surprisingly, this situation made it difficult for the PRI to maintain the same sort of electoral legitimacy as it had had in the past against a stronger, more viable opposition. During the 1979 elections, several party members bemoaned the impotence of elected deputies, who, they pointed out, were the only elected officials in the Federal District. In response, one district organizer insisted that the *juntas de vecinos* had been nurtured by the PRI and that, somehow, the PRI must reinstate its influence over them, although many *delegados* professed that they would resist such moves.[41] With such internal divisions and conflicts as 1982 neared, the CNOP was mortally wounded. Urban populations were questioning urban policies, local political structures, and the PRI. And with the debt crisis looming on the horizon, the continuation of one-party rule no longer appeared to be a foregone conclusion. With the PRI quickly scrambling to recover lost ground in Mexico City, despite the gloomy economic prospects that lay ahead, talk of a proposed urban democratic reform for the capital hit the presidential campaign. Many in the party felt this urban reform would help the PRI capture lost legitimacy; but implementing the change was easier said than done. The intraparty struggles that ensued challenged long-standing structures of corporatism and brought the ruling party closer to dissolution than any other issue had in decades. As such, it was to be the last leg of a conflicted journey for the PRI that both started and ended in the nation's capital city.

8

URBAN DEMOCRATIC REFORM

AS CHALLENGE TO CORPORATIST

POLITICS, 1982–1988

Given the magnitude of fiscal problems in both Mexico City and the nation at large, Mexico's debt crisis captured public attention during the 1982 electoral campaign, forcing the PRI once again to rethink its strategy of national development and the capital's role in this larger picture. The party leadership began to ponder the extent to which they could continue pouring resources into the infrastructural development of Mexico City and still meet austerity objectives. Many in the PRI worried that increased urban expenditures in the capital would lead to greater national indebtedness and negatively affect plans for national economic recovery. Yet to reduce or even stall public expenditure on urban servicing in Mexico City, the nation's most populous and mobilized locale, might give fuel to the city's rapidly expanding urban social movements and thus nurture greater political opposition from the general citizenry. This posed a dilemma: how best to balance the ruling party's pressing national macroeconomic priorities with long-standing political and fiscal objectives in Mexico City?

This question of local-national articulation had a familiar ring. Concerns about balancing local and national political and economic objectives had been the ruling party's principal concern after the Revolution; again in 1928, when municipal rule in the capital was abolished; in the early 1940s, with the CNOP's foundation; during the 1950s and early 1960s, when Uruchurtu managed Mexico City for the middle classes and shunned fiscal insolvency; and again during the Echeverría and López Portillo administrations. In each of these periods, the ruling party had tinkered with Mexico City's existing structures of political participation in order to create the maneuvering room for introducing local policies that would both aid national economic development objectives and keep key urban populations politically loyal, especially those outside the labor and peasant sectors whose interests were not well served by national policies or the party's corporatist structures. But now, in 1982, the fiscal situation in both the capital city and the nation was much weaker than in previous periods; and urban service scarcities and local political demands were much greater, too, given the city's massive size. This situation called for a dramatic response. Complicating matters, by this time Mexico City populations had already lived through a series of institutional reforms in local structures of participation that had clearly been unsuccessful in stemming urban social movements, fully appeasing dissatisfied urban populations, or guaranteeing their gainful involvement in politics, either local or national. Given this immediate legacy, any additional small-scale tinkering in mechanisms for urban political participation in the capital might automatically be seen as inadequate to achieve desired legitimacy objectives.

Leading the way in addressing these dilemmas was the party's newly appointed presidential candidate, Miguel de la Madrid. A Harvard-trained economist clearly inspired by a mandate to restore Mexico's macroeconomic credibility, de la Madrid came to the presidency with a publicly articulated commitment to urban political and economic reform. He began by appointing a fiscally sensitive political ally, Ramón Aguirre, as mayor of Mexico City. Aguirre was an astute accountant and fellow *técnico* who had worked with de la Madrid in the Secretaría de Programación y Presupuesto. Aguirre was considered a member of de la Madrid's political "team" and was expected to keep local politics and policymaking in line with national stabilization objectives. Thus, with Aguirre at his side in Mexico City, de la Madrid pushed the privatization of several key urban services and renewed a policy emphasis on urban and administrative decentralization, including the development of secondary cities. His intent in introducing a national decentralization policy was not only to expand investment in outlying regions, as had been Echeverría's objective with decentralization, but also to restructure decision-making responsibility so that fewer resources were spent on urban policy, especially in Mexico City.

One way de la Madrid aimed to accomplish both fiscal and urban goals simultaneously was by eliminating the Secretaría de Asentamientos Humanos (SAHOP), which had originated with Echeverría, and replacing it with the Secretaría de Desarrollo Urbano y Ecología (SEDUE). In the previous administration of López Portillo, the SAHOP had implemented thousands of programs for housing and urban development; so with its elimination many of these projects went to the back burner. In its stead, the newly formed SEDUE concerned itself with the ecological consequences of concentrated urbanization and worked to stem the rising costs of urban land, materials, and interest rates, which worried de la Madrid because they "provoked a reduction in private sector construction activities and the consistent under-utilization of installed capacity."[1] In addition to moving the emphasis away from land regularization and toward a more efficient and privatized servicing and provision of urban services, de la Madrid used the new SEDUE to improve his own political relations with the CNOP, which still held old-guard PRIistas suspicious of modern "técnicos" like de la Madrid and Aguirre. The hope was that by strengthening institutional connections between SEDUE and the CNOP, the president might minimize any ill political or urban effects of privatization or austerity in the city. This was evidenced by the fact that during his first year as president, de la Madrid used the SEDUE to sign an agreement with the CNOP to jointly "implement programs of urban development, housing, and ecology" that appealed to one of the CNOP's principal constituencies, the urban poor and non-wage-earning workers whose illegal settlement on virgin lands in the urban periphery were adding to the metropolitan area's ecological demise. With this agreement, the CNOP would fight to protect "the territorial reserves of its constituents," and in turn, the SEDUE was "obliged to give attention to the demands of the CNOP."[2]

President de la Madrid's commitment to administrative reform and decentralization extended beyond Mexico City, however, such that he mandated changes in the way that all local, state, and national jurisdictions made decisions about urban policy and services, too. In so doing, his ultimate objective was to "rationalize" economic planning and policymaking by reducing the bureaucratic constraints and old-guard political pressures associated with highly centralized decision making. These changes were considered a corner-stone of de la Madrid's governing strategy, and decentralization soon came to define his administration in much the same way that shared development defined Echeverría's. Like Echeverría's support for shared development, more-over, de la Madrid's advocacy of administrative decentralization had both a political and an economic logic. In Mexico City at least, the expectation was that a more rationalized and streamlined decision-making structure would be more in tune with local service and population needs, and less influenced by the personal and political objectives of government bureaucrats. As such, it would help eliminate duplication of urban services and serve the purpose of balancing local fiscal accounts while still aiding in the city's development. Indeed, to the extent that de la Madrid's reforms sought to shift decision making to the local level, decisions about Mexico City's servicing were now to be made with an eye to local revenues. This meant that the federal govern-ment—or foreign lenders, for that matter—would no longer be the preferred financier for urban services, as during previous administrations, and that the city would have to balance its books on its own.

All in all, the de la Madrid–Aguirre partnership broke from past practices in three critical ways. First, it was one of the first in postrevolutionary Mexico to work seriously throughout an entire administration to reduce overall urban service expenditures in the capital. It also was the first to emphasize urban decentralization and regional development at Mexico City's expense. Fiscal austerity for Mexico City had been one of Mayor Uruchurtu's objectives, of course, but this had been an unpopular stance with national leaders, like President Díaz Ordaz, who argued instead for greater investment in the capi-tal city. Also, Echeverría's commitment to decentralization, while in many ways similar to de la Madrid's, was always conceived in tandem with gener-ous service support and social expenditures for Mexico City's populations. De la Madrid's strategy, in contrast, afforded no such political or fiscal lee-way in the capital. Second, de la Madrid was one of the first contemporary presidents to move his administration away from specific high-profile urban policy stances for Mexico City, like housing development or transport infra-structure, and toward the problematic issues of administration. That is, de la Madrid was committed to rethinking general procedures of urban policy-making, not primarily their content. Of course, all previous presidents and mayors were clearly as much interested in procedure as in the content of urban service provisions, owing to the fact that the unpopularity of certain urban service policy positions had clear implications for procedure. Yet not since the elimination of municipal governance in Mexico City in 1928 and the foun-dation of the CNOP in 1943 had Mexico's national administration been more preoccupied with administrative procedure than with servicing, per se, in the capital. Last, President de la Madrid was the first postrevolutionary president to rhetorically link decentralization to democracy as much as to economic development. Echeverría, of course, had advocated both a democratic opening and regional decentralization during his administration. But rarely did he link the two; and decentralization for him was more a means for economically benefiting rural populations and regions.

De la Madrid's approach was slightly different. From early in his campaign, de la Madrid touted the decentralization of urban decision making as strengthening democratic principles and practices. He also underscored a commitment to revitalizing the CNOP's participatory bases by reintroducing the territoriality of politics. Both issues went straight to the heart of the PRI's growing political problems with Mexico City and national populations and as such they helped offset the negative effects of previous practices. With de la Madrid at the helm, Mexico's states and local jurisdictions were granted substantially more responsibility and autonomy in electing representatives to the national Congress. Granted, local jurisdictions may have had fewer resources to invest in municipal services after 1984, but local politicians were more administratively connected to their constituencies, which changed the nature of both demand making and urban policymaking in Mexico's municipalities.

Despite these overall gains, de la Madrid's successes were much more qualified in Mexico City than in the regions. Why? Because de la Madrid's efforts to place Mexico City's growth and development on the back burner, put procedure over policy, and more democratically restructure local political processes by reviving *municipios* generated considerable conflict and controversy within the PRI. While many in Mexico lauded these efforts, because they sought to politically and economically reenfranchise regional populations who had been excluded by decades of urban bias, or because they provided a means to address the nation's fiscal crisis, those populations and politicians in Mexico City who stood to lose with these types of reforms put up a battle from the very beginning. This was demonstrated by the fact that de la Madrid successfully reintroduced urban and administrative reforms in all states and municipalities in Mexico *except* for Mexico City, despite his efforts. During his first year in office, for example, as he announced measures to grant more administrative autonomy to the regions, de la Madrid also proposed an urban democratic reform for Mexico City. Similar in objective to several of de la Madrid's new policies, the purpose of the proposed urban democratic reform was to fundamentally restructure the nature and extent of urban policymaking and political participation in Mexico City. This was to be accomplished by establishing a locally elected legislative body to represent the capital's residents and by introducing direct popular election of Mexico City's mayor, two rights of democratic participation denied Mexico City residents but granted to all other urban residents of Mexico. Unlike de la Madrid's proposed municipal reforms for the regions, however, which were implemented, the democratic reform for Mexico City was rejected after five years of behind-the-scenes struggle and debate.

In its place the PRI introduced an advisory body with no legislative power. Thus the fate of de la Madrid's democratic reform in Mexico City was much the same as the administrative and political reforms during the Echeverría period, which resulted in a *junta de vecinos* system that was easily manipulated by the presidentially appointed mayor and other party leaders. The crux of the problem for de la Madrid stemmed from the fact that the proposed urban democratic reform magnified the growing conflicts over urban priorities and their articulation with national political institutions, economic development, and now democratization. The proposal also raised difficult questions about the extent to which political, as opposed to economic, objectives should guide urban policymaking in the capital city. As such, the proposal exacerbated conflicts between powerful state actors, especially the president and Mexico City's mayor, who split over the proposed urban democratic reform, depending on whether they were concerned most with the urban or the national domain and depending on their commitment to corporatist, rather than democratic, institutions. Under contention was the fact that this mechanism would allow citizens to participate in local politics as individuals rather than as members of corporate institutions; it would also allow them to make demands about urban rather than class concerns. Both of these changes held the potential to challenge national corporatist structures, since these long-standing structures of participation were based primarily on class identities.

In this chapter I discuss the intraparty conflicts over de la Madrid's proposed urban democratic reform, their origins in past urban political practices, their implications for urban governance, service provision, and development in Mexico City, and their larger impact on corporatist politics in Mexico. I begin with an analysis of the reform itself, and how and why de la Madrid envisioned the proposed urban democratic reform as both changing the nature of urban servicing and facilitating macroeconomic growth in the nation as a whole. I then analyze the ensuing conflicts between President de la Madrid, Mexico City's mayor, and the party leadership, which eventually stalled the implementation of the reform. Next I examine the political responses of Mexico City's populations to the government's internal conflicts, as well as the ways in which mobilization of the city's residents, in response to this state inaction, in turn affected the terms of debate within the party over urban and national democratic reform. I conclude with a brief discussion of the fundamental changes—in both corporatist politics and urban redevelopment practices in Mexico City—that resulted from de la Madrid's proposed urban reform and the conflicts it produced.

RESTRUCTURING LOCAL POLICY AND POLITICS

When Miguel de la Madrid first introduced his ideas for democratic reform in Mexico City during the 1981 presidential campaign, he was careful to avoid taking a controversial stand on urban service provision in the capital, focusing instead on the administrative decision-making process used to achieve urban policy outcomes. This was good politics, given the advent of an urban and national fiscal crisis that ensured that any changes in urban servicing would be either costly or contentious. His efforts to discuss the reform primarily as a means for ensuring greater democratization were clear during the presidential campaign, as de la Madrid tailored many of his statements about urban reform in Mexico City to traditional middle classes, who were seen to be most concerned with the absence of democratic institutions in the capital. During his campaign, de la Madrid also aimed his discussion of urban democratic reform at so-called popular, low-income populations, who sought new, more open institutional mechanisms to help them address the pressing urban problems they faced, and who protested through their participation in urban social movements. By raising issues of administrative and procedural reform in urban policymaking, and by highlighting the democratic potential of these changes, de la Madrid avoided disagreements over specific urban policies, transport or otherwise, which in the past had set the terms for debilitating conflicts and fiscal crisis in Mexico City. His political objectives, nonetheless, were similar to those of presidents Echeverría and López Portillo, who had openly expressed allegiance to specific urban policies in the past. All three sought to bolster the PRI's popularity among urban residents in the capital, especially those middle classes and non-wage-earning workers not represented in the labor sector of the party, who felt increasingly betrayed by the CNOP and who were now inclined to bypass the PRI by joining autonomous social movements or actively supporting opposition parties.

At first, de la Madrid's campaign promises about urban democratic reform in Mexico City were mostly abstract claims, more slogans than concrete plans. For example, in his stump speeches, de la Madrid was no more specific than to suggest that Mexico "find democratic formulas . . . for the Distrito Federal . . . to establish organisms and processes assuring a greater citizen representation in governance."[3] Once in office, however, de la Madrid moved forward forcefully, ordering his closest allies in the Secretaría de Gobernación (Governance) to develop a plan for a feasible democratic reform in Mexico City. The president's allies in Gobernación responded to the challenge. Less than six months later, they proposed the creation of a new political jurisdiction in the Mexico City metropolitan area, one that would replace the old Distrito Federal and that would be governed by the principles of direct election and governance guaranteed in the constitution for all other states and municipal jurisdictions in Mexico. The right to directly elect a governor, or for all practical purposes a mayor, was a principal feature of the proposed jurisdictional change. Although it was not clear exactly which jurisdictional form would be best—one that limited the Federal District to a small geographic area in the center of Mexico City and then created a totally new state surrounding the district, or one that limited the size of the Federal District but that integrated the remaining Mexico City populations into the already-established surrounding states—the main idea was to create a new jurisdiction with direct electoral privileges that would fundamentally alter past structures of decision making for Mexico City.

In addition to meeting the objectives of providing direct representation for residents of Mexico City and thereby preempting any more serious political challenges that might come with the implementation of harsh stabilization policies, the proposed plan to create a totally new political jurisdiction in the capital fulfilled another of the urban policy objectives of the de la Madrid team, which was the so-called rationalization of public spending in Mexico City. The urban democratic reform, its proponents gambled, would wrench power out of the hands of those who had consolidated control over much public spending and urban service provision in Mexico City: a collection of industrial and construction interests, transport and public service contractors, and local patronage bosses, many linked to the CNOP, who rarely limited their own expenditures. De la Madrid saw the power of these local groups—among which ICA, the Alianza de Camioneros, and local *delegados* of the *junta* system figured most notably—as obstacles to the principal austerity components of his national economic restructuring and stabilization programs. Indeed, the president and his allies attributed much of the nation's enormous foreign debt to growing urban expenditures in Mexico City, and he feared that if groups with too much local influence were not sufficiently contained, they would hinder his well-elaborated plans to drastically reduce public spending in Mexico City. By allowing Mexico City's residents more participation, then, de la Madrid expected either to undermine the power of these locally entrenched political interests and lobbies, or at least to counterbalance their spending priorities. If the urban democratic reforms were successfully achieved, de la Madrid could redirect federal resources away from the Mexico City budget and use them to nurture productive and foreign-capital-generating investments in border and coastal regions of the country, a shift in focus that would be quite difficult if big-spending interests still controlled Mexico City policymaking.

All these concerns suggest that the initial proposal for urban democratic reform offered by the president and his national cabinet allies at Gobernación grew out of a commitment to facilitating national recovery, maintaining international creditworthiness, and creating an efficient and productive economic environment for the nation's largest and most promising industries. Without question, de la Madrid's priority was to revive and bolster the Mexican economy as a whole. He hoped to accomplish this in an economically conservative manner, responding to the demands and restrictions of the IMF while at the same time creating favorable economic conditions for a more competitive—less subsidized and protected—private sector to grow. However, given the relationship between urban expenditures and both local and national fiscal crisis, de la Madrid felt a good place to start was Mexico City administration. The logic was that the proposed urban democratic reform would (1) incorporate potential opposition groups into the PRI-dominated formal political process, and thus preempt any popular social protests or support for opposition parties that might either diminish the government's legitimacy or serve as impediments to the implementation of this austerity plan; and (2) at the same time create favorable conditions for structuring an efficient and decentralized administration of that economic recovery plan.

Coming full circle, then, this proposal brought to the political agenda some of the same concerns pondered by Mexico leaders in 1928 when they eliminated municipal rule in the first place. Would Mexico City be governed by democratic elections, or could local politics be subordinated to national corporate structures and national politics? Now, however, these issues were intricately linked to the government's efforts to separate local from national politics, rather than fuse them. Indeed, in stark contrast to 1928, when eliminating direct elections in the capital was seen as key to giving national political leaders sufficient political maneuvering room to revive the Mexico City economy and achieve national development objectives, in 1982 it was necessary to reintroduce separate and autonomous democratic structures in the capital in order to achieve national economic objectives. Yet for precisely this reason, the proposal for a democratic reform in Mexico City brought nationally powerful political and economic elites into conflict with local populations over a change that would alter the local and national articulations of classes and institutions within the ruling party. Clearly, this urban democratic reform proposed by de la Madrid involved much more than "home rule," or the struggle for local representation in the capital city—a common concern in places like Washington, D.C., or Paris. At stake was not just the possibility of grassroots political participation in local governance. Also under contention was a restructuring of the ways that urban services would be provided and administered in the capital; and because this had local and national consequences that were both political and economic, the proposal was understandably controversial. The establishment of a local democratic body for urban policymaking in Mexico City might make the CNOP obsolete and possibly even undermine the political power of other corporatist sectors, which would threaten the political system upon which the PRI had based close to seventy years of one-party rule. At a minimum, it would eliminate the *junta* and *delegado* system and challenge the mayor's capacity to direct Mexico City's urban development. At a maximum, however, it would separate local and national political practices enough to both restore legitimacy to local politics and revive the national economy, and, in turn, give the PRI a new lease on national power.

MANAGING MEXICO CITY: ADMINISTRATIVE CONCERNS TRIUMPH OVER POLITICS

Precisely because the proposed democratic reform would fundamentally alter local power structures and their articulation with national politics, it produced opposition from those forces in Mexico City who had the most to lose if such reforms were implemented. Mexico City Mayor Ramón Aguirre was one of the strongest opponents to the proposed reform, mainly because a democratic reform would curtail his policymaking power and its national importance. In particular, Mayor Aguirre feared that by bringing direct accountability to the local citizenry in the capital city, the proposed democratic reform would markedly alter the existing structure of urban decision-making power in Mexico City as well as the types of policies and services implemented there. The new mayor did not necessarily express his opposition in those terms, however; he argued, instead, that the current *junta* system could adequately serve the purpose of legitimizing the political system through popular participation and absorbing future urban grievances. With a system of limited participation already in place, one that was complementary rather than threatening to the existing structure of power, the mayor saw little need to suport the president's proposed urban reform.

Because Mexico City's mayor is appointed by the president, because Mayor Aguirre was considered one of de la Madrid's strongest political and ideological allies, and because Aguirre supported de la Madrid on similar regionally directed reforms, it is at first difficult to understand why he would oppose the president on this issue. Why would the mayor place concerns about accountability and administration in Mexico City before national economic concerns or the wishes of President de la Madrid and his powerful political allies? Why would Aguirre support the old *junta* system, which President de la Madrid and many urban residents saw as incapable of offering mechanisms for true grassroots participation in decisions about urban redevelopment and policy? After all, Aguirre had been appointed mayor in the first place because he was considered a strong team player and unquestionable de la Madrid supporter. Thus, an understanding of Aguirre's opposition to the reform lies as much in a better understanding of the structure of political and economic power in Mexico City as in a focus on the man himself. As discussed thoroughly up to this point, decision making and urban administration in Mexico City have long been influenced by powerful, locally entrenched private sector lobbies, urban service providers, local career bureaucrats, patronage and party bosses, and more recently, by a neighborhood-level system of *delegados* wielding power through the *junta* system. It was these groups who felt most threatened by the proposed changes and who brought Aguirre to his oppositional stance on the reform.

When de la Madrid went beyond campaign rhetoric and used the first months of his administration to formulate a real plan of action, private sector lobbies with years of invested political capital, like ICA and the Alianza de Camioneros jumped into action. They worried that the proposed changes could undermine their ability to set the urban policymaking agenda in Mexico City in accordance with their own interests. Principal among their concerns was the fear that they might lose the power to monopolize contracts, set profitable prices, and influence service levels for transport, housing, sewage, and water projects from which they had directly benefited in the past. Many local *delegados* and participants in the *junta* system also opposed the plan, in large part because it would eliminate the need for this system. Urban projects and programs in Mexico City were a source of power and patronage for these local leaders. Thus they too had much to lose if a democratically elected deliberative body were to replace the *junta* and *delegados* systems.[4] Most city planners, technicians, and career bureaucrats in the Distrito Federal followed suit. Many believed it would infringe upon their professional autonomy and responsibility, since the reform would increase citizen access to and participation in programming and policymaking.

Though both the PRI and Mexico City bureaucrats and administrators had long given lip service to the importance of grassroots participation, the likelihood of true citizen involvement in urban servicing decisions was a concern for several reasons. For one, many in the Mexico City bureaucracy were directly involved in private sector networks. A common pattern has been for planners and other technicians—generally engineers or architects—to move back and forth between public and private sector jobs, relying on contacts and expertise in each domain to grease the wheels of policy implementation and contracting. This was especially the case in 1982, after the conservative de la Madrid government brought many like-minded technocrats with an openness to the private sector into the government. Because the democratization of urban decision making might end this beneficial system of exchange, it stirred controversy among bureaucrats and local private businesses who gained from this nearly institutionalized set-up. For another, there were some local planners who took their responsibilities seriously and felt that introduction of participatory democracy would necessitate responding inordinately to local pressures in highly mobilized (if not overly politicized) neighborhoods or around certain urban policy services. Thus they would be prevented from introducing the technically sophisticated and efficient measures they sought to counteract urban problems in one of the world's largest, most polluted, underserviced, and overcongested cities.

Local planners' opposition to the urban democratic reform may be somewhat surprising, especially since many of these professionals considered themselves the voice of progress and reason in a domain that previously had been dominated by corrupted *políticos*. It was only with the Echeverría administration, in fact, that technically efficient planners and policymakers had joined city government in great numbers and started to make headway in local affairs; and many had experienced political opposition from old-guard CNOPistas and other political forces who opposed the urban policy changes under Echeverría, as noted in the last chapter. But now this corps of planners faced different obstacles to policymaking if the democratic reform was to be introduced. Most specifically, many worried that purely political concerns imposed from the grassroots would drive local involvement in urban policymaking. Of course, even among local technocrats there were different reasons—some more noble than others—for wanting to maintain technocratic autonomy. There were those who wanted the freedom to cut local service provisions in order to comply with austerity objectives, others who wanted the autonomy to work against local entrenched lobbies or party bosses in order to produce more progressive, citizen-oriented changes, and still others who, plain and simply, expressed little confidence in the teeming masses. Additionally, granting political favors while discharging bureaucratic duties is often a means of direct political advancement in Mexico, and many planners and technicians continued to see work for the public sector as a way to advance their political careers. This was true for both the younger, highly educated technicians and old-guard bureaucrats involved in Mexico City administration, who had many years invested in the CNOP and party politics. For these so-called dinosaurs, the proposed changes in urban administration would rob them of political advantages gained in past struggles over urban policy or urban reform.

Nonetheless, knowing that many politicians and policymakers with a hand in Mexico City governance opposed the reform does not fully explain why Mexico City's mayor also opposed the urban democratic reform, especially given his obvious ties to de la Madrid. After all, it has been well demonstrated in both Díaz Ordaz's and Echeverría's cases that presidents are frequently able to push through their own policy objectives and priorities for Mexico City, even when they are opposed by local bureaucratic or class forces. Moreover, there is plenty of evidence that under certain conditions, Mexico City's mayors themselves have sufficient political and institutional power to impose their preferred urban policies, as was certainly the case with both Uruchurtu and Martínez Domínguez, and even Sentíes. When each of these men was in power in Mexico City, their positions on urban policy generally reigned; it was only after their forced removal that opponents were able to push through alternative measures. So why would Aguirre not have ignored the opposition of these locally entrenched interests and supported the proposed reform of his mentor, de la Madrid? Probably the most fundamental difference was that Mayor Aguirre faced a series of problems and obstacles to urban governance that previous mayors had avoided.

For one thing, by 1981, just before Aguirre took office, urban social movements in Mexico City reached new heights, owing to the debt crisis and the revitalization of the *junta* system discussed in the last chapter. To the extent that extensive urban mobilization was expected to continue with the introduction of austerity so desired by de la Madrid, Mayor Aguirre knew he would be facing difficulties in urban administration and policymaking. For another, the limited fiscal resources that were available for Mexico City governance also threatened to make the job of administering this metropolis even more difficult. Unlike many previous mayors, Aguirre had no special political or personal ties to urban service providers—either the Alianza or ICA—or with old-guard bureaucrats in the CNOP on whom he could rely to carry out the formidable task of governing one of the largest cities in the world. Under these circumstances, and with only a few months as mayor under his belt,

Aguirre was reluctant to alienate the forces that wielded so much political power and technical expertise in the capital city. As such, when local *caciques* and technocrats opposed the urban democratic reform, Aguirre was reluctant to buck them. Mayor Aguirre needed local administrators and urban service providers on his side if he was to effectively administer Mexico City in times of fiscal crisis and intense popular mobilization. Also, private sector lobbies and urban service providers with past experience in policymaking and governance in the capital, like ICA, already held a substantial amount of political and technical leverage. Their strong involvement in many projects and programs over the years had made them indispensable, because they provided technical assistance from both within and outside the bureaucracy and because they facilitated the rapid and efficient implementation of urban policy. Last, even the *delegados* were important allies to a man like Aguirre, who had little experience in urban policymaking and who worried about urban mobilizations growing out of hand. The *delegados* and representatives in the *junta* system already controlled access to the local population, absorbed grievances, and thus held the power to generate local political support for, or opposition to, the mayor. They too were important forces to keep on his side, especially since in mid-1982, when the Gobernación reform was first proposed, Mayor Aguirre was still new in his job as mayor and wished to avoid unnecessary political problems with local *delegados*.

This is not to say that Mayor Aguirre did not have his own reasons for opposing the democratic reform. It was widely known that he had presidential aspirations and wanted an unblemished image as one with full control over Mexico City. Given its clause for popular election of Mexico City's mayor, if implemented, this reform would make Aguirre a lame duck and prevent him from building more political connections. Still, Aguirre's position on the reform was probably as much grounded in his network of administrative allies as in his own personal ambitions, which in turn institutionally distanced him from de la Madrid's stance. Indeed, the mayor did not come into conflict with the president over the proposed urban democratic reform because of stark ideological differences with the president and his team. Both were considered right of center in the Mexican political spectrum, both were publicly committed to the general idea of austerity and economic recovery, and the mayor was still universally considered a loyal member of de la Madrid's political team. Otherwise he might have been forcibly removed, as were Uruchurtu and Martínez Domínguez. Nor was it that the president and the mayor expressed different degrees of concern about urban social protests and dissatisfaction in Mexico City. Both were fully cognizant of growing social pressures in the capital and aware that this could pose serious political problems in the near future. The problem, rather, was that the mayor and the president were situated in different administrative and class networks, respectively local and national, which gave them different objectives, responsibilities, and obligations, and which compelled them to respond in different ways to the idea of urban democratic reform and the possibility of greater citizen participation in Mexico City governance.

Although an intraparty split between those with local and national political obligations was not an entirely new phenomenon, having shown its head in the Uruchurtu–Díaz Ordaz and Martínez Domínguez–Echeverría conflicts, the positions taken by Mayor Aguirre and Presient de la Madrid in this particular controversy unfolded differently from past conflicts, because of the debt crisis. By 1982, with austerity presenting itself as the most urgent problem on the national political agenda, Mexico's president had little recourse but to foster good relations with a network of powerful financial institutions (national and international), bankers, and industrialists concerned with national economic recovery and restructuring, overall fiscal solvency, and the international competitiveness of the economy. He gained the party's presidential nomination, in fact, largely because as an economist with conservative leanings, he was politically and ideologically amenable to national-level industrial and financial interests and their concerns about setting the macroeconomy back on track. Once in power, he controlled the national cabinet positions and institutions that directed macroeconomic policy, thereby further cementing his political and social relationships with these same class forces. During the same time, however, much of the PRI leadership intensified its relationships with other classes (mainly labor, the peasantry, and the urban poor and middle classes), further disassociating the presidency from the party leadership and linking the former to dominant class interests. President de la Madrid accordingly saw urban democratic reform as something that would give him political space to achieve these difficult economic objectives and thus respond to the demands of his network of nationally dominant private sector allies, while at the same time appealing directly to the urban grassroots with the promise of democracy.

Mayor Aguirre, on the other hand, saw the exact same reform as preventing him from fulfilling his principal administative objectives and responding to the political and class-specific obligations presented by his own network of allies: local business elites, patronage bosses, and Mexico City planning administrators. In order for Aguirre to maintain legitimacy as mayor by offering viable urban services, he needed to maintain strong working relationships with the class, political, and technocratic forces in Mexico City, few of which supported the political reform—though often for different reasons. All this suggests that the mayor and the president were embedded in distinct political and class networks that colored their views of the urban democratic reform and the problems or solutions associated with greater local participation in urban decision making. While the mayor wanted to protect the jurisdictional and administrative system of centralized decision making in Mexico City, because it sheltered the interests of his class and political allies, the president wanted to restructure this system of urban policymaking precisely because it undermined his national administrative objectives of economic restructuring.[5] The political ramifications of urban democratic reform also differed for Mayor Aguirre and President de la Madrid. Aguirre expected it to give dissatisfied urban residents and their potential leadership in leftist opposition parties the means to wrest control of Mexico City administration from local business lobbies, patronage bosses, and local technocratic elites—his own base of administrative and political power. Such a possibility had never existed before; and had previous nationally imposed urban reforms proposed the same democratic measures, we might have seen a similar split between the president and the mayor. But all urban reforms to date merely offered limited mechanisms for urban political participation. None questioned the overwhelming power of the mayor or the president to administer Mexico City. The president and his allies, however, supported the reform for precisely this reason. It would enable urban residents to voice dissatisfaction, elect their own mayor, and thus directly mold the way urban policy was made.

This contest over the urban democratic reform in 1982 echoed the past in many ways, especially the state of affairs in 1928, the last time democratic rule in Mexico City had truly been up for grabs. For example, as in 1928, both the process and the outcome of the debate over urban democratic reform held ramifications for one-party rule and for Mexico's political and economic future, except now positions in the party were switched. In 1982, Mexico's president and party leaders tended to support urban democratic rule, while local *políticos* opposed it; whereas in 1928, national political leaders opposed urban democratic structures and local *políticos* like Luis Morones supported them. And as we shall see, the positions were switched because of the changing political and economic conditions in the capital—which themselves were produced by decades of urban policy decisions and administrative reforms made in the absence of local democratic structures. Mexico's PRI was now at a crossroads, especially with respect to its capacity to manage articulations between urban and national development, between mayor and president, and between politics and economy. By the early eighties, both the urban and the national domains were sufficiently distinct in terms of class or political forces, and in terms of the institutional mechanisms for wielding power, that the party's respective political figureheads took entirely different positions with respect to procedures for urban administration and democratic content. Still, the mayor's and the president's urban policy objectives and macroeconomic priorities were not completely distinct, as seen in their shared desire to limit urban expenditures and privatize urban service provision. That is, even while the close fit between urban and national priorities evident in earlier decades within the ruling party still held in terms of national economic priorities, it had now broken down with respect to issues of local political participation. And it was the issue of local participation that brought yet a third set of actors into the controversy.

THE PRI LEADERSHIP, LOCAL LEGITIMACY, AND LIMITED URBAN DEMOCRATIC REFORM

With President de la Madrid and his allies in Gobernación at odds with the mayor's office over the proposed reform, the party leadership worked frantically to stem the conflict before the opposing factions wrought too much political damage to the party. In an effort to minimize antagonism, the PRI's leaders offered a compromise reform, one that was much less extreme than Gobernación's proposal to introduce a wide-reaching urban democratic reform and much more accommodating than the mayor's position that no such urban reform was necessary. Specifically, the PRI leadership proposed the creation of a new legislative body of popularly elected representatives in Mexico City. This new proposal was intended as a more moderate reform, one that implied no changes in the boundaries or the nature of the existing administrative structure in the Distrito Federal, and that held no provisions for overturning presidential appointment of Mexico City's mayor.

The PRI proposed this compromise version for several reasons. For one, many in the PRI leadership did not support President de la Madrid's idea of creating a new and autonomous jurisdiction in the capital, because they wanted to maintain presidential appointment of the mayor, a situation that they saw as safeguarding the power of the presidency. This was considered important because many considered Mexico's "presidentialism" essential to the historical successes of the PRI-dominated political system: A strong and autonomous president was seen as having the power to balance incorporated sectors in conflict. For another, many in the PRI leadership worried that urban democratic reform would give opposition parties or other dissident voices a chance to capture political control in Mexico City, especially over the mayor's office. This in turn could challenge the power of the president in a way that produced potentially disastrous national political repercussions. These fears were not unfounded. After hovering in the low thirties during the Uruchurtu administration, and rising only slightly with Sentíes, the percentage of Mexico City residents who supported opposition parties during congressional elections in Mexico City had shot up to 41.6 percent in 1979 and 51.65 in 1982 (see Appendix C). With close to 51 percent of the Mexico City population already abandoning the PRI, an opposition victory in an open electoral contest for mayor and local congressmen was in fact quite likely. Many in the PRI did not want to take that risk, especially in the midst of a serious debt crisis that reduced the party's popularity anyway.

A second but related reason some within the party leadership were reluctant to support de la Madrid's proposal for urban democratic reform was their concern that this plan was part of an effort to diminish the influence of Mexico City–based *políticos*, or old-guard party activists and bureaucrats, and heighten the power and influence of the *técnicos*. Competition between these young *técnicos* and older, more traditional *políticos* had first appeared with a vengeance during the Echeverría administration. As we saw in the last chapter, it continued during the López Portillo administration, particularly in Mexico City, as mechanisms for wielding power independent of the party, like the *junta*, were constructed. By 1982, this conflict had reached new heights, as de la Madrid brought into his cabinet an entire slate of foreign-trained economists and MBAs who sought to recast party politics and national policy in a more U.S.-oriented mold. By 1982, de la Madrid's efforts had not yet totally undermined the political power of old-guard party activists in the capital, and in the PRI as a whole; but urban democratic reform threatened to speed the process in potentially damaging ways. If implemented, the urban democratic reform might diminish the capacity of the party and its old cadres of *políticos* to make urban policy and thus generate strong patron-client linkages, since it institutionalized the capacity of ordinary citizens to participate in politics. And without power and patronage in Mexico City, old *políticos* would have little to buttress their political power in the party, while *técnicos* would be able to rise to more influential heights. To the extent that the PRI might be fundamentally transformed in the process, this possibility raised serious concerns among some of its leadership.

Although the PRI had good reasons to be cautious about changing urban political procedures in Mexico City, this did not necessarily mean that they favored the status quo and sided fully with Aguirre. In fact, many in the PRI questioned the mayor's position that no reform was necessary. Most of the party leadership felt that the PRI's principal goals should be to maintain the long-term stability of corporatism and one-party rule; and they recognized that the weakest link in the corporatist system as a whole, and in the CNOP in particular, was in Mexico City. A steady rise in urban political abstentionism and support for opposition parties over the previous decade signaled the declining legitimacy of the PRI and the CNOP. From a peak of close to 70 percent electoral support for the PRI in Mexico City during Uruchurtu's term as mayor, support steadily declined to near 43 percent in the mid-1980s, as opposition party support jumped to a high of 51 percent. Particularly threatening for the PRI was the fact that in 1982, large numbers of Mexico City voters, who in the past had merely abstained, now gave their support to opposition candidates. Many in the PRI saw this as a result of the growing dissatisfaction within the CNOP's constituency vis-à-vis urban policy and national politics, which was first seen after Uruchurtu's forced departure and which accelerated in subsequent administrations. Accordingly, reviving the party's legitimacy with respect to Mexico City residents was of special concern to the party leadership. The legitimacy issue took on urgency after 1981, as social movements in Mexico City began to coordinate among themselves for the first time. Before 1982, Mexico City's urban social movements had been based primarily in specific neighborhoods, which made it easier for the CNOP and other party activists to co-opt or accommodate urban demands. But when these urban social movements joined together into the CONAMUP in late 1981 and 1982, they became a danger to the CNOP's institutional efficacy. Making matters worse, it was becoming clear to residents themselves that the CNOP was losing control over low-income populations and middle classes in the capital city, which gave further incentive to bypass the party and join urban movements. It can be estimated that by 1982 there were close to 180,000 residents active in urban social movements in Mexico City.[6]

Given these political problems with residents in the capital, the PRI leadership felt that a new legislative body in Mexico City might be a good idea, especially if mayoral appointment remained in the president's hands. Party leaders reasoned that introducing a body of popularly elected representatives to help manage and implement urban policy for Mexico City might help the PRI counterbalance its declining legitimacy vis-à-vis dissatisfied Mexico City populations. Such actions might even give the PRI more room to manage the fiscal crisis, because such a body would be charged with the difficult task of making tough urban policy choices in conditions of austerity. To the extent that the new legislative body—and not the party leadership itself—would be forced to take on the increasingly contradictory demands of Mexico City populations, the change might actually reduce the urban pressure on the weakening CNOP. According to one high-level PRI member active in the CNOP, in fact, many felt that a new legislative body would help legitimize the party because it would provide a format for urban groups to recognize that "their conflicts and problems are among themselves, not between them and the [PRI-dominated] government." [7] To some in the party, in fact, a legislative reform—especially without changes in mayoral appointment—was seen as holding the potential to *strengthen* both the CNOP and the PRI, since the CNOP's strong historical presence in Mexico City and the presidentially appointed mayor's safeguarded position still made some party activists confident that PRI members would be most likely to control the legislative body, anyway. The PRI's proposed urban reform, then, would demonstrate commitment to democratization and thus generate support for the PRI, without creating an institution that would truly challenge its power and control.

The PRI's moderate reform clearly served its own institutional objectives, which grew out of the social and class networks in which it was embedded, and which revolved around presidential power and legitimacy concerns. Moreover, the PRI's compromise proposal did not antagonize Mayor Aguirre or President de la Madrid and their respective allies, which also served the PRI's larger political objectives. For a president to be rebuked on a principal campaign promise and policy decision so early in his administration might reveal to the public a critical weakness in the party or the political system. To the extent that this would suggest the PRI's declining hegemony, or even signal presidential weakness with respect to other groups within the PRI, the PRI leadership wished to avoid this outcome at all costs. However, the party leadership also knew that it would be equally disastrous to humiliate Mayor Aguirre by fully undermining his power and prerogatives, since this might bring all-out conflict between the president and the mayor and thus tarnish the political system's image of stability and relative consensus. Thus, even in terms of salvaging internal party stability, the PRI saw the proposed urban legislative reform as a sound compromise option.

This is not to say that there was full consensus about the compromise reform. The mayor and the president both had strong links to certain factions of the party. And even within the PRI's coordinating committee—which consisted of the labor (CTM) and peasant (CNC) sectors as well as the CNOP—there were substantial differences over the reform that were never fully resolved. While the CNOP leadership enthusiastically supported the PRI's compromise reform, the CTM leadership, whose constituents were national labor groups and not a specifically urban population, tended to oppose it, as did much of the CNC. [8] There was also some dissension within the CNOP itself, understandably. Many of the technocrats working in Mexico City government, mentioned earlier as opponents of the initial proposal for democratic reform, were active in the CNOP and unwilling to lose their control over urban policy. Yet despite this internal dissension, the PRI leadership still took a clear and relatively decisive position on the reform, primarily because Mexico City populations in general, and the CNOP's urban constituents in particular, were so essential to party legitimacy. To most outside observers, moreover, the easiest and most logical solution would have been the intermediate reform, the compromise advocated by the PRI. Yet this was not to be. De la Madrid's administration was new enough that the president and his allies at Gobernación were reluctant to budge, afraid of showing political weakness to their macroeconomic and party allies so early in the game. The president felt himself to be on strong footing, since he relied on the increasingly powerful international and national economic elites and institutions for his political support. The mayor and his allies, moreover, who undoubtedly counted on factions of supporters within the party, also had enough at stake and sufficient power in the urban domain that they were also unwilling to compromise. Their ability to bring Mexico City to a standstill gave them a large bargaining chip. Yet in all this, the PRI leadership held fast to the middle ground, still seeing their alternative as the best solution for all.

A FISCAL CHALLENGE TO THE COMPROMISE

Just as it began to appear that the equal distribution of power and intransigence among the three networks of actors would keep the debate over urban democratic reform stalled indefinitely, an important event broke the stalemate. In July 1983, a year after the presidential election that brought de la Madrid to power, Mexico held its first state and local elections under the new administration. In the balloting for governors in several states, the PRI triumphed with little more than the usual public outcry of fraud and ballot fixing. And this, in turn, rekindled the intraparty conflict over urban democratic reform by reinforcing the two extreme differences in opinion over the reform's necessity in the context of debt crisis. The mayor and other opponents of the reform claimed that the positive electoral results were further evidence that *no* reform was actually necessary. Despite the fact that Mexico City voters themselves had not gone to the ballot box, the argument was that even in conditions of debt crisis, the PRI had maintained political legitimacy and strength. Yet the president and the Gobernación were equally convinced that this would actually be the perfect time for a reform, since conditions were sufficiently stable. That is, the midyear election results suggested to the president that electoral support for opposition parties was not so great after all, even in times of economic crisis. Accordingly, he and his allies argued that the PRI could still hold power even if the urban democratic reform was implemented.

With the president's and mayor's forces now even more polarized, party leaders intervened once more in order to quell the controversy. This time, however, the relative smoothness of the 1983 elections persuaded the PRI leadership to side with the mayor. For the well-seasoned party leadership, "If it ain't broke don't fix it" served as a guide for assessing the election's implications and the need for reform. The PRI subsequently abandoned the idea that even a moderate political reform was necessary, or that active debate on the topic should continue. If anything, the party leadership felt it was time to move beyond the conflict, which was beginning to paralyze the government and reinforce divisions that needed to be unified in order to deal with the multitude of more pressing economic and potential political problems on the horizon. When the PRI leadership dropped its active support for even a moderate reform, the debate was temporarily closed. Of course, not all members within the PRI were happy or willing to drop the idea of reform; nor were all those in the mayor's office or Gobernación in agreement with their respective leaders. But again, in terms of identifiable political positions on the part of each of these three sets of actors, changing conditions diminished the urgency for the PRI leadership to support the reform as much as did any sudden revelations about the appropriateness or inappropriateness of the policy. When the party leadership failed to push its compromise, the balance of opinion changed and the reform was effectively tabled, since no firm position could be reached.

For over two years the proposal for urban democratic reform remained stalled. But not so the city's fiscal crisis, the pressure for austerity, or urban social movements. Within a scant two years, by early 1985, political dissatisfaction in the capital was reaching dangerous heights, as it was becoming evident to politicians and citizens alike that de la Madrid's austerity plan was not bringing rapid or visible benefits to the common people, particularly in the capital. As the economy stagnated, opposition to the government heightened. So too did pressures on authorities to further cut urban policy expenditures, especially in the capital, where economic stagnation meant that local revenues were also sharply on the decline. As a result, in 1985 both de la Madrid and the PRI leadership began to think once again about implementing some form of urban democratic reform. Only now, they responded with greater urgency than before, since the economy was sliding down quickly. Between 1983 and 1984 alone, private sector investment fell 22.6 percent and consumption fell 7.7 percent; inflation reached 80 percent, and purchasing power fell 30 percent.[9] Not only did this provoke a new round of protest from the population, it further hurt the industrial sector and thus diminished the private sector's capacity to generate taxable revenues. Together, these pressures suggested that the 1983 decision to table the proposal might have been too hasty. Keeping the status quo intact had made sense when urban servicing was expected to continue at the same modest rate. But as of early 1985, when it became apparent that the debt crisis was also hurting domestic revenue generation and pushing the limits of social sacrifice, it was clear that urban investment in Mexico City would have to take a drastic downturn if the country was to meet its austerity obligations.

But why did Mexico City bear the brunt of pressure for austerity such that the urban reform looked so urgent now? Indeed, the debt crisis and attendant stabilization policies introduced by de la Madrid in 1983 and 1984 hurt many firms, both in and outside of Mexico City. What is significant, however, is that those firms most able to weather the mounting economic problems were the internationally linked companies that had already started to leave Mexico City in the early 1970s. They accelerated their flight when the crisis hit, thereby depriving the city of much-needed revenues. Smaller and medium-sized firms were most injured by the debt crisis and stabilization schemes, yet they tended to stay in the capital. Accordingly, the percentage of national tax revenue generated in the capital city plummeted, dropping 18 percent between 1980 and 1983 alone.[10] Through their impact on the location and prosperity of certain segments of the business sector, then, austerity measures introduced after 1983 and the continually deteriorating economy further undermined Mexico City's already precarious fiscal base, which in turn reduced local resources for urban expenditures. The implications of this pattern for both employment levels and fiscal solvency in Mexico City were disastrous.[11]

Because the urban fiscal crisis was so intricately linked to the weakening condition of the national economy, moreover, it was difficult for the federal government to bail out Mexico City. Even if business revenues outside the formal boundaries of the Distrito Federal were not diminishing as rapidly, they were not available for Mexico City authorities because they were needed to help the federal government pay off its own foreign debt. Indeed, Mexico City had no direct claim on them, and once they went directly to de la Madrid's allies in national government, it was even less likely that they would end up subsidizing urban expenditures in the fiscally bloated capital. Figures on social spending in the capital reveal the extent of the crisis. Squeezed both locally and nationally, in 1985 alone resources for Mexico City were so scarce that expenditures on critical urban services in the capital plummeted 12 percent on transport, 25 percent on potable water, 18 percent on health services, 26 percent on trash collection, and 56 percent on land regularization.[12] Making matters worse, as expenditures on urban services fell, employment dropped, poverty increased exponentially, and the costs of housing and much-needed urban expenditures rose at an unprecedented rate as the debt crisis intensified. In the three-year period starting in 1984, prices of dietary staples in Mexico City rose at phenomenal rates—757 percent for beans, 480 percent for eggs, 454 percent for fish, 340 percent for milk, and 276 percent for cornmeal.[13] Spiraling consumer costs were a particularly serious concern in Mexico City because speculation on scarce commodities was pervasive. In 1985, the Mexico City government even closed over two thousand commercial establishments in Mexico City for price gouging.[14]

These rapidly deteriorating conditions not only deepened Mexico City's fiscal crisis, they set the stage for a dramatic rise in political opposition among residents in the capital. Some of the strongest public protests in Mexico City came in response to the rising food prices that resulted from the termination of food subsidies. Others came in response to rising transport costs imposed by Mexico City authorities. Still others came as urban residents saw government prioritizing industrial development or austerity objectives over their own urban service concerns. This was exemplified in the actions of residents of one Mexico City barrio, who organized a massive protest against the ruling party because authorities were spending scarce resources on "soda factories but not public services." [15] These were not minor disturbances: At another rally over the paucity of urban services, the crowds neared three hundred thousand.[16]

As urban protest activities and social movements intensified rapidly between 1983 and 1985, President de la Madrid and the PRI leadership once again considered the tabled urban democratic reform. Much of their concern was with economic conditions and the political problems that might ensue in Mexico City if President de la Madrid continued with harsh stabilization policies. Yet de la Madrid and party leaders were also becoming especially concerned about the ways in which the crisis was weakening national corporatist structures—especially the CNOP. They felt that the debt crisis' negative impact on the PRI's legitimacy was intricately linked to the growing feelings of national political exclusion among those who were supposed to be formally represented by the CNOP. Party leaders were most troubled by the fact that the crisis was now being experienced equally by many of the CNOP's constituents. While in the past the CNOP leadership had to worry about dissatisfaction from one group of constituents or another, urban poor or middle classes, high-level bureaucrats or rank and file, rarely had it faced common levels of dissatisfaction from almost all its members simultaneously. But two years of severe debt crisis changed this. Urban residents from low-

and middle-income families shared a common economic crisis, but more important, they shared a feeling that they could not effect change through the CNOP; while old-guard bureaucrats, who were losing their power owing to the rising influence of *técnicos* in managing the crisis, now found themselves in a disadvantaged position similar to that of rank-and-file state workers, who were steadily losing their jobs to austerity cuts in the public sector.

Mexico City's middle classes, in particular, began to feel the pinch in several critical areas of urban consumption that in the past had been relatively immune from economic downturns, including the rising cost of luxury imports, a scarcity of affordable housing, steep increases in gas prices, and cutbacks in expenditures on education, including up to 100 percent increases in the costs of private education.[17] Of course, the so-called urban middle class was clearly not homogeneous, holding within it many different income and occupational groups, including small businessmen and shopkeepers, white-collar workers, and professionals, many of whom worked in the government sector. Yet these were among the groups most affected by the national debt crisis, they were the groups most concentrated in Mexico City, and they were the occupational groups formally represented within the CNOP. Several years of austerity made a big difference for them. Additionally, the elimination of subsidies and protective measures—principal components of stabilization and austerity policies demanded by the IMF—were harshly felt by small and medium-sized businesses in the capital, and this created a basis for concern among this vocal and well-organized sector of Mexico's urban middle class. Reduced government expenditures over 1983 and 1984, mandated by stabilization policies, also meant that middle-class employees in the government, such as doctors, teachers, and lower-level bureaucrats, were now directly threatened, since layoffs in the public sector had become a common cost-cutting measure by 1985.[18]

The urban poor, many of whom, like the urban middle classes, were members of the CNOP, shared the same dire straits. As inflation rates continued to rise during the mid-1980s, so too did costs of basic goods and services like housing, education, and health care. Carlos Tello notes that between 1982 and 1985, unemployment rose from 5 percent to 15 percent of the work force, real salaries *fell* 65 percent, and housing shortages hit a new high.[19] All this lent urgency to the demands of existing urban social movements. As urban social expenditures were cut and the costs of urban services climbed, the urban poor focused their political demands even more on consumption and production rather than workplace issues. Declining numbers of formal sector jobs and the dramatic increase in informal sector employment in Mexico City, which came as the crisis intensified, lent fuel to this tendency to struggle at the neighborhood level rather than at work. As formal employment opportunities declined precipitously, urban populations shifted their focus to home and neighborhood. Because informal sector workers lack steady employment, are rarely unionized, and often hold multiple jobs, their organization in and around workplace issues is difficult. As the crisis hit, many supported themselves with informal work at home (such as illegal subcontracting) or used their home or residential location to give them specialized access to neighborhood markets. Accordingly, demands for urban services like electricity, water, housing, or even transport became especially critical to their livelihoods as the crisis wore on.

Of course, the growth of the urban informal sector in Mexico City was not a new phenomenon, and it was a result of more than just the debt crisis. Street vendors and informal sector workers had for years lived in Mexico City, as noted in previous chapters. Yet the debt crisis of the mid-1980s brought even more of the unemployed and underemployed to the capital. As many of the city businesses became less profitable with the economic crisis, some of the smaller ones actually folded and their owners also took to more informal employment. Formal sector employment declined accordingly, and wages fell so low that many who were lucky enough to have steady employment also entered the ranks of the informal sector to make up the income difference. This further limited the pervasiveness and strength of workplace struggles as the main form of political protest. The result was a dramatic rise in urban struggles and social movements and a steady weakening of Mexico's corporatist political system, which was structured around class identities formulated primarily in the workplace.

The strengthening of urban social movements constituted a challenge to the CNOP and the PRI because these movements purposefully sought organizational autonomy and rejected more formal channels of political participation. As such, they could not be easily absorbed into the PRI-controlled institutions that made up the corporatist political system. To the extent that the debt crisis limited authorities' fiscal capacity to respond to urban poor and middle-class dissatisfactions with increased urban expenditures, this, too, fueled urban social movements and their challenge to the party. In the past, especially during the López Portillo and Echeverría administrations, party leaders and government officials had been able to respond to urban discontent by expanding city services and programs, especially transport and housing. Although such expenditures never matched in quantity those in major infrastructure for industrial and construction interests, they did appease popular demands somewhat, albeit selectively. Yet the declining tax revenues and attendant fiscal crisis made such policy actions increasingly impossible, as was evidenced by the 56 percent drop in expenditures for land regularization, as noted earlier.[20] One of the greatest problems for the de la Madrid administration, then, was the debt crisis, which heightened the demands of urban residents as it reduced the resources available to respond to those demands.

The economic crisis not only weakened the corporatist political system because it limited the CNOP's capacity to keep its constituents politically loyal; it also exacerbated the tensions between the CNOP's constituents and the labor sector, which in turn had serious repercussions within the party as a whole. Whatever scarce resources the government had available to address popular demands of Mexico City residents were generally directed to the organized working classes affiliated with the CTM. This was apparent in urban housing programs for workers and in the granting of inflation-indexed wage increases for organized laborers once the debt crisis hit. The purpose of this "solidarity pact" between capital, labor, and the state, as the PRI called it, was to gain organized labor's acquiescence and support for stabilization and the controversial process of macroeconomic restructuring. But its effect was to privilege the CTM and organized labor's demands, in comparison to the nonwage urban poor, informal sector workers, and middle classes, who could not rely on the CNOP or Mayor Aguirre to spend for them, either. As a result, the corporatist political system threatened to split wide open, since the debt crisis revealed that, of the three corporatist sectors, only the CTM had sufficient national and local political power to achieve wage and employment benefits for its industrial labor constituents in these difficult times. Greater demands for urban services, in contrast, were a low priority, because they would deepen the urban fiscal crisis if they were met, and because these sectors were seen as less critical to national economic recovery plans.

No matter the reason, the result of just three years of deepening economic crisis was politically devastating for the PRI. By 1985 party leaders were openly under the gun. During that year, the CONAMUP, or confederation of urban social movements, which was considered to have "consolidated" its power in 1985, began a public attack on the government.[21] Associations representing small industries and commerce in Mexico City also joined with many of the city's urban social movements in making open calls for a change in the government's macroeconomic strategy.[22] With urban poor and middle classes united against the government, opposition sentiment crystallized in the 1985 Mexico City elections for the national legislature. Citywide, the PRI gained only 42.63 percent of the local (eligible) vote, almost 6 percent less than in 1979, and a full 22 percent less than the national rate of support for the party, while the opposition parties combined captured over 57 percent of the vote.

Abstentions, moreover, reached almost 45 percent citywide, and were as high as 50 percent in some particularly mobilized districts of the capital.[23]

EARTHQUAKE JOLTS THE PRI

As electoral results in the capital city showed unprecedented levels of political dissatisfaction with the PRI, the issue of urban democratic reform again surfaced. In a public statement late in 1985, CNOP officials openly acknowledged that the PRI would continue to lose elections unless it could select candidates and restructure politics and policy in a way that would appeal to the city's dissatisfied poor and middle classes.[24] In order to address this concern, the PRI leadership reversed its 1983 opposition to urban democratic reform. They now joined de la Madrid and his allies in Gobernación in a push to reintroduce the proposal for legislative reform. Yet scarcely two months after the disastrous July electoral results, and before the issue could even be pursued further, a massive earthquake rocked Mexico City. The September 1985 quake threw millions onto the street and wrought widespread infrastructural destruction. Equally important, the quake tarnished the reputation of Mayor Aguirre and shook the faith of many in the Mexico City government, the PRI, and the Mexican political system as a whole by exposing the inability of local and national politicians to manage the city's most basic services in a time of disaster.

Widespread questioning of the ruling party and politics as usual rose to the surface because the earthquake hit three of the most mobilized and politically active neighborhoods of the city, where local residents were already well organized in urban social movements and beginning to challenge the evident neglect of popular demands. Several of the key areas hardest hit also happened to be older sections of the city that were peopled by traditional middle-class residents, as in the Colonia Roma, or that were home to shopkeepers, street vendors, and low-level government employees who lived in the popular neighborhoods a few kilometers around the *zócalo*. These neighborhoods held a relatively stable population and boasted a strong sense of community, in no small part because 1940s rent control regulations, restrictions on downtown development, and past favoritism granted by Mayor Uruchurtu and others had limited resident turnover during the past four decades. The residents of these areas also tended to be formal constituents of the CNOP, many of whom had successfully opposed and stalled the urban reconstruction plans of earlier administrations. In fact, one of the most seriously damaged locales was Colonia Roma, a charming old neighborhood with colonial buildings, parks, and wide boulevards that bordered the lavish Zona Rosa (or Pink Zone)—which hosted several principal metro stations and a thriving tourist entertainment center that local residents had opposed because they feared its disruptive potential. The remaining neighborhoods with heaviest destruction bordered the city's traditional center, not far from Calle Tacuba, where earlier struggles over street widening and downtown development had played themselves out. The residents of these particular neighborhoods, then, had long seen the PRI's authoritarian hand in the urban domain and its willingness to ignore local demands and urban service priorities when larger political objectives were involved.

Another reason the earthquake gave life to long-standing urban opposition to the PRI was that both local and national governing agencies failed to rapidly or efficiently assess the political and material damage. As a result of the inadequate response by local authorities, combined with an unparalleled level of community solidarity in the neighborhoods, people in the area hit hardest by the quake organized themselves rapidly, even within a few hours, to deal with the injured and with damaged property. These local groups maintained and expanded their organizations month after the quake, as the government continued to flounder in its efforts to care for the injured and the thousands of homeless. Not only did these conditions breed even greater support for grassroots democratic control, they directly challenged the PRI's legitimate claim to authority, at least in Mexico City, which in previous administrations had been based in large part on the party's ability to deliver the goods. The party's failure to respond adequately to the circumstances motivated citizens to question past political practices and to take control of the urban situation themselves. Indeed, the earthquake spurred Mexico City residents to struggle for greater participation and control over urban servicing and their own political destinies, which challenged the PRI as never before. This spelled disaster for the PRI; and with the elections and the earthquake occurring back to back, many in the party thought something had to be done immediately to restore public confidence. Another prolonged debate over urban political reform would only hurt the PRI more, so actions were quickly taken to indicate both resolve and decisiveness.

A few weeks after the quake, PRI representatives in Congress announced a plan to create a new, albeit still unarticulated, type of political mechanism for citizen participation in the event of disaster.[25] This general proposal served as a feeler for both party members and citizens about the appropriate level of grassroots participation in urban politics. Once the plan received strong support and public acclaim, party leaders renewed the behind-the-scenes discussion over de la Madrid's original proposal for democratic governance in Mexico City. In the discussion that followed, the intermediate option's success appeared most likely: creating a new legislative body without altering provisions for presidential appointment of the Mayor. Of course, de la Madrid and his allies at Gobernación still supported the more wide-reaching reform and felt that given the unique post-earthquake conditions, something drastic could and should be done as soon as possible. Yet the PRI leadership still believed the president's reform to be overly guided by technocratic considerations of economic restructuring and recovery, expressing insufficient cognizance of the political history as well as the current temperature of the nation.[26]

The party leadership's capacity to successfully push the compromise position in early 1986 was made easier by the fact that Aguirre also softened his earlier position of extreme opposition to urban political reform. It was now quite clear to the mayor that the recent protests and problems associated with the earthquake had challenged his reputation and political efficacy. Moreover, in the wake of the local bureaucracy's initial failure to respond, President de la Madrid had already created a new semiautonomous agency, the Renovación Popular, to coordinate earthquake reconstruction in the capital city. Although there were still thousands of homeless residents in the city's streets, this new agency had achieved remarkable success in allocating new property titles, constructing new housing, and working with existing urban social movements that had used the earthquake to rally popular support. This demonstrated to Aguirre and all other parties concerned that the city could be coordinated without the cadre of local bureaucrats, *delegados*, and urban service providers who had held their political and technical skills as ransom for accommodating their opposition to the reform. These developments, then, limited Aguirre's capacity to push for his original stand, and it forced him to seek a way to restore his own rapidly diminishing reputation with both the president and Mexico City populations. With both the mayor and the president in weak positions to make extreme proposals on democratic reform, the party leadership was able to push its original position, the modified democratic reform.[27]

Nonetheless, between the initiation of public hearings on the urban reform in June 1986, and the formal submission of an initiative to the national Congress in early December 1986, something rather surprising occurred: This well-crafted compromise was abandoned, even after intraparty consensus had been struck. The origins of the rapid about-face lay once again in electoral results, but in northern regions of the country, like Chihuahua, where the right-wing PAN was strong, rather than in Mexico City. Although the PRI claimed a triumph in these elections, charges of electoral fraud abounded in greater numbers than usual. Even the United States and other international forces joined the chorus, chastising the PRI for declaring a clear victory when it was apparent that electoral dissatisfaction was widespread. Furthermore, in the wake of the elections and cries of fraud, the PAN organized a series of protests and marches that garnered international attention and at times became violent. Representatives of autonomous social movements, many of whom had strong connections with movements in Mexico City, joined the PAN marches.

This delicate situation with respect to both electoral and popular opposition made several within the PRI again change their stand, as they became reluctant to follow through with even the limited legislative reform agreed upon earlier, and now proposed for discussion in the public hearings. At issue for the first time in decades was the extent to which political developments in regions outside the capital would have an impact on Mexico City politics. In the previous decades, since the consolidation of politics and power in the capital city during the 1920s and 1930s, party leaders had been able to separate out political challenges from center and region by keeping provincial politics out of the national political limelight and by concentrating national political attention on the concerns of the capital city's residents. While corporatist structures of politics aided in these procedures by downplaying territorial bases of political demand making and highlighting class identities instead, more often than not the PRI met these goals by using repression in the provinces and mayoral accommodation in Mexico City. But with debt crisis eliminating the party's fiscal capacity to accommodate urban populations and with Mexico City's urban problems reaching a point where accommodating so many disparate urban policy preferences was nearly impossible, the complicity of Mexico City populations in this national political division of labor became increasingly untenable.

The fraud and corruption of the July 1986 northern elections were not only a stark reminder of this unspoken complicity, they also were seen as a portent of what might occur in the capital if residents did not continue to openly and actively challenge the ruling party. Accordingly, after the July 1986 elections in the north, the likelihood of a PAN victory in several districts in Mexico City seemed even greater than it had nine months earlier, when the moderate reform had been approved. This was due to both the continued strength of middle-class urban organizations organized in the aftermath of the earthquake—many of which either ideologically sympathized with the PAN or merely supported it as an act of protest against the PRI—and to the PAN's heightened national profile during the Chihuahua challenge. Complicating matters for the PRI, by July 1986 many of these urban movements in Mexico City were making demands about urban services and employment and linking them to larger political and economic issues, including the repudiation of the foreign debt. By tying the macroeconomic situation to local conditions, urban movements further challenged the separation of Mexico City politics from other national developments, as had occurred with the Chihuahua elections. After mid-1986, representatives of these urban movements also argued that the government's unwillingness to fund large-scale reconstruction derived from its commitment to fiscal austerity over political responsibility or humanitarian concerns, a position that brought the tensions between urban service priorities and national economic development to the forefront of political debate.

Equally salient, by linking the intensity of the destruction in the Mexico City built environment to the complicity of past administrations in corrupt urban construction practices, after 1985 many of Mexico City's urban movements also focused on the willingness of previous administrations to accommodate the construction industry's interests at the expense of residents' lives and livelihood. This spurred residents to push for stricter urban building and construction regulations, as well as to question the history of complicity between local officials and private sector forces with national power (like ICA). In making these connections, each of which meant moving beyond a singular concern with urban services, in one way or another Mexico City's social movements became a serious political threat to the PRI and to its larger development objectives.

With Mexico City populations linking their circumstances to national political and economic conditions, the urban democratic reform tentatively agreed upon for Mexico City just two months earlier was no longer seen as a moderate or expedient compromise that could preempt opposition, but as a risky measure that might give away too much power to opposition forces wishing to challenge the party's hold on both local and national politics. Thus contention reemerged and soon opponents to the urban democratic reform became a majority voice. In a striking abrogation of their original position, officials in Gobernación also abandoned the idea. Not only did urban social movements' demands for repudiation of foreign debt obligations worry the proposals' original protagonists, they were now as concerned about the *costs* of successfully maintaining political power in the face of greater democratization as with the political possibilities of doing so. One official argued that what really dampened Gobernación's enthusiasm—in addition to concerns about popular demands for debt repudiation and other calls for major changes in macroeconomic policy—was the massive amount of money the PRI had poured into the campaign in northern states. Rumors abounded that the PRI's coffers were nearly depleted after spending inordinate sums of money to secure an electoral victory that many refused to accept as legitimate anyway. This suggested to de la Madrid and his allies at Gobernación that to maintain power in a more open political system, whether in Mexico City or the regions, might require even greater amounts of money, which were clearly lacking in these austere times. This realization hit the de la Madrid team where it hurt the most: It directly jeopardized their austerity programs and macroeconomic recovery plans.

MEXICO'S CITY'S ASAMBLEA DE REPRESENTANTES: SIDESTEPPING URBAN DEMOCRATIC REFORM

Without support by governing authorities or party leaders for any form of real democratic reform of local electoral practices in the capital, the question was what to do. Because public audiences had already been held and citizen expectations raised about some form of democratic change in the institutional structure of Mexico City governance, even a moderate one, it would be very difficult for party leaders to drop the idea entirely. Doing so would have been a clear indication that the PRI lacked any commitment at all to grassroots democratic participation in Mexico City, an allegiance that was already being treated with a large dose of skepticism given the limited nature of the compromise reform offered in 1986. To avoid political suicide in the capital, the PRI felt that its only remaining alternative was to implement a plan that included mechanisms for direct local elections, but that eliminted the legislative power of the elected body. In this way, the PRI hoped to display at least some superficial commitment to the idea of urban political reform, while still limiting and controlling the extent of popular participation in urban policymaking. The bill finally offered to the national Congress by the PRI, which was approved in April 1987, established a local assembly for Mexico City residents, called the Asamblea de Representantes del Distrito Federal. The new Asamblea was touted as a representative body, but it held no legislative power. Rather, the new body's activities were limited to passing recommendations and nonbinding initiatives concerning programs and policies administered in Mexico City. As with the modified reform, there was no provision for direct election of the mayor. Thus the reform was more symbolic than substantive, and many considered it only a slightly more sophisticated version of the existent *delegado* and *junta de vecinos* systems in Mexico City. Residents still had very little formal power to participate locally in decision making about the urban services and policies that affected their daily lives.

The reform was not totally useless for everybody. Though it did little to provide for democratic political participation of the urban poor and middle classes in Mexico City policymaking, the new Asamblea permitted the PRI to negotiate a new lease on urban governance. During the weeks and months surrounding the proposed Asamblea's approval, local authorities carried out several fiscal reforms that they had been trying to achieve for years in Mexico City without success, including a tripling of the subway fare, which had remained at the same low rate for practically two decades. Mexico City authorities also announced plans to triple local real estate taxes.[28] In other words, with the Asamblea in place, local and national politicians now actually had enough maneuvering room to move forward with a more stringent austerity plan for the capital city, one of their original objectives in proposing urban democratic reform in the first place. And these connections were well articulated to the public. Government spokesmen were among the first to highlight the relationship between fiscal crisis and political change in the capital when they announced in May 1987 that their plans to sell locally based state industries, liquidate trusteeships, and fuse several dependencies were an integral part of government efforts to "reorder and politically reform" Mexico City.[29]

In terms of giving Mexico's leaders the opportunity to introduce fundamental changes in the financing and provision of urban services in Mexico City, then, the Asamblea can be considered a relatively successful reform. But the political benefits were, at best, limited. Given its advisory character, the Asamblea turned out to be as much an embarrassment for the PRI as anything else. In very uncharacteristic fashion, the plan itself received very little public fanfare after its approval. One national subsecretary privately called it "the reform that nobody wanted," and several prominent PRI leaders criticized the plan in public.[30] Their biggest complaint was that the reform's limited scope reinforced the image of a political system unwilling—or at least unable—to respond to calls for true urban democratic reform from local populations. Rather than legitimizing or strengthening the established political system and the PRI's power within it, at least in Mexico City, the troubled process and the watered-down institutional reform it produced helped tarnish the PRI's reputation from within its own ranks, perhaps the most fatal indictment of all. By 1987, when the new presidential campaign started to unfold, this issue was the sword upon which the PRI would be irreparably wounded. Even after the introduction of the Asamblea, urban social movements in the city were alive with demands about declining basic services, rising costs of transport and electricity, the negative effects of austerity, and their limited political participation in Mexico City governance. Moreover, precisely because the government moved forward with full fiscal austerity measures in Mexico City, despite the limited democratic rights offered in exchange, resident populations were eager to repudiate the PRI.

Riding the crest of these concerns, PRI activist Cuauhtémoc Cárdenas captured the imagination of Mexico City's masses, especially its cadres of urban social movements. Although Cárdenas's opposition voice first beckoned informally, as a wake-up call to the CNOP and fellow PRIistas for failing to protect the political and economic rights of populations hurt by de la Madrid's austerity plans, it soon became much more. Starting only as an insurgent ideological current within the party itself, Cárdenas and his allies within the PRI soon shifted their position to that of opposition challengers. By 1988, Cárdenas's criticisms began to fuel the development of a well-organized grassroots movement that questioned party policies from the outside as well as within.

Cárdenas's shift from internal critic to external opponent came in large part because of the strong support lent him by Mexico City's urban movements and residents dissatisfied with austerity-produced urban service scarcities and the lack of democratic rights in the capital. Indeed, even though Cárdenas probably never intended his opposition to be mainly urban-based, by taking on the issues of austerity and the party's failure to democratize internally, his own political objectives intersected with the pressing concerns of already well-organized Mexico City's residents. This was made clear in a speech given at a public rally in Mexico City, when Cárdenas proudly noted that his supporters—by rallying behind the Frente Democrático Nacional rather than the PRI—not only voted against "economic dependency" and deteriorating social and employment conditions, but that they also voted "for the recuperation of full citizenship for the residents of the Distrito Federal."[31] In other words, not only were the economic crisis and the failed democratic reform intricately linked in the Cárdenas campaign; Cárdenas drew much of his political support from those groups in Mexico City who were most disenfranchised by the debt crisis and the PRI's highly circumscribed policy response to popular pressures for basic services and urban democratic reform.

A look at electoral results reveals the urban bases of Cárdenas's support and their national impact. Cárdenas ran on an opposition party ticket and gathered almost as much support nationally (39 percent) as did the PRI's candidate, Carlos Salinas (41 percent). For the first time in fifty years, opposition parties combined gained more national electoral support (59 percent) than did the PRI's candidate. Yet despite his failure to triumph nationally, Cárdenas swept Mexico City, where the strength of his electoral support was matched only in his home state of Michoacan. Not only did Cárdenas's participation in the election take support away from the ruling party's candidate in presidential elections, it also spilled over into Distrito Federal elections for Congress, which further demonstrates the extent of Mexico City opposition to the PRI. In 1988, the PRI captured only 27.6 percent of the eligible vote in Mexico

City, a rate almost half the national average (51.1 percent). Most important, perhaps, in this election support for the PRI in Mexico City hit an all-time historic low (never having dropped below 30 percent in any election since the PRI's foundation). The 27 percent support rate for the PRI in Mexico City in 1988 compared to 68 percent in 1958 during the height of Uruchurtu's term and to 48 percent scarcely six years earlier. Accordingly, Cárdenas's near-win in the 1988 national election rested almost fully on his overwhelming success in the capital, which held close to one-fourth the national population.

In addition to the ties Cárdenas cultivated with Mexico City's urban social movements over issues of austerity and failed democratic reform, another factor that undoubtedly helped him tap Mexico City's support was his past connection to the CNOP and democratizing forces within it. This observation, however, also returns us to a focus on the urban conflicts and policy dissatisfactions of Mexico City populations. Cárdenas and his most visible political allies, like Porfirio Muñoz Ledo, were powerful and active ex-PRIistas who made their reputations and cemented their political networks within the CNOP. It was through years of activism in the CNOP, in fact, that they had been able to develop strong ties to many grassroots organizations in Mexico City. Thus it was also through the CNOP that Cárdenas developed a constituency of Mexico City residents dissatisfied with the ways that the national political leadership and corporatist institutions of the party operated, especially the way they dealt with urban problems. Perhaps the best evidence that Cárdenas challenge was firmly grounded in the PRI's problems with the CNOP's declining responsiveness to its urban bases is seen in the CNOP's public support for Cárdenas when leaders of the PRI and the remaining two sectors demanded his expulsion in spring 1987. And after the 1988 election it was publicly acknowledged that many in the CNOP had rallied behind Cárdenas and lent covert institutional support to his campaign.

These past linkages to the CNOP, then, may also help explain why urban populations supported Cárdenas much more strongly than they did the right-wing PAN, which in past elections had been the party that appealed to the growing numbers of middle classes—and some urban poor—unhappy with the PRI. Despite the dramatic fall in support for the PRI in 1988, the PAN fared no better at the polls than it had in the previous presidential election, indicating that the strength of new urban opposition fell almost fully behind Cárdenas. This is not so surprising when we consider that Cárdenas's political platform included nationalist programs of protection for smaller industries, support for urban poor and middle classes, and a repudiation of speculators and international banking institutions. All these issues had been raised on behalf of Mexico City populations by Echeverría, Uruchurtu, and others who in earlier periods also sought to focus national politics either on servicing and growth problems in Mexico City or on the absence of mechanisms for political participation in the capital. Of course, Uruchurtu, Echeverría, and Cárdenas were all defeated in their efforts to keep the concerns of Mexico City populations and their urban service demands as central on the national political agenda. What was different about the 1988 version of this undertaking, however, was that Cárdenas never even made it to a position of national political power, having been expelled from the party early on in the campaign and then prevented from claiming a national electoral triumph after the results were in. This suggests that the long-standing concerns of Mexico City's urban poor and middle classes were sufficiently banished from within the party's inner circles of deliberation by 1988, both institutionally and in terms of politics and policymaking, that national political leaders no longer felt compelled to let Mexico City's populations strongly factor into the national political agenda. If Cárdenas had triumphed nationally, this situation might have been reversed. But with his ouster from the party and his official defeat, the PRI now had a clear path to pursue its national economic agenda and place issues of popular participation and servicing in Mexico City on the back burner.

A NEW ARTICULATION OF URBAN AND NATIONAL POLITICS

With Cárdenas's failure to capture the presidency, the urban popular challenge to national politics that had been growing in Mexico City also receded to the background. Urban social movements did not disappear, of course, nor did all party leaders' efforts to show responsiveness to concerns about urban services and popular demands in Mexico City. But by and large, it was pretty clear that after 1988 demands relating to Mexico City's servicing and urban development were to be subordinated to the PRI's national macroeconomic priorities, at least in the course of local politics. The economic crisis of the eighties, in short, gave Mexico's PRI both the rationale and the urgency to institutionally unlink urban and national politics. The Asamblea stood as testament to this separation. Actions taken in the Asamblea superseded those that the nationally constituted CNOP might have implemented on the urban level, making the CNOP almost obsolete in local politics and thus silencing the voices of Mexico City populations in the party's national policymaking. Because the new Asamblea lacked statutory power, however, its existence did not stop the national government from directing the course of local policymaking. Indeed, the Asamblea's limited power gave Mexico City's mayor the freedom to follow national directives by lessening any political obligation the mayor might feel to chart a course different from that of the president, if local populations so demanded. That is, with the Asamblea's establishment as a "representative" body, even a limited one, the mayor's office no longer bore the entire burden of legitimizing the national party in the eyes of Mexico City populations, as had been the case with Uruchurtu and his successors; and thus it had even more freedom to follow national directives. The result of this shift in affairs was a series of urban policy changes after 1988 that were made more with an eye to national economic recovery than to the concerns of local populations.

The new dynamics of urban policymaking first became clear in rate hikes and the privatization of urban services that followed the creation of the new Asamblea. Yet the new direction in urban policymaking became especially evident in decisions made about urban services and redevelopment policy in the capital once Mexico's new president, Carlos Salinas de Gortari, came to office and appointed another mayor. Mexico City's new mayor, Manuel Camacho, rode into office with ambitious plans for downtown development and gentrification of several old central city neighborhoods, ideas that had been formulated during his tenure as secretary of SEDUE under de la Madrid and his previous involvement in the urban reconstruction of post-earthquake Mexico City. Despite strong resistance to the plan in the Asamblea, Camacho's urban redevelopment projects aimed to restore and revitalize downtown areas in order to attract visitors and displace low-income residents, as well as to spur the revival of an urban land market that was just beginning to see signs of life with the transfer of land titles and urban property rights during the earthquake renovation. This new project called for a renovation of old housing stock in downtown areas and a commitment to preserving the historic potential of downtown, not only for purposes of national patrimony but also to encourage upper-income housing development and tourism, a principal source of foreign exchange. It also called for massive displacement of street vendors and other informal sector workers who clogged downtown streets.

With these new plans now in the implementation stage, Camacho accomplished what no other mayor or presidential administration had been able to do: He overcame the political opposition of poor and lower-middle-class residents in downtown areas and introduced large-scale urban redevelopment of Mexico City. In past administrations, the persistence of rent control and the self-organization of residents brought a stability of residence and a degree of political efficacy that buttressed the power of downtown districts and traditional low-income neighborhoods to reject such plans. But by 1988, both the local and national power of the downtown neighborhoods and communities had been broken. Some of this was due to the earthquake, which gave the government an opportunity to offer new property titles, and thus eliminate the straitjacket of rent control. Some was due to Camacho's skills as a negotiator. Equally important, however, was the fact that local politics changed dramatically when the ineffectual Asamblea superseded the CNOP as the mechanism for structuring local politics. Indeed, the widespread transformation of downtown areas now seen in Mexico City became possible precisely because the nationally powerful CNOP disappeared as a potent political force representing these very same downtown residents, like street vendors and shopkeepers, and because its replacement, the Asamblea, still allows the politically appointed mayor to balance or override requests generated by local residents in the service of integrated urban and national economic objectives, like tourism. That is, past political structures like the CNOP that gave Mexico City residents a say (albeit limited) in national debates over urban policymaking have been made obsolete by purely local ones that lack sufficient power to stand up against nationally controlled structures or national priorities, including the development of Mexico City–based tourism and the vitalization of the downtown land market for the country's growing financial sector.

The capacity of local residents to fight downtown development is now limited, not only because the Asamblea lacks legislative power and is controlled by a presidentially appointed mayor, but also because this new superficially democratic body presupposes the political participation of individuals as representatives of different subterritorial domains in the city, rather than groups or classes. To the extent that corporatist identification with the CNOP, or patron-client relations between Mexico City residents and the mayor or residents and community *junta* leaders, are no longer the basis for the political participation of Mexico City populations, certain neighborhoods—especially downtown—will no longer be able to use national political structures or specialized class-based political relations with the mayor or other governing officials to successfully press for their concerns. As a result, the PRI can use the Asamblea to divide and conquer local opposition to urban growth or redevelopment, while offering the illusion of urban democratic participation. This is not to say that with the Asamblea in place, patron-client relations have been eliminated from Mexico City politics, or that local constituents fully lack political power. Indeed, Mayor Camacho's skills in dealing with downtown shopkeepers and street vendors, either directly in a traditional patron-client style or through the machinations of the Asamblea, have afforded him great latitude to introduce downtown development plans; and some fortunate groups of vendors and shopkeepers have received clear benefits. Yet much of the new mayor's maneuvering room owes to the isolation of specific groups of Mexico City residents from each other and from class-based or clientelistic structures of political participation that in previous periods linked them to other classes or citywide groups, and by so doing buttressed their political power within the PRI and local governance. In short, with larger institutions like the CNOP institutionally unlinked from their urban constituencies, and with Mexico City's mayor partially freed from the political obligation to serve as the voice for disenfranchised Mexico City residents, the nature of urban policymaking and the city's spatial composition are now being fundamentally transformed.

Along the way, so too is Mexico's corporatist political system and the role of Mexico City's urban poor and middle classes within it. That changes in urban policymaking should have some national political impact can be of no surprise to those who recognize that urban policy and national politics have long been linked. The party's principal corporatist institution, the CNOP, was founded largely to accommodate the urban policy demands of excluded Mexico City populations. So now with the Asamblea fully superseding the CNOP and other party-dominated mechanisms as the principal political structure for Mexico City's residents to press their demands, the CNOP has lost one of its principal functions and much of the constituency that gave it voice and power within the party in the first place. Accordingly, the internal structures of the party are also undergoing a fundamental transformation as the CNOP is slowly receding to the background. That the internal structure of the PRI, and thus Mexican politics, is in the midst of a fundamental transformation was first made manifest in February 1990, a little more than one year after Carlos Salinas took office, when the PRI announced that it was going to disband the CNOP and create an entirely new institutional apparatus for urban poor and middle classes to participate in national politics. The new sector of the party was called UNE, Ciudadanos en Movimiento,[32] and it held within its ranks groups as diverse as labor, community, and ecological organizations, many of which are active primarily in Mexico City. By eliminating the CNOP at this time, the PRI may have implicitly acknowledged that the key to its near electoral defeat in 1988, and its own internal political problems before and after, lay with the conflict over the role and functioning of the CNOP. And as we have seen here, many of these conflicts resulted from disagreements over urban policy and administration in Mexico City, especially over the CNOP's ability to accommodate urban social movements and their demands about urban services and administration in the capital.

It may not be too early to know whether a new structure like the UNE will be successful where the CNOP failed: By 1993, even this new body was disbanded and replaced by yet another called the Frente Nacional de Organizaciones y Ciudadanos (FNOC), in an institutional about-face that suggests the party's difficulties in reforming the old CNOP and accommodating its constituents. But one thing is certain: If this new organization, whatever its name or structure, no longer has to take principal responsibility for Mexico City residents' demands about local politics and the problematic issues of urban development, and if it can relegate these obligations to the new Asamblea, the PRI may have much greater freedom to negotiate the uncertain terrain of urban policy and politics in Mexico. Without the burden of Mexico City and its urban problems hanging heavy on its back, moreover, the PRI may have maneurvering room to address the accelerating regional conflicts and provincial challenges to one-party rule that increasingly mark Mexican politics and national political debate as we round out the decade of the nineties.

9

RECASTING THE DYNAMICS

OF URBAN AND POLITICAL

CHANGE IN MEXICO

As one of the world's largest cities and capital of one of Latin America's most industrialized and prosperous nations, Mexico City hardly looks the part. Both a journey through this book and a stroll down the streets and downtown neighborhoods of Mexico's capital give rise to the feeling that Mexico City may be a city lost in time. Small shops and specialized trades mix colorfully with residential buildings and a few scattered government offices and prep schools to produce an astonishingly low-density land usage in the city center, uncannily reminiscent of prerevolutionary days at the turn of the century. Street vendors vie with cars, buses, hand-driven carts, and pedestrians for right-of-way on narrow streets still barely wide enough for one-way traffic, let alone motorized vehicles. With the exception of a single, lone sky-scraper known as the Torre Latinoamericana, which hovers awkwardly above downtown blocks of primarily two- and three-story buildings, as of 1990 corporate or residential high-rises have been virtually absent in downtown Mexico City. In their stead stand monumental edifices from the eighteenth and nineteenth century and a smattering of low-rise office buildings dating to the early twentieth century. It is only now that Mexico City is starting to host the high-density, capital-intensive infrastructural development of its built environment that marks almost every other world city of measurable size.

Mexico City's traditional, quasi-colonial character and low-density land usage stand in stark contrast to patterns seen in other huge metropolises of Latin America, like São Paulo and Rio de Janeiro, Buenos Aires, Caracas, and Santiago, Chile, where dense and highly developed downtowns host count-less skyscrapers, banks, and corporate headquarters. Decades ago, as their national economies first began to prosper, historic areas and colonial buildings were destroyed and downtown streets were transformed with the construc-tion of massive government and commercial buildings, hotels, and middle- or upper-income residential high-rises. This urban redevelopment usually had a visible impact on the structure of the entire metropolitan area and on the daily conditions of urban life, from transport infrastructure and extension in space to class concentration and community. In clear contrast to Mexico City, for example, these Latin American cities proudly display wide streets and modern urban infrastructure that have both facilitated the journey outward and valo-rized the urban land market, especially downtown.

To those who know Latin America's principal urban centers, Mexico City also stands apart as a city in especially grave peril. Intolerable pollution, para-lyzing traffic congestion, urban infrastructural deficiencies, and population overload characterize Mexico's capital city much more visibly than most other principal cities of Latin America, even those whose host countries evidence a similar stage of industrial development as Mexico, like São Paulo or Rio de Janeiro. Thus it is not only Mexico City's unparalleled size and several decades of concentrated and uncontrolled growth that have produced these debilitating urban problems. Mexico City's internal structure and unusual downtown land use patterns both exemplify its exceptionality and contribute to the lamentable urban chaos.

While in Mexico City there is no systematic pattern of increasing density from the metropolitan core to its outskirts, in other major Latin American cities one sees much clearer evidence of a steady decrease in high-rises and a steadily declining density of land usage when moving from costly central city properties to the inaccessible and less prestigious areas of the periphery. This landscape frequently hides within it an identifiable pattern of income differentiation, evident not necessarily in concentric circles but in the blossoming of distinct neighborhoods whose age and location belie an articulation with an active and steadily expanding urban land market. But in Mexico City such differentiated patterns are much less visible or systematic. Decades without a truly dynamic downtown urban land market have made their mark on the entire built environment, which has grown in space but not in height. Even though specific neighborhoods manifest the lifestyles of their residents, lower and middle classes live all over the metropolitan area, in both center and periphery, with only the very rich spatially separated from the rest. The slow pace of urban land development within Mexico City's formal bounds further hides differences in income and land usage that in other cities have come with historical waves of continuous land turnover and downtown development. Only in the capital's outmost periphery, in fact, are income differences among the urban population, both rich and poor, clearly etched in territory and space.

So what explains the distinct patterns of urban development in Mexico City? How is it that the world's largest city has extended in space so rapidly, yet at the same time afforded so little investment in the built environment and downtown development? There is, of course, much to be said for the preservation of Mexico's colonial heritage and the slowness with which this teeming metropolis adopted the urban construction patterns that accompanied rapid modernization in so many other cities. Downtown Mexico City retains a charm and infrastructural heritage that will attract tourists and sustain innovations in architectural preservation for decades to come. Yet there are also many urban problems that have emerged hand in hand with Mexico City's unique development patterns, including catastrophic pollution levels, transportation gridlock, and basic infrastructural scarcities that limit the opportunities of its residents. Accordingly, the question of why Mexico City displays this exceptional character is an enormously important one, both practically and for the field of urban studies.

In this book we have found answers to these and other questions through a focus on postrevolutionary political dynamics, both local and national: not only the ways in which party leaders and governing officials either promoted or shunned particular urban development policies for the capital in order to generate political alliances or popular support, but also the ways in which political alliances or popular pressures mandated certain urban development policies and administrative strategies in the capital city. Of course, almost all urban development decisions are embedded in politics in one way or another, no matter what city or country you consider. Accordingly, to invoke a focus on political dynamics, per se, does not go nearly far enough in explaining Mexico City's exceptionality, especially its enormous size combined with relatively limited downtown development. Rather, what makes Mexico City's urban development patterns so unique are two interrelated factors historically specific to postrevolutionary Mexico: one-party rule and the overlap of local and national institutions and objectives.

One-party rule placed unique pressure on local officials to be politically responsive—not just technically proficient—in administering Mexico City, where the nation's largest and best-organized concentration of people resided. Because of the peculiar structure and nature of one-party rule, moreover, Mexico's leaders made political accommodations to urban middle and working classes simultaneously, some of whom used local and some of whom used national political institutions to express grievances about urban policy and development. Yet middle and working classes frequently had very different urban policy orientations, because of their distinct occupational needs and their distinct residential locations in Mexico City itself. In this circumscribed social and spatial terrain, where the ruling party tried to balance multiple class interests and foster industrial development in the capital at the same time, Mexico City officials introduced urban service and administrative policies that best allowed them to keep the loyalty of a broad spectrum of forces. These particular urban policies, in turn, contributed to a rare combination of low-density downtown land usage and urban sprawl.

Complicating matters, governing officials had to worry about balancing local and national developmental concerns at the same time as they sought to balance the cross-class demands of different corporatist constituents within the capital city itself. These ongoing tensions arose from the fact that Mexico City was home to national political institutions, the greatest concentration of population and economic investment, and most of the nation's industrial and financial infrastructure. Thus, to foster urbanization-led industrialization in Mexico City meant to foster the nation's economic development and to give employment and services to large numbers of the nation's most vocal and organized social and class forces (manufacturing industrialists, their laborers, and middle classes). If Mexico City went belly-up, or its populations abandoned the ruling party and supported opposition forces because they were dissatisfied with local policies and conditions, the national political repercussions would have been monumental. What determined policy or economic "success" in Mexico City, however, was frequently up for grabs. Actors with a view to purely local dynamics of life and livelihood did not always see eye to eye with actors concerned primarily with the national economy, or actors organized in national political federations rather than local ones. Accordingly, the extent to which political, social, and spatial developments in Mexico City articulated with national developments has been a source of constant concern to Mexico's leaders for decades. With the ruling party aware of both local-national and cross-class constraints, the involvement of competing local and national actors with different visions of the city further restricted the options for urban policymaking. The city's growth and spatial development, accordingly, emerged as the by-product of political leaders' conflicting attempts to coordinate local and national domains while still maintaining the class and institutional balance of power underlying one-party rule.

Given the jurisdictional overlaps and class tensions manifest in and over development of the nation's capital, the privileging and extraordinary growth of Mexico City, as well as the cap on downtown development, were by no means simple or even well-articulated tasks facilely imposed by a unified political leadership on a willing public in agreement on the city's future. Nor were they automatic responses to economies of scale or the investment decisions and urban priorities of Mexico's capitalists. The unique patterns of urban development of Mexico's capital were as much a result of the unsteady and shifting balance of political and class power, both local and national, as a coherent product of the ruling party or specific class forces. In the limited common ground for striking a balance between the competing and often incompatible concerns of different classes, both local and national, officials frequently introduced contradictory and ever more costly urban policies. The result was not only fiscal crisis, which itself had devastating political and urban developmental repercussions, but also a rapid and extended urban growth combined, most anomalously, with relatively limited downtown development. Mexico City's internal structure and growth, in short, were highly contested and interrelated processes that brought local and national state and class actors into conflict with each other and among themselves in ways that affected both urban development and the nation itself.

TRANSPORT CONFLICTS IN RETROSPECT

The long view of political struggles over the urban development of Mexico City presented here has shown that speicific conflicts over transport services were among the most controversial and consequential determinants of urban land use patterns and urban sprawl, as well as of the shifting balance of political power that engendered these urban development patterns. This was due not only to the fact that transport servicing had a direct impact on the composition, character, and spatial bounds of the capital, but also to the fact that some of Mexico's most powerful class actors, nationally speaking, were involved in the production or supply of transport services for Mexico City. In the early years of Mexico City's development, for example, trolley workers were among the most active and organized of the working classes. As demonstrated in Chapters 2 and 3, the urban reconstruction and development of Mexico City in the 1920s was intricately linked to the governing coalition's ability to establish good political relations with these *transportistas*, mainly trolley workers and bus drivers, just as political leaders' capacity to establish good relations with the city's business elite was contingent on their ability to ensure reconstruction and efficient urban services, especially transport. Both objectives required alliance building and compromise, negotiations that presupposed certain political deals and that in turn set limits on certain urban redevelopment policies while engendering others. As part of the process, revolutionary leaders established new corporatist organizations that empowered certain class forces but not others. In this early period, the losers were trolley workers and their radical allies in the labor movement. The winners were a federation of bus drivers, who would shun the party's labor sector, become members of the CNOP, and establish extraordinarily strong political ties to the mayor's office. Together, these new class and institutional dynamics influenced both party politics and urban development policy in the capital for decades to come.

In the fifties, transport policies again lay at the forefront of contentious political debates over political power and Mexico City's urban development. A first round of conflicts pitted bus drivers who wanted to widen downtown streets against central city residents who protested the resulting disruption and displacement. Once that controversy was resolved through the implementation of regulatory urban transport policies amenable to both parties, new strains emerged from other class forces with yet a third vision of the city and downtown development. This conflict was not so easily resolved in the urban policy domain because it pitted those who sought to keep Mexico City contained, manageable, and structured around small-scale commerce, services, and light industry, especially downtown, against those who saw the capital city altogether differently: not as a compilation of traditional neighborhoods that should be protected as part of the national patrimony, but rather, as the engine of the nation's industrial and financial development.

As demonstrated in Chapters 4 and 5, by the 1960s these conflicts peaked in the struggle over a proposed mass rapid transit project, or subway, known as the METRO, which mobilized two competing coalitions of state-class forces around entirely different plans for the city's composition and growth. Insofar as this subway project held the potential to alter central city residential and employment patterns, and thus many residents' social networks, daily experiences, and urban identities, it generated active opposition from many among the city's middle classes, particularly shopkeepers, small business owners, and longtime residents in central areas, most notably along Calle Tacuba. In a shift of political alliances, the urban bus industry and its allies in Mexico City government sided with downtown residents and also decried the plan, not only because it would undermine the centrality of urban bus transport but also because it would accelerate Mexico City's already chaotic growth patterns and thus create problems for urban transport service provision.

Yet subway supporters were a formidable force to challenge because of their power in the national economy and national politics. They included the construction industry, large financiers, real estate developers, promoters of foreign tourism, several of the nation's most successful commercial conglomerates, and internationally owned producers and suppliers of mass rapid transit equipment who saw the city more as a machine to generate profit than as a space that embodied a social identity. Complicating matters, leaders of the organized labor sector nationally powerful in the PRI were among the advocates of the subway project; they supported many of the economic modernization objectives of the private sector proponents of the subway and their nationally powerful political allies within the ruling party in order to repudiate a local mayor who frequently bypassed their class-specific priorities. Also, for many in the organized labor sector, physical restructuring of Mexico City's colonial center and elimination of the urban bus industry's monopoly control were necessary conditions for better urban servicing, for the triumph of labor activism, and for Mexico City's sound economic modernization—which meant more employment opportunities. Competing positions on mass rapid transit for Mexico City, then, came to symbolize a particular view of equality, class, power, and Mexico's developmental future. Most important perhaps, the pro-METRO controversy pitted one sector of the PRI—organized labor—against another—the ruling party's so-called middle-class constituents in the CNOP, including artisans, shopkeepers, and small factory owners, all of whom were politically linked to Mexico City's mayor and all of whom argued against urban restructuring, rapid economic growth, and the economic modernization that would eliminate the urban bases of their livelihoods and the territorially bounded networks and identities they presupposed. In many ways reminiscent of conflicts surrounding trolley workers in the 1920s, the proposed subway project split the PRI, pitting national and local politicians against each other at the same time as it generated antagonisms within and between the two separate corporatist sectors representing working classes, middle classes, and the urban poor.

When subway proponents triumphed in the controversy, the political repercussions were so great that after 1970 both local and national politicians found themselves introducing ambiguous, if not contradictory, urban transport policies in order to restore the political balance put in jeopardy by the previous administration's position on the METRO and urban development. As a result, during the 1970s Mexico City's transport and servicing conditions deteriorated, while the city continued to expand outward and downtown land usage patterns remained relatively intact. Clearly then, political conflicts over the subway and its impact on downtown development and urban growth over the sixties and seventies molded the contours of Mexico City's urban development and produced ambiguous urban policies. These conflicts ran as a thread through the major political upheavals and institutional reforms introduced in Mexico during the seventies. As such, urban transport conflicts have been to twentieth-century Mexico what railroads were in the nineteenth century: both symbol and object of local and national contention over state power, class power, and the vision of the future. Like Max Weber's switchmen of history, the institutional responses, economic policies, social and political conflicts, and lived experiences engendered by the provision and administration of particular urban transport services altered relationships within and between classes and the state, both local and national, pushing Mexico City down an urban development path that greatly affected the nature and future of one-party rule.

FROM POLICY TO URBAN POLITICAL PARTICIPATION

Second only to transport perhaps, conflicts over the nature and extent of political participation in urban policymaking played an especially critical role in Mexico City's urban development and in the balance of political and class power underpinning certain urban policy stances. This is not so surprising, of course: It is logical that the content and nature of urban development policies are very much a product of who, exactly, is institutionally empowered to make those decisions. It is also not so surprising that any efforts to deny or assure urban political participation to certain class forces will be controversial, determining the balance of political and class power and thus the overall urban orientation of an administration. Accordingly, issues of urban political participation and urban policymaking, transport-related or otherwise, are intricately intertwined. Without sound and efficacious mechanisms for political participation, specific policies become even more politically controversial, and vice versa.

All this was first clear in the 1920s, when the overwhelming political power of certain sectors of the urban working class to determine urban and administrative policy in Mexico City, especially those providing urban services and empowered by the CROM, led to labor unrest, grassroots opposition, intraclass tension, and intrastate conflict. In a strange twist, these conditions induced political leaders to eliminate democratic mechanisms for municipal rule in the capital, a decision that not only gave the ruling party leadership more leeway to introduce urban policies consistent with their own urban redevelopment priorities, but that also generated more popular unrest. Together, resident unhappiness about limited political participation in Mexico City's administration and policymaking, combined with the class biases of the ruling party's urban policies, led to massive urban social unrest in the 1930s and to the establishment of a new political structure to guarantee the participation of urban popular and middle classes: the CNOP. It was at this point, moreover, that Mexico City started to grow with full force at the expense of the nation's provinces and peripheral regions.

Once the CNOP was established, Mexico saw more than rapid urbanization-led industrial development; the ruling party also passed a critical juncture in stabilizing national politics and consolidating one-party rule. With local populations now provided with political structures for equal participation in corporatist politics, the tensions between Mexico City residents and national political leaders were temporarily shelved, as were tensions between urban and national developmental objectives, and Mexico saw remarkable political tranquility for a period of close to three decades. In fact, from 1940 to 1965 it appeared that what was good for Mexico City's economy and servicing was also good for national politics and the macroeconomy. During this period of remarkable urban and economic growth, Mexico City's mayor began playing an especially critical role in integrating local with national politics and balancing the urban concerns of local populations with the developmental objectives of the national government. The latter was accomplished by establishing firm control on servicing and the administration of Mexico City, especially by keeping downtown development off the policy docket and by limiting the city's growth. However, this stable political situation and the balance struck between local and national objectives was equally contingent on the mayor's ability to keep questions of urban political participation on the back burner, which was generally accomplished by forging strong patron-client relations through the mayor's office with those urban populations most dissatisfied with the national political leadership.

When the mayor's network of patron-client relationships was challenged and eventually disrupted, because of the controversial urban development policies imposed by the president and national party leaders in the 1960s, questions about local political participation again emerged with force and affected the urban policymaking environment. After the 1960s, urban transport was still an issue of concern, of course; but with subway construction already under way little could be done to reverse the continued expansion of the city, a path pretty much set in stone with the subway's opening in 1969. At best, political demands could be directed at preventing the full-scale downtown redevelopment that subway proponents originally envisioned. With these constraints, by the early 1970s local residents turned their attention even more actively to the limited mechanisms for political participation in the capital and the ways in which they could better use local mechanisms to make demands for protecting downtown neighborhoods and bettering basic urban infrastructural services in the burgeoning metropolis.

The growing preoccupation with questions of urban political participation was especially clear in the Echeverría and López Portillo administrations, during which grassroots pressures in Mexico City spurred each president and his allies in the party and the mayor's office to introduce entirely new local institutional mechanisms for political participation in the capital. While on the surface these institutional transformations generally were touted as democratic outlets through which resident populations could articulate their concerns about urban services and administration, they were easily controlled from above and generally provided only limited opportunities for political participation and urban policymaking. In addition, these institutional reforms were not so different from earlier ones undertaken in the thirties and again in the fifties, insofar as they linked the lives and activities of Mexico City residents to the mayor's office or to other new national agencies that also sought to integrate urban with national developmental objectives. Accordingly, the urban political reforms of the seventies and early eighties failed to either redress popular grievances about local political exclusion or to fundamentally alter the hierarchical and highly centralized ways that major decisions about urban growth and redevelopment were made. Most important, these new structures for urban policymaking did not supersede old ones, but rather existed side by side. The consequent fragmentation of structure for urban political participation further limited the political power of Mexico City residents to autonomously determine urban policy. This both generated greater political dissatisfaction and did little to change the urban policymaking status quo, which remained riddled with conflicts and ambiguous urban policy stances.

By the time Miguel de la Madrid came to the presidency in 1982, the question of Mexico City's administration and who was to be politically empowered to make urban policies became the most critical urban issue under debate. Several government officials considered changes in urban adminis-tration and urban political participation to be the best way to restructure or reverse Mexico City's developmental patterns, especially its trajectory of unlimited urban growth. Because the ruling party's previous efforts to syn-chronize urban and national development objectives generally occurred at the expense of residents' local political autonomy, especially their power to make independent decisions about urban development policy, Mexico City resi-dents were eager to break with past patterns and support the urban political reform. With the CNOP all but inoperative and the mayor's office no longer an ally, Mexico City residents were pushing for urban democratic reform in hopes that this would establish a local body through which they could successfully pose their specific urban policy demands about the city's servic-ing and growth. Downtown residents, in particular, were convinced that the only way to ensure control over their urban communities and livelihoods was to maintain their own independent political power, since national political actors and institutions increasingly supported urban redevelopment plans that had disruptive consequences for downtown areas. For these residents of the city's traditional neighborhoods, to fight for the introduction of democratic structures for urban political participation in Mexico City was to challenge past ways of developing, servicing, and administering the capital. The fact that past efforts to balance class antagonisms and integrate local and national development objectives had increasingly led to ambiguous, contradictory, or extraordinarily costly urban policies, further fueled both state and popular support for urban democratic reform.

What all this suggests is that as time progressed and the city grew larger and more unmanageable, mechanisms for urban administration and urban political participation became as crucial for determining the nature and spa-tial character of the city as did specific urban policies, like transport, which were more salient in earlier periods. Yet this was not a one-way street: As the structures of local politics changed over time, so did the nature and direction of urban development. Starting with the elimination of municipal rule and moving to the establishment of the Consejo Consultivo in the 1930s, the for-mation of the CNOP in the 1940s, the implementation of the *delegado* system in the 1970s, the establishment of the Asamblea de Representantes del Dis-trito Federal in 1987, and finally the elimination of the CNOP in 1989, each change in the principal institutional structure for local participation altered the balance of political power between different classes in Mexico City and between local and national actors. This not only had an impact on which class and social forces were directly involved in local decision making, and thus on the nature and content of urban redevelopment policies, it also reintroduced legitimacy concerns that frequently pushed political leaders to craft new urban policy compromises.

FROM URBAN DEVELOPMENT CONFLICTS TO NATIONAL POLITICS

My primary intent here has been to document the political struggles surrounding the servicing and administration of Mexico City and to consider their impact on urban development in the capital. Yet precisely because we have found Mexico City's servicing, administration, and urban development to be intricately linked to the dynamics of one-party rule, as well as both product and producer of tensions between local and federal domains, this study also sheds some new light on national politics in Mexico. We have seen that, in many ways, conflicts over Mexico City were part and parcel of larger political struggles over the consolidation of postrevolutionary governance and over the direction of national political and economic development pursued by Mexico's PRI. Accordingly, as an analytic focus, urban development conflicts help us navigate through the long sweep of twentieth-century Mexican politics. Though such an analytic focus may not be as telling in other country contexts, Mexico's unique history ensures that a focus on Mexico City and its peculiar patterns of urban development will illuminate critical dimensions of the national experience, both political and economic.

It started with the capital city's undisputedly central role during and immediately after the 1910 Revolution. Efforts by the revolutionary leadership to generate or sustain popular political support in Mexico City after 1910 influenced urban development policies, and vice versa, such that one set of objectives became increasingly linked to the other. The subsequent territorial and institutional overlap of local and national political domains, which eventually reinforced this initial dynamic, further ensured that urban development conflicts articulated directly with national politics. Mexico's postrevolutionary political consolidation and corporatist state building were in large part contingent on restoring prosperity and economic growth in Mexico City, on ensuring urban service workers' loyalty by offering privileged political access to the state and services, on keeping residents happy through favorable urban redevelopment policies, and on institutionally and economically linking urban and national development policy and politics. This, in turn, helps explain why some of the fundamental institutional contours of corporatism first established in the late 1910s and 1920s, like the formation of the CROM, were grounded in state-labor collaborations over urban service provision and why, conversely, the success and stability of these corporatist pacts rested on the successes of urban service provision in the capital.

Once this local-national dynamic was entrenched in the structure of corporatist politics, the articulation of urban servicing and administration with national politics continued. When Mexico City populations expressed political dissatisfactions over urban service provision or political exclusion, for example, national party leaders responded by establishing new political connections—through national institutions as frequently as local—with class or social groups not previously involved in the governing franchise. The CNOP is a case in point. The result was a broad-based social and class inclusiveness that made corporatism in Mexico distinct from almost all other Latin American variants of corporatism. One unfortunate by-product of this inclusiveness was a more extensive and controlling state apparatus; another was a conflictual mix of local and national politics and policymaking that helped produce Mexico City's rapid growth, urban sprawl, and low-density land use patterns. When large numbers of the capital city's residents later joined urban social movements in a challenge to these urban political practices and developmental patterns, national political structures and the stability and one-party rule they had sustained also faced a challenge. Party leaders scrambled to restructure both national political institutions—especially the CNOP—and the place of Mexico City residents within them.

Patching up the damage was difficult, however, because the now well-entrenched intraparty dynamics depended on the cross-class and local-national balances forged in earlier decades. When the fit between local and national political institutions was shaken, as were cross-class sectoral alliances, the ruling party faced debilitating internal conflicts with national repercussions for urbanization, industrialization, and the corporatist structures of one-party rule. This is perhaps clearest with a view to the late 1970s and 1980s, as Mexico City populations increasingly began to link deteriorating urban conditions, the character of urban life, and the problems of one-party rule to the nature of urban policymaking and the absence of local structures of political participation in the capital. When residents began to join urban social movements, to reject the avenues for political participation offered by the nonterritorial, nationally constituted corporatist political system, and to withdraw electoral loyalty from the PRI, the party scrambled to reintroduce new, more democratic mechanisms for urban political participation and for the local administration of Mexico City's urban services.

If we examine the long sweep of changes from 1910 to 1988, then, we see that conflicts over the city's servicing, political administration, growth, and sociospatial character emerged and reemerged as central during several watershed points in the development of Mexico's national political institutions, especially when changing political or macroeconomic conditions required a shift in urban policymaking or when local populations—especially the middle classes and the urban poor—found themselves with urban policy priorities and demands for political participation that did not square well with national development objectives. Throughout the decades, the PRI experimented with different ways of linking or separating urban policy, urban politics, and national development objectives, generally in response to the extent of mobilization in the capital city over service or participatory concerns. In the process, the country experienced a slow but steady transformation in the articulation of local and national politics, a transformation that manifested itself in fundamental changes in the institutional structure and operation of Mexico's corporatist political system.

In theoretical terms, the crux of the problem lay in the uneasy fit between corporatism, rapid and uncontrolled urbanization, concentrated industrialization, and one-party rule. As Mexico City grew in size and industrial prominence, the class-based corporatist political system and its national structures of participation became increasingly unable to accommodate the growing— and often competing—urban service demands that came with rapid, sprawling urbanization and concentrated industrialization. This difficulty also resulted largely from the fact that urban problems were frequently cross-class concerns, while Mexico's structures of corporatism were class-based. With the PRI's institutional capacity to respond to accelerating urban demands ever more limited, urban populations bypassed formal state structures in growing numbers, either withdrawing electoral support from the ruling party or mobilizing into autonomous urban social movements outside the party structure. Because, by then, Mexico City held the largest and most vocal concentration of people in the country, and because it housed all significant institutions of party and state power, these developments posed a mortal challenge to the PRI and to the legitimacy of one-party rule, both locally and nationally. The result was a steady weakening of the PRI both electorally and institutionally. And now, it appears that a new phase of Mexican politics has begun. The PRI is no longer capable of sustaining its power by tinkering with corporatist structures or local governing mechanisms. Fundamental political changes in institutions and practices now mark the party's agenda. This became apparent after the introduction of the Asamblea de Representantes del Distrito Federal in the late 1980s, when the party leadership disbanded the CNOP and replaced it with the UNE, and then the FNOC, bodies that repudiate the class-based political identities around which the corporatist system was constructed.

That the sector chosen for elimination was the one originally built to appease the urban demands of Mexico City's popular and middle classes, and that it was the sector that had become so divided and inoperable in the face of intrastate and intraclass conflicts over urban priorities, drives home the argument that many important facets of national politics in Mexico have revolved in no small part around urban dynamics. Equally telling, with corporatist politics crumbling at the geographic and political center, so to speak, the PRI's hold in the outlying regions also appears in question. Before, when prosperity in Mexico City articulated smoothly with national development objectives, and both Mexico City's and the nation's fiscal and political future looked rosy, regional political problems were always relatively well managed by the PRI. Although this frequently occurred through co-optation, corruption, and sometimes even repression, regional challenges to the PRI never managed to disrupt the ruling party's hold on power when prosperity and stability in Mexico City led the nation onward. But now, with the party's foothold in Mexico City under threat, conditions have changed, such that the PRI may be unable to keep both urban and regional opposition under wraps without showing signs of stress. For the first time in years, in fact, the PRI is now focusing its attention on rural and regional policy changes—like the elimination of the *ejido* system of communal property—as much as on urban issues in order to capture the political high ground. As the regional question comes to the surface again, as it did during the Revolution and its aftermath, questions about Mexico's political future loom larger. With political opposition growing in both the center and the regions, and with the PRI eliminating fundamental institutions that guaranteed support from both urban and rural populations for so many years, the CNOP and the *ejido*, Mexico appears to be on the precipice of some of the most salient political changes seen since the consolidation of corporatism and one-party rule close to half a century ago.

POLITICS, CLASS, AND HISTORIOGRAPHY IN MEXICO

To focus on political conflicts over Mexico City's urban development and explore their articulation with national politics is not to deny the myriad other factors that have influenced corporatism and the dynamics of one-party rule in Mexico. But this approach nonetheless highlights several critical issues generally left unexamined in studies of Mexico, and by so doing introduces a slightly new way of interpreting corporatist politics and trajectories of social and political change that have unfolded over the last several decades.

Many sociological and historiographical accounts of fundamental political transformations in the immediate postrevolutionary period show a rural bias: They start from the premise that rural populations, particularly *campesinos* and their concerns, have been central in establishing the initial ideological contours and institutional foundations of national politics. This is especially true in the scholarly work on agrarian movements, or on Lázaro Cárdenas's relationship to the peasantry in the development of populism, corporatism, and one-party rule in Mexico.[1] There is of course no denying that peasant forces were critical in the Mexican Revolution and its aftermath, or that they continue to make their mark on national politics. Yet much of this scholarship may suffer from a romanticization, if not overvaluation, of the determinative impact of rural struggles on Mexican politics in this early period. After all, we have seen that Mexico City was the nation's single most critical locale after the 1910 Revolution. Had Mexico's political leaders been unable to consolidate popular support in the capital city in the late 1930s, for example, regional opposition might have triumphed. Thus developments within Mexico City itself were central to the ruling party's successes in centralizing political power and institutional decision making, as well as in triumphing over regional forces.

Granted, scholars have already argued that the process of postrevolutionary consolidation and state building was contingent on the consolidation of state power over Mexico's rebellious regions and provinces. Nonetheless, most have made this argument from the point of view of co-optation and defeat in the ultimately conquered regions. None has charted this process from the vantage point of the capital city itself, or through a focus on what it took to triumph in the center, as opposed to the regions, as we have here. And our concern with postrevolutionary political conflicts in Mexico City is not merely gratuitous, equivalent in intellectual weight to one more regional study that fills out the complex whole of Mexican politics. Rather, when the core, meaning Mexico City, does not hold politically, and state or class conflicts there challenge the power of the revolutionary leadership, the ruling party's claims to national power are in serious jeopardy. The same could not be said for any other single city or region in the country. This was true not only in the decade immediately after the Revolution, it also became clear when Monterrey-based opposition candidate General Juan Andreu Almazán was unable to sustain his position in national politics after 1940. In this critical period, the ruling party's success in holding national power lay in its ability to reorient urban development policies toward protesting groups in the capi-

CHAPTER NINE

tal, who had been dispossessed by past urban policies and thus inclined to support Almazán. To the extent that, after the Almazán challenge, the PRI then altered urban policies and national political structures in order to accommodate Mexico City's urban popular and middle-class residents and give them a forum for voicing their specific urban development concerns, both their local and national support for the PRI was assured and one-party rule was effectively consolidated.

These findings about the importance of urban development conflicts in the 1930s and the reforms in national political structures that they generated in the 1940s stand in contrast to prevailing opinion that Cárdenas's class-specific orientation toward rural peasants and industrial laborers established the principal contours of Mexico's corporatist and populist political development. We have seen that during the Cárdenas administration, it was urban populations as much as rural ones who set limits to national politics and policymaking; and within urban populations, it was middle and not only industrial working classes who were salient in driving the ruling party's actions. In other words, it was not just Cárdenas's peasant-labor pacts or his founding of the CNC and the CTM that mattered. Rather, it was the ruling party's successful efforts to incorporate Mexico City populations into the CNOP in the early 1940s that rounded out Mexico's class-inclusive political system and established the formal institutional contours of Mexico's corporatism. And the initial demands and concerns of these urban populations, as well as how they were institutionally incorporated in the CNOP, were in no small measure linked to patterns of servicing and administration in the capital. After the inclusion of urban popular and middle classes into the party through the formation of the CNOP, moreover, rural populations were pretty much relegated to the sidelines of national politics, especially as the party leadership crafted its political and economic development strategies around the political and economic prominence of Mexico City, through urban policies that were intended to foster urbanization-led industrialization and simultaneously keep the loyalty of the Mexico City-based CTM and CNOP constituents. As such, the PRI's capacity to administer Mexico City, foster its growth, and offer infrastructural services to its businesses and residents served it well both locally and nationally for several decades. When party leaders failed in these regards, and urban development and policy decisions created more conflict than consensus in the capital, as occurred first in the late 1960s and then intensified during the 1970s and 1980s, the PRI's hold on both local and national political power weakened.

In addition to the preoccupation with rural populations and the failure to take urban dynamics seriously in national politics, another bias that runs like a thread through much sociological and historiographical work on politics and state building in Mexico is the assumption that capital-labor or capital-state conflicts and alliances are perhaps the most central set of relationships in determining general trajectories of political development. Many scholars have suggested that the consolidation of corporatism and one-party rule in Mexico lay in institutionalized pacts forged between capital and labor through the active mediation of the PRI-dominated state. They also argue that the state's ability to co-opt labor and the urban poor also helped keep the economy afloat and the PRI in power.[2] The preoccupation with labor and capital is so widespread that it has pushed scholars to argue that growing political problems for the ruling party in the 1970s and 1980s were also rooted in the mounting conflicts between capital and labor or in the bureaucratization of the labor movement and the ruling party.[3]

Although the focus on capital-labor tensions or capital-labor-state pacts is critical in helping us understand some of the principal developments in twentieth-century Mexico, it occasionally leaves important questions unanswered. What conditions made it possible for the Mexican state to institutionalize its pacts with capital and labor, and why did this occur first in Mexico City? Why did Mexico's service workers, artisans, shopkeepers, professionals, and employees, who outnumbered industrial laborers in the early period, not oppose these political pacts or the rapid industrialization they presupposed? Why was opposition to the ruling party greater in Mexico City during the 1970s and 1980s than in most other locales or regions, especially if the source of problems was merely a distancing of civil society from the state? Last, how does a focus on capital-labor-state conflicts or alliances account for the fact that urban concerns shared by different classes—as much as the workplace concerns of any particular class—have in recent decades become the source of some of the most active grassroots mobilization seen in Mexico since the Revolution, or the fact that state actors themselves were often divided when it came to major urban policy decisions?

With these questions we become aware of several critical gaps in our understanding of Mexican political development that can be filled with a more deliberate focus on Mexico City's self-employed and its nonindustrial, non-wage-earning and informal sector workers, especially the urban poor and middle classes. In our account of the local and national politics of urban development, we found that these broadly defined middle sectors have played an absolutely essential role in determining state policies, political conflicts and reforms, and even economic development trajectories. Indeed, Mexico's poor and traditional middle classes have been vital in determining the strength and composition of certain state-class and cross-class alliances by uniting with

CHAPTER NINE

local state actors against national state actors, by uniting with certain local factions of capital against others, and by siding with local state actors against organized industrial workers then in alliance with national state actors. Of course, the alliances that the urban popular and middle classes have formed with other classes or with state actors have been much less durable than state-capital-labor alliances or capital-labor conflicts. Yet that is precisely what makes the urban poor and middle classes so politically significant. The contingent and ever-shifting nature of middle-class political alliances owes mainly to their contradictory class location, as Erik Olin Wright would argue, which makes them as open to the concerns of capital as of labor. Because of this, the urban poor and middle classes have been a critical swing force in determining the balance of state and class power and some of the most critical aspects of Mexico's urban and national development. However, such findings elude those who focus primarily on the relationships between big capitalists and industrial working classes, or who identify the urban poor as characteristically pitted against the state or allied with industrial labor in its relationship with capital.

In calling attention to the role of the so-called middle sectors in Mexico's politics, both urban and national, I echo the focus on middle classes used by Soledad Loaeza in her seminal work on education policy in Mexico during the 1950s and 1960s. Yet I depart from her perspective and break ground by identifying middle sectors as institutional actors placing pressure on the state or other classes through the CNOP or through the Mexico City mayor's office, rather than solely as class or opposition forces standing outside corporatist politics, as does Loaeza. By so doing, I underscore the critical role of the CNOP in party politics, a focus that has been absent in most studies of Mexican corporatism, mainly because the prevailing wisdom is that the CNOP was merely a token sector of the party, a mechanism to generate electoral support with little impact on policy and national politics. If any sector matters in party or policymaking dynamics, the argument goes, it is the CTM, and less so, the CNC—that is, the industrial labor or peasant sectors. Yet as is clear in this study, the CNOP has been a very influential sector in the development of Mexico's political system, in the formation of the nation's populist agenda, and in the fundamental institutional and political transformations of the last five decades. Moreover, as discussed earlier, the actions and activities of the CNOP and its constituents have played an essential role in several critical conflicts within the PRI, including those involving other sectors and the nation's principal administrators and politicians.

Granted, much of the CNOP's institutional impact on Mexican politics can be traced not to its institutional strength per se, but to problems with its organizational structure and internal composition, both of which created internal dissention over the sector's appropriate role and its political agenda. Also, although the CNOP formally represents the "popular middle classes," not all eligible constituents have joined or are active. Yet many of its problems stem from the fact that the CNOP was intended—and fully expected by its constituents—to serve as a format for wielding demands and influencing policies, mainly urban. When it did not function as such, constituents and urban citizens alike often felt betrayed, political conflicts accelerated, and conflicts with other sectors frequently arose. Urban popular and middle-class disenfranchisement and CNOP-related conflicts together spurred some of the most fundamental policy changes and institutional reforms introduced in Mexico, including those that have responded most directly to the population's demands for new mechanisms of democratic participation.

Once we focus on the CNOP as one of the principal institutional bases of the three-tiered corporatist system, we also are able to challenge the assumption present in much of the literature on Mexico that the concerns and interests of popular classes are identical to those of the organized working class. In Latin America in general and Mexico in particular, the term *popular classes* is frequently used interchangeably with *working classes*. Thus there are very few studies of the institutional behavior or class orientation of the so-called popular middle classes—or those poorly paid, frequently self-employed, non-wage workers who do not work directly for big capitalists; this diverse group would include street vendors, taxi drivers, and small shopkeepers, among others. Placing these people in the same category as the working class, or treating them as analytically indistinguishable, overemphasizes their affinity with labor and underestimates the characteristics they share with the professional middle classes or small capitalists. And as we have seen in this study, the interests, actions, nature of organization, and political orientation of the popular classes in Mexico have often differed markedly from those of the industrial working classes.

Granted, in both theory and practice, which occupations should be considered popular classes, which working classes, and which middle classes may be debatable; and any such categorizations tend to vary as the economy and employment practices change. Determining class affiliations may be even more confusing in the case of Mexico, where the formal institutional separation of so-called popular and working classes is sometimes unclear and where both popular and professional middle classes are organized and institutionally incorporated within the same sector. But given the fact that the party's popular sector, or CNOP, has even existed as institutionally separate from the confederation of workers, and that it emerged as a political force in the 1940s precisely because the language, experience, and policy concerns of so-called popular classes were so different from those of the industrial working class, it is reasonable to claim that we must begin to analyze popular classes on their own. Under what conditions will they unite with working or middle classes, and to what extent does this determine political development trajectories or color our theoretical understanding of change in Mexico?

Through this study of political conflicts over urban development, we have just started to scratch the surface of such an inquiry. We have found that struggles over urban policy, for example, played a critical role in the dynamics of popular class formation by differentiating the interests and identities of the urban poor and popular middle classes from industrial working classes. Accordingly, we can interpret the account presented here as more than a story of how classes use urban concerns to fight for their own class interests; it is also a story of how and why classes or class segments, in this case popular and middle classes, care enough about urban development to struggle over it, and pit themselves against working classes in the process, a dynamic that transforms these classes and their power as much as the urban domain itself.

REEXAMINING THE STATE AND POLICYMAKING

This book, however, is not intended to shed light on class formation and class relations as much as on the Mexican state and the underpinnings of its policy actions. In the body of literature on the Mexican state and policy, although scholars have explored different aspects of the policymaking process, several shared assumptions prevail. One is that the nation is governed by a system of presidentialism, which means that Mexico's president is considered virtually omnipotent in guiding policy and development. Presidentialism has been considered a key element of political stability in Mexico, to the extent that the president's autonomous capacity to make policy decisions enables the party to overcome internal differences.[4] A second shared assumption is that the bureaucracy—which is assumed to answer largely to the president and to comprise networks of actors sharing common educational and political experiences—is the single most powerful force in the policymaking process. A third assumption, related to the second, is that bureaucrats—and thus the state—are relatively independent from both the party and class forces in making policy decisions.

All three assumptions lead most scholars of policymaking in Mexico to focus on the training of state bureaucrats, their social and political relationships to each other and to the president, the institutional dynamics within particular policymaking agencies, and sometimes on international pressures that either facilitate or impede bureaucratic decision-making processes.[5] These factors no doubt are critical for understanding much policymaking in Mexico. Yet it is striking that each somehow misses the mark in explaining the most salient aspects of urban development policymaking presented here. Some assumptions, in fact, like that of presidentialism and the relative autonomy of bureaucrats, seem to be completely off target. For example, we have found that Mexico's president was frequently unable to push through his preferred urban policies, especially if Mexico City's mayor, an appointed member of his own so-called bureaucratic team, opposed the policy. That is, even though Mexico's president has clearly held inordinate power within the political system, he has by no means been unchallenged, or politically guaranteed the capacity to impose his will in all situations. The president's ability to push certain policies has depended on the social and class forces allied with and against him, and on the institutional power that opposing or supporting forces bring to bear on behalf of his policy stances. In short, policymaking power is not merely a matter of the president's institutional prerogatives or close personal and political ties to appointed members of his cabinet.

The empirical challenge to prevailing theories of presidentialism and related arguments about social networks linking state actors is seen in the frequency of presidential-mayoral conflicts in Mexico. Not only was the president often thwarted by Mexico City's mayor in policymaking, occasionally the same presidential and mayoral players in policy dramas disagreed on some policy issues but agreed on others, or even changed positions from disagreement to agreement on the same policy issue over the course of a single administration. Both scenarios suggest several new ways of thinking about the relationships among politicians, government officials, and the president as well as their impact on policy. First, if the president's policy preferences (de la Madrid's urban democratic reform or Díaz Ordaz's subway project, for example) can be undermined by appointed members of his own government, who at other times may even have supported presidential policy stances wholeheartedly, factors like knowing who studied with whom, or who was appointed by whom, or even what the president desired, are clearly not enough to explain policy outcomes. Second, and even more important, analyzing presidentialism or the president's institutional power in policymaking tells us absolutely nothing about why presidents would take certain policy stances. That is, presidentialism—even at its best—tells us only about process and nothing about content. To find out why presidents take certain policy positions, and to ascertain why they may be different from positions taken by their appointed mayors, we frequently must look beyond the individuals themselves and toward the political and institutional relationships these two distinct actors cultivate with different class actors and party operatives.

These conclusions also suggest a more careful examination of the second assumption about politics and policymaking that prevails among political scientists of Mexico: that state bureaucrats are the most critical and powerful—if not singular—determinants of policy. It follows from our observations that if urban policy emerges out of the institutional obligations and class networks of presidents and mayors, much more is at stake than the will of state bureaucrats. This is clear in several ways. For one thing, it is major political players—like the mayor, the president, and the PRI leadership—who determine policy consistently across the decades, not an anonymous cadre of bureaucrats. For another, precisely because highly visible actors like the president and Mexico City's mayor occasionally disagree over policy, other class and social forces often enter the picture to shift the political balance. Prominent among those forces that allied with certain high-level government officials or that influenced certain policy stances by placing pressure on political leaders were the class or social actors associated with certain sectors of the party, especially the CNOP and the CTM; although occasionally it was forces who were excluded from these sectors, like disenfranchised middle classes and the urban poor, who mattered most. Accordingly, these findings suggest that when bureaucrats were involved in policymaking, they were not so much autonomous forces pursuing their own independent decisions as they were spokesmen for other more powerful political actors with acknowledged institutional and political power, for certain classes, and even for certain sectors of the party.

These findings make it clear that in seeking a framework for understanding both conflicts over policy and the resolutions that eventually emerged from these conflicts, we need to look beyond so-called autonomous bureaucrats and cultivate a better understanding of their relationships to the party and to classes as well as their impact on intraparty dynamics and class relations. Moreover, we must be cognizant not only of bureaucrats' relationships to the PRI leadership but also of their relationships with class-based incorporated sectors and their constitutents. Indeed, the policy positions taken by powerful political actors like Alfonso Martínez Domínguez are more easily understood with a view to his background in the CNOP, the class and social relations he cultivated there with the state workers' union, and the larger debates within the party about the obligations of the CNOP leadership to its poor and middle-class constituents, than to his personal relationship with President Díaz Ordaz or to his bureaucratic position in the government.

The proposition that party politics and their uniquely institutional class dynamics matter in state policymaking in Mexico stands in contrast to the bureaucratic autonomy approach found in most literature on the Mexican state, an approach that at times appears to make a claim for "free-floating" bureaucrats acting on the basis of their own interests. Scholars may be reaching this conclusion because they assume that decades of one-party rule have insulated state bureaucrats from the rank-and-file members of the party and its corporatist sectors. Yet our evidence suggests otherwise. We have seen that even those bureaucrats with a long history of government service may be beholden to influential political leaders who themselves are responding to class or party pressures. Most important perhaps, state bureaucrats, themselves, are formally members of the party and of the largest of its three class-based institutional sectors, the CNOP; and because state workers are the single largest union within the CNOP, over the years they have expanded their role in party politics, influenced intraparty conflicts, and generated intraclass controversy, especially with respect to other constituents within the CNOP. So how can we consider workers in state agencies merely bureaucrats, autonomous from the party and classes?

To the extent that many state bureaucrats are themselves members of the party, and identify themselves as middle-class constituents of the CNOP, we must also critically examine one last prevailing assumption about the state and politics in Mexico: that the state is an ever more powerful and autonomous collection of bureaucrats hovering over a weakening civil society. Assumptions like this are frequently hidden in the argument that the PRI's principal political problems lie in its incapacity to maintain its legitimacy and popularity with society at large.[6] Of course, there is some truth to that argument. The PRI's electoral popularity and the numbers formally organized in its ranks (especially as a percentage of total population) have been declining steadily over the years. To the extent that the PRI cannot maintain sufficient electoral support to remain in power, political changes—up to and including the slow democratization of one-party rule—may indeed be forthcoming. Yet much more is going on here than initially meets the eye, and it should spur some critical questioning of the argument that the PRI's problems rest in its estrangement from civil society. As demonstrated in this account of the local and national politics of urban development, there have been as many serious and consequential political conflicts between party leaders, and between the corporatist sectors and their constituents, as between the PRI leadership and the so-called masses of civil society over the most appropriate policy. Clearly then, there is no clear pattern of state-civil society distinction: Party, state, and class actors have united and split in remarkable ways that challenge prevailing assumptions about autonomous bureaucrats and their policymaking.

Of course, the PRI has faced considerable grassroots opposition over the years; and it is no secret that the PRI has been worried enough to offer opposition forces prime political positions or greater say in backroom party politics. Many see this as a sign of the PRI's proclivity to co-opt grassroots opposition. Yet as we have seen here, the institutional accommodations frequently made in order to bring grassroots opposition into the PRI were a principal factor in party consolidation, as occurred with the CNOP in 1943 and other urban political reforms before and after that. These institutional accommodations have also extended the PRI's lease on political life with urban populations, such that this so-called co-optation of opposition from civil society—or those initially outside the party's formal political structures—has been part and parcel of state building. Along the way, the PRI's franchise has broadened to include many forces in society and to give grassroots organizations institutional forums for limited political participation.

There is no denying that these ever more inclusive institutional mechanisms for political participation never function as fully in practice as they do in party rhetoric. But until recently, they have worked sufficiently well to keep a broad variety of social groups loyal to the PRI and one-party rule. Therefore one can conclude that a substantial portion of the PRI's problems lie not with grassroots opposition outside the party, or civil society pitted against an all-powerful state, as much as with the internal problems produced by these ever-expanding institutional structures. As the party's franchise becomes ever more inclusive, old-guard activists and their well-entrenched patron-client relations are frequently called into question; and the PRI's problems in this regard seem to be sector- and thus class-specific. As a result, the PRI's most serious political obstacles rest in its inability to keep the CNOP's urban popular and middle-class constituents loyal and to overcome these larger intraparty conflicts (frequently revealed in tensions between the president and mayor), not necessarily in an equally declining popularity from all corners of society.

Clearly then, the sources of the PRI's accelerating political problems may lie not so much in an antistatism generated from civil society against bureaucrats, or an outpouring of grassroots opposition to the principles and objectives of the PRI, as in a series of institutional weaknesses and intraparty conflicts that have prevented the PRI from achieving its original objectives while still remaining open to new forces with new agendas or different visions.

THE PRI, THE STATE, AND CORPORATIST POLITICS RECONSIDERED

What can we conclude about the Mexican state, policymaking and the nature of political development and one-party rule in Mexico? If we take our study of the local and national politics of Mexico City's urban development as the point of departure, clearly the PRI-dominated state is not a Leviathan standing over society, but a fluid and relatively malleable political organization whose changing institutional structures are responsive to the changing social and class dynamics of Mexico's urbanization-led industrialization. Far from the monolithic, Machiavellian party with absolute and willful control over policy and civil society, the PRI has shown itself to be a heterogeneous concoction of social classes and political factions holding little consensus over critical issues, especially urban services and administration in the capital. Some of the most insurmountable intraparty conflicts have been intensified by the economic crisis, of course, which limits the state's capacity to continue administering Mexico City's development and fostering its growth and servicing in the same unlimited manner as before. Yet we have shown that some of the more debilitating and politically significant intraparty divisions were evident as early as the late 1950s and early 1960s, as seen in the conflicts within and between the different corporatist sectors and between different administrative domains in the state about the nature and direction of Mexico City's urban development. These urban development conflicts accelerated during the 1970s and into the 1980s to the point that the PRI was so internally divided that taking forceful action about an issue as central as urban democratic reform was extraordinarily difficult. Thus, Mexico's true Leviathan, so to speak, may be its capital city, as much as its expanding bureaucratic state.

It makes perfect sense, of course, that a large and complex party like the PRI would suffer internal conflicts over urbanization, among other things, especially since, in order to institutionalize one-party rule, it frequently finds itself working hard to appeal to a great variety of groups with competing interests. Yet despite the predictability of such divisions, scholars have ignored them in an effort to paint state policymaking under one-party rule as governed by well-connected bureaucrats operating with institutional autonomy from both class and party forces. This may be a serious misreading. Bureaucratic conflicts, especially over urban policy and between the president and Mexico City's mayor, were deeply embedded in conflicts within the party, especially those grounded in tensions within and between its class-based sectors. Moreover, these conflicts and divisions were not brief encounters or benign disagreements between individuals, between right and left, or between hard-line and soft-line groups within the party. They were ongoing conflicts unfolding through the decades that consistently set the president against the mayor, often pitted one corporatist sector against another, and generally affected the party's popular sector in irreversible ways with mortal implications for the CNOP and maybe even the PRI.

The institutional embeddedness of state, class, and party structures recounted here may also help explain the PRI's earlier historical successes and its recent near downfall. For decades before 1980, the PRI's capacity to incorporate new social and class forces by creating new party institutions or developing new governmentally administered political mechanisms has enabled it to sustain an incredible degree of legitimacy and electoral support, especially from Mexico City populations who make up the largest and most active concentration of the nation's residents. These new institutions and practices, which generally involved the CNOP and the Mexico City mayor's office, opened the PRI to the nation's "middle sectors" and set the stage for several decades of political stability. Yet there reforms also brought their own problems. With ever more social and class forces institutionally absorbed into party structures or state agencies' administrative circles of patron-clientelism, there was less room to maneuver. Accommodating one set of demands frequently put party or state actors at odds with others. Moreover, as social and class conflicts emerged, so too did intraparty and intrastate conflicts. And as state and party conflicts emerged, classes were reintroduced into the fray through their respective party structures or administrative networks, which further bloated the size and scope of the state. As a result, it has become ever more difficult for the PRI to reach a consensus about important political and economic policy decisions.

The question arises as to whether this view of the Mexican state as embedded in class and party structures, and debilitated by conflicts in and over Mexico City, can—or should—sustain an entirely new view of corporatist rule and political development in Mexico. Or, is it a view that relates only to a study of urban policymaking and thus has limited applications? The answer is probably both yes and no. After all, urban policies and the conflicts they generate are in many ways unique in comparison with other policy conflicts. For one, urban service problems and concerns engage a remarkably wide variety of state and class actors in unpredictable ways. For another, the state cannot maintain legitimacy only by balancing the urban service demands of capital and labor, as is frequently possible with other policy issues or in other bureaucratic domains. The state also has to accommodate the urban demands and concerns of the self-employed and the unemployed and underemployed who are often directly dependent on the urban environment and who, in combination with professional middle classes, constitute a much larger portion of the population in developing countries like Mexico than do industrial laborers focused on workplace concerns. In addition, although urban concerns frequently pit residents against the state, they can also pit residents against private capital or capital against the state and vice versa. Unlike some other policy issues, moreover, the state and private capital do not always see eye to eye on what urban services are necessary, how they will be financed, and whose interests will be sacrificed in the process; nor do capitalists themselves, since they frequently vary by size and location in ways that affect their urban policy concerns. This is especially so in developing countries like Mexico, where rapid industrial development was forcefullly imposed on a community-based local economy of small factories and shops.

Complicating matters, cities and the urban experience are etched in the life and mind of a nation's citizenry, such that urban problems frequently take on symbolic as well as substantive meaning. This, and the fact that urban problems are frequently more pervasive than workplace problems in newly industrializing countries where only a small proportion of the population can be considered wage-labor, makes the population highly vocal about urban policies. Yet the service activities around which citizens mobilize as consumers must be provided, and conflicts over who provides these urban services further complicate the state's role and limit its room to maneuver. All these factors, then, make policymaking in the urban domain somewhat distinct: Unlike many other bureaucratic domains, cities are complex organisms involving the state and almost all class forces, with some acting as producers, others as consumers, and still others as regulators. To the extent that our findings about the Mexican state and its policymaking reflect this complexity, and push us to reject assumptions about the autonomous power of state bureaucrats, we may want to be cautious about making broad generalizations about the Mexican state and policy.

Nonetheless, there are good reasons to believe that some generalizations about the state and politics in Mexico can be made from this study, despite the unique character of urban services and urban policy conflicts. In highly urbanized countries like Mexico, where population, economic investment, and political activities are all concentrated in one large primary city, the urban domain is at least as consequential as any other single bureaucratic domain of national importance. As just one area of national policymaking, it may be perhaps the most consequential. So why not explicitly recognize it as such? Scholars have made generalizations about the Mexican state based on studies of oil, food, or profit-sharing policy, so why not urban policy? Indeed, Mexico City's urban development has been intricately linked to processes of national industrialization and to the establishment of state-labor collaborations and the party's three-tiered structure of corporatism. This alone lends credence to its potential to generate insight into national politics and development in Mexico.

Yet perhaps the strongest argument for developing a new and somewhat challenging view of Mexican politics through a focus on urban policymaking in Mexico City comes from our findings about the critical impact of urban development conflicts on changes in party structures and practices. As shown here, rapid and concentrated urbanization in Mexico City produced political dissatisfactions among urban popular and middle classes not easily addressed by Mexico's class-based nationally constituted incorporated political system. Mexico's three-tiered corporatist political structure, in short, has been ill-equipped to deal with urban servicing and administrative problems or the conflicts produced by different visions of urban development, such that urban questions, by their very nature, have split corporatist structures internally and pit one corporatist structure against other. As a result, new patron-client practices that were initially developed to accommodate the institutional weaknesses of the corporatist structures vis-à-vis urban populations frequently have exacerbated these problems by creating shadow structures for political participation that either competed with party structures or that fragmented the institutional power of residents in local and national politics. Moreover, state actors often went head to head over urban policies or urban development priorities, depending on whether they were more concerned with the urban or the national domain and depending on their state, class, and party allegiances. Over time, these urban conflicts, and their repeated emergence, irreparably weakened old national structures and practices of corporatism.

The PRI may still be standing; but the institutional edifice that gave it power and authority for so many decades is crumbling from within. In Mexico today, this situation is so critical that some state actors have disassociated themselves from these weakening and delegitimized party structures, while still maintaining the PRI facade. This may be the arena where we see the most fundamental political changes in the future. Efforts by the Salinas administration to separate the PRI from its rank-and-file sectoral constituents in Mexico City, by eliminating the CNOP, suggest that many governing officials in Mexico now see the PRI's sectoral structure to be a severe handicap. This is further evidenced by President Salinas's development of the PRONASOL poverty alleviation program, which bypasses party structures, is run directly out of the president's office, and whose intent is to reach targeted clientelistic populations seen as key to building a new political base. These new practices, moreover, have focused on regional—and not Mexico City—populations to an extent unparalleled in Mexico's postrevolutionary politics, although some visible communities of the urban poor in Mexico City have also been targeted and many of the rural poor—the indigenous communities—have also been ignored. If Salinas and his team of institutional reformers are successful, and the PRI sheds its old corporatist structures and class embeddedness while taking on a new commitment to economic liberalism in the regions, it may be able to fundamentally alter the direction of national economic development, too. Current presidential support for the North American Free Trade Agreement can be understood in light of these objectives, since its economic benefits may flow to the country's northern regions more than Mexico City, diminishing the capital city's unparalleled economic position while also changing trade balances, external linkages, and the sectoral composition of the national economy.

But redirecting political attention away from Mexico City will not be that easy. This is best evidenced by the return, in 1993, of contentious debate over the future of democratic politics and administration in Mexico City, an issue that clearly was not resolved with the establishment of the Asamblea de Representantes del Distrito Federal in 1988. Again, as under President de la Madrid and others before him, citizens within and outside the party are debating whether new democratic structures should be established in the capital, whether Mexico City's mayor should still be presidentially appointed, whether local representatives should have juridical power to make urban policy, and whether any such changes would buttress or undermine the PRI's power, both locally and nationally. So the debate goes on. With the mayor of Mexico City, Manuel Camacho, tapped as one of the leading precandidates as the 1994 presidential campaign unfolded, these questions took on special urgency and obvious national political importance. In the long run, their resolution will no doubt depend on who takes over as Mexico's next president and whether he can integrate both Mexico City and rural demands for political democracy and economic prosperity. If Camacho triumphs, and his past actions are any clue, there may be new efforts to recoordinate urban and national politics through a revised or restructured party apparatus as much as through democratic reform. If a candidate without a good political understanding of Mexico City politics and corporatist practices becomes Mexico's next president, however, it may signal an end to the capital's political dominance, a shift in political and economic focus, and, most important perhaps, an immanent metamorphosis of the PRI and its corporatist structures. The challenge for future scholars will be to figure out what happens next, not just in Mexico City, but in its relation to the regions and the nation as a whole.

APPENDIXES

APPENDIX A: METHODOLOGY AND SOURCES

What has emerged in this book can be thought of as a "life account" of Mexico City. A life account, as C. Wright Mills would have it, exists at the intersection of biography and history. Just as Mills sees the sociological imagination as giving us the tools to see our own individual problems in light of society's problems, our own lives in the context of history, and our own actions as constituting this history, so we can view Mexico City similarly. Mexico City's urban development problems have, in many ways been the problems of the nation. The ways these so-called local problems of spatial development have been situated and worked out in the context of national problems, by state and class actors both local and national, has constituted a powerful driving force in the history of both the city and the nation.

In gathering materials for this study and constructing a biographical account of the capital city and its relationship to Mexican political history, I turned first to the "subject" itself: Mexico City government documents that gave some insight into the capital's growth and principal problems. I also analyzed secondary accounts from others—mainly residents—about the city and its problems. Last, I relied on materials that could contextualize both sets of accounts: that is, documents and interviews from scholars, journalists, residents, and city officials about what they saw as the principal urban problems and trajectories of change in the capital city. For each of these three sets of accounts, moreover, I surveyed parallel documents for the nation as a whole: that is, national government documents, accounts of national bureaucrats and party activists (PRI), and secondary materials on history and politics in Mexico.

Given the book's broad historical scope and the attendant difficulties in obtaining personal accounts of urban services and national politics after the 1910 Revolution, different types of sources and materials predominate in the different periods under study. For example, early chapters that cover developments between 1910 and 1934 rely heavily on secondary materials and archival sources. While much of the discussion in Chapter 2 of urban conditions in general and transport in particular is based on historical evidence collected by other scholars, none have linked these conditions to local-national conflicts over urban development, as I have done here. In making these connections, moreover, my own archival resources are especially relevant. The three archives used most frequently for this study are the Archivo General de la Nación (AGN); the Museo de la Ciudad de

México, and a semiprivate archive in the Departamento del Distrito Federal. At the latter archive, the main sources of information were the *Actas y Versiones del Consejo Consultivo de la Ciudad de México (AVCC)*, or minutes from the Consultative Council of Mexico City.

Materials for the period between 1934 and 1960 are drawn mainly from the AGN, from unpublished documents of the Distrito Federal, from an occasional interview, and from periodicals, primarily newspapers. In general, newspaper accounts of developments used in this work must be taken with a grain of salt, given the limits on press independence. But newspapers also are important sources of information on who is in and who is out politically and the rhetorics they employ to appeal to certain social or class constituencies, which itself says much about the political orientations of critical actors. Moreover, in the service of demonstrating public accommodation to social demands, newspapers are frequently some of the best sources for identifying points or themes of conflict and tension between citizens and the government, both local and national.

Later chapters on the 1960s and 1970s combine secondary documents with approximately fifty personal interviews conducted in 1980 and 1981. Primary data for the final chapters on the most recent period is based on approximately fifty interviews conducted in 1987, along with very few secondary materials, owing to the nearness of the events and their political sensitivity. Some quantitative data is peppered throughout the text, to the extent that it is illuminating and available. But by and large, this is a quasi-ethnographic study of political relationships and conflicts; qualitative evidence that contextualizes the city's development and the problem it and corporatist politics suffered along the way is best suited for such a study.

With respect to particular urban transport policy conflicts, several sets of sources were used. Information on the labor struggles of Mexico City's *tranviarios* during the 1920s and 1930s comes mainly from documents compiled by Mexican labor historians, although primary materials are also used and cited in the notes. Despite employing secondary accounts, the argument I present about the development and urban-based splits within the Mexican labor movement in this early period is entirely original. Information on conflicts within and between urban bus drivers and Mexico City administrators during the 1940s and 1950s came mainly from newspapers and government documents. The bulk of the findings about the METRO and internal state conflicts in the 1960s through the 1980s however, came from personal interviews conducted with leading members of Mexico's PRI, and bureaucrats and politicians in the Departamento del Distrito Federal (Mexico City's governing agency), especially its transport division, known as the Comisión de Vialidad y Transporte Urbano (COVITUR). Information on the METRO project also was gathered during interviews with engineers and architects from Ingenieros Civiles Asociados (ICA), the engineering conglomerate responsible for constructing Mexico City's subway.

My personal interviews with members of Mexico's PRI, with bureaucrats in government agencies, and with private sector spokesmen provided critical information about urban transport policy processes and the interplay between these different groups and interests within and outside the state. Participant observation in Mexico City's transportation agency (COVITUR) throughout 1981, moreover, provided a valuable backdrop for understanding how the Mexican bureaucracy works, how decisions about urban transport service provision and administration are made, and how and why political alliances and compromises form the basis for many urban policy actions. It also provided a basis for understanding the urban policy process and the interplay between public and private sector actors, not only with regard to transport policy but also with respect to national development policy and politics. This made it possible to discard inappropriate questions and to formulate more incisive ones for subsequent interviewing with public and private sector actors involved with the METRO in the periods under study.

The affiliation with COVITUR, and the contacts made while there, expedited the process of interviewing, since personal contacts and networks were used to identify and arrange appointments with key actors who had been involved in the METRO controversy and other urban policy deliberations. This meant that a snowballing technique was used for selection of interviews more than any specific and rigid sampling procedure. In the Mexican case this technique is probably the best way of collecting information, since only those highly integrated into public and private sector networks are able to pinpoint who in the network has the most relevant and critical information. It is also worth noting that a great portion of interviewing about the METRO and Mexico City's Asamblea de Representates del Distrito Federal was conducted in informal settings outside government offices, at times with "off the record" responses and pleas for anonymity. For that reason, names of interviewees are not provided as a matter of course, though some are included in the text and the notes.

Information on the urban democratic reform proposed for Mexico City in the early 1980s, the Asamblea de Representantes, primarily comes from interviews that were conducted with approximately seventy planners, engineers, and both federal and Mexico City public officials between December 1980 and December 1981, and for three months in the spring of 1987, as noted earlier. Among the agencies contacted were (1) Government dependencies or agencies: Secretaría de Programación y Presupuesto, Secretaría de Gobernación, Gobierno del Distrito Federal, Secretaría de Desarrollo Urbano y Ecología, Renovación Popular, Comisión de Vialidad y Transporte Urbano (COVITUR), Sistema de Transporte Colectivo, and Comisión Nacional de Salubridad Popular; (2) Political parties: Partido Revolucionario Institucional (PRI) (including special interviews in the Confederación Nacional de Organizaciones Populares, or CNOP), Partido Acción Nacional (PAN), Partido Socialista Unido de México (PSUM); and (3) Urban social movements: Confederación Nacional de Movimientos Urbanos Populares (CONA-

MUP), Asamblea de Barrios, and Mujeres para el Diálogo. Interviews were also conducted with private sector spokesmen for organizations and companies in the transport industry, particularly those who actively opposed or promoted the METRO project, such as Ingenieros Civiles Asociados (ICA) and Ingeniería de Sistemas de Transporte Metropolitano (ISTME).

Population Growth in Mexico City, the Federal District, and the Metropolitan Area, 1900–1990 (thousands)

	1900	1910	1921	1930	1940	1950	1960	1970	1980	1990	1940–70	1970–90
											Percentage Change	
Mexico City[a]	345	471	615	1,029	1,448	2,249	2,829	3,003	2,686	1,930	107%	−36%
Federal District[b]	542	730	903	1,221	1,645	3,240	5,178	7,327	9,165	8,236	345%	12%
Metropolitan Area[c]	NA	NA	NA	NA	1,758	3,136	5,381	9,211	14,419	15,048	424%	63%

[a]Mexico City is the smallest and oldest jurisdiction used in census documents, and comprises four *delegaciones*: M. Hidalgo, Cuauhtémoc, B. Juárez, and V. Carranza.

[b]The Federal District is the second largest demographic unit in census documents. It is comprised of the four Mexico City *delegaciones* listed above and twelve others: Azcapotzalco, Coyoacán, Cuajimilpa, Villa G. Madero, Ixtacalco, Ixtapalapa, Magdalena Contreras, Milpa Alta, Villa Alvaro Obregón, Tlahuac, Tlalpan, and Xochimilco.

[c]The Metropolitan Area includes the four *delegaciones* of Mexico City, the twelve *delegaciones* of the Federal District, and several contiguous urban areas in the state of Mexico.

Sources: Atlas de la Ciudad de México, 1900–1980, México, D.F.; México Dirección General de Estadística, *Censo General de Población*, México, D.F., 1990; and Luís Unikel, *El Desarollo Urbano de México: Diagnóstico e Implicaciones Futuras*, 2d ed., Mexico City: El Colegio de México, 1978.

Patterns in Federal Elections for Congressional Representatives, 1946–1988

Percentage of Votes Cast for PRI and Opposition Parties

Year	Nationwide		Federal District	
	PRI	Opposition	PRI	Opposition
1946*	73.52	26.48	50.34	49.66
1949	89.32	10.67	61.90	38.10
1952*	74.31	25.69	49.01	50.99
1955	87.27	12.73	56.05	43.81
1958*	88.33	11.67	68.59	31.27
1961	90.23	9.32	63.94	35.45
1964*	86.26	13.60	65.98	33.71
1967	83.32	16.49	65.34	34.02
1970*	80.07	15.74	55.41	33.40
1973	69.66	30.44	43.74	40.27
1976*	80.09	19.91	55.62	28.97
1979	69.74	30.26	46.71	41.64
1982*	69.25	30.75	48.35	51.65
1985	64.81	35.19	42.63	57.37
1988*	51.11	48.89	27.61	72.39

*Presidential election year

Patterns of Abstentionism (as a Percentage of Registered Voters)

Year	Nationwide (1)	Federal District (2)	Difference (2/1)
1946*	13.55	39.47	+25.92
1949	27.69	33.41	+5.82
1952*	25.51	34.22	+8.71
1955	31.18	37.00	+5.82
1958*	28.44	31.47	+3.03
1961	31.67	37.73	+6.06
1964*	33.39	37.26	+3.87
1967	31.34	35.45	+4.11
1970*	35.83	32.92	−3.91
1973	39.68	35.61	−4.07
1976*	37.95	37.16	−0.34
1979	50.67	42.48	−8.19

Patterns of Abstentionism (as a Percentage of Registered Voters)

Year	Nationwide (1)	Federal District (2)	Difference (2/1)
1982*	34.14	29.29	−4.85
1985	50.68	44.84	−5.84
1988*	47.54	45.23	−2.31

*Presidential election year

Sources: Jaqueline Peschard, "Las elecciones en el Distrito Federal (1946–1970)," *Revista mexicana de sociología* 50 (July–September 1988): 232; Comisión Federal Electoral.

APPENDIX D

Presidents of the Mexican Republic and Mayors of Mexico City, 1915–1994

President	Term of Office	Mayor	Term of Office
F. Lagos Cházaro	1915	G. Magaña	1915
		C. López de Lara	1915
V. Carranza	1917–1920	G. de la Mata	1917
		C. López de Lara	1917
		A. Breceda	1918
		A. González	1918
		A. Breceda	1919
		B. Flores	1919
		M. Rueda Magro	1919
		M. Gómez Noriega	1920
A. de la Huerta	1920	C. Gasca	1920–1923
A. Obregón	1920–1924	R. Ross	1923
		A. Rodríguez	1923–1924
		R. Ross	1924
P. Elías Calles	1924–1928	F. R. Serrano	1926–1927
		P. Villa Michel	1927–1928
E. Portes Gil	1928–1930	M. M. Puig Casauranc	1929–1930
		C. Ibañez	1930
		Lamberto Hernández	1930–1931
P. Ortiz Rubio	1930–1932	E. Romero Courtade	1931
		Lorenzo Hernández	1931
		V. Estrada Cajigal	1932
A. L. Rodríguez	1932–1934	M. Padilla	1932
		J. G. Cabral	1932
		A. Sáenz	1932–1935
L. Cárdenas	1934–1940	C. Hinojosa	1935–1938
		J. Siurug	1938
		Raúl Castellanos	1938–1940
M. Ávila Camacho	1940–1946	J. Rojo Gómez	1940–1946
M. Alemán Valdez	1946–1952	F. Casas Alemán	1946–1952
A. Ruiz Cortines	1952–1958	E. P. Uruchurtu	1952–1958
A. López Mateos	1958–1964	E. P. Uruchurtu	1958–1964
G. Díaz Ordaz	1964–1970	E. P. Uruchurtu	1964–1966
		A. Corona del Rosal	1966–1970
L. Echeverría Alvarez	1970–1976	A. Martínez Domínguez	1970–1971
		O. Sentíes	1971–1976

President	Term of Office	Mayor	Term of Office
J. López Portillo	1976–1982	C. Hank González	1976–1982
M. de la Madrid Hurtado	1982–1988	R. Aguirre Velázquez	1982–1988
Carlos Salinas de Gortari	1988–1994	M. Camacho Sólis	1988–1993

Source: Instituto Nacional de Estudios Historicos de la Revolución Mexicana, *Participación Ciudadana en el Gobierno del Distrito Federal*, Mexico City: Secretaria de Gobernación, 1987.

NOTES

CHAPTER ONE

1. Octavio Paz, *Return to the Labyrinth of Solitude*, p. 343.
2. Unless otherwise specified, population figures refer to the Mexico City metropolitan area. For detailed numbers, see Appendix B.
3. See Aníbal Quijano, "Dependencia, cambio social, y urbanización en latinoamérica"; Manuel Castells, *Multinational Capital, Nation-States, and Local Community*; Christopher Chase-Dunn, "Urbanization in the World System"; Alejandro Portes and John Walton, *Labor, Class, and the International System*; Michael Timberlake, ed., *Urbanization in the World Economy*.
4. Gustavo Garza, *El proceso de industrialización en la Ciudad de México, 1821–1970*.
5. Alan Gilbert and Peter Ward, *Housing, the State, and the Urban Poor*, p. 60.
6. Susan Eckstein, *The Poverty of Revolution*, p. 208.
7. Edward Soja, "The Spatiality of Social Life: Towards a Transformative Retheorisation," p. 90.
8. John Urry, "Some Notes on Realism and the Analysis of Space," p. 123.
9. Michael Storper and Richard Walker, *The Capitalist Imperative: Territory, Technology, and Industrial Growth*, p. 1.
10. Soja, "Spatiality of Social Life," pp. 81, 173.
11. Jonathan Arac and Barbara Johnson, eds., *The Consequences of Theory*.
12. Andrew Sayer, "The New Regional Geography and Problems of Narrative," pp. 258–59, 263.
13. Manuel Castells, *The Urban Question*, and "Is There an Urban Sociology?"
14. For Novo the history of transport is in many ways the history of politics:

Retrospectivamente, no es pues sino natural que la Revolución, ese sacudimiento de nuestra inercia porfiriana, anterior a las guerras mundiales y a la Revolución rusa, coincidiera en la ciudad de México con una aceleración de los transportes que deparó a los generales el privilegio de su iniciación, cuando fueron los generales los primeros en circular por nuestras calles en grandes automóviles. . . . Se creaba en ellos el tipo de un chofer temerario, cuya importancia sociológica, filosófica, diagnosticaría el conde de Keyserling, y que ya era distinto del chauffeur morandiano de 1900. . . . Los choferes de los generales, bien remunerados, jóvenes, hábiles; primeros hijos de la Revolución, sobrevivirían a la fugaz prosperidad derrochadora de sus patronos. Exiliados por chaqueteo, arruinados por la política o—lo que era ciertamente menos frecuente—muertos gloriosamente en campaña, los generales se extinguían, y sus choferes, dueños a la vez de una técnica y de unos ahorros, se compraban un coche propio, un enemigo de las carretelas de bandera, que les permitiera alquilarlo y dispensar la apetecida velocidad del desplaza-

miento popular al mayor número posible de ciudadanos y a un precio módico.
Había tal coche. La "ingenuidad," como ellos dicen por ingenio, de los norte-
americanos, lo había producido; era el Ford en 1917. Año de la Constitución. . . .
Era el Ford, origen último, causa primera del ruleteo, y joven abuelo de los camiones. . . . Se creó asi, en los camiones que de la operación resultaron, el nuevo oficio
del cobrador, cuya ubicación no importaba. Secretario ejecutivo del chofer, tro-
taba en pie sobre el estribo trasero. . . . Mucho de nuestro folklore expresivo al
ingenio verbal de aquella nueva casta de choferes y cobradores, y es muy de desear
que algún académico alerta rastree hasta su origen gasolinero tantos dichos nuestros . . . "ruletear," verbo excelente que implica el *peddling*, la oferta trashumante
de los servicios, conserva una clara raíz dentro de su hoy más amplia conotación
de actividades; y en igual diáfano caso filológico se encuentra la expresión "hacer
coche"—o "hacer Tacuba." Pero es muy justo acreditar al gremio la invención de
la palabra "mordida," hoy de tan general vigencia, cuando el gremio dio el nombre
de "mordelones" a los primeros agentes de tránsito que la proliferación de vehículos, extintos ya los coches de caballos, indujo a las autoridades a crear, como
reguladores oportunos de una circulación que empezaba a hacerse densa.

Translation:

In retrospect, it is only natural that the Revolution, which shook us from our Porfirian inertia and preceded the World Wars and the Russian revolution, would
coincide in Mexico City with an increase in vehicles, introduced by the generals,
who were the first to circulate in our streets in large automobiles. . . . They created
a type of daring driver whose sociological and philosophical importance was discovered by the count of Keyserling, and who was already different from the chauffeur of 1900. . . . The drivers of the generals, well paid, young, and competent, the
first sons of the Revolution, would live in the flighty and spendthrift prosperity of
their patrons. Exiled after internal factionalism, ruined by politics or—certainly
less frequently—perishing heroically in military campaign, the generals died off;
their drivers, owners of both a special skill and some savings, purchased their own
cars—enemies of the standard horse-drawn carriages—rented themselves out, and
provided the longed-for speed and mobility to the greatest number of individuals
at a moderate price. There was such a car. The ingenuity, as they call talent, of
the North Americans had produced it; it was the Ford of 1917. Year of the Constitution. . . . It was the Ford, the source, the main cause of the rise of the taxi,
the young grandfather of the omnibus. . . . From the buses that grew out of this
operation, the new occupation of fare-collector emerged, whose location was un-
important. The driver's executive secretary trotted alongside, hitching a ride on the
back footboard. Much of our expressive folklore has its roots in the verbal inven-
tiveness of that new caste of drivers and fare-collectors, and some alert academic
would do a great service by tracing the gas-related etymologies of so many of our
sayings . . . "ruletear," an excellent verb implying peddling, the nomadic offering
of services, conserves a clear root within its most broad connotation of activities;
and in the same diaphanous philological case is the expression "hacer coche" [to
take a ride]—or "hacer Tacuba" [to cruise; n.b. that Mexico City's main down-

town shopping district lies on Calle Tacuba, where almost all public transport passed or originated]. But it is quite just to credit that sector with the invention of the word "mordida" [bribe], of such generalized usage today, when the guild gave the name of "mordelones" to the first transport agents whom the authorities established as timely regulators of the increasingly dense circulation produced by the proliferation of vehicles that replaced the now extinct horse-drawn carriages.

Salvador Novo, "Caballos, calles, trato, cumplimiento," pp. 103–5.

CHAPTER TWO

1. María Dolores Morales, "La expansión de la Ciudad de México en el siglo XIX: el caso de los fraccionamientos," pp. 191–92.

2. Rodney Anderson, *Outcasts in Their Own Land: Mexican Industrial Workers, 1906–1911*, p. 46.

3. Ibid., p. 44.

4. Morales, "La expansión de la Ciudad de México," p. 194.

5. Roberto Eibenschutz, "Evolución de la Ciudad de México," p. 134.

6. Manuel Perlo Cohen, "Política y vivienda en México, 1910–1952."

7. Departamento del Distrito Federal, "Antecedentes de la formación de la industria camionera," pp. 1–3.

8. Carlos Aguirre, "La promoción de un fraccionamiento: San Tomás," p. 218.

9. Manuel Vidrio C., "Sistemas de transporte y expansión urbana: los tranvías," pp. 201, 212–15.

10. Perló Cohen, "Política y vivienda," p. 4.

11. Miguel Rodríguez, *Los tranviarios y el anarquismo en México (1920–1925)*, p. 101.

12. When the Compañía de Tranvías laid trolley tracks, it also paved the streets, a service that the city had come to depend upon. Thus the city's financial obligations to the Compañía were twofold: for direct service provision and for credit. See Departamento del Distrito Federal, *Memoria de los trabajos realizados durante el ejercicio de 1926*, p. 52.

13. *Actas y versiones del Consejo Consultivo del Distrito Federal*, April 9, 1930, p. 10.

14. Perlo Cohen, "Política y vivienda," p. 5.

15. Moisés González Navarro, *Población y sociedad en México, 1900–1970*, p. 176.

16. Frank Tannenbaum, *The Making of Modern Mexico*, p. 238.

17. Luis Araiza, *Historia del movimiento obrero*, vol. 3, pp. 74–75.

18. Perlo Cohen, "Política y vivienda," p. 6.

19. Jean Meyer, "Los obreros en la revolución mexicana: los batallones rojos," p. 12.

20. Raul Trejo Delarbre, "The Mexican Labor Movement, 1917–1975," pp. 178–79. See also Levy and Székely, *Mexico: Paradoxes of Stability and Change*, pp. 55–57.

21. Rosendo Salazar, *Las pugnas de la gleba*, p. 79.

22. Trejo Delarbre, "Mexican Labor Movement," p. 179.

23. Arnaldo Córdova, *La ideología de la revolución mexicana*, p. 16.

24. Ramon Eduardo Ruiz, *Labor and the Ambivalent Revolutionaries*, p. 35.

25. John Mason Hart, *Revolutionary Mexico*, p. 271.

26. Araiza, *Historia del movimiento obrero*, p. 10.

27. John Mason Hart, *Anarchism and the Mexican Working Class*, p. 130.

28. Ruiz, *Labor*, p. 41.

29. Hart, *Anarchism*, p. 149.

30. Araiza, *Historia del movimiento obrero*, vol. 3, pp. 20–22. In these documents the word *mesero* is used, which I would translate as waiter rather than restaurant worker (as Hart suggests in *Anarchism*, p. 149).

31. Tannenbaum, *Peace by Revolution*, p. 233.

32. Robert Paul Millon, *Mexican Marxist: Vincente Lombardo Toledano*, esp. pp. 3–42, for a discussion of the Casa during the early years of the Mexican labor movement.

33. Anderson, *Outcasts in Their Own Land*, pp. 77–79.

34. As late as 1930, factories (800) in the capital did not greatly outnumber small-scale artisan workshops (657), known as *talleres*. See *Atlas del Distrito Federal: geográfico, histórico, comercial, estadístico, agrario*, p. 28.

35. Ruiz, *Labor*, p. 50.

36. "Sección editorial: la defensa de Mexico," *Nueva Era*, March 7, 1912, p. 7.

37. "Los obreros de la capital," *Nueva Era*, March 8, 1912, p. 5.

38. *Nueva Era*, March 7, 1912, p. 3.

39. Ruiz, *Labor*, p. 50.

40. James D. Cockcroft, *Intellectual Precursors of the Mexican Revolution*, p. 225.

41. Hart, *Anarchism*, p. 178.

42. Araiza, *Historia del movimiento obrero*, vol. 3, p. 112.

43. Rocío Guadarrama, *Los sindicatos y la política en México: la CROM, (1918–1928)*, p. 45.

44. Notably, the few Mexico City syndicates that joined the CGT represented the most proletarianized and ideologically radicalized professions, like spinners and weavers employed in the textile industry, bakers, and Mexico City electricians, who were not urban artisans but strictly supervised workers in the foreign-owned Ericsson telephone company. Local communists also joined.

45. Rodríguez, *Los tranviarios*, pp. 145–46; and Ernesto de la Torre Villar, "Notas para la historia del trabajo," p. 670.

46. *Nueva Era*, March 8, 1912, p. 3.

47. Ruiz, *Labor*, pp. 51–52.

48. Rodríguez, *Los tranviarios*, p. 150.

49. Ibid., pp. 129–30, 151.

50. Ibid., p. 76.

51. Ibid., pp. 80, 83–84.

52. Ibid., p. 161.

53. Hart, *Anarchism*, p. 151.

54. Ruiz, *Labor*, p. 55.

55. *Informe de la gestión administrativa del Lic. D. Benito Flores*, p. 5.

56. Instituto Nacional de Estudios Históricos de la Revolución Mexicana, *Participación ciudadana en el gobierno federal*, p. 45 (hereafter cited as INEHRM).

57. *Informe de la gestión administrativa*, p. 43.

58. Ibid., p. 25.

59. *Informe del gobierno del Distrito Federal*, p. 5.

60. Araiza, *Historia del movimiento obrero*, vol. 4, p. 110.

61. Cf. Rodríguez, *Los tranviarios*, p. 191.

62. Hart, *Anarchism*, p. 163.

63. *Atlas del Distrito Federal*, p. 130; and Rodríguez, *Los tranviarios*, p. 171.

64. *Informe del gobierno del Distrito Federal*, pp. 72–73.

65. Ernesto de la Torre Villar, "Notas para la historia de las comunicaciones y el trabajo: la Compañía de Tranvías y las luchas obreras, 1900–1945," p. 699.

66. A word of caution: There is little consistency in accounts of the formation of the Alianza, or of when it became independent. According to Héctor Manuel Romero, in *Historia del transporte* (pp. 122–24), the Alianza was founded in 1919 and gained independence from the Centro Social de Choferes in 1926. Yet in *Transporte y contaminación en la Ciudad de México*, Jorge Legoretta dates the founding of the Centro Social de Choferes to 1923, and notes that the Alianza emerged from the Federación Camionera del Distrito Federal, and not the Centro. The point is that by the mid to late 1920s, urban bus services displaced trolleys as the principal mode of transport, and the Alianza de Camioneros organizationally and politically cemented its political power.

67. Perló Cohen, "Apuntes para una interpretación," p. 9. President Alvaro Obregón was known to be closely linked to the Alianza, and appointed Alianza members to numerous political posts.

68. Arnaldo Córdova, *La formación del poder político en México*, p. 103.

69. The Partido Laborista Mexicano controlled the municipality of Mexico for roughly four years, 1925–1928. Perló Cohen, "Apuntes," p. 13.

70. José Rivera Castro, *La clase obrera en la historia de México*, pp. 102–3.

71. *Informe del gobierno del Distrito Federal*, p. 18.

72. INEHRM, *Participación*, p. 46.

73. While some unionists did remain in the CROM, most deserted and became independent or formed their own local unions while awaiting developments. Hart, *Anarchism*, p. 175; see also Araiza, *Historia del movimiento obrero*, vol. 4, pp. 140–50.

CHAPTER THREE

1. Juan Felipe Leal, "The Mexican State: An Historical Interpretation," p. 27 (emphasis mine).

2. *Ley Orgánica del Distrito Federal y de los Territorios Federales*, p. 24.

3. *Departamento del Distrito Federal: reorganización administrativa del Departamento*, Sección 1: Consejos Consultivos, pp. 5–6.

4. *Actas y versiones del Consejo Consultivo del Distrito Federal*, April 9, 1930, pp. 8–9 (hereafter cited as *AVCC*).

5. Between 1925 and 1928 alone, more than fifty-five new groups joined the CROM, among which were the *Unión de Oficinistas Ferrocarrileros* (railroad office workers), the *Gran Sindicato de Comerciantes Ambulantes de la Ciudad de México* (Mexico City street vendors), the *Sindicato de Comerciantes*, the *Federación de Cólonos* (neighborhood organizations), the *Sindicato de Cólonos* (residents) *del Ex-Hipódromo de Peralvillo*, and numerous other organizations that included both *empleados* and *obreros*. For elaboration, see Rocío Guadarrama, *Los sindicatos y la política en México: la CROM (1918–1928)*, pp. 200–202.

6. *AVCC*, April 9, 1930, pp. 8–9.

7. *AVCC*, August 13, 1930, p. 2.

8. *AVCC*, March 12, 1930, p. 3a.

9. *AVCC*, March 12, 1930, p. 3e.

10. Ibid.

11. *AVCC*, March 12, 1930, p. 5a.

12. Underlying these conflicts was growing competition for market shares in Mexico City, such that large commerce voiced concerns that small *comerciantes* had more flexibility in work hours (i.e., they could be open longer than eight hours and on Sundays) because—being self-employed—they did not have to comply with the recent national legislation guaranteeing workers' rights and protections. With so many of the nation's industrial and commercial firms located in Mexico City, these local deliberations clearly took on national importance. Yet their resolution in the capital city relied on the balance of forces within the Consejo; and in this context, as in the nation itself where labor federations had substantial political power, it was difficult for them to prevail.

13. *AVCC*, August 29, 1930, p. 10.

14. *AVCC*, August 29, 1930, p. 7. The exact words: "Yo quisiera que . . . nuestra ciudad sea—hablando con una frase popular—menos 'pomadosa' pero más util. Yo creo que si somos hombres modernos, que si somos humanos, debemos delinear este programa, en el sentido de dar oportunidad a la gente pobre que quiere buscar honestamenta el pan."

15. See Adrian García Cortés, *La reforma urbana de México: crónica de la Comisión de Planificación del DF*, p. 24 (fn 9).

16. Starting in the early 1930s, we see evidence that several federations of shopkeepers and small *comerciantes* frequently connected with women's groups whose principal objectives were to provide charity for the non-working-class poor. Among the common urban policy concerns that unified these groups were efforts to establish food co-ops and to guarantee rent control. See Archivo General de la Nación, exp. 702.2/655.2, Galería de Presidentes, Cárdenas period.

17. Manuel Perló Cohen, "El cardenismo y la Ciudad de México: historia de un conflicto," p. 7.

18. Manuel Perló Cohen, "Política y vivienda en México, 1910–1952," pp. 30–39;

and Beatriz García Peralta and Manuel Perló Cohen, "El estado, sindicalismo oficial, y políticas habitacionales," pp. 99–101.

19. Perló Cohen, "El Cardenismo," pp. 8–9.

20. José Antonio Rojas Loa O., "La transformación de la zona central, Ciudad de México," p. 225.

21. Perló Cohen, "El cardenismo," p. 5. Between 1935 and 1940, Mexico City expenditures as a proportion of national expenditures dropped to 12.5 percent, whereas between 1929 and 1934 they approached 14.8 percent. Manuel Perló Cohen, *Estado, vivienda, y estructura urbana en el cardenismo*, p. 77.

22. Perló Cohen, "El cardenismo," p. 2.

23. Perló Cohen, *Estado, vivienda, y estructura urbana*, p. 11.

24. Ricardo Pérez Montfort, *Los empresarios alemanes, el tercer reich, y la oposición a Cárdenas*, p. 6.

25. Carlos Sirvent, *La burocracia política central en el sistema de dominación mexicano*, pp. 108–9.

26. Nora Hamilton, "State and Class Conflict," p. 354.

27. The military sector, however, was not granted the same privileges as the other sectors. According to Pablo González Casanova, it represented military men as "citizens and not as a corporate grouping" (*El estado y los partidos políticos en México*, p. 119). By grouping the military into one sector that had a formalized institutional relationship with the state, Cárdenas was able to ensure that military forces supportive of his political projects had privileged access to party operations, even if the military as a sector did not participate on equal footing with the others.

28. Soledad Loaeza, *Clases medias y política en México*, p. 96.

29. Trolley workers were among the few urban service workers who remained in the labor federation, owing to their "red" history in the CGT. Thus they shunned restrictions on strikes, a stance they took with support from the labor federation's leadership.

30. Archivo General de la Nación, Series 2, 331.9 (29) expediente 14, Galería del Dirección General de Gobierno.

31. Perló Cohen, *Estado, vivienda, y estructura urbana*, pp. 72, 75.

32. Ibid., p. 50.

33. Archivo General de la Nación, exp. 545.3/94, Galería de Presidentes, Cárdenas period.

34. Perló Cohen, *Estado, vivienda, y estructura urbana*, p. 14.

35. CANACINTRA, *Análisis económico nacional, 1934–1940*, p. 93.

36. Ibid.

37. CONCANACOMIN, *Memoria de la Cámara Nacional de Comercio e Industria de la Ciudad de México*, p. 71.

38. Archivo General de la Nación, expediente 545.3/94, Galería de Presidentes, Cárdenas period.

39. See CONCANACOMIN, *Memoria de la Cámara Nacional de Comercio e Industria*, p. 71.

40. Albert Michaels, "Las elecciones de 1940;" cf. Loaeza, *Clases medias y política*, p. 98.

41. Archivo General de la Nación, expediente 473.3/130, Galería de Presidentes, Cárdenas period.

42. Partido Revolucionario Institucional (PRI), *Historia documental de la CNOP*, vol. 1, pp. 40, 43, 136, 188.

43. Ibid., p. 46.

44. PRI, *Historia documental de la CNOP*, vol. 1, p. 76, for a listing of the different occupations grouped within the CNOP. For 1938 and 1946 figures on party membership, see Luis Javier Garrido, "Un partido sin militantes," p. 75.

45. Garrido, "Un partido sin militantes," p. 61.

CHAPTER FOUR

1. Leticia Juárez González, "La organización empresarial en México durante el Cardenismo," p. 71.

2. Cámara de Comercio de la Ciudad de México, *Informe anual*, p. 9.

3. This is not to say that northerners shunned industrial projects. The Garza Sada family is a case in point: Their Cerveceria Cuahtemoc, in Monterrey, the capital city of the northern state of Nuevo Leon, was one of the first and most successful industrial enterprises in Mexico.

4. Teresa Franco, *Ensayo sobre la historia de la Cámara Nacional de la Industria de Transformación*, p. 20.

5. Franco, *Ensayo sobre*, p. 20.

6. Brachet Márquez, *The Pact of Domination*, p. 10.

7. Bernardo Mendez Lugo, "Desarrollo y industrialización subordinada en México," p. 125; Stephen H. Haber, *Industry and Underdevelopment: The Industrialization of Mexico, 1910–1940*, pp. 80–83.

8. While there were a few industrial firms from northern regions involved in the CANACINTRA in its first years, due to their participation in consumer goods production, processing, or packaging (including the Compañía Fundidora de Fierro Acero de Monterrey and Talleres Monterrey) the majority of firms were located in Mexico City. See Franco, *Ensayo sobre*, passim.

9. Marco Antonio Alcazar, *Las agrupaciones patronales en México*, p. 39; and Jorge Piñeda Palacios, *CANACINTRA: semblaza histórica, 1941–1985*, p. 10.

10. Franco, *Ensayo sobre*, pp. 24–25; and Alcazar, *Las agrupaciones patronales*, p. 47.

11. Javier Aguirre et al., *El Partido de la Revolución: historia, estructura, y predominio del Partido Revolucionario Institucional*, p. 35.

12. Dale Story, *Industry, the State and Public Policy*, p. 85. See also Vincent L. Padgett, *The Mexican Political System*, p. 131.

13. Franco, *Ensayo sobre*, p. 37.

14. A Mexico City journalist wrote that Alemán based much of his urban political support in the 1946 elections on the numerous contingents of *paracaidistas* (illegal land invaders) who claimed property titles, one of the policies introduced along with the formation of the CNOP. Cf. Manuel Perló Cohen, "Política y vivienda en México, 1910–1952," p. 49.

15. Soledad Loaeza, *Clases medias y política en México*, pp. 143, 147–50.

16. Uriel Jarquín Gálvez and Jorge Javier Romero Vadillo, *Un PAN que no se come: biografía de Accion Nacional*, p. 45.

17. Priscilla Connolly, Oscar Nuñez, and Enrique Ortiz, *Las políticas habitacionales del estado mexicano*, p. 23.

18. Gustavo Garza, *El proceso de industrialización en la Ciudad de México, 1821–1970*, apéndice estadístico, pp. 394–426.

19. Beatriz García Peralta and Manuel Perló Cohen, "Estado, sindicalismo oficial, y políticas habitacionales: análisis de una década de Infonavit," pp. 100–101.

20. Perló Cohen, "Política y vivienda," p. 51.

21. *El Universal*, April 25, 1948; cf., Perló Cohen, ibid., p. 54.

22. García Peralta and Perló Cohen, "Estado y sindicalismo oficial," pp. 103–4.

23. Oliver Oldman et al., *Financing Urban Development in Mexico City*, pp. 25–26; and Priscilla Connolly, "Finanzas públicas y estado local: el caso del Departamento del Distrito Federal," p. 84.

24. At issue was how Mexico City would be funded. The most heated debate unfolded between the Secretaría de Hacienda (Treasury), which originally supported the proposition that the Distrito Federal be funded fully by the federal government, and the Mexico City mayor's office, which supported the Distrito Federal's fiscal independence. Ultimately, with pressure from then-president Obregón, the Treasury Department changed its position. The argument was that it would be "dangerous to accept a mixing of national finances" with local ones, particularly in the first year of Mexico City's reorganization. And while the treasury secretary based his position on technical concerns about the city's capacity to run itself on the basis of "destroyed plans and disappeared documentation," the political implications of fiscal dependence on the national government were undoubtedly a concern—especially since Obregón's decision to remove democratic rule in the capital had been highly contentious. *Actas y versiones del Consejo Consultivo del Distrito Federal*, June 25, 1930, pp. 1a–3a (hereafter cited as *AVCC*).

25. This tax structure has always been controversial. As early as 1929, Mexico City officials requested exemptions from federal rates for Mexico City industries in order to keep them from leaving the capital to seek cheaper labor and lower taxes. They claimed that not only "because the Distrito Federal was the heart and brain of Mexico," but also because the federal government imposed its "moral and material presence," the national government had the obligation to help the Distrito Federal in this matter. However, treasury officials refused to waive the exemption and the dual tax burden still remains. *AVCC*, May 21, 1930, pp. 13–15.

26. Garza, *Proceso de industrialización*, p. 210.

27. Bertha Lerner and Susana Ralsky, *El poder de los presidentes*, p. 395.

28. In response to one such public charge, Uruchurtu claimed that he was only trying to prevent Mexico from being "converted into the latrine of the world" by keeping out immigrants and illegal goods traffickers who "give nothing of a spiritual or material order to Mexico." In another telling comment, Uruchurtu stated his disgust with the "invasion" of "millions of men of all races, who we receive as the blind without knowing their origins, who are taking positions that give them economic power and that prevent us from fully investigating their activities." The

comment about the "blind" refers to the fact that for many decades, street vending and hawking had been the exclusive domain of handicapped residents. Gonzalo de la Parra, "Puntos de vista: primero echar a los indeseables que ya entraron; después lo demás," n.p.

29. Jose Antonio Rojas Loa O., "La transformación de la zona central, Ciudad de México, 1930–1970," p. 228.

30. "Promete Uruchurtu mejorar los servicios y frenar la carestía en el D.F." *Excélsior*, December 6, 1952.

31. Angel Andonegui, "Meritoria labor del Regente Uruchurtu."

32. Oldman et al., *Financing Urban Development*, p. 28.

33. Garza, *Proceso de industrialización*, p. 172, 225–26; and Alexander Bohrisch and Wolfgang Konig, *La política mexicana sobre inversiones extranjeras*, pp. 43–45, 70.

34. Cámara Nacional de la Industria de la Transformación, *La Cámara Nacional de la Industria de la Transformación y el Consejo de Planeación Económica y Social en el D.F.*, pp. 3–4.

35. Oldman et al., *Financing Urban Development*, pp. 25, 31.

36. "La labor de Uruchurtu," *El Universal*, November 12, 1953; and "Culminó la obra de 12 años de Ernesto Uruchurtu," *Excélsior*, November 22, 1964.

37. Oldman, et al., *Financing Urban Development*, p. 25.

38. "El complemento de una obra," *El Universal*, April 25, 1957.

39. "Uruchurtu y la administración pública," *Novedades*, August 19, 1957.

40. "Elogia la obra del Lic. Uruchurtu," *El Universal*, January 3, 1957.

41. "Uruchurtu mejorá al DF," *El Universal*, May 5, 1954.

42. Wayne Cornelius, *Politics and the Migrant Poor in Mexico City*, p. 203.

43. Uruchurtu was even able to make his policy of no new land development fit nicely with the high moral tone he had set publicly. He once justified his actions in this regard as an honest "campaign against developers (*fraccionadores*) who commit true fraud, who sell plots of land they do not own and for which they have no authorization for public works." "Un vasto programa de obras publicas por 400 milliones, esta en marcha en el DF," see *El Nacional*, April 15, 1959.

44. Jarquín Gálvez and Romero Vadillo, *Un PAN*, p. 52.

45. "Interés esencial en tener la colaboración del pueblo," *El Nacional*, March 2, 1954.

46. "Recibió una medalla y un pergamino el Lic. Ernesto P. Uruchurtu," *El Nacional*, February 27, 1958.

CHAPTER FIVE

1. "Convenio entre General Motors de México y la Alianza de Camioneros," *Novedades*, n.d., 1949.

2. Rubén Figueroa Figueroa personifies the power of the Alianza within the PRI. He has been both a congressional representative and governor, and his son has been a congressman.

3. "El monopolio camionero, en 8 lineas," *Excélsior*, December 1, 1971.

4. "Los camioneros anuncian que fabricarán sus propias llantas," *Excélsior*, April 30, 1958; "Llamado a la unidad del gremio camionero," *El Universal*, November 4, 1958.

5. "La Alianza de Camioneros de Mexico denuncia una calumniosa campaña, *El Nacional*, November 17, 1957.

6. ISTME, *Sistema de transporte colectivo (METRO) de la Ciudad de México*, p. 3.

7. "Con esfuerzo renovado se supera en el Distrito Federal el servicio de pasajeros en autobuses," *Siempre*, July 13, 1966, p. 70.

8. Adrian García Cortés, *La reforma urbana de México*, pp. 19–20.

9. Victor Manuel Villegas, *Un pleito tristemente célebre en la Ciudad de México en el siglo XX*, p. 99.

10. Villegas, *Un pleito tristemente célebre*, p. 111.

11. Ibid., pp. 22, 46.

12. Ibid., pp. 60, 61.

13. Frank Brandenburg, *The Making of Modern Mexico*, p. 306.

14. Villegas, *Un pleito tristemente célebre*, p. 42.

15. Ibid., pp. 213, 221.

16. Antonio Caram, "Campesinos víctimas de inspectores."

17. Adrian García Córtes, *Urbes y pueblos*, p. 234. See also "El pequeño comerciante es muy necesario," *Excélsior*, January 11, 1960.

18. ICA was no small construction firm. It was one of the most economically successful firms in Mexico. In 1966, for example, ICA was generating more than 1 percent of Mexico's gross national product and its projects were among Mexico's finest: the Ciudad Universitaria, the Mexico City drainage system, the transpeninsular highway of Baja California, El Centro Médico (Mexico City's principal medical center), Conjunto Urbano Nonoalco-Tlatelolco, the Palacio de Deportes and all other major Olympics constructions, the Periférico (Mexico City's largest freeway), several of the city's finest hotels (María Isabel, Alameda, Camino Real, Presidente Chapultepec), the American Embassy, and Perisur (the first and largest commercial shopping center in the capital). See Ingenieros Civiles Asociados, *XXX años de realizaciones*, p. 1.

19. "Un realizador de 'imposibles,'" *Excélsior*, September 29, 1977. Some of ICA's most visible officials were Javier Barros Sierra, who became secretary of public works as well as rector of the national university; Raul Sandoval, who became a high official in the Department of Water Resources; and Fernando Espinoza, subsecretary of public works. See "3 Engineering Units Expand," *Journal of Commerce*, p. 1. In a listing of seven of ICA's deceased engineers taken from a thirtieth-anniversary publication of the firm in 1967, it is telling that all but one had held positions of importance in national or Distrito Federal government departments charged with infrastructure development.

20. Antonio Rodríguez, "La solución: El METRO o el monorriel?" p. 14.

21. Villegas, *Un pleito tristemente célebre*, p. 114.

22. Ibid., p. 231.

23. Ibid., p. 112.

24. For the so-called technical rationale for the subway project, see ISTME, *Sis-*

tema de transporte colectivo (METRO) de la Ciudad de México. The "technological solution" was built upon questionable studies. The initial feasibility study compared mass rapid transit to automobiles rather than to buses, and employed doubtful estimates of the METRO's target population. Costs also were grossly underestimated.

25. All nine firms charged with construction and engineering tasks were wholly owned subsidiaries of Grupo ICA: Ingenieros Civiles Asociados, S.A.; Preforzadas Mexicanas, S.A.; Solum, S.A.; Industria de Hierro, S.A.; Construcciones, Conducciones, y Pavimentos, S.A.; Equipos Nacionales, S.A.; Ingeniería y Puertos, S.A.; Ingenieros y Arquitectos, S.A.; and Estructuras y Cimentaciones, S.A. Also, ICA was linked with French financial institutions and French transport technology exporters, connections that further motivated this firm to promote the subway project, which when built utilized French technology and French financing.

26. Marta Schteingart Kaplan, "La promoción inmobiliaria en la área metropolitana de la Ciudad de México, 1960–1980," p. 16.

27. Villegas, *Un pleito tristemente célebre,* p. 61.

28. Ingenieros Civiles Asociados, *Grupo ICA: qué es el Grupo ICA?* p. 6.

29. "Entrevista con Héctor Hernández Casanova," *Año V,* p. 40.

30. "Uruchurtu no va a dejar deudas: los compromisos del Departamento del DF serán cubiertos," *Excélsior,* March 19, 1962.

31. "Seguirá la obra constructiva de la capital: México es una ciudad sin deudas, le dijo Uruchurtu a Dubost," *Excélsior,* November 6, 1962.

32. "En 1970, no habrá problemas de agua ni transporte en el DF," *Excélsior,* August 12, 1965.

33. "Los franceses tienen plan y dinero para construir aquí un ferrocarril subterráneo," *Excélsior,* November 9, 1964.

34. Rodríguez, "La solución," p. 14.

35. "Los problemas del Distrito Federal," *Excélsior,* May 7, 1963.

36. Oliver Oldman et al., *Financing Urban Development in Mexico City,* p. 28.

37. ISTME, *Estudio completo de movimientos de personas en el primer cuadro,* p. 27.

38. Oldman et al., *Financing Urban Development,* p. 38. See also Alejandra Moreno Toscano, *Ciudad de México: ensayo de construcción de una historia.*

39. CANACINTRA, *La Cámara Nacional de la Industria de Transformación y el Consejo de Planeación Económica y Social en el DF,* pp. 3–4.

40. "No se establecerán nuevas empresas industriales en el Distrito Federal," *El Nacional,* February 14, 1964.

41. See Timothy King, *Mexico: Industrialization and Trade Policies Since 1940,* pp. 68–69; and Leopoldo Solis, *Economic Policy Reform in Mexico: A Case Study for Developing Countries,* p. 18.

42. Gustavo Garza, *El proceso de industrialización en la Ciudad de México, 1821–1979,* esp. pp. 154, 172.

43. Clark Reynolds, "Why Mexico's Stabilizing Development Was Actually Destabilizing," p. 1006.

44. Oldman et al., *Financing Urban Development,* p. 10.

45. Enrique Valencia, *La Merced: estudio ecológico y social de una zona de la Ciudad de México,* p. 20.

46. Schteingart Kaplan, "La promoción inmobiliaria." Members of Grupo Industria y Comercio's founding family, the Saenz family, were shareholders and directors of the Grupo del Valle de México, a mortgage bank whose activities centered on the development of the metropolitan area and that was directly connected with ICA's Banco del Atlántico. Grupo DESC was also linked with Grupo Industria y Comercio. Perhaps the most central node in all these connections was ICA. Grupo ICA and Grupo Industria y Comercio shared directors and joint ownership in the Banco Internacional del Fomento Urbano, S.A. (International Bank of Urban Development), whose directors and shareholders, in addition to members of the Saenz family, have included ICA's Gustavo Velasco, Julio Poulat, Luis Garcia Barbachano, and Manuel Rojo. ICA was also tied to Grupo Industria y Comercio through the Banco Internacional Inmobiliario (Real Estate Bank International).

47. José Luis Cecena is cited in "Industria: asamblea de los aliados," *Siempre*, p. 14.

48. Berta Lerner and Susana Ralsky, *El poder de los presidentes: alcances y perspectivas (1910–1973)*, p. 372; and Luis Gonzaga y Armendariz, "Díaz Ordaz, sucesor de López Mateos," p. 45.

49. According to Linda Sutherland, *Transport Planning in Mexico City*, p. 75, members of the family of Díaz Ordaz's wife were among the founding members of ICA. Guadalupe Borja de Díaz Ordaz was related to founders Angel Borja Navarette and Gilberto Borja de Navarette.

50. "Mas fuerza al 'control' público," *Política*, January 1, 1965.

51. Antonio Elizondo, "De ardor mueren los quemados y los enanos," p. 26.

52. Ibid.

53. "Uruchurtu come con los diputados," *Siempre*, July 28, 1965.

54. "Uruchurtu como el objetivo de todos los demagogos," *Siempre*, August 4, 1965.

55. Antonio McDonald, "Tratan de convertir la Ciudad de México en botín político," p. 24.

56. "La nacion: 'bulldozer' presidencial," *Política*, September 15, 1966.

57. "1700 camioneros pararon durante cuatro horas," *El Universal*, November 30, 1965.

58. "Desean los camioneros 60 pesos de salario mínimo," *Novedades*, August 30, 1965.

59. "Huelga camionera," *Política*, May 1, 1966. In Mexico the judicial system, controlled by the PRI, retains the power to determine a strike's legality.

60. "La huelga y los permisionarios," *Política*, June 1, 1966.

61. "Sugieron una sistema mixto para la administración del transporte urbano," *Excélsior*, July 19, 1966.

62. "Transporte en el Distrito Federal," *Política*, August 15, 1966.

CHAPTER SIX

1. See Roberto Newell and Luis Rubio, *The Political Origins of Mexico's Economic Crisis*; David Barkin and Gustavo Esteva, "Social Conflict and Inflation in

Mexico," who argue that growing inflation associated with stabilizing development in Mexico brought capital-labor tensions and social conflicts to a peak starting in 1968 (see esp. pp. 137–40); and Miguel Angel Rivera Rios, *Crisis y reorganización del capitalismo en México.*

2. "La sucia campaña contra Uruchurtu," *Siempre*, October 20, 1966.

3. See *Diario de los Debates*, Cámara de Diputados, September 13, 1966. Cf. Lucía Ramírez Ortiz, *Enrique Ramíez y Ramírez: obras legislativas*, p. 221.

4. Renato Leduc, "Bulldozer y diputados," p. 18.

5. After years of service as the secretary-general of the FSTSE (the National State Workers Federation, the largest single organization within the CNOP), and a term as secretary-general of the FTDF (or state workers within the Distrito Federal), Martínez Domínguez became secretary-general of the CNOP. He held the last post from 1961 to 1965, when he was appointed a congressional *diputado* to represent the CNOP.

6. Personal interview, ex-mayor Octavio Sentíes, Mexico City, July 16, 1987.

7. In their collective statement, labor leaders claimed that "Uruchurtu ha[s] not attended or resolved the social problems in the capital," in large part because he dedicated his time to primarily ornamental public works, and that "urban transport ha[s] not improved—and in fact it worsened" during his tenure. See "Cuatro centrales obreras se habían pronunciado contra la actividad de Uruchurtu," *El Día*, September 15, 1966.

8. Confederación de Trabajadores Mexicanos, "Segundo consejo nacional de la CTM: octubre 19 al 24, 1936," n.p.

9. "Uruchurtu hizo un milagro," *Siempre*, September 21, 1966.

10. Personal interview, Lic. Manuel Orijel Salazar of the CNOP, Mexico City, July 16, 1987.

11. See Lerner and Ralsky, *El poder de los presidentes*, p. 407.

12. "Deporte: el compromiso olímpico," *Política*, May 1, 1965.

13. Tarcisio Ocampo, *México, huelga de la UNAM, marzo–mayo, 1966*, v. 5, p. 316.

14. For a detailed account of middle-class student involvement, see Rafael Segovia, "The Mexican University Strike."

15. Berta Lerner and Susana Ralsky, *El poder de los presidentes*, p. 394.

16. Jacqueline Peschard, "El PRI: partido hegemónico (1946–1973)," p. 212.

17. Madrazo died mysteriously in a plane crash less than a year later, and Rector Chávez was replaced by Javier Barros Sierra, one of ICA's most prominent members. Rafael Segovia, "The Mexican University Strike," p. 314.

18. Manuel Castells, "Apuntes para un análisis de clase de la política urbana del estado mexicano," p. 1178.

19. José Antonio Rojas Loa O., "La transformación de la zona central, Ciudad de México," p. 228.

20. Alejandra Massolo, *Memoria del pedregal, memoria de mujer: testimonio de una colonia*, p. 44.

21. Rolando Cordero, "México, alternativas y contradicciones," *Siempre*, January 17, 1973.

22. Alfonso Martínez Domínguez, moreover, was "rewarded" by being named president of the PRI in early 1967 after serving one year in the Cámara de Diputados and after leading the congressional debate against Uruchurtu.

23. Mario Ojeda, *Alcánces y límites de la política exterior de México*, p. 166.

24. Sergio Zermeño, *México: una democracia utópica*, p. 40.

25. Luis Javier Garrido, "Un partido sin militantes," p. 75.

26. Leopoldo Solís, *Economic Policy Reform in Mexico: A Case Study for Developing Countries*, p. 31. Also, public expenditures under the Díaz Ordaz administration relied much more heavily on foreign imports and credit for foreign technology aid schemes than any other previous Mexican administration, thereby worsening the nation's balance of payments and fueling inflation. Rosario Green, *El endeudamiento público externo de México, 1940–1973*, esp. pp. 97–103.

27. Timothy King, *Mexico: Industrialization and Trade Policies Since 1940*, pp. 64–65.

28. Clark Reynolds, "Why Mexico's 'Stabilizing Development' Was Actually Destabilizing," p. 1008.

29. Beatríz García Peralta and Manuel Perló Cohen, "Estado, sindicalismo oficial y políticas habitacionales: análisis de una década de INFONAVIT," p. 105.

30. Lerner and Ralsky, *El poder de los presidentes*, p. 430.

31. Cf. Business International Corporation, *Mexico: Operating for Profit in a Changing World*, p. 27.

32. Ibid., p. 27.

33. Ibid.

34. Solís, *Economic Policy Reform in Mexico*, p. 44.

35. Ibid., p. 47.

36. Guillermo Ochoa, "Incoherencía en el gobierno del D.F."

37. See Judith Adler Hellman, *Mexico in Crisis*, pp. 161, 170.

38. *Quarterly Economic Review of Mexico* (July 1971): p. 31.

39. *El pulso de los sexeñios: 20 años de crísis en México*, p. 42.

40. Sanabria González also claimed that under Uruchurtu, the Consejo had a "certain authority," which it subsequently lacked under Corona del Rosal and Martínez Domínguez. "Desde 1969, el Consejo Consultivo de la Ciudad de México no ha sido tomado en cuenta," *Excélsior*.

41. Hellman, *Mexico in Crisis*, p. 161.

42. *Quarterly Economic Review of Mexico* (February 1971): pp. 2–3.

43. Hellman, *Mexico in Crisis*, pp. 163, 170.

44. "El gabinete," *Expansión*, December 16, 1970, p. 11.

45. "Ampliaron el viaducto y planean un monorriel," *El Universal*, April 1, 1971.

46. Personal interview, Pablo Sandoval, Sindicato de Profesores de la Universidad Autónoma de Guerrero, November 11, 1981. See also *Quarterly Economic Review of Mexico* (July 1974): p. 5. Echeverría and Rubén Figueroa had been friends since childhood, another relatively significant factor ensuring political relationships in Mexico.

47. "La era de obras suntuarias e innecesarias ha concluido, declaró el Regente Senties," *Novedades*, October 28, 1971.

48. "Garantía de desarrollo," *El Universal*, July 9, 1971.

49. "Más que una obra monumental, emprende Sentíes una de auxilio a los necesitados," *Novedades*, n.p.

50. "Garantía de desarrollo," *El Universal*.

51. "Preferencia a colonias pobres por encima de obras suntuarias: plan de Sentíes para el sexenio: drenaje, regularización, viviendas, escuelas, no piensa ampliar el METRO, sustituirán a La Merced," *Excélsior*, August 22, 1971.

52. "Ha tenido éxito el desalojo de los comerciantes ambulantes ordenado por el Lic. Octavio Sentíes Gomez," *El Nacional*, September 20, 1971.

53. "Más que una obra monumental," *Novedades*.

54. "El sector empresarial manifestó su apoyo a la obra para resolver problemas del D.F.," *Excélsior*, November 11, 1971.

55. Ibid.

56. "En 15 dias un plan a Echeverría para decentralizar servicios en el DF," *Excélsior*, July 21, 1971.

57. Interview with engineer Fernando Giffard of COVITUR, Mexico City, May 12, 1981. According to architect Fernando Islas (personal interview, July 27, 1981) of ISTME, the transport-planning subsidiary of ICA, part of this is explained by the fact that the director of public works during the Echeverría administration wanted to build his career as a so-called *técnico*, and thus he shunned ICA and used other contractors in order to build his own, alternative political networks.

58. This information is drawn from computer printouts obtained from ICA's construction division (Estructuras y Cimentaciones, S.A.). It does not reflect the considerable number of contracts for consulting, personnel, or equipment purchased from ICA by the Distrito Federal.

59. See Estructuras y Cimentaciones, *Obras ejecutadas*, pp. 17–33. During the Echeverría administration ICA continued to undertake government projects, but they took place primarily in other regions or for dependencies other than the Distrito Federal, and they fit more into Echeverría's shared development plans. For example, many of ICA's public contracts in this period were for the construction of new public housing and for roads, bridges, and other infrastructural projects in rural areas.

60. "Burócratas capitalinos visitaron al Regente," *Novedades*, January 12, 1972.

61. Gilbert and Ward, *Housing, the State, and the Poor*, p. 179.

62. Ibid., p. 191.

63. Beatríz García Peralta and Manuel Perló Cohen note that this change of affairs also created serious problems between Echeverría and the union bureaucracy, which had been accustomed to using party and sector structures to control housing credit and allocation for workers. "Estado, sindicalismo oficial y políticas habitacionales," p. 120.

64. Gilbert and Ward, *Housing, the State, and the Poor*, p. 191.

65. Partido Revolucionario Institucional, *Historia documental de la CNOP*, vol. 3, pp. 59–84.

CHAPTER SEVEN

1. Miguel Basañez, *El pulso de los sexenios.*

2. "Supresión de rutas y juxtapuestas y complementación de un transporte con otro, anuncia el Regente Sentíes," *Excélsior*, February 2, 1972.

3. *Quarterly Economic Review of Mexico* (April 1973): p. 7.

4. As Leopoldo Solís notes, with Echeverría's rapid reversal on spending cuts, "the priorities of his inauguration speech were submerged under the ready-to-be activated investments dear to the bureaucratic establishments; . . . agencies with a capacity to deliver had their whims fulfilled and previously-shelved programs reappeared and were upgraded and quickly improved." *Economic Policy Reform in Mexico: A Case Study for Developing Countries.*

5. Ibid., p. 201.

6. "Nuevos enfoques en obras públicas," *Expansión*, October 4, 1972, p. 22. Echeverría believed that coastal tourism would strengthen the national economy and move investment away from the capital city, thereby sustaining a more equitable regional distribution of wealth. His intent was also to encourage foreign investment and capture foreign exchange (tourism was Mexico's number-one export), which would restore some of the lost confidence of large commercial and industrial groups. It was even expected that coastal tourism would help some Mexico City capitalists too, because most foreign tourists stayed in the capital city before or after visiting coastal tourist destinations. *Quarterly Economic Review of Mexico*, January 1973, pp. 4–6.

7. Many of these new cities housed a high proportion of state-owned industries involved in capital-intensive production and served as the cornerstones of Echeverría's nationalist industrial development policy. Gustavo Garza, "El desarrollo urbano de México." Cf. Manuel Perló Cohen and Marta Schteingart Kaplan, "Movemientos sociales urbanos en México."

8. *Quarterly Economic Review of Mexico* (July 1973): p. 2; and (April 1973): p. 2.

9. Solís, *Economic Policy Reform*, p. 71.

10. "El IV informe: precisiones," *Expansión*, September 18, 1974, p. 9.

11. Personal interview, engineer Angel Alceda (ICA), Mexico City, October 1, 1981. See also Comisión Técnica de Mexicanización y Supervisión de la Construcción de los Coches del METRO, *Informe general No. 1*, January 31, 1974.

12. The French extended 1,800 million pesos in credit to the Mexican government to cover the costs of the Mexicanization of the project.

13. Each 12 kilometers of track required 102 new cars, and an extension of 12.7 kilometers of track, alone, cost the government 2.1 billion pesos. *Expansión*, October 31, 1973, p. 26; *Quarterly Economic Review of Mexico* (January 1974): p. 11.

14. Valentín Ibarra, "El Autotransporte de pasajeros en el área metropolitana de la Ciudad de México," p. 79; Dirección General de Ingeniería de Tránsito y Transportes, *Plan rector de vialidad y transporte para el Distrito Federal*, pp. 4, 75.

15. As defined by the agency that administers the METRO, the Sistema de Transporte Colectivo (STC), saturation refers to the weakness of metal parts in trains due to overcrowding.

16. Comisiones Unidas de Comunicaciones y Transportes del Distrito Federal, *Acta de la comida reunión de trabajo de las subcomisiones de hecho y análisis técnico de dictamen*, pp. 20, 25.

17. Dirección General de Estadística, *Plan rector de vialidad y transporte*. Cf. Ibarra, "El autotransporte de pasajeros," Table 9.

18. "Mexico City's METRO: Doubling in Size by 1982," *Railway Age*, October 9, 1978.

19. These numbers are derived from figures presented in Jorge Legoretta, *Transporte y contaminación en la Ciudad de México*, p. 39.

20. Alan Gilbert and Peter Ward, *Housing, the State, and the Poor*, p. 94.

21. Antonio Azuela de la Cueva, *La ciudad, la propiedad privada, y el derecho*, p. 47.

22. Gilbert and Ward, *Housing, the State, and the Poor*, p. 193.

23. Juan Manuel Ramírez, *El movimiento urbano popular en México*, pp. 62–63, 66.

24. Ibid., pp. 159–64.

25. There are two telling indicators of the contradictory and competing directions the economy followed under López Portillo. First, monetary policies were an unwieldy hybrid of money creation and foreign borrowing, a combination that weakened Mexico's economic position on two fronts simultaneously by bringing both inflation and an overvalued peso. Second, under López Portillo Mexico rejected formal entry into GATT, while at the same time liberalizing trade barriers. See Bela Balassa, "Trade Policy in Mexico," pp. 802–4.

26. Gilbert and Ward, *Housing, the State, and the Poor*, pp. 97, 167, 194.

27. Ibid., p. 95.

28. Peter Ward, *Welfare Politics in Mexico: Papering Over the Cracks*, p. 98.

29. Ibid., p. 98.

30. Gilbert and Ward, *Housing, the State, and the Poor*, p. 195.

31. Ibid., p. 195.

32. Ibid., p. 194.

33. "Optimizar la vialidad," *El Universal*, April 6, 1981.

34. "Espera el DDF," *El Universal*, January 3, 1981.

35. Patricio Iglesias, "La política financiera pública del DF, 1970–1983," p. 111.

36. Ibid., Table 2.

37. Priscilla Connolly, "Finanzas públicas y estado local," Cuadro 1.

38. Iglesias, "La política financiera pública," p. 116; Connolly, "Finanzas públicas," p. 87.

39. Manuel Perló Cohen and Marta Schteingart Kaplan, "Movimientos sociales urbanos en México," p. 120.

40. Gilbert and Ward, *Housing, the State, and the Poor*, p. 195.

41. Ibid., p. 196.

CHAPTER EIGHT

1. Alicia Ziccardi, "Problemas urbanos: proyectos y alternativas ante la crisis," pp. 58–59.

2. Convenio SEDUE-CNOP, México, August 11, 1983; cf. Ziccardi, ibid., p. 71.

3. Miguel De la Madrid, *Nacionalismo revolucionario*, p. 26.

4. Though it is true that these local delegates never had fully autonomous power to make urban policy, given the centralized power the mayor's office holds over the *delegado* system, they did hold a notable degree of influence in the neighborhood. Alan Gilbert and Peter Ward corroborate this when they claim that several of these *delegados* had actually become relatively powerful urban *caciques* over the years, thus indicating that they would indeed have much to lose with the introduction of the local legislature. *Housing, the State, and the Poor*, p. 195.

5. It is also noteworthy that Mayor Aguirre has been the only cabinet member to reject the secretary of planning and budgeting's (Programación y Presupuesto) six-year development plan. In keeping with the president's administrative decentralization and economic recovery objectives, this plan had also called for an administrative reform in Mexico City that would reallocate decision-making and investment responsibilities in the Mexico City area on the basis of economic sectors (i.e., transport, housing, etc.). Yet Aguirre adamantly opposed the plan because it suggested that major decisions made in Mexico City were to fall under the jurisdiction of the respective national cabinets, and the Mexico City mayor's office would be left only as an administrative body, with very little decision-making power.

6. Juan Manuel Ramírez names eighty-seven different urban movements as active in the Mexico City metropolitan area, and estimates that they have approximately two thousand members. *El movimiento urbano popular en México*, p. 141.

7. Personal interview, Miguel Covián Pérez, Mexico City, June 1987.

8. See S. Sánchez Vázquez, "La CTM y la renovación electoral en el D.F.," *El Día*, August 2, 1986, n.p.; and "El partido contra el presidente?" *La Jornada*, July 25, 1986, p. 2.

9. See *Quarterly Economic Review of Mexico*, 1984, p. 10; and *Comercio exterior*, February 1984, p. 1.

10. "El endeudamiento externo y la crisis en México," *Estrategia*, p. 2.

11. A 1983 survey conducted by one of Mexico's principal private financial institutions, BANAMEX, indicated that medium-sized industries in thirteen different sectors, most of which were located in Mexico City, were plagued by insufficient liquidity, lack of primary materials, high interest rates, high financing costs, and low sales. Fewer than 30 percent of these industries operated at as much as 80 percent capacity ("El endeudamiento externo," p. 2). CANACINTRA spokesmen claimed "that small and medium-sized industry were 'desperate' for credit"; and in response to CANACINTRA's demands, even government spokesmen acknowledged "that the effects [of the crisis] on business and the consumer of the fall in demand and loss of purchasing power had reached the 'limits of social sacrifice' " (*Quarterly Economic Review of Mexico*, 1984, no. 2, p. 10).

12. Cámara de Diputados, *Comparecencia de Ramón Aguirre*, p. 42.

13. F. Calzada Falcon and F. Hernández y Puente, "Mil días de deterioro," p. 22.

14. "Distribución de comestibles en la MCMA," *Unomásuno*, October 2, 1985, p. 1.

15. SIPRO, *Cronologías e indicadores internacionales y nacionales*, (1986), p. 60.

16. Ibid., p. 60.

17. *Comercio exterior*, June 1982, p. 205.

18. See Soledad Loaeza, "Las clases medias mexicanas y la coyuntura económica actual," esp. pp. 233–34; and "Las capas medias entre la espalda y la pared," *Estrategia*, pp. 54–58.

19. "La crisis en 1985: saldos y opciones," pp. 405–6.

20. Peter Ward, *Welfare Politics in Mexico*, p. 9.

21. Ricardo Hernández, *La Coordinadora Nacional de Movimientos Urbanos Populares*, p. 61.

22. *Quarterly Economic Review of Mexico*, 1984, pp. 10–14.

23. "DF: 50% de abstención y 40 triunfos del PRI," *Unomásuno*, July 15, 1985, p. 1.

24. "El PRI afronta problemas y pierde elecciones cuando selecciona a malos candidatos: CNOP," *Unomásuno*, December 18, 1985, p. 4.

25. "Proponen diputados PRIistas crear un plan nacional de participación ciudadana en casos de desastre," *Excélsior*, October 1, 1985.

26. "El próximo presidente debe ser un político y no un tecnócrata, manifestó Ardavin Miguni," *Unomásuno*, July 3, 1987, p. 8.

27. "El partido contra el presidente?" *La Jornada*, July 25, 1986.

28. SIPRO, *Cronologías e indicadores*, January 1987, p. 53; July 1987, p. 381.

29. "Se democratizará el capital con la venta de paraestatales," *Excélsior*, May 31, 1987, p. 1a.

30. SIPRO, *Cronologías e indicadores*, January 1987, p. 55.

31. Cuauhtémoc Cárdenas, *Nuestro lucha apenas comienza*, p. 146.

32. "UNE, ciudadanos en movimiento, nuevo nombre: Silvia Hernández fue reelecta al frente del sector popular," *La Jornada*, September 26, 1990, p. 6.

CHAPTER NINE

1. See Friedrich Katz, ed., *Riot, Rebellion, and Revolution: Rural Social Conflict in Mexico*; and Arturo Warman, *We Come to Object: The Peasants of Morelos and the National State*.

2. See Jose Luis Reyna, "Control político, estabilidad, y desarrollo en México"; Raul Trejo Delarbre, "The Mexican Labor Movement: 1917–1975"; James Cockcroft, *Mexico: Class Formation, Capital Accumulation, and the State*; Nora Hamilton, *The Limits to State Autonomy*; and Susan Eckstein, *The Poverty of Revolution: The State and the Urban Poor in Mexico*.

3. See Roberto Newell and Luis Rubio, *Mexico's Dilemma: The Political Origins of Economic Crisis*; and Barry Carr and Ricardo Anzaldua Montoya, eds., *The Mexican Left, the Popular Movements, and the Politics of Austerity*.

4. Daniel Cosio Villegas, *El sistema político mexicano* and *El estilo personal de gobernar*; and Jorge Carpizo, *El presidencialismo mexicano*.

5. See Peter H. Smith, *Labyrinths of Power: Political Recruitment in Twentieth-Century Mexico*; Judith A. Teichman, *Policymaking in Mexico: From Boom to Crisis*; Merillee S. Grindle, *Bureaucrats, Politicians, and Peasants in Mexico*; Roderic A. Camp, *The Making of a Government: Political Leaders in Modern Mexico*; and Daniel Levy and Gabriel Székely, eds., *Mexico: Paradoxes of Stability and Change*.

6. See Miguel Basañez, *El pulso de los sexenios: 20 años de crisis en México*.

BIBLIOGRAPHY

BOOKS AND ARTICLES

Aguirre, Carlos. "La promoción de un fraccionamiento: Santo Tomas." In *Ciudad de México: ensayo de contrucción de una historia*, edited by Alejandro Moreno Toscano. Mexico City: Instituto Nacional de Antropología e Historia, 1978.

Aguirre, Javier, et al. *El partido de la revolución: historia, estructura, y predominio del Partido Revolucionario Institucional*. Mexico City: Estudios Políticos, Económicos y Sociales del Distrito Federal (CEPES), 1985.

Alcázar, Marco A. "Las agrupaciones patronales en México." *Jornadas* 66 (1970): 15–101.

Anderson, Rodney D. *Outcasts in Their Own Land: Mexican Industrial Workers, 1906–1911*. DeKalb: Northern Illinois University Press, 1976.

Andonegui, Angel. "Meritoria labor del regente Uruchurtu." *El Universal*, January 20, 1953.

Anguiano, Arturo. *El estado y la política obrera del cardenismo*. Mexico City: Ediciones Era, 1975.

Ankerson, Dudley. "Saturnino Cedillo: A Traditional Caudillo in San Luis Potosí, 1890–1938." In *Caudillo and Peasant in the Mexican Revolution*, edited by D. A. Brading. Cambridge: Cambridge University Press, 1980.

Arac, Jonathon, and Barbara Johnson, eds. *Consequences of Theory*. Baltimore: Johns Hopkins University Press, 1991.

Araiza, Luis. *Historia del movimiento obrero mexicano*. Four volumes. Mexico City: n.p., 1964–65.

Arreola, Alvaro, et al. "Memoria: los primeros ocho días." *Revista Mexicana de Sociología* 48 (April–June 1986): 105–21.

Arriaga Lemus, María de la Luz. "Austeridad y bajos salarios, premisas de la reconversión." *Excélsior*, June 15, 1987, p. 4-M.

Arriola, Carlos, and Juan Gustavo Galindo. "Los empresarios y el estado en México (1976–1982)." *Foro Internacional* 225 (1981): 118–137.

Arroche Parra, Miguel. "Privilegiados: el gran transporte." *Excélsior*, October 3, 1981.

Aubin, Henry. *City for Sale*. Montreal: Editions l'Etincelle, 1977.

Azuela de la Cueva, Antonio. *La ciudad, la propiedad privada, y el derecho*. Mexico City: El Colegio de México, 1989.

Bailey, David C. *Viva Cristo Rey: The Cristero Rebellion and the Church-State Conflict in Mexico*. Austin: University of Texas Press, 1974.

Balassa, Bela. "Trade Policy in Mexico." *World Development* 9 (1983): 795–811.

Barbosa Cano, Favio. *La CROM: de Luis N. Morones a Antonio J. Hernández*. Puebla: Editorial Universitaria, 1980.

Barkin, David, and Gustavo Esteva. "Social Conflict and Inflation in Mexico." In *Modern Mexico: State, Economy, and Social Conflict*, edited by Nora Hamilton and Timothy Harding. Los Angeles: Sage Publications, 1986.

Bartra, Roger. *Estructura agraria y clases sociales en México*. Mexico City: Ediciones Era, 1974.

Basañez, Miguel. *La lucha por la hegemonía en México*. Mexico City: Siglo Veintiuno Ediciones, 1981.

———. *El pulso de los sexenios: 20 años de crisis en México*. Mexico City: Siglo Veintiuno, 1990.

Bassols Batalla, Narciso. *La revolución mexicana cuesta abajo*. Mexico City: Impresiones Modernas, S.A., 1960.

Bassols, Mario, and Alfredo Delgado. "La CNOP y las organizaciones de colonias." Unpublished manuscript, 1985.

Basurto, Jorge. *El proletariado industrial en México (1850–1930)*. Mexico City: Universidad Nacional Autónoma de México, 1975.

Bohrisch, Alexander, and Wolfgang Konig. *La política mexicana sobre inversiones extranjeras*. Mexico City: El Colegio de México, 1976.

Borja, Angel. "Programa del gobierno 1977–82." In *Vialidad y transporte*. Mexico City: Secretaría de Asentamiento Humano y Obras Públicas, 1976.

Brachet Márquez, Viviane. *The Pact of Domination: State, Class, and Social Reform*. Unpublished manuscript, 1990.

Brading, D. A., ed. *Caudillo and Peasant in the Mexican Revolution*. Cambridge: Cambridge University Press, 1980.

Bradenburg, Frank. *The Making of Modern Mexico*. Englewood Cliffs, N.J.: Prentice-Hall, 1974.

Bravo Ahuja Ruíz, Victor E., and Marco Antonio Michel. "Alianza de clases y dominación: México, 1930–1946." *Historia y Sociedad* 9 (1976): 31–53.

Business International Corporation. *Mexico: Business Problems and Opportunities*. New York: Business International Corporation, 1962.

———. *Mexico: Operating for Profit in a Changing Market*. New York: Business International Corporation, 1971.

Cal y Mayor, Rafael. *El transporte público en las ciudades mexicanas*. Mexico City: Dirección General de Ingeniería de Transporte y Tránsito, 1973.

Calvert, Peter. *Mexico*. New York: Praeger, 1973.

Calzado Falcón, Fernando, and Francisco Hernández y Puente. "Mil días de deterioro." *La Jornada*, June 29, 1987.

Camp, Roderic. "Education and Political Recruitment in Mexico." *Journal of Interamerican Studies and World Affairs* 18 (1976): 295–323.

———. *Intellectuals and the State in Twentieth Century Mexico*. Austin: University of Texas Press, 1985.

———. *The Making of a Government: Political Leaders in Modern Mexico*. Tucson: University of Arizona Press, 1984.

Caram, Antonio. "Campesinos víctimas de inspectores." *Novedades*, November 28, 1961.

Cárdenas, Cuauhtémoc. *Nuestra lucha apenas comienza*. Mexico City: Editorial Nuestro Tiempo, 1988.

Cardoso, Fernando Henrique, and Enzo Faletto. *Dependency and Development in Latin America*. Rev. ed. Translated by Marjory Mattingly Urquidi. Berkeley: University of California Press, 1979.

Carpizo, Jorge. *El presidencialismo mexicano*. Mexico City: Siglo Veintiuno Editores, 1979.

Carr, Barry. "The Mexican Economic Debacle and the Labor Movement: A New Era or More of the Same?" In *Modern Mexico: State, Economy, and Social Conflict*, edited by Nora Hamilton and Timothy Harding. Los Angeles: Sage Publications, 1986.

—————. *El movimiento obrero y la política en México, 1910–1929*. Volumes 1 and 2. Mexico City: Secretaría de Educación Pública, 1976.

Carr, Barry, and Ricardo Anzaldua, eds. *The Mexican Left, the Popular Movements, and the Politics of Austerity*. Monograph Series 18. La Jolla: Center for U.S.-Mexican Studies, 1986.

Castells, Manuel. "Apuntes para un análisis de clase de la política urbana del estado mexicano." *Revista Mexicana de Sociología* 39 (1977): 1161–91.

—————. *The City and the Grassroots: A Cross-Cultural Theory of Urban Social Movements*. Berkeley: University of California Press, 1983.

—————. *City, Class, and Power*. New York: St. Martin's, 1978.

—————. *Crisis urbana y cambio social*. Mexico City: Siglo Veintiuno Editores. 1981.

—————. "Is There an Urban Sociology?" In *Urban Sociology: Critical Essays*, edited by Christopher G. Pickvance. London: Tavistock Publications, 1976.

—————. *Multinational Capital, Nation-States, and Local Community*. Berkeley: Institute of Urban and Regional Research, 1979.

—————. *The Urban Question*. London: Edward Arnold Ltd., 1977.

Ceceña, José Luis. *México en la órbita imperial*. Mexico City: Ediciones El Caballito, 1978.

Chase-Dunn, Christopher. "Urbanization in the World System: New Directions for Research." In *Cities in Transformation*, edited by Michael Peter Smith. London: Sage Publications, 1984.

Chevalier, François. "The Ejido and Political Stability in Mexico." In *The Politics of Conformity in Latin America*, edited by Claudio Vélez. New York: Oxford University Press, 1967.

Cinta, Ricardo. "Burguesía nacional y desarrollo." In *El perfil de México*. 7th ed. Mexico City: Siglo Veintiuno Editores, 1980.

Clark, Marjorie Ruth. *Organized Labor in Mexico*. Chapel Hill: University of North Carolina Press, 1934.

Coatsworth, John. "Los orígines del autoritarismo moderno en México." *Foro Internacional* 16 (1975): 205–32.

Cobos, Emilio Pradilla, comp. *Democracia y desarrollo urbano en la zona metropolitana de la Ciudad de México*. Vol. 1, *Expansión de la mancha urbana*. Vol. 2, *Planeación urbana y bienestar social*. Vol. 3, *Impacto del movimiento*. Vol. 4, *Proyectos urbanos de los partidos políticos*. Vol. 5, *Cultura urbana*. Mexico City: Editorial Antártica, 1990–1991.

Cockburn, Cynthia. "The Local State Management of Cities and People." *Race and Class* 18 (Spring 1977): 363–76.

Cockcroft, James D. *Intellectual Precursors of the Mexican Revolution, 1900–1913.* Austin: University of Texas Press, 1968.

———. *Mexico: Class Formation, Capital Accumulation, and the State.* New York: Monthly Review Press, 1980.

Cohen, Michael A. *Urban Policy and Political Conflict in Africa: A Study of the Ivory Coast.* Chicago: University of Chicago Press, 1974.

Coleman, Kenneth M. "The Capital City Electorate and Mexico's Accion Nacional: Some Survey Evidence on Conventional Hypotheses." *Social Science Quarterly* 56 (1975): 503–9.

Collier, David. *Squatters and Oligarchs: Authoritarian Rule and Policy Change in Peru.* Baltimore: Johns Hopkins University Press, 1976.

———, ed. *The New Authoritarianism in Latin America.* Princeton, N.J.: Princeton University Press, 1979.

Connolly, Priscilla. "Finanzas públicas y estado local: el caso del Departamento del Distrito Federal." *Revista Azcapotzalco* 5 (1984): 57–91.

———. "Programa nacional de desarrollo urbano y vivienda, 1984: desconcentración planificada o desconcentración de carencias?" In *Una decada de planeación urbano-regional en México, 1978–1988,* edited by Gustavo Garza. Mexico City: El Colegio de México, 1989.

Connolly, Priscilla, et al. *Las políticas habitacionales del gobierno mexicano.* Mexico City: Centro Operacional de Vivienda y Poblamiento, A.C., 1977.

Contreras, Ariel José. *México 1940: industrialización y crisis política.* Mexico City: Siglo Veintiuno Editores, 1977.

Contreras Santiago, José M. *Justificación de la inversión en sistemas de transporte colectivo por el beneficio económico y social que genera: el caso de México.* Mexico City: Camara de Diputados, 1980.

Cordero, Rolando. "México, alternativas y contradicciones." *Siempre,* January 17, 1973, pp. ii–viii.

Cordero H., Salvador. "Concentración industrial y poder económico en México." *Cuadernos del CES,* Number 18. Mexico City: Centro de Estudios Sociológicos, El Colegio de México, 1977.

Cordero, Salvador, and Rafael Santin. "Los grupos industriales: una organización económica en México." *Cuadernos de CES,* Number 23. Mexico City: Centro de Estudios Sociológicos, El Colegio de México, 1977.

Córdova, Arnaldo. *La formación del poder político en México.* Mexico City: Ediciones Era, 1972.

———. *La ideología de la revolución mexicana: la formación del nuevo régimen.* Mexico City: Editorial Era, 1989.

———. *La política de masas del cardenismo.* Mexico City: Serie Popular Era, 1974.

Cornelius, Wayne, Jr. "Political Instability: The Case of Mexico." *American Political Science Review* 63 (1975): 853–59.

———. *Politics and the Migrant Poor in Mexico City.* Stanford, Calif.: Stanford University Press, 1975.

Corona Rentería, Alfonso. *La economía urbana.* Mexico City: UNAM, Instituto de Investigaciones Económicas, 1974.

Cosío Villegas, Daniel. *El estilo personal de gobernar*. Mexico City: Joaquin Mortiz, 1974.

———. *El sistema político mexicano*. Mexico City: Joaquin Mortiz, 1972.

Davis, Diane E. "The Rise and Fall of Mexico City's Subway (METRO) Policy: Pro and Anti-Urban Growth Coalitions, National Development Strategies, and the State." Ph.D. dissertation, University of California at Los Angeles, 1986.

de la Madrid, Miguel. *Los grandes problemas nacionales de hoy*. Mexico City: Editorial Diana, 1982.

———. *Nacionalismo revolucionario: siete tesis fundamentales de campaña*. Mexico City: PRI, 1982.

———. *Primer informe de gobierno*. Mexico City: Presidencia de la República, 1983.

de la Parra, Gonzalo. "Puntos de vista: primero echar a los indeseables que ya entraron, después los demás." *El Universal*, September 15, 1950.

de la Peña, Moses T. *El servicio de autobuses en el Distrito Federal*. Mexico City: Departamento del Distrito Federal, 1943.

de la Torre Villar, Ernesto. "El ferrocarril de Tacubaya." *Historia Mexicana* 35 (1987): 377–90.

———. "Notas para la historia de las comunicaciones y el trabajo en México: la Compañía de Tranvías y las luchas obreras, 1900–1945." In *Humanitas*. Mexico City: Universidad de Nuevo Leon, 1974.

Delgado Crespo, Romulo. "Valor de la tierra en tres calles típicas de la Ciudad de México." *Estudios de Valuacion*. Segunda Convención Panamericana de Valuación, Santiago, October 12–18, 1952.

DeRossi, Flavia. *The Mexican Entrepreneur*. Paris: OECD, 1971.

Díaz Arias, Julian. *La operación del METRO*. Mexico City: Sistema de Transporte Colectivo, 1978.

Domingo, Alberto. "Los enanos están de fiesta! Convierten a Uruchurtu en ogro de drama de Shakespeare." *Siempre*, September 28, 1966, pp. 8–9.

Duncan, S. S., and M. Goodwin. "The Local State and Restructuring Social Relationships: Theory and Practice." *International Journal of Urban and Regional Research* 6 (June 1982): 157–85.

Dunleavy, Patrick. *Urban Political Analyses: The Politics of Collective Consumption*. London: MacMillan Press Ltd., 1980.

Eckstein, Susan. *The Poverty of Revolution: The State and the Urban Poor in Mexico*. Princeton, N.J.: Princeton University Press, 1977.

———. "Urbanization Revisited: Inner-city Slum of Hope and Squatter Settlement of Despair." *World Development* 18 (1990): 165–81.

Edel, Matthew, and Ronald Hellman. *Cities in Crises: The Urban Challenge in the Americas*. New York: Bildner Center for Western Hemispheric Studies, 1989.

Eibenschutz, Roberto. "Evolución de la Ciudad de México." *Expansión*, October 26, 1977, pp. 130–34.

Elizondo, Antonio. "De ardor mueren los quemados y los enanos: la sistemática campaña contra Uruchurtu es producto de la ineptitud de unos y la envidia de todos." *Siempre*, July 20, 1966.

———. "Uruchurtu como objectivo de todos los demagogos." *Siempre*, August 4, 1965, pp. 12–13.

Enciclopedia de México. "METRO." Mexico City: Editorial Internacional, 1974.

Ertze Garamendi, Ramón de. "Ernesto P. Uruchurtu: regente humanista." *Siempre*, October 12, 1966.

Escalante, Alvaro. "El vía crucis de la vialidad." Cartoon in *La Prensa*, August 11, 1981, p. 50.

Espinosa Sánchez, Irma Elizabeth. "Costos del transporte urbano en la Ciudad de México." Master's thesis, Universidad Nacional Autónoma de México, 1977.

Espinoza Ulloa, Jorge. *El METRO: una solución al problema del transporte urbano.* Mexico City: Representaciones y Servicios de Ingeniería, S.A., 1975.

Evans, Peter, and Gary Gereffi. "Inversión extranjera y desarrollo dependiente: una comparación entre Brasil y México." *Revista Mexicana de Sociología* 42 (January–March 1980): 9–71.

Fainstein, Susan S., et al. *Restructuring the City.* New York: Longman Books, 1986.

Falcón Romana. *El agrarismo en Veracruz: la etapa radical (1928–1935).* Mexico City: El Colegio de México, 1977.

Fernández Boyoli, Manuel. *Lo que no sabe de la rebellión cedillista.* Mexico: Grafi Art, 1938.

Flores, Edmundo. *Tratado de economía agrícola.* Mexico City: Fondo de Cultura Económica, 1961.

Flores Olea, Victor. "Poder, legitimidad y política en México." In *El perfil de México.* 7th ed. Mexico City: Siglo Veintiuno Editores, 1980.

Flores Rico, Carlos. "Democratización del Distrito Federal." *El Dia*, July 24, 1986.

Fragoso, Juan Manuel, et al. *El poder de la gran burguesía.* Mexico City: Ediciones de Cultura Popular, 1978.

Franco, Teresa. *Ensayo sobre la historia de la Cámara Nacional de la Industria de Transformación.* Mexico City: CANACINTRA, 1980.

Friedland, Roger. *Power and Crisis in the City: Corporations, Unions, and Urban Policy.* New York: Macmillan, 1982.

Fuentes Díaz, Victor. *Los partidos políticos en México.* Vol. 3, *de Carranza a Ruíz Cortines.* 3d ed. Mexico City: Altiplano, 1956.

Gálvez, Uriel Jarquin, and Jorge Javier Romero Vadillo. *Un PAN que no se come: biografía de Accion Nacional.* Mexico City: Ediciones de Cultura Popular, 1985.

Garcia Briseño, Filberto. "Apuntes históricos sobre el movimiento obrero tranviario." *El Popular*, December 23, 1951.

García Cantú, Gastón. *El pensamiento de la reacción mexicana: historia documental, 1810–1962.* Mexico: Empresas, 1965.

García Cortés, Adrian. *La reforma urbana de México: crónica de la Comisión de Planificación.* Mexico City: Bay Gráfica y Ediciones, 1972.

———. *Urbes y pueblos.* Mexico City: La Enciclopedia Urbana, S.A., 1967.

García Mundo, Octavio. *El movimiento inquilinario de Veracruz 1922.* Mexico City: Septesentas, 1976.

García Peralta, Beatriz, and Manuel Perló Cohen. "Estado, sindicalismo oficial y políticas habitacionales: análisis de una década de INFONAVIT." In *El Obrero Mexicano.* Vol. 2. Mexico City: Siglo Veintiuno Editores, 1984.

García Rojas, Luis. "A partir de septiembre aumentará en 50% el pago por agua para industrias y comercios." *Unomásuno*, May 28, 1987, p. 10.

Garrido, Luis Javier. *El Partido de la Revolución Institucionalizada: la formación del nuevo estado en México.* Mexico City: Siglo Veintiuno Editores, 1982.

———. "Un partido sin militantes." In *La vida política mexicana en crisis*, edited by Soledad Loaeza and Rafael Segovia. Mexico City: El Colegio de Mexico, 1987.

Garza, Gustavo. "Concentración espacial de la industria en la Ciudad de México: 1930–1970." *Revista Mexicana de Sociología* 18 (1984): 3–16.

———. "Desarrollo económico, urbanización y políticas urbano-regionales en México (1900–1982)." *Demografía y Economía* 18 (1983): 157–88.

———. *Industrialización de las principales ciudades de México: hacia una estrategia espacio-sectoral de descentralización industrial.* Mexico City: El Colegio de México, 1980.

———. *El proceso de industralización en la Ciudad de México, 1821–1970.* Mexico City: El Colegio de México, 1985.

Germani, Gino. *Authoritarianism, Fascism, and National Populism.* New Brunswick, N.J.: Rutgers University Press, 1978.

Gershensen, Antonio. "Reconocimiento y evidencia de la necesidad de cambios." *La Jornada*, May 31, 1987, p. 22.

Giddens, Anthony. "Time, Space, and Regionalization." In *Social Relations and Spatial Structures*, edited by Derek Gregory and John Urry. New York: St. Martin's Press, 1985.

Gilbert, Alan, and Peter Ward. *Housing, the State, and the Poor: Policy and Practice in Three Latin American Cities.* Cambridge: Cambridge University Press, 1985.

Gil Villegas, F. "Descentralización y democracia: una perspectiva teórica. In *Descentralización y democracia en México*, edited by Blanca Torres. Mexico City: El Colegio de México, 1986.

Gómez Tagle, Silvia. *Insurgencia y democracia en los sindicatos electricistas.* Mexico City: El Colegio de México, 1980.

Gonzaga y Arméndariz, Luis. "Díaz Ordaz, sucesor de López Mateos." *Impacto*, July 29, 1981, pp. 44–46.

González Angúlo, Jorge. "Los gremios de artesanos y la estructura urbana." In *Ciudad de México: ensayo de construcción de una historia*, edited by Alejandra Moreno Toscano. Mexico City: Instituto Nacional de Antropología e Historia, 1978.

González Casanova, Pablo. *Democracy in Mexico.* New York: Oxford University Press, 1970.

———. *El estado y los partidos políticos en México.* 3d ed. Mexico City: Ediciones Era, 1986.

González Navarro, Moises. *Población y sociedad en México (1900–1970).* Vol. 1. UNAM: Serie de Estudios No. 42, 1974.

Gordon, David. "Capitalist Development and the History of American Cities." In *Marxism and the Metropolis: New Perspectives in Urban Political Economy*, edited by William Tabb and Larry Sarvers. New York: Oxford University Press, 1984.

Green, Rosario. *El endeudamiento público externo de México: 1940–1973*. Mexico City: El Colegio de México, 1976.

Gregory, Derek, and John Urry, eds. *Social Relations and Spatial Structures*. New York: St. Martin's Press, 1985.

Grindle, Merilee Serrill. *Bureaucrats, Politicians, and Peasants in Mexico: A Case Study in Public Policy*. Berkeley: University of California Press, 1977.

———, ed. *Politics and Policy Implementation in the Third World*. Princeton, N.J.: Princeton University Press, 1980.

Guadarrama, Rocío. *Los sindicatos y la política en México: la CROM (1918–1928)*. 2d ed. Mexico City: Ediciones Era, 1984.

Gulalp, Haldun. "Capital Accumulation, Classes, and the Relative Autonomy of the State." *Science and Society* 51 (1987): 287–313.

Haber, Stephen H. *Industry and Underdevelopment: The Industrialization of Mexico, 1910–1940*. Stanford, Calif.: Stanford University Press, 1989.

Hamer, Andrew Marshall. *The Selling of Rail Rapid Transit*. Lexington, Mass.: Lexington Books, 1976.

Hamilton, Nora. *The Limits of State Autonomy: Postrevolutionary Mexico*. Princeton, N.J.: Princeton University Press, 1984.

———. "The State and Class Conflict During the Cárdenas Period." In *Classes, Class Conflict, and the State*, edited by Maurice Zeitlin. Cambridge: Winthrop, 1980.

Hansen, Roger D. *The Politics of Mexican Development*. Baltimore: Johns Hopkins University Press, 1971.

Hart, John Mason. *Anarchism and the Mexican Working Class, 1860–1931*. Austin: University of Texas Press, 1978.

———. *Revolutionary Mexico: The Coming and Process of the Mexican Revolution*. Berkeley: University of California Press, 1987.

Harvey, David. *The Urbanization of Capital: Studies in the History and Theory of Capitalist Urbanization*. Baltimore: Johns Hopkins University Press, 1985.

———. "The Urban Process Under Capitalism: A Framework for Analysis." *International Journal of Urban and Regional Research* 2 (1978): 101–31.

Hellman, Judith Adler. *Mexico in Crisis*. New York: Holmes and Meyer, 1978.

Hernández S., Ricardo. *La Coordinadora Nacional del Movimiento Urbano Popular (CONAMUP): su historia 1900–1986*. Mexico City: Equipo Pueblo, 1987.

Hernández Gutiérrez, Ignacio. "La burguesia comercial nativa y el capital extranjero." In *La burguesía mexicana*, edited by Ramiro Reyes Esparza et al. Mexico City: Editorial Nuestro Tiempo, S.A., 1973.

Hirsch, Joaquim. "The State Apparatus and Social Reproduction: Elements of a Theory of the Bourgeois State." In *State and Capital: A Marxist Debate*, edited by J. Holloway and S. Picciotto. London: Edward Arnold, 1978.

Hodgson, J. L., F. W. Schloesser, and W. Z. Bairey, eds. "Selected Papers on the Mexican and International Economies from 1966 to 1968 by Redvers Opie." *Tlatelolco Economic Monographs*, Tianguisco Series 1 (November 1968).

Huacuya, Mario, and José Woldenberg. *Estado y lucha política en el México actual*. Mexico City: Ediciones El Caballito, 1976.

Ibarra, Valentín. "El autotransporte de pasajeros en el área metropolitana de la Ciudad de México." Master's thesis, El Colegio de México, 1981.

Iglesias, Patricio. "La política financiera pública del DF, 1970–1983." *Revista Azcapotzalco* 6 (1985): 107–23.

Jacobs, Ian. "Rancheros of Guerrero: The Figueroa Brothers and the Revolution." In *Caudillo and Peasant in the Mexican Revolution*, edited by D. A. Brading. New York: Cambridge University Press, 1980.

Jeux, Alain. "La SOFRETU et la Cooperation Technique dans les Transports Urbains." *Revue Général de Chemins de Fer* 52 (March 1983): 139–44.

Johnson, Kenneth F. "Mexico's Authoritarian Presidency." In *Presidential Power in Latin American Politics*, edited by T. DiBacc. New York and London: Praeger, 1977.

Juárez González, Leticia. "La organización empresarial en México durante el cardenismo: implicaciones internas e internacionales." Master's thesis, Universidad Nacional Autónoma de México, 1983.

Kandell, Jonathan. *La Capital: The Biography of Mexico City*. New York: Random House, 1986.

Katz, Friedrich. "Pancho Villa, Peasant Movements and Agrarian Reform in Northern Mexico." In *Caudillo and Peasant in the Mexican Revolution*, edited by D. A. Brading. New York: Cambridge University Press, 1980.

———, ed. *Riot, Rebellion, and Revolution: Rural Social Conflict in Mexico*. Princeton, N.J.: Princeton University Press, 1988.

Katznelson, Ira. *City Trenches: Urban Politics and the Patterning of Class in America*. New York: Pantheon Books, 1981.

———. *Marxism and the City*. New York and London: Oxford University Press, 1992.

King, Timothy. *Mexico: Industrialization and Trade Policies since 1940*. New York: Oxford University Press, 1970.

Knight, Alan. *The Mexican Revolution*. Vol. 1, *Porfirians, Liberals, and Peasants*. Vol. 2, *Counter-Revolution and Reconstruction*. Cambridge: Cambridge University Press, 1986.

———. "Peasant and Caudillo in Revolutionary Mexico." In *Caudillo and Peasant in the Mexican Revolution*, edited by D. A. Brading. New York: Cambridge University Press, 1980.

Krause, Enrique. *Historia de la Revolución Mexicana*. Mexico City: El Colegio de México, 1977.

Krieger, Ronald. *Mexico: An Economic Survey*. New York: First National Bank, 1971.

Labastida Martin del Campo, Julio. "Los grupos dominantes frente a las alternativas de cambio." In *El perfil de México*. 7th ed. Mexico City: Siglo Veintiuno Editores, 1980.

———. "Proceso político y dependencia en México (1970–1976)." *Revista Mexicana de Sociología* 39 (January–March 1977): 193–227.

Lajous, Alejandra. *Los orígines del partido único en México*. Mexico City: Universidad Nacional Autónoma de México, 1979.

Larrosa, Manuel. *Marío Pani: arquitecto de su época*. Mexico City: Universidad Nacional Autónoma de México, Facultad de Arquitectura, 1985.

Leal, Juan Felipe. "The Mexican State, 1915–1973: An Historical Interpretation." In *Modern Mexico: State, Economy, and Social Conflict*, edited by Nora Hamilton and Timothy F. Harding. Los Angeles: Sage Publishers, 1986.

———. *México: estado, burocracia y sindicatos*. Mexico City: Ediciones El Caballito, 1985.

Leduc, Renato. "Bulldozers y diputados." *Siempre*, September 21, 1966, p. 18.

———. "Esta monstruosa ciudad: culpa de quién?" *Siempre*, October 12, 1966, p. 30.

Legoretta, Jorge. *Transporte y contaminación en la Ciudad de México*. Mexico City: Centro de Ecodesarrollo, 1989.

Lerner de Sheinbaum, Berta, and Susana Ralsky de Cimet. *El poder de los presidentes: alcances y perspectivas (1910–1973)*. Mexico City: Instituto Mexicano de Estudios Políticos, A.C., 1976.

Levy, Daniel, and Gabriel Székely. *Mexico: Paradoxes of Stability and Change*. Boulder, Colo.: Westview Press, 1987.

Loaeza, Soledad. "Las clases medias mexicanas y la coyuntura económica actual." In *México ante la crisis: el impacto social y cultural de las alternativas*, edited by Pablo González Casanova. Mexico City: Siglo Veintiuno Editores, 1986.

———. *Clases medias y política en México*. Mexico City: El Colegio de México, 1988.

Looney, Robert E. *Development Alternatives of Mexico*. New York: Praeger, 1982.

———. *Economic Policy Making in Mexico: Factors Underlying the 1982 Crisis*. Durham, N.C.: Duke University Press, 1985.

López Monjardín, Adriana. "El espacio en la producción: Ciudad de México, 1850." In *Ciudad de México: ensayo de construcción de una historia*, edited by Alejandra Moreno Toscano. Mexico City: Instituto Nacional de Antropología e Historia, 1978.

Mabry, Donald J. *Mexico's Acción Nacional: A Catholic Alternative to Revolution*. Syracuse, N.Y.: Syracuse University Press, 1974.

McDonald Vargas, Antonio. "Un día de luto para el pueblo: de fiesta para tanto autorizado." *Siempre*, October 5, 1966, p. 24.

———. "Tratan de convertir la ciudad en botín político." *Siempre*, November 24, 1965.

Márquez Fuentes, Manuel, and Octavio Rodríguez Araujo. *El Partido Comunista Mexicano*. Mexico City: Ediciones El Caballito, 1973.

Martínez Assad, Carlos, and Alicia Ziccardi. "El municipio libre: entre la sociedad y el estado." *Revista Mexicana de Sociología* 48 (1986): 7–51.

Martínez de la Vega, Francisco. "Signos de la época: el trabajo al día; la renuncia lista." *Siempre*, October 5, 1966.

Marván Laborde, Ignacio. "La dificultad del cambio." In *El partido en el poder: seis ensayos*. Mexico City: Partido Revolucionario Institucional–IEPES, 1990.

———. "Evolución de la competencia electoral en el Distrito Federal." Paper presented at the annual meeting of the Latin American Studies Association, Washington, D.C., April 1991.

Massolo, Alejandra. *Memoria del Pedregal, memoria de mujer: testimonio de una colonia*. Mexico City: Mujeres Para el Diálogo, 1988.

———. "Que el gobierno entienda, lo primero es la vivienda!" *Revista Mexicana de Sociología* 48 (April–June 1986): 195–239.

Medina Peña, Luis. *Del cardenismo al avilacamachismo. Historia de la Revolución Mexicana*. Mexico City: El Colegio de México, 1976.

Medina Valdés, Gerardo. "El Metro: tarde o temprano tronarán las tarifas políticas." *El Diario de México*, August 27, 1981, p. 8.

Mejiás, José Luis. "Municipalizar." *Excélsior*, October 14, 1981, p. 1A.

Mendez Lugo, Bernardo. "Desarrollo e industrialización subordinada en México." Master's thesis, Ciencias Políticas y Sociales, Universidad Nacional Autónoma de México, 1976.

Meyer, Jean. *La Cristiada*. 3 vols. Mexico City: Siglo Veintiuno Editores, 1974.

———. "Los obreros en la revolución mexicana: los batallones rojos." *Historia Mexicana* 81 (July–September 1971): 1–38.

———. *Le sinarquisme: Un fascisme mexicain?* Paris: Libraire Hachette, 1977.

Michaels, Albert L. "Las elecciones de 1940." *Historia Mexicana* 21 (July–September 1971): 80–134.

Miliband, Ralph. *The State in Capitalist Society*. New York: Basic Books, 1969.

Millon, Robert Paul. *Mexican Marxist: Vicente Lombardo Toledano*. Chapel Hill: University of North Carolina Press, 1966.

Mills, C. Wright. *The Power Elite*. New York: Oxford University Press, 1956.

Mollenkopf, John. *The Contested City*. Princeton, N.J.: Princeton University Press, 1983.

Molotch, Harvey. "City as a Growth Machine: Toward a Political Economy of Place." *American Journal of Sociology* 82 (1976): 309–32.

Molotch, Harvey, and John Logan. *Urban Fortunes: The Political Economy of Place*. Berkeley: University of California Press, 1987.

Montero Zendejas, Daniel. *Estado, democracia y partido*. Mexico City: B. Costa-Amic Editorial, 1979.

Morales, Mariá Dolores. "La expansión de la Ciudad de México en el siglo XIX: el caso de los fraccionamentos." In *Ciudad de México: ensayo de construcción de una historia*, edited by Alejandra Moreno Toscano. Mexico City: Instituto Nacional de Antropología e Historia, 1978.

Moreno Toscano, Alejandro. *Ciudad de México: ensayo de construcción de una historia*. Mexico City: Instituto Nacional de Antropología e Historia, 1978.

———. "La crisis en la ciudad." In *México hoy*, edited by Pablo González Casanova and Enrique Flores. Mexico City: Siglo Veintiuno Editores, 1979.

Mosk, Sanford. *Industrial Revolution in Mexico*. Berkeley and Los Angeles: University of California Press, 1954.

Muñoz, Hilda. *Lázaro Cárdenas: síntesis de su campaña presidencial*. Mexico City: Fondo de Cultura Económica, 1976.

Murray, Robin. "The Internationalization of Capital and the Nation-State." *New Left Review* (May–June 1971): 84–109.

Navarro, Bernardo, and Ovidio González. *Metro, metrópoli, México*. Mexico City: UNAM-Xochimilco, 1989.

Needler, Martin C. *Mexican Politics: The Containment of Conflict.* New York: Praeger, 1982.

Newell, Roberto, and Luis Rubio. *Mexico's Dilemma: The Political Origins of Economic Crisis.* Boulder, Colo.: Westview Press, 1984.

Novo, Salvador. "Caballos, calles, trato, cumplimiento . . ." In *Seis siglos de la Ciudad de México,* edited by Salvador Novo. Mexico City: Fondo de Cultura Económica, 1974.

Ocampo, Tarcisio. *México, huelga de la UNAM, marzo–mayo, 1966.* 5 vols. Cuernavaca, Mexico: Centro Intercultural de Documentación, 1976.

———, ed. *Los médicos y la socialización de la medicina: documentatos y reacciones de prensa.* Cuernavaca, Mexico: Centro Intercultural de Documentación Dossier No. 18, 1968.

———, and Humberto Jurando. *México: reeleción de diputados 1964–1965, reacciones de prensa.* Cuernavaca, Mexico: Centro Intercultural de Documentación Dossier No. 29, 1969.

Ochoa, Guillermo. "Incoherencia en el gobierno del D.F." *Excélsior,* July 21, 1976.

Ojeda, Mario. *Alcances y límites de la política exterior de México.* Mexico City: El Colegio de México, 1976.

Oldman, Oliver, Henry T. Aaron, Richard M. Bird, and Stephen L. Kass. *Financing Urban Development in Mexico City.* Cambridge, Mass.: Harvard University Press, 1967.

Padgett, L. Vincent. *The Mexican Political System.* New York: Houghton Mifflin, 1976.

Paoli Bolio, Francisco J. "El cambio de presidente: elecciones mexicanas de 1976." *Revista Mexicana de Sociología* 41 (January–March 1979): 325–52.

Paz, Octavio. *The Labyrinth of Solitude.* New York: Grove Press, 1985.

Perló Cohen, Manuel. "Apuntes para una interpretación en torno al proceso de acumulación capitalista y las políticas urbanas del Distrito Federal, 1920–1980." Mimeo, Instituto de Investigaciones de la UNAM, 1981.

———. "El cardenismo y la Ciudad de México: historia de un conflicto." Paper presented at the seminar "México: 1931–1980," Coordinacion de Humanidades, UNAM, March 1988.

———. "De como perdió la Ciudad de México su municipalidad sin obtener en cambio ni una democracia de manzana." *Siempre,* July 2, 1980.

———. *Estado, vivienda y estructura urbana en el cardenismo.* Instituto de Investigaciones Sociales: UNAM, 1981.

———. "Política y vivienda en México, 1910–1952." Mimeo, Instituto de Investigaciones Sociales de Sociales de la UNAM, 1981.

———, and Marta Schteingart Kaplan. "Movimientos sociales urbanos en México." *Revista Mexicana de Sociología* 46 (1984): 105–27.

Perez Lopez, Enrique. "The National Product of Mexico: 1895 to 1964." In *Mexico's Recent Economic Growth: The Mexican View,* edited by Enrique Perez Lopez. Austin: University of Texas Press, 1967.

Perez Montfort, Ricardo. *Los empresarios alemanes, el Tercer Reich, y la oposición a Cárdenas.* Master's thesis, El Colegio de México, 1984.

Peschard, Jacqueline. "El PRI: partido hegemónico (1946–1973)." In *El partido en el poder: seis ensayos*. Mexico City: PRI-IEPES, Publicaciones Mexicanas, 1990.

Pineda Palacios, Jorge. *CANACINTRA: semblanza histórica, 1941–1985*. Mexico City: CANACINTRA, 1986.

Piñeiro, José Luis. *Structure of Power and Rules of the Political Game in Mexico*. Mexico City: Instituto de Investigaciones Sociales, Universidad Nacional Autonoma de México, 1980.

Pred, Alan. *Constructing Human Geographies: The Local Transformations of Practice, Power Relations, and Consciousness*. Boulder, Colo.: Westview Press, 1990.

Polsby, Nelson W. *Community, Power, and Political Theory*. New Haven, Conn.: Yale University Press, 1963.

Poniatowska, Elena. *La noche de Tlatelolco*. Mexico City: Editorial Era, 1971.

Portes, Alejandro, and John Walton. *Labor, Class, and the International System*. New York: Academic Press, 1981.

———. *Urban Latin America: The Political Condition from Above and Below*. Austin: University of Texas Press, 1976.

Portes Gil, Emilio. *Quince años de política mexicana*. Mexico City: Editorial Botas, 1954.

Puig Cassauranc, Jose Manuel. *La galetea rebelde a varios pigmaleones: de Obregón a Calles*. Mexico: Impresores Unidos, 1938.

Purcell, John F. H., and Susan K. Purcell. "Machine Politics and Socio-Economic Change in Mexico." In *Contemporary Mexico*, edited by J. Wilkie, M. Meyer, and E. Monzon de Wilkie. Berkeley: University of California Press, 1976.

Purcell, Susan K. *The Mexican Profit-Sharing Decision: Politics in an Authoritarian Regime*. Berkeley: University of California Press, 1975.

———, and John F. H. Purcell. "Community Power and Benefits from the Nation: The Case of Mexico." In *Latin American Urban Research*, edited by F. Rabinovitz and F. Trueblood. Beverly Hills, Calif.: Sage Publications, 1973.

Quarterly Review of Mexico. London: The Economist Intelligence Unit. No. 1 (February 1971); No. 3 (July 1971); No. 1 (January 1973); No. 1 (January 1974); No. 3 (July 1974); No. 1 (1983); Nos. 2, 10, 11 (February, October, November 1984).

Quijano, Anibal. "Dependencia, cambio social y urbanización en latinoamérica." *Revista Mexicana de Sociología* 30 (1969).

Ramírez, Juan Manuel. *La ley general de asentamientos humanos: carácter y contradicciones*. Master's thesis, Universidad Nacional Autónoma de México, 1980.

———. *El movimiento urbano popular en México*. Mexico City: Siglo Veintiuno Editores, 1986.

Ramírez Ortiz, Lucía. *Enrique Ramírez y Ramírez: obras legislativas*. Mexico City: Editorial Popular de los Trabajadores, 1982.

Rangel, José Calixto. "La clase media en 1980." In *El perfil de México*. 7th ed. Mexico City: Siglo Veintiuno Editores, 1980.

———. *La pequeña burguesía en la sociedad mexicana, 1895–1960*. Mexico City: Instituto de Investigaciones Sociales, UNAM, 1972.

Rebolledo Gout, Juan. *Participación ciudadana en el gobierno del Distrito Federal*. Mexico City: INEHRM, 1987.

Reyes Rios, Fernando. "Aspectos generales del servicio de autotransporte urbano de pasajeros en la Ciudad de México." Master's thesis, Universidad Nacional Autónoma de México, 1963.

Reyna, José Luis. *Control político, estabilidad y desarrollo.* Centro de Estudios Sociológicos, El Colegio de México, 1974 (Cuadernos de CES #3).

————. *An Empirical Analysis of Political Mobilization: The Case of Mexico.* Ithaca, N.Y.: Cornell University Press, 1971.

————. "Movilización y participación política: discusión de algunas hipótesis para el caso mexicano." in *El perfil de México.* 7th ed. Mexico City: Siglo Veintiuno Editores, 1980.

————. "El movimiento obrero en 1952–1964." *Historia de la Revolucion Mexicana.* Mexico City: El Colegio de México, 1978.

Reynolds, Clark. *The Mexican Economy: 20th Century Structure and Growth.* New Haven, Conn.: Yale University Press, 1970.

————. "Why Mexico's 'Stabilizing Development' Was Actually Destabilizing (With Some Implications for the Future)." *World Development* 6 (1978): 1005–18.

Rivera Castro, José. *La clase obrera en la historia de México.* Vol. 8. Mexico City: Instituto de Investigaciones Sociales, UNAM, 1983.

Rivera Ríos, Miguel Angel. *Crisis y reorganización del capitalismo mexicano: 1960–1985.* Mexico City: Ediciones Era, 1986.

Rivera Urrutia, Eugenio, and Ana Sojo. "Movimiento popular, conflicto social, y democracia." *Revista Mexicana de Sociología* 47 (October–December 1985): 17–38.

Robles, Gonzalo. "El desarrollo industrial." In *México: cincuenta años de revolución.* Vol. 1, *La Economía.* Mexico: Fondo de Cultura Económica, México, 1960.

Rodríguez, Antonio. "La solución: el METRO o el monorriel?" *Siempre*, September 1, 1965, pp. 14–15.

Rodríguez, Miguel. *Los tranviarios y el anarquismo en México (1920–25).* Puebla, Mexico: ICUAP, 1978.

Rodríguez Piña, Jaime. "Venta de inmuebles en la Ciudad de México, 1850–1852." In *Ciudad de México: ensayo de construcción de una historia*, edited by Alejandra Moreno Toscana. Mexico City: Instituto Nacional de Antropología e Historia, 1978.

Rodríguez Salas, J. "Finanzas públicas y política urbana en el DF. CONAMUP-UAG." *Testimonios* 1 (May 1983): 89–101.

Rojas Loa O., José Antonio. "La transformación de la zona central, Ciudad de México, 1930–1970." In *Ciudad de México: ensayo de construcción de una historia*, edited by Alejandra Moreno Toscana. Mexico City: Instituto Nacional de Antropología e Historia, 1978.

Rojas Nieto, J. Antonio. "Algunas implicaciones sociales de la estrategia económico-social del regimen." In *México ante la crisis: el impacto social y cultural de las alternativas*, edited by Pablo González Casanova. Mexico City: Siglo Veintiuno Editores, 1986.

Romero, Héctor Manuel. *Historia del transporte en la Ciudad de México: de la trajinera al METRO.* Mexico City: Secretaría General de Desarrollo Social, 1987.

Roxborough, Ian. "Mexico: The Charrazo of 1940." In *Crisis and Containment in Latin America, 1944–1948*, edited by Leslie Bethell and Ian Roxborough. Cambridge: Cambridge University Press, 1992.

———. *Unions and Politics in Mexico*. Cambridge: Cambridge University Press, 1984.

Rueschemeyer, Dietrich, and Peter Evans. "The State and Economic Transformation: Toward an Analysis of the Conditions Underlying Effective Intervention." In *Bringing the State Back In*, edited by Peter Evans et al. Cambridge: Cambridge University Press, 1985.

Ruiz, Ramón Eduardo. *Labor and the Ambivalent Revolutionaries: Mexico, 1911– 1923*. Baltimore: Johns Hopkins University Press, 1976.

Ruíz Massieu, José F. *Fuentes legales de financiamiento a la vivienda popular*. Mexico City: INFONAVIT, 1976.

Russell, Philip. *Mexico in Transition*. Austin, Tex.: Colorado River Press, 1977.

Salazar, Rosendo. *Historia de las luchas proletarias en México: 1923–1946*. México City: Ediciones Avante, 1956.

———. *Las pugnas de la gleba*. Mexico City: Partido Revolucionario Institucional, Comisión Nacional Editorial, 1972.

Saldaña, Adalberto. *El estado en la sociedad mexicana: filosofía, estructura, influencia, y perspectivas del estado*. Mexico City: Editorial Porrúa, S.A., 1981.

Saldívar, Américo. *Ideología y práctica del estado mexicano: el conflicto estado-iniciativa privada, 1970–1976*. Mexico City: Universidad Nacional Autónoma de México, 1981.

Sánchez Vásquez, Salvador. "La CTM y la renovación electoral en el Distrito Federal." *El Día*, August 2, 1986.

Saunders, Peter. *Urban Policies: A Sociological Interpretation*. London: Hutchinson, 1979.

Sayer, Andrew. "The Difference that Space Makes." In *Social Relations and Spatial Structures*, edited by Derek Gregory and John Urry. New York: St. Martin's Press, 1985.

———. "The New Regional Geography and Problems of Narrative." *Environment and Planning* 7 (1989): 253–76.

Schers, David. *El sector popular del PRI*. Master's thesis, El Colegio de México, 1973.

Schmitter, Philippe C. "Still the Century of Corporatism." In *The New Corporatism: Social Political Structures in the Iberian World*, edited by F. Pike and T. Stritch. Notre Dame, Ind.: University of Notre Dame Press, 1974.

Schteingart Kaplan, Marta. *Los productores del espacio habitable: estado, empresa y sociedad en la Ciudad de México*. Mexico City: El Colegio de México, 1989.

———. "La promoción inmobilaria en el área metropolitana de la Ciudad de México, (1960–1980): articulaciones entre prácticas privadas y públicas en la producción de vivienda." Working paper, El Colegio de México, 1981.

———. "Sector inmobiliario capitalista y formas de apropiación del suelo urbano: el caso de México." *Demografía y Economía* 13 (1979): 449–67.

Secretaría de Patrimonio Nacional. *Encuesta nacional de hogares: área metropolitana de la Ciudad de México, 1976*. Mexico City: Estados Unidos Mexicanos, 1977.

Segovia, Rafael. "The Mexican University Strike." In *Political Power in Latin America: Seven Confrontations*, edited by R. Fagen and W. Cornelius. Englewood Cliffs, N.J.: Prentice-Hall, 1970.

———. "La reforma política." *Foro International* 14 (January–March 1974): 314–16.

Shafer, Robert J. *Mexico: Mutual Adjustment Planning*. Syracuse, N.Y.: Syracuse University Press, 1966.

Shulgovsky, Anatol. *México en la encrucijada de la historia*. México City: Ediciones de Cultura Popular, 1968.

Silva, Fernando. "Planeación regional y descentralización." In *Descentralización y democracia en México*, edited by Blanca Torres. Mexico City: El Colegio de México, 1988.

SIPRO. *Cronología e indicadores internacionales y nacionales: síntesis de prensa mensual*. Mexico City: Servicios de Prensa Procesados, A.C., 1986–1987.

Sirvent, Carlos. "La burocracia política central en el sistema de dominación mexicano." Ph.D. diss., Universidad Nacional Autónoma de México, 1975.

Smith, Michael P. *The City and Social Theory*. New York: St. Martin's Press, 1979.

Smith, Peter H. *Labyrinths of Power: Political Recruitment in Twentieth Century Mexico*. Princeton, N.J.: Princeton University Press, 1979.

Soja, Edward W. *Post-Modern Geographies: The Reassertion of Space in Critical Social Theory*. London: Routledge and Kegan Paul, 1987.

———. "The Spatiality of Social Life: Towards a Transformative Retheorisation." In *Social Relations and Spatial Structures*, edited by Derek Gregory and John Urry. New York: St. Martin's Press, 1985.

Solís, Leopoldo. *Economic Policy Reform in Mexico: A Case Study for Developing Countries*. New York: Pergamon Press, 1981.

Stevens, Evelyn P. *Protest and Response in Mexico*. Cambridge, Mass.: MIT Press, 1974.

Storper, Michael, and Richard Walker. *The Capitalist Imperative: Territory, Technology, and Industrial Growth*. New York: Basil Blackwell, 1989.

Story, Dale. *Industry, the State, and Public Policy in Mexico*. Austin: University of Texas Press, 1986.

Sutherland, Linda. "Transport Planning in Mexico City." Master's thesis, University College, London, 1978.

Swanstrom, Todd. *The Crisis of Growth Politics*. Philadelphia: Temple University Press, 1985.

Tamayo, Jaime. *La clase obrera en la historia de México*. Vol. 7. Mexico City: Instituto de Investigaciones Sociales, 1987.

Tannenbaum, Frank. *Peace by Revolution*. New York: Columbia University Press, 1933.

Taylor, Lance. "Mexico's Adjustment in the 1980's: Look Back Before Leaping Ahead." In *Adjustment Crisis in the Third World*, edited by R. Flinberg and V. Kallab. New Brunswick, N.J.: Transaction Books, 1984.

Ten Kate, Adrian, and Robert B. Wallace. *Protection and Economic Development in Mexico*. New York: St. Martin's Press, 1980.

Tello, Carlos. *La política económica en México, 1970–1976.* Mexico City: Siglo Veintiuno Editores, 1979.

———. "La crisis en 1985: saldos y opciones. In *México ante la crisis: el impacto social y cultural de las alternativas,* edited by Pablo González Casanova. Mexico City: Siglo Veintiuno Editores, 1986.

Tenorio, Jesus Paolo. "Se sigue hundiendo la Ciudad de México?" *Revista Comercio* 22 (April 1981): 244.

Timberlake, Michael, ed. *Urbanization in the World Economy.* Orlando, Fla.: Academic Press, 1985.

Timberlake, Michael, and Jeffrey Kentor. "Economic Dependence, Overurbanization, and Economic Growth: A Study of Less Developed Countries." *Sociological Quarterly* 24 (1983): 489–508.

Torrealba, Luis Leon. "Mexico City's METRO: Subway Construction Begins." *Headlights* 29 (August 1967): 12.

Trejo Delarbre, Raul. "The Mexican Labor Movement, 1917–1975." In *Modern Mexico: State, Economy, and Social Conflict,* edited by Nora Hamilton and Timothy Harding. Los Angeles: Sage Publishers, 1986.

Turner, Frederick C. "Mexican Politics: The Direction of Development." In *Críticas constructivas del sistema político mexicano,* edited by W. Galde and S. Ross. Austin: University of Texas, Institute of Latin American Studies, 1973.

Unikel, Luis, Crescencio Ruiz Chiapetto, and Gustavo Garza Villareal. *El desarrollo urbano de México: diagnóstico e implicaciones futuras.* Mexico City: El Colegio de México, 1976.

Unger, Kurt. "México: transferencia de tecnología y estructura industrial." In *Libros del CIDE.* Mexico City: Centro de Investigaciones de Demografía y Economiá, El Colegio de México, 1984.

Unzueta Lorenzana, Gerardo. *Testimonio ante la comisión de dictamen de las comisiones unidas del Distrito Federal de comunicaciones y transportes.* República de México: Camara de Diputados, 1980.

———. "Intervención de Gerardo Unzueta." *Oposición,* October 5, 1980, pp. 4–5.

Urry, John. "Localities, Regions and Social Class." *International Journal of Urban and Regional Research* 5 (1981): 455–75.

———. "Social Relations, Space, and Time." In *Social Relations and Spatial Structures,* edited by Derek Gregory and John Urry. New York: St. Martin's Press, 1985.

———. "Some Notes on Realism and the Analysis of Space." *International Journal of Urban and Regional Research* 7 (1983): 122–29.

Valencia, Enrique. *La merced: estudio ecológico y social de una zona de la Ciudad de México.* Mexico City: Instituto Nacional de Antropología e Historia, Universidad Nacional Autónoma de México, 1965.

Van Ginneken, Wouter. *Socio-Economic Groups and Income Distribution in México.* New York: St. Martin's Press, 1980.

Vellinga, Menno. *Economic Development and the Dynamics of Class: Industrialization, Power, and Control in Monterrey, Mexico.* Amsterdam: Van Gorcum and Company, 1979.

Vernon, Raymond. *The Dilemma of Mexico's Development: The Roles of the Private and Public Sectors.* Cambridge: Harvard University Press, 1963.

Vidrio C., Manuel. "Sistemas de transporte y expansión urbana: los tranvías." In *Ciudad de México: ensayo de construcción de una historia*, edited by Alejandra Moreno Toscano. Mexico City: Instituto Nacional de Antropología e Historia, 1978.

Villa, Manuel. "Las bases del estado mexicano y su problemática actual." In *El perfil de México*. 7th ed. Mexico City: Siglo Veintiuno Editores, 1980.

Villegas, Victor Manuel. *Un pleito tristemente célebre en la Ciudad de México en el siglo XX*. Toluca, Mexico: Biblioteca de Cooperación Universitaria, S.A., 1979.

Viniegra, Salazar. *Problemas del transporte en el Distrito Federal*. Mexico City: Banco de México, 1950.

Walsh, M. W., and S. K. Witcher. "As Debt Turmoil Ebbs and Flows in Mexico, Human Misery Persists." *Wall Street Journal*, June 12, 1986, p. 1.

Walton, John. *Elites and Economic Development: Comparative Studies in the Political Economy of Latin American Cities*. Austin: University of Texas Press, 1977.

Ward, Peter. "Political Pressure for Urban Services: The Response of Two Mexico City Administrations." *Development and Change* 12: 379–407.

———. *Welfare Politics in Mexico: Papering Over the Cracks*. Boston: Allen and Unwin, 1986.

Warman, Arturo. *We Come to Object: The Peasants of Morelos and the National State*. Baltimore: Johns Hopkins University Press, 1980.

Wasserman, Mark. *Capitalists, Caciques, and Revolution: The Native Elite and Foreign Enterprise in Chihuahua*. Chapel Hill: University of North Carolina Press, 1984.

Whitt, J. Allen. *Urban Elites and Mass Transportation: The Dialectics of Power*. Princeton, N.J.: Princeton University Press, 1982.

Wilkie, James W. *The Mexican Revolution: Federal Expenditures and Social Change Since 1910*. Berkeley: University of California Press, 1970.

Womack, John, Jr. *Zapata and the Mexican Revolution*. New York: Alfred A. Knopf, 1969.

Yáñez Reyes, Sergio L. *Génesis de la burocracia sindical cetemista*. Mexico City: Ediciones El Caballito, S.A., 1984.

Zabludovsky, Jacobo. "El gobierno del Distrito Federal." *Novedades*, October 27, 1964.

Zazueta, Cesar, and Ricardo de la Pena. *La estructura del Congreso del Trabajo*. Mexico City: FCE, 1984.

Zeitlin, Maurice. *The Civil Wars in Chile (Or the Bourgeois Revolutions that Never Were)*. Princeton, N.J.: Princeton University Press, 1986.

Zepeda M., and J. Marco. "El Reto inflacionario." *Unomásuno*, Suplemento Político, June 28, 1987, p. 2.

Zermeño, Sergio. *México: Una democracia utópica*. Mexico City: Siglo Veintiuno Editores, 1978.

Ziccardi, Alicia. "Grandes obras en la Ciudad de México." In *Una década de planeación urbano-regional en México: 1978–1988*, edited by Gustavo Garza. Mexico City: El Colegio de México, 1989.

———. "Problemas urbanos: proyectos y alternativas ante la crisis." In *México ante la crisis: el impacto social y cultural de las alternativas*, edited by Pablo González Casanova. Mexico City: Siglo Veintiuno Editores, 1986.

NEWSPAPER ARTICLES

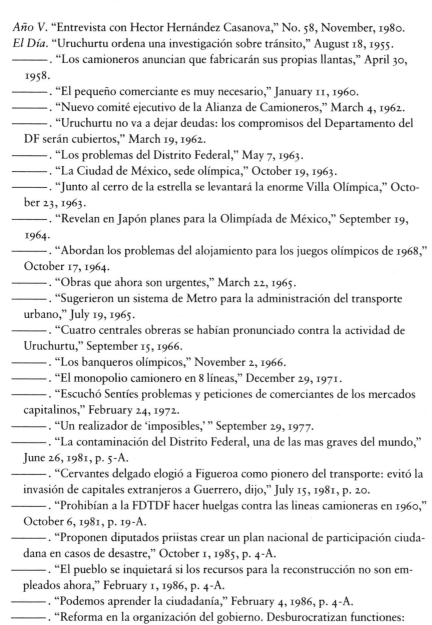

Año V. "Entrevista con Hector Hernández Casanova," No. 58, November, 1980.

El Día. "Uruchurtu ordena una investigación sobre tránsito," August 18, 1955.

———. "Los camioneros anuncian que fabricarán sus propias llantas," April 30, 1958.

———. "El pequeño comerciante es muy necesario," January 11, 1960.

———. "Nuevo comité ejecutivo de la Alianza de Camioneros," March 4, 1962.

———. "Uruchurtu no va a dejar deudas: los compromisos del Departamento del DF serán cubiertos," March 19, 1962.

———. "Los problemas del Distrito Federal," May 7, 1963.

———. "La Ciudad de México, sede olímpica," October 19, 1963.

———. "Junto al cerro de la estrella se levantará la enorme Villa Olímpica," October 23, 1963.

———. "Revelan en Japón planes para la Olimpíada de México," September 19, 1964.

———. "Abordan los problemas del alojamiento para los juegos olímpicos de 1968," October 17, 1964.

———. "Obras que ahora son urgentes," March 22, 1965.

———. "Sugerieron un sistema de Metro para la administración del transporte urbano," July 19, 1965.

———. "Cuatro centrales obreras se habían pronunciado contra la actividad de Uruchurtu," September 15, 1966.

———. "Los banqueros olímpicos," November 2, 1966.

———. "El monopolio camionero en 8 líneas," December 29, 1971.

———. "Escuchó Sentíes problemas y peticiones de comerciantes de los mercados capitalinos," February 24, 1972.

———. "Un realizador de 'imposibles,'" September 29, 1977.

———. "La contaminación del Distrito Federal, una de las mas graves del mundo," June 26, 1981, p. 5-A.

———. "Cervantes delgado elogió a Figueroa como pionero del transporte: evitó la invasión de capitales extranjeros a Guerrero, dijo," July 15, 1981, p. 20.

———. "Prohibían a la FDTDF hacer huelgas contra las lineas camioneras en 1960," October 6, 1981, p. 19-A.

———. "Proponen diputados priistas crear un plan nacional de participación ciudadana en casos de desastre," October 1, 1985, p. 4-A.

———. "El pueblo se inquietará si los recursos para la reconstrucción no son empleados ahora," February 1, 1986, p. 4-A.

———. "Podemos aprender la ciudadanía," February 4, 1986, p. 4-A.

———. "Reforma en la organización del gobierno. Desburocratizan functiones: C. Mireles," February 7, 1986, p. 2.

————. "Voz popular: municipios sí, delegaciones, no," July 22, 1986.

————. "Democratización del DF; el estado inconveniente," July 24, 1986.

Estrategia. "El endeudamiento externo y la crisis en México," 2 (1983).

————. "Las capas medias entre la espada y la pared," 51 (1983): 54–58.

Excélsior. "Cámara," August 20, 1940.

————. "Los camioneros anuncian que fabricarán sus propias llantas," April 30, 1958.

————. "Sugieron una sistema mixto para la administración del transporte urbano," July 19, 1966.

————. "Desde 1969 el Consejo Consultivo de la Ciudad de México no ha sido tomado en cuenta," July 11, 1971.

————. "En 15 días un plan a Echeverría para descentralizar servicios en el D.F.," July 21, 1971.

————. "Preferencia a colonias pobres por encima de obras suntuarias; plan de Sentíes para el sexenio: drenaje, regularización, viviendas, escuelas. No piensa ampliar el METRO y sustituirán a la merced," August 22, 1971.

————. "Planean enviar a las marías a sus pueblos," September 12, 1971.

————. "El sector empresarial manifestó su apoyo a la obra para resolver problemas del D.F.," November 11, 1971.

————. "Supresión de rutas juxtapuestas y complementación de un transporte con otro anuncia el Regente Sentíes," February 2, 1972.

————. "Sentíes informó a los Hoteleros sobre el crédito para el Metro," November 24, 1973.

————. "Se democratizará la capital con la venta de parestatales," May 7, 1987, p. 1a.

Expansión. "Como aprovechar la experiencia del exterior," April 23, 1969, pp. 17–22.

————. "Identificación inmediata del candidato del PRI," November 5, 1969, pp. 6–10.

————. "Noticias mexicanas," November 4, 1970, p. 12.

————. "El gabinete," December 16, 1970, pp. 6–13.

————. "Nuevos enfoques en obras públicas," October 4, 1972.

————. "El IV informe: precisiones," September 18, 1974.

————. "Diez años de expansión: legislación," July 21, 1976, pp. 57–109.

————. "Autotransportes: no más arranques y bocinazos," November 22, 1978, pp. 44–54.

————. "Las 500 empresas más importantes de México," August 20, 1980, p. 30.

————. "Transporte urbano: un conflicto con dimensiones de tragedia," October 15, 1980, pp. 62–73.

El Heraldo de México. "Uruchurtu no autorizó los 'mercados sobre ruedas,'" February 16, 1977.

La Jornada. "El partido contra el presidente," July 25, 1986.

————. "Cierre de pequeña empresa por la apertura comercial," June 19, 1987, p. 15.

————. "La crisis ha representado un riesgo para la estabilidad social: MMH," June 20, 1987, p. 3.

BIBLIOGRAPHY

——————. "El PAN, en la mejor etapa de su historia: Vincenio Tovar," June 29, 1987, p. 4.

——————. "La CNOP no pidío la expulsión de la Corriente Democrática, aseguró Guillermo Fonseca Alvarez," June 30, 1987, p. 4.

Journal of Commerce. "3 Engineering Units Expand," February 8, 1962, p. 1.

Mass Transit. "Suppliers Guide," 9 (1983), p. 54.

——————. "French Rail Listings," 10 (1983), pp. 14–17.

El Nacional. "La Alianza de Camioneros de México denuncia calumniosa campaña," November 17, 1957.

——————. "Valdovinos renunció a la secretaría general de la Alianza de Camioneros," November 1, 1958.

——————. "Los estudios para construir el METRO finalizarán en julio," April 29, 1965.

——————. "Comité organizador de los XIV juegos de la olimpiada," August 29, 1965.

——————. "Por medio de trabajadores sociales el D.F. esta buscando solución al problema de los comerciantes ambulantes," March 2, 1971.

——————. "Los camioneros—un gremio incomprendido—colaboran a la solución de nuestros problemas de transporte," July 16, 1971.

——————. "Amplio programa de justicia social en las areas marginadas del D.F., proyecta el regente," August 22, 1971.

——————. "Ha tenido éxito el desalojo de los comerciantes ambulantes ordenado por el Lic. Octavio Sentíes Gómez," September 30, 1971.

——————. "El monopolio camionero, en 8 líneas," December 1, 1971.

——————. "La industria de la construcción en nuestro país es autosuficiente," April 29, 1972.

The News. "Hank González Outlines Seven Capital Sins," April 2, 1981, p. 6.

New York Times. "Mexico Gets Monorail Plan," October 28, 1965.

Nueva Era. "Editorial: La defensa de México," March 7, 1912, p. 3.

——————. "Los obreros de la capital," March 8, 1912, pp. 3, 5.

Novedades. "Energía contra 'coyotes' y vigilancia en la frontera: el Subsecretario de Gobernación habla sobre hechos denunciados," September 8, 1950.

——————. "Uruchurtu y la administración pública," August 19, 1957.

——————. "Muere por inanición la Alianza de Camioneros de México, A.C.," February 24, 1959.

——————. "Importará 1600 millones municipalizar los transportes," July 15, 1965.

——————. "Desean los camioneros 60 pesos de salario mínimo," August 30, 1965.

——————. "Mas que una obra monumental, emprende Sentíes una de auxilio a los más necesitados," August 22, 1971.

——————. "La era de obras suntuarias e innecesarias ha concluido, declaro el Regente Sentíes," October 28, 1971.

——————. "Mas seguridad en las calles y moralización de funcionarios," January 4, 1972.

——————. "Burócratas capitalinos visitaron al regente," January 13, 1972.

——————. "Lucha contra la corrupción," January 14, 1972.

——————. "En ciudad satélite y el norte de la ciudad, se agudiza la neurosis," January 18, 1981, p. 1.

——————. "Mil millones de pesos en productividad y males nerviosos al Distrito

Federal: el congestionamiento vial," February 9, 1981, p. 1.

———. "Consequencia del tránsito mal humor y ahora la enfermedad psíquica de la capital es el insomnio," April 26, 1981, p. 2.

———. "La diaria pesadilla de Metro: autodestrucción y próximo colapso," August 26, 1981, p. 1.

Ovaciones. "Calvario para los usuarios del Metro: hasta la vida se arriesga, abundan jalones y golpes, demoras en el servicio," August 19, 1981.

Política. "Mas fuerza al 'control' público: re-elección de diputados," January 1, 1965, p. 12.

———. "Deporte: el compromiso olímpico," May 1, 1965, p. 28.

———. "Trabajo," May 1, 1965, pp. 14–15.

———. "Transportes: monopolio y huelga," August 1, 1965, p. 19.

———. "Distrito Federal: a gusto al PAN?" December 1, 1965, pp. 24–25.

———. "Huelga camionera," May 1, 1966, pp. 25–26.

———. "La huelga y los permisionarios," June 1, 1966, pp. 13–14.

———. "Transporte en el Distrito Federal," August 15, 1966.

———. "La nación: 'bulldozer' presidencial," September 15, 1966.

———. "CANACINTRA: industria sin competencia," December 1, 1968, p. 25.

Railway Age. "Mexico City's Metro: Doubling in Size by 1982," October 9, 1978.

Revista Grupo ICA. "Construcción urbana," No. 11, June 1980, pp. 13–16.

Siempre. "Control de transportes," January 7, 1959, p. 9.

———. "Uruchurtu come con los diputados," July 28, 1965, p. 7.

———. "Uruchurtu como el objetivo de todos los demagogos," August 4, 1965, pp. 12–13.

———. "Vida política: programa de Uruchurtu," November 3, 1965, p. 9.

———. "Industria: asamblea de los 'aliados,'" April 1, 1966.

———. "Con esfuerzo renovado se supera en el Distrito Federal el servicio de pasajeros en autobuses," July 13, 1966, p. 70.

———. "Uruchurtu hizo un milagro," September 21, 1966, p. 5.

———. "La sucia campaña contra Uruchurtu," October 20, 1966, pp. 16–17.

———. "Piedra olímpica," October 21, 1966, p. 9.

———. "CANACINTRA: industrias sin competencia," December 1, 1966.

El Sol de México. "El cambio de autoridad en el asunto olímpico," July 26, 1966.

———. "Quitarán estaciones camioneras en torno a terminales del METRO," April 21, 1981, p. 11.

El Universal. "Uruchurtu mejora al DF," May 5, 1954.

———. "Llamado a la unidad del gremio camionero," November 4, 1958.

———. "México cumplirá los compromisos contraidos aseguró el gral. Clark en Nombre del Lic. D. Ordaz," October 9, 1964.

———. "Obras que ahora son urgentes," March 22, 1965.

———. "Servicio camionero," July 7, 1965.

———. "Se iniciaron en marzo las construcciones olímpicas," October 19, 1965.

———. "1700 camioneros pararon durante cuatro horas," November 30, 1965.

———. "Ampliaron el viaducto y planean un monorriel," April 1, 1971.

———. "Garantia de desarrollo," July 9, 1971.

———. "Frena al progreso turístico la Alianza de Camioneros," November 23, 1972.

———. "Optimizar la vialidad, tarea prioritaria de DDF en '81," January 3, 1981.

———. "En protesta por el alza de los pasajes, secuestran autobuses," February 20, 1981, p. 12.

———. "Espera el DDF recaudar este año más de 55,000 millones de pesos," April 8, 1981, p. 1.

———. "La mitad de las enfermedades del corazón las causan el cigarro, la contaminación y el 'estres,'" April 20, 1981, p. 19.

Unomásuno. "Las grandes vías del DF, sin longitud suficiente," January 18, 1981, p. 1.

———. "Ciudad y gobierno," June 28, 1981, p. 25.

———. "Discrepancias entre especialistas sobre las causas del hundimiento en Tacubaya," July 23, 1981, p. 21.

———. "Instructivo," cartoon, September 7, 1981, p. 21.

———. "Reconoce el PSUM su derrota en los 40 distritos del Distrito Federal, pero no porcentages," July 13, 1985, p. 3.

———. "Pide la CANACINTRA que se postergue la política de liberalización comercial: perjudicará gravamiento a la planta productora," July 14, 1985.

———. "Distrito Federal: 50% de abstención y 40 triunfos del PRI," July 15, 1985, p. 1.

———. "Proponen priístas crear un plan nacional de participación ciudadana en casos de desastres," October 1, 1985, p. 11.

———. "Distribución de comestibles en la MCMA," October 2, 1985.

———. "El PRI afronta problemas y pierde elecciones cuando selecciona a malos candidatos: CNOP," December 18, 1985, p. 4.

———. "Las medidas económicas de México basadas en el FMI, son el camino adecuado: Mendoza Fernández," May 27, 1987, p. 14.

———. "Desconocen el desalojo de comerciantes en el centro," June 25, 1987, p. 10.

———. "Queja de residentes del fraccionamiento girasoles," June 28, 1987, p. 10.

———. "El próximo presidente debe ser un político y no un tecnócrata, manifestó Ardavín Migani," July 3, 1987.

Wall Street Journal. "French Group gets $250 mill. Job for Caracas Subway," May 16, 1978, p. 12.

———. "Nation in Jeopardy: Mexico City's Growth, Once Fostered, Turns into Economic Burden," October 4, 1987, pp. 1, 8.

OTHER PERIODICALS

Comercio Exterior
Quarterly Economic Review of Mexico

GOVERNMENT DOCUMENTS, ARCHIVAL RESOURCES, AND MISCELLANEOUS REPORTS

Actas y versiones del Consejo Consultivo del Distrito Federal (AVCC). June 5, 1929–January 15, 1930; March 12, 1930; July 23, 1930; August 13 and 29, 1930.

Atlas del Distrito Federal: geográfico, histórico, comercial, estadístico, agrario.
Mexico City: Talleres Gráficas de la Nación, 1925.
American Chamber of Commerce of Mexico. *Business/Mexico*. Mexico City, 1968.
Asociación de Banqueros de México. *Anuario financiero*. Mexico City, 1950.
————. *Anuario financiero*. Mexico City, 1960 and 1970.
Banco de México. *Anuario finanaciero de México*. Mexico City, 1960 and 1970.
Banco Nacional de Comercio Exterior. *Obras públicas para México*. No. 18, 1968.
————. *México: la política económica*. Mexico City, 1971.
Banco Nacional de Comercio Exterior, S.A. "Intercambio comercial Mexico-
Francia," *Comercio exterior* 28 (March 1978): 359–70.
Banco Nacional de Obras y Servicios Públicos, S.A. *Obras para México*. No. 16,
1967.
Bank of London and South America. *BOLSA Review* 1 (1967): 222.
————. *Informe anual*, 1967.
Banque Nationale de Paris. *Mexico: Jeux Olympiques 1968*. Paris, 1968.
Cámara de Comercio de la Ciudad de México. *Informe anual de la Cámara de
Comercio de la Ciudad de México, 1942–1943*. Mexico City, 1944.
Camara de Diputados. *Comparecencia del jefe del Departamento del Distrito Fed-
eral, Ramón Aguirre Velázquez, ante la LIII legislativa*. Mexico City: Cámara de
Diputados, 1985.
————. *Subcomisiones de hechos y análisis técnico y de dictamen de las comisiones
unidades de comunicaciones y transportes del DF*. Mexico City: Cámara de Dipu-
tados, 1980.
Cámara Franco-Mexicana. *Directorio: Cámara Franco-Mexicana de Comercio e
Industria, A.C.* Mexico City, 1982.
Cámara Nacional de la Industria de la Transformación. *Análisis económico nacional,
1934–1940*. Mexico City: CANACINTRA, 1940.
————. *La Cámara Nacional de la Industria de la Transformación y el Consejo de
Planeación Económica y Social en el D.F.* Mexico City: CANACINTRA, 1958.
————. *20 años de lucha, 1941–1961*. Mexico City: CANACINTRA, 1961.
Comisión de Vialidad y Transporte Urbano. *Estudio de origen-destino del área
metropolítana de la Ciudad de México*. Mexico City, 1981.
————. *Anuario de vialidad y transporte del Distrito Federal: antecedentes y estado
a 1980*. Mexico City: Secretaría de Obras y Servicios, Departamento del Distrito
Federal, 1981.
Comisión Técnica de Mexicanización y Supervisión de la Construcción de los
Coches del METRO. *Informe General no. 1*, January 31, 1974.
————. *Informe General no. 2*, November 30, 1974.
Comisiones Unidas de Comunicaciones y Transportes del Distrito Federal. *Acta de
la comida reunión de trabajo de las subcomisiones de hecho y análisis técnico de
dictamen*. Mexico City: Cámara de Diputados, 1980.
CONCANACOMIN. *Memoria de la Cámara Nacional de Comercio e Industria
de la Ciudad de México (trabajos desarrollados en 1938)*. Mexico City: Departa-
mento de Estudios Económicos, 1939.
Confederación de Trabajadores Mexicanos. "Segundo consejo nacional de la CTM:

octobre 19 al 24." In *Historia documental. 50 años de lucha obrera*. Vol. 1. Mexico City: CTM, 1936.

———. "Tercer consejo de la CTM: enero 26 al 27." In *Historia documental. 50 años de lucha obrera*. Vol. 1. Mexico City: CTM, 1937.

Departamento del Distrito Federal. *Anuario de vialidad y transporte del Distrito Federal: antecedentes y estado a 1980*. Mexico City: Secretaría de Obras y Servicios, Comisión de Vialidad y Transporte Urbano, 1981.

———. *Presentación de un esfuerzo sexenal*. Mexico City, 1971.

———. *Antecedentes de la formación de la industria camionera*. Departamento del Distrito Federal: Banco de Datos Reg. #T-3, 252, n.d.

———. *Memoria de los trabajos realizados del 1926*. Mexico: Talleres Gráficas de la Nación, 1927.

———. *Cuenta pública del Departamento del Distrito Federal, 1973–1980*. Dirección General de Ingeniería de Tránsito y Transporte. *Estudio sobre la factibilidad de la prolongación del Metro Netzahualcoyotl, Estado de México*. Mexico City, 1972.

———. *Informe de labores, 1972*. Mexico City: Departamento del Distrito Federal, 1972.

———. *Plan rector de vialidad y transporte para el Distrito Federal*. Mexico City, 1976.

Estructuras y Cimentaciones. *Obras ejecutadas*. Mexico City: ICA, n.d.

Informe de la gestión administrativa del Licenciado D. Benito Flores (primero como secretario general encargado del despacho y despues como gobernador del Distrito Federal). Archivo del Ayuntamiento de México. Mexico City: Talleres Gráficos de la Nación, 1919.

Informe del gobierno del Distrito Federal 1923. Archivo del Ayuntamiento de Mexico. Mexico City: Talleres Gráficos de la Nación, 1923.

Ingenieros Civiles Asociados (ICA). *XXX años de realizaciones*. Mexico City: ICA, 1967.

———. *El grupo ICA a 1967*. Mexico City: ICA, 1967.

———. *Memoria: METRO de la Ciudad de México*. Mexico City: ICA, 1977.

———. *Grupo ICA: que es el grupo ICA?* Mexico City: ICA, 1979.

———. *Grupo ICA: memoria de la XXXIII asamblea del Grupo ICA*. Mexico City: ICA, 1980.

———. *Antecedentes de la formación de la Industria Camionera*. Mexico City: ICA, n.d.

Instituto Nacional de Estudios Históricos de la Revolución Mexicana (INEHRM). *Participación ciudadana en el gobierno del Distrito Federal*. Mexico City: INEHRM, 1987.

Instituto de Ingeniería. "Transporte de pasajeros en la Ciudad de México: estudio preliminar." Reporte no. 150. Mexico City: Universidad Nacional Autónoma de México, 1967.

ISTME. *Sistema de Transporte Colectivo (METRO) de la Ciudad de México*. Mexico City: Ingenieros Civiles Asociados, S.A., 1967.

———. *Estudio completo de movimiento de personas en el primer cuadro. Habi-*

tantes puestos de trabajo, asistentes por cualquier motivo y total de viajes genera-dos. Mexico City: Ingenieros Civiles Asociados S.A., 1968.

ISTME/SOFRETU. *Determinación del número de usuarios que utilizarán el sistema metropolitano (en base a estimación teórica de origen y destino, y a la actual fiso-nomía de los sistemas de transporte con que cuenta el Distrito Federal*. Mexico City: Ingenieros Civiles Asociados, S.A., 1968.

Ley Orgánica del Distrito y de los Territorios. Mexico City: Talleres Gráficos de la Nación, 1929.

Partido de la Revolución Mexicana (PRM). *Memorias del Partido de la Revolución Mexicana: 33 meses al servicio de la Revolución, 1940–1943*. Mexico City, 1943.

Partido Revolucionario Institucional (PRI). *Luis Eceverría: práxis política*. Mexico City, 1971.

———. *Historia documental de la CNOP*. Vol. 1, 1945–1959. Vol. 2, 1959–1970. Vol. 3, 1970–1984. Mexico City: Edicap, 1984.

Presidencia de la República, Unidad de la Crónica Presidencial. "Terremotos de sep-tiembre: sobretiro de las razones y las obras crónica del sexenio 1982–1988." DF: Fondo de Cultura Económica, 1986.

Registro de Propiedad. "ICA Industrial, S.A.; ICA International, S.A.," July 17, 1981.

Secretaría de Asentamientos Humanos y Obras Públicas. *Programa para la descen-tralización territorial de las actividades industriales*. Mexico City, 1979.

Sistema de Transporte Colectivo. *Presencia del Metro*. Mexico City, 1975.

———. *El Metro para la Ciudad de México*. Mexico City, 1979.

Union Internationale de Transport Publique (UITP). *UITP Handbook*. Brussels, 1983.

INDEX

101; white-collar, 52. *See also* middle
classes, popular classes, state workers
Wright, Erik Olin, 313

Zapata, Emiliano, 21, 22, 34, 36, 42–
44, 52